eTRUST

eTRUST

FORMING RELATIONSHIPS IN THE ONLINE WORLD

KAREN S. COOK, CHRIS SNIJDERS,
VINCENT BUSKENS, AND COYE CHESHIRE,
EDITORS

A VOLUME IN THE RUSSELL SAGE FOUNDATION SERIES ON TRUST

Russell Sage Foundation • New York

The Russell Sage Foundation

The Russell Sage Foundation, one of the oldest of America's general purpose foundations, was established in 1907 by Mrs. Margaret Olivia Sage for "the improvement of social and living conditions in the United States." The Foundation seeks to fulfill this mandate by fostering the development and dissemination of knowledge about the country's political, social, and economic problems. While the Foundation endeavors to assure the accuracy and objectivity of each book it publishes, the conclusions and interpretations in Russell Sage Foundation publications are those of the authors and not of the Foundation, its Trustees, or its staff. Publication by Russell Sage, therefore, does not imply Foundation endorsement.

Library of Congress Cataloging-in-Publication Data

eTrust / Karen S. Cook ... [et al.].
    p.   cm. – (The Russell Sage Foundation series on trust)
    Includes bibliographical references and index.
    ISBN 978-0-87154-311-0 (alk. paper)
    1. Trust. I. Cook, Karen S.
    BF575.T7T785 2009
    158.2—dc22

                    2009011415

Text design by Suzanne Nichols.

RUSSELL SAGE FOUNDATION
112 East 64th Street, New York, New York 10065
10 9 8 7 6 5 4 3 2 1

The Russell Sage Foundation
Series on Trust

The Russell Sage Foundation Series on Trust examines the conceptual structure and the empirical basis of claims concerning the role of trust and trustworthiness in establishing and maintaining cooperative behavior in a wide variety of social, economic, and political contexts. The focus is on concepts, methods, and findings that will enrich social science and inform public policy.

The books in the series raise questions about how trust can be distinguished from other means of promoting cooperation and explore those analytic and empirical issues that advance our comprehension of the roles and limits of trust in social, political, and economic life. Because trust is at the core of understandings of social order from varied disciplinary perspectives, the series offers the best work of scholars from diverse backgrounds and, through the edited volumes, encourages engagement across disciplines and orientations. The goal of the series is to improve the current state of trust research by providing a clear theoretical account of the causal role of trust within given institutional, organizational, and interpersonal situations, developing sound measures of trust to test theoretical claims within relevant settings, and establishing some common ground among concerned scholars and policymakers.

Karen S. Cook
Russell Hardin
Margaret Levi

SERIES EDITORS

Previous Volumes in the Series

Contents

About the Authors

Vincent Buskens is associate professor in the Department of Sociology/ICS at Utrecht University.

Coye Cheshire is assistant professor at the School of Information at University of California, Berkeley.

Karen S. Cook is Ray Lyman Wilbur Professor of Sociology, current chair of the Department of Sociology, and director of the Institute for Research in the Social Sciences at Stanford University.

Chris Snijders is professor of sociology of technology and innovation at the School of Innovation Sciences at Eindhoven University of Technology.

Judd Antin is Ph.D. candidate at the School of Information at University of California, Berkeley.

Brandy Aven is Ph.D. candidate in the Department of Sociology at Stanford University.

Davide Barrera is assistant professor in the Department of Sociology/ICS at Utrecht University.

Gary E. Bolton is professor in the Smeal College of Business at Penn State University and director of the Laboratory for Economic Management and Auctions (LEMA).

Andreas Diekmann is professor of sociology at ETH Zurich.

Alexandra Gerbasi is assistant professor of sociology at California State University, Northridge.

Ben Jann is research scientist at ETH Zurich.

Tapan Khopkar received a Ph.D. from the School of Information at the University of Michigan.

Azi Lev-On is senior lecturer and head of new media track at the Ariel University Center.

Masafumi Matsuda is research scientist at NTT Communications Science Laboratories, Hokkaido.

Uwe Matzat is assistant professor at the School of Innovation Sciences at Eindhoven University of Technology.

Axel Ockenfels is professor in the Department of Economics at the University of Cologne.

Paul Resnick is professor at the School of Information at the University of Michigan.

Hiroyuki Takahashi is research scientist at NTT Resonant, Inc., Tokyo.

Yukihiro Usui is research scientist at NTT Advanced Technology Corporation, Tokyo.

Sonja Utz is assistant professor for Internet and new media in the Department of Communication Science at VU University, Amsterdam.

Jeroen Weesie is associate professor in the Department of Sociology/ICS at Utrecht University.

David Wyder is a former student of Andreas Diekmann and now works for PostFinance Swiss Post.

Toshio Yamagishi is professor in the Department of Behavioral Science at Hokkaido University, Sapporo.

Noriaki Yoshikai is professor in the School of Engineering at Nihon Daigaku, Tokyo.

Introduction

KAREN S. COOK, CHRIS SNIJDERS, VINCENT BUSKENS, AND
COYE CHESHIRE

TRUST FACILITATES social interaction. When it exists, it strengthens cooperation, provides the basis for risk-taking, and grants latitude to the parties involved. When it does not exist, various mechanisms are required to protect against exploitation. In its most basic form, trust can be reduced to a situation where A knows that if she hands over the control of the situation to B, B can choose between an action X or Y. Trust is involved when there is a real probability that B will choose the action A does not prefer (Coleman 1990). Many trust-related distinctions, which are often implicit, can be clarified using this simple metaphor. Perhaps the most obvious distinction is that between trust, which is connected to A, and trustworthiness, which is connected to B (Hardin 2002), so that a trusting A in itself is not complete without a trustworthy B. One can also distinguish between trust as a behavioral measure ("A trusts: she chooses to let B choose") versus trust as a subjectively perceived probability that is attached (perhaps unconsciously) to the event that B will choose the action that A prefers ("A trusts: she feels that it is likely that B will choose the action A prefers"). Another distinction can be made according to what kind of entity B actually is. B can represent a brand or a product, an institution such as the government, or perhaps an abstract entity such as the general public. Throughout this book, however, the focus is on both A and B being persons. A related issue is whether trustful and trustworthy behavior are largely attitudinal ("some persons A have a stronger disposition to trust") or contextual ("under some conditions, persons A tend to trust more often"). We will encounter examples of both throughout this volume.

For trust to actually work, the trusted party must be both willing and able to honor the trust placed in her. In the absence of clear information about these two dimensions, trust reduces to risky decision making under uncertainty (Snijders 1996). If the risks are too high or the uncertainty too great, potentially valuable social interactions will not occur. In

1

such environments, various institutional and organizational mechanisms are typically established to facilitate interaction. Sometimes third-party institutions, which offer assurance that all parties live up to their promises, can overcome the need for trust between persons. One could see banks and credit card companies as attempts to realize an impartial third party (though the recent credit crisis has raised doubts as to the trustworthiness of this particular third party).

A mechanism that can help in the absence of stabilizing third parties is repeated interaction. In repeated interactions, each actor can test the other to determine whether the partner is both capable and willing to perform as desired (Axelrod 1984; Kreps 1990; Gibbons 2001). The repetition of moves helps because actors in a trust relationship can learn by observing the behavior of their partner and can control opportunistic behavior by using future sanctions more or less tit-for-tat. Moreover, repetition gives partners real incentives to invest in their reputations. In this case, the exchange of information is between two parties in a dyadic relationship. However, many interactions are embedded in a larger context of interactions in which repeated interaction with the same party is either not likely or not that frequent. Buyers and sellers on eBay are an example. In such settings, reputation can play a vital role in establishing trust in the absence of a long-term dyadic relationship. Even though the direct pathway of information flow from A to B and back is lacking, information can flow through third parties and mutually cooperative relations can be built, in principle in the same general way as in dyadic relationships.

This volume on trust and reputation is complementary to earlier volumes in the Russell Sage Trust series in the sense that we focus attention on reputation as a specific mechanism that can be used in many ways to facilitate interactions not likely to occur in the absence of such information. This mechanism in relation to trust and trustworthiness has been mentioned only occasionally in earlier volumes in the series.

Although reputation can also play a role in repeated interactions between the same two actors, in this volume we focus on the effects of third-party information on trust. In a larger context, actors can build reputations for being trustworthy if information about their benevolent, reliable behavior reaches their potential future partners (Granovetter 1985). Information about a partner's capabilities and intentions flows through the network of actors, allowing all to learn about their potential future trust partners. On the other hand, partners can reward or punish trustworthy or untrustworthy actors if they can change existing reputations by distributing information about their experiences with specific actors in the network of possible future partners (for longer informal accounts of learning and control in such settings, see Yamagishi and Yamagishi 1994; Buskens and Raub 2002; for more formal theoretical discussions on such reputation effects in social networks, see Raub and Weesie 1990; Buskens 2002). Most of the chapters in this volume do not focus on disentangling reputation mechanisms in different contexts, but emphasize instead the effectiveness of and problems associated with reputation mechanisms in various situations.

In contexts in which direct informal communication in a network is difficult to achieve, it becomes worthwhile to provide such information in a more institutionalized way. There are a number of historic examples of such institutions (for example, Greif 1989, 2006; Klein 1997). More recently, reputation systems have also become well known in the world of Internet-based interactions. Typically, users can leave some kind of feedback about cooperation with their previous partner (as on eBay or LinkedIn), or about the quality of the goods they supplied (as on Amazon). This feedback is then made available to all other users, and those with a good reputation can benefit from their trustworthy behavior because their attractiveness as a future partner increases.

Many chapters in this volume explicitly address the problems that arise in environments often characterized by anonymity and faceless interaction, such as Internet commerce and computer-mediated interaction more generally. And there are good reasons to place specific emphasis on these types of interactions. Information technology has made the problem of trust more salient. Many of the trust problems that can occur in the "real" world now have a virtual counterpart, but the conditions under which one has to solve trust problems online strongly differ from the conditions under which people are accustomed to solving such problems. Several factors make trusting behavior online much more difficult than offline. For instance, on the Internet one cannot see the other party face to face, and single-shot encounters are very common. However, the Internet also offers many new possibilities and innovative solutions to trust problems. Use of the reputation of the interacting partners is one potential solution, and is being used in many online settings (see, for example, Kollock 1999; Resnick and Zeckhauser 2002).

Many research questions related to anonymous interactions in which reputation mechanisms are used to solve trust problems are addressed in this volume. How are such interactions made possible organizationally? What safeguards are necessary and what role does reputation play? What types of reputation systems work best to provide the needed clues to trustworthiness or ready access to organizational and legal means of redress? How are reputations repaired if damaged? Can they be? What are the determinants of effective monitoring in the world of online interaction and commerce? What role does reputation information play in the effort to provide assurance and some control over malfeasance? In the next section, we discuss briefly the nature of the contributions of each chapter in this volume and conclude with a postscript to identify important questions for future research that the work reported here raises.

Organization

This volume is divided into three parts. The first offers four experimental studies in which hypotheses are tested relating to the effects of different kinds of reputation systems on trust. Subjects in the laboratory are involved in trust situations, but the conditions and amount of information that subjects have about interactions of other subjects are varied. Some of the systems resemble Internet auctions like eBay. The main issue underlying these studies is which kinds of reputation systems allow markets to be more cooperative. The second part of the volume includes two field studies on actual Internet-related transactions or exchanges. These studies apply different approaches to study the extent to which reputation in online interactions facilitates trust for the actual users: is there an empirical basis for the claim that reputation can have value in online settings? The third part of the volume is devoted to challenges related to creating trust from a more general point of view in an online setting. What kinds of information do trust partners find important under which conditions? For instance, are partners more interested in learning about a partner's general disposition to behave in a trustworthy manner or in the partner's external incentives that determine the likelihood of such behavior? When do which kinds of trust stabilizing mechanisms work and how can we extend the findings from auction settings to the broader arena of online interactions?

Part I: Effects of Reputation Systems on Trust

In chapter 1, Gary Bolton and Axel Ockenfels provide an overview of a series of studies conducted in the laboratory to understand the effect of different reputation mechanisms on trust. Their subjects play a trust game framed as a buyer-seller interaction (see Dasgupta 1988; Camerer and Weigelt 1988; Kreps 1990). A buyer has to decide whether he will buy a product from a seller. The seller then has to decide whether to ship the product. This way, implementation of trust remains purely behavioral. It is assumed that the buyer must pay first and that the seller has an incentive to not ship the product. In isolated encounters, when buyers buy just once from the same seller and no information about the behavior of sellers is distributed among the buyers, the market will collapse as soon as buyers learn that the sellers are frequently not trustworthy. Bolton and Ockenfels compare this baseline setting with a treatment in which buyers still interact only once with each seller, but now obtain information about other buyers' previous encounters with the seller.

They discover that this eBay-like institution facilitates trust as well as trustworthiness, but that the market is still far from perfect, in the sense that products are not always bought and, if they are bought, the products are not always shipped. In the remainder of the chapter, Bolton and Ockenfels focus on explaining these market imperfections and conclude that there are two main reasons for them. First, some sellers simply do not realize that not shipping affects their future dealings with other buyers. Second, buyers are not always willing to trust sellers with relatively bad reputations, because they are not confident enough about the sellers' trustworthiness. This implies, however, that future buyers from this seller do not obtain new or updated information on which they can base their decisions about this seller's trustworthiness.

In chapter 2, Davide Barrera and Vincent Buskens use an experimental design that is a bit further away from direct translation to eBay interactions. In their study, subjects are involved in repeated trust situations. More specifically, subjects play repeated investment games (see Berg, Dickhaut, and McCabe 1995), a continuous version of the trust game, in which trustors can determine how much they want to send to the trustee from a given amount of money or points. The amount sent is then tripled and given to the trustee. The trustee decides how much he returns from what he has received. Barrera and Buskens vary the amount of information trustors obtain from other trustors, and the trustors play repeated games with the same trustee. They find that the subjects' experiences are most important in guiding future behavior. They also find that trustors become more trustful if they find out that other trustors have trusted the same trustee, confirming once more that information from third parties can indeed affect trust behavior.

In chapter 3, Toshio Yamagishi, Masafumi Matsuda, Noriaki Yoshikai, Hiroyuki Takahashi, and Yukihiro Usui reproduce a lemons market in an experimental lab, in which subjects can choose a level of quality for their product and then sell the product claiming a higher quality than the product actually has—a typical feature of online auctions in second-hand goods. They find that when sellers are anonymous, the quality of the products sold reduces to the lowest level. Because this then causes the market for high-quality goods to collapse, we end up with a real lemon's market, in the sense that high-level quality goods are no longer offered for sale because the likelihood of the goods being lemons is too high. The main research question is whether reputation systems can help prevent the decline of quality in this market. The authors indeed find that if buyers can identify sellers and can adapt their behavior toward specific sellers in subsequent interactions, then the quality of the products offered is significantly higher. Because in online reputation systems changing one's identity is sometimes relatively easy, Yamagishi and his colleagues consider alternative experimental designs in which sellers can change their identities. It turns out that the effect of reputation is indeed smaller if sellers can change identities. This effect is especially striking if buyers can give only neutral or negative ratings. The detrimental effect of changing identities is smaller if buyers can also give positive ratings.

In chapter 4, Tapan Khopkar and Paul Resnick provide their subjects with trust games similar to those Bolton and Ockenfels offered. Subjects face decisions about buying and shipping goods. The implementation of the game slightly differs because buyers and sellers decide simultaneously. Khopar and Resnick also include a reputation system in which buyers can rate their previous interactions with the sellers. One of the main research questions is whether Indian and American subjects differ in trust and trustworthiness and whether this difference disappears when a reputation system is in place. Such a finding would strongly support the use of reputation systems online. Although Khopkar and Resnick did find that the American subjects are more trusting and more trustworthy than the Indian subjects, they did not find that the reputation system affected either trust or trustworthiness.

Part II: Field Studies on the Reputation Premium

In chapter 5, Andreas Diekmann, Ben Jann, and David Wyder use data from the auction platform QXL ricardo (now Tradus) to examine the effects of reputation on the probability of a successful deal, the mode of payment, and the selling price. Using classic sociological examples to show that the idea of a reputation system in itself is not new, they consider how reputations work in practice, utilizing data from mobile phone auctions. One of the main advantages of using Tradus instead of eBay is that on Tradus there are many more sellers with relatively low reputation scores. The value of reputation as a solution to the potential lack of trust is less apparent when comparing a seller with a score of +5,000 with one with a score of +10,000, as can easily occur on eBay. Diekmann and his colleagues find that there indeed is a small *reputation premium*: the phones are sold for higher prices when the reputation score of the seller is higher, previous findings concerning the reputation premium aside. Moreover, reputation also seems to influence the characteristics of the auction itself, such as the choice of payment mode and the choice of a starting bid. Whereas sellers typically choose payment modes that protect them from opportunistic buyers, making the interaction a trust game with the buyer as the trustor, buyers are reasonably well protected against opportunistic sellers through the reputation mechanism.

In chapter 6, Chris Snijders and Jeroen Weesie also consider the effects of reputation on selling prices, but use data from a completely different kind of online market, the market for computer programmers (coders). Their research is guided by the finding that though a reputation premium indeed seems to exist, it often appears to be rather small. At the heart of their chapter lies the notion that auction data of the eBay kind typically cannot consider which other goods on offer were considered but not chosen. That someone buys a certain phone implies that other phones or the same phone from another seller were rejected. Snijders and Weesie use data that incorporates these rejected possibilities using data from RentACoder.com, which allows them to shed some light on the existence of a reputation premium. On RentACoder, buyers can post a *bid request*, a description of a certain computer programming task a buyer wants to have carried out. Coders then bid for the project and the buyer chooses the preferred coder. After the job is finished, both buyer and coder rate each other, just as in the case of eBay or QXL ricardo. The critical difference from standard auction sites is that this setup allows Snijders and Weesie to use these data to distinguish between what buyers are willing to pay for a coder with a high reputation and what they have to pay for a high reputation. These are not the same, and Snijders and Weesie find that the difference between the two is striking. Whereas the effect of reputation on the actual selling price is positive but relatively small, as in many auction studies, the effect of reputation on the willingness to pay is large. Hence buyers would be willing to pay a high price for reputation, but in markets such as RentACoder they simply do not have to. So reputation has value, but because the competition between sellers is tough, the extent to which reputation affects the selling price is small.

Part III: Assessing Trust and Reputation Online

In chapter 7, Karen Cook, Coye Cheshire, Alexandra Gerbasi, and Brandy Aven examine how individuals use limited information when attempting to determine the trustworthiness of providers of online goods and services. They concentrate on first-time buyer-seller relationships, in which potential buyers must assess the trustworthiness of sellers without the aid of third-party reputation mechanisms. Drawing on theory and empirical work on trust, trustworthiness, and social exchange, these authors argue that the competence and motivations of the exchange partner (that is, seller) are two key factors individuals use to make inferences about trustworthiness, especially when uncertainty and risk are not managed or reduced through third-party institutions. Using a survey-based experiment design, the authors demonstrate that the combined effect of high competence and high motivation is clearly important for assessing the trustworthiness of sellers in online goods and service markets. However, they also provide evidence that perceived competence and motivation have different relative degrees of importance in online goods markets compared to online service markets. Using both experimental results and open-ended qualitative responses, they show that information about the motivation of the provider is more salient than competence information in their example service market. We encounter a related issue when it comes to rebuilding trust, which Sonja Utz addresses in chapter 8. However, in the online goods markets, information about the seller's competence is more important than that about the motivation of the provider. Cook and her colleagues argue that understanding how individuals use different types of information when making assessments of trustworthiness in first-time interactions is essential for exchange in both online and offline markets.

In chapter 8, Utz tackles a topic that is often neglected when it comes to trust—the way in which trust can be rebuilt. Because many trust issues take place in a setting not free from noise, accidental abuse of trust can be catastrophic if rebuilding the trust in some way is not possible. Especially in online settings, rebuilding trust has characteristics that make it an intriguing subject. First, because many online interactions are one-shot interactions with strangers, the rebuilding is for the most part not aimed at the current partner but instead at future other partners. What makes the challenge greater is that the possibilities to repair trust are limited. For instance, in online auctions typically the only thing business partners can do is exchange relatively brief and public text messages. This creates a situation in which communication about what went wrong is a delicate matter: the only thing that potential future business partners have to judge trustworthiness on is a couple of lines of text, so those lines had better be convincing. In a series of experiments, Utz shows that eBay users are aware of the possibility of noise, but that trust in the partner can decrease even if the problem is caused by noise. She also shows that the content of the messages between buyer and seller affects the extent to which trust is affected when something went wrong during the transaction. Extending and combining research from different areas, Utz demonstrates that the kind of problem, either competence based or morality based, makes a difference to the business partner, and affects which kind of messages work best to minimize the damage.

This congruency between the goals and intentions of the partners, and the way in which trust and cooperation problems are handled, is also at the core of Uwe Matzat's study. In chapter 9, Matzat argues that the trust and public good problems online groups or communities face should be managed in accordance with the kind of relational interests members feel toward each other. Matzat distinguishes three kinds of control. The weakest forms are the so-called frame stabilizing tools. These increase the cognitive salience of the group, emphasize the common norms and values of a group, or compare one group with others.

For instance, in many online groups, specific symbols or icons are used, or a common set of behavioral rules are followed. The second kind are indirect monitoring tools and give members the opportunity to show disapproval to other members who do not live up to the group standard. The strongest forms of social control are the direct control tools, which affect the costs and benefits of the behavioral alternatives of the members directly. The most extreme example is expelling members from a group, but milder and positive forms, such as publishing a list of the most active members, are also used. Matzat contends that the effectiveness of these tools depends on the relational interests group members feel toward each other. Comparing data from a sample of Dutch eBay users with a sample of members from knowledge-sharing communities, it is immediately apparent that users in the knowledge-sharing group show a stronger tendency to share relational interests. In particular, the data reveal that care should be taken when it comes to standard recommendations in the literature concerning how to manage online communities. The tools available to an online community manager to exert social control are of different value depending on both the kind of problem and the kind of user group.

In chapter 10, Coye Cheshire and Judd Antin focus on systems of online collective action in which individuals contribute small amounts of information and generate shared information pools, thus creating public or club goods. Categorizing online information exchange systems along the dimensions of *order*, the organization of individual contributions and the clarity of the intended collective outcome, and *coordination*, the organization of contributors around roles, duties, and defined responsibilities, Cheshire and Antin argue that order and coordination shape the base levels of system uncertainty individuals face in different types of online services. Through examples, the authors show that online systems with higher levels of order and coordination have transparent exchange processes, thereby raising user confidence in the achievement of expected outcomes. Systems with lower levels are largely undefined and have vague or indeterminate collective outcomes. Furthermore, the authors argue, the online environment in which individuals interact with an information system can create perceptions of uncertainty that negatively impact participation. Cheshire and Antin apply their categorization scheme to the study of system uncertainty, environmental uncertainty, and information sharing behavior by presenting the results of two Internet field experiments. Using an archetypal ordered and coordinated information exchange system, their study examines the independent effects of highlighting the recipient of participants' efforts and associating with commercial advertisements on contribution behavior. Cheshire and Antin demonstrate that, under some conditions, emphasizing the recipient of one's efforts can increase user contributions to online information systems. Furthermore, associating with commercial advertising can act like third-party reputations, altering the users' awareness of environmental uncertainty and reducing contribution behavior.

In chapter 11, which concludes this volume, Azi Lev-On explores some of the key mechanisms that help individuals overcome risks in online environments and facilitate the development of cooperation. Lev-On characterizes two main ways of managing trust problems in online environments. First, individuals can generate trust by altering agents' expectations about the future behaviors of others without other institutional reinforcements. The second method involves the introduction of third-party systems or institutions, which shift the problem from relational trust to a focus on the institution's perceived competence. Using contemporary examples, Lev-On shows how the Internet can become a breeding ground for the rapid growth of institutional innovations that facilitate interaction yet restrict the development of trust. He argues that reputation management systems also enable the inexpensive production and dissemination of reputations—thus facilitating cooperation without the need for interpersonal trust. Using current experimental evidence, Lev-On demonstrates the difficulty of building trust through lean media forms, which he refers to as "poor" Internet communication channels. Following recent research, Lev-On argues that the Internet presents several unique hazards over offline interactions, especially those relating to identity persistence and the poverty of social context cues. When contrasted with the de facto standard of interpersonal face-to-face interaction, he argues that poor Internet channels put users in a disadvantaged cognitive position to overcome risk and generate trust-based cooperation.

Postscript

This volume includes both experimental work and field research from a variety of disciplines on trust and reputation systems in a variety of online settings, from ongoing social networks and groups to short-term economic transactions for goods and services. The reputation systems vary from institutionalized and formal as in eBay and QXL ricardo to more informal as in the case of some online community groups and systems of generalized exchange of information. Bringing this research together in one place allows us to focus attention on the types of reputation mechanisms that solve trust problems in various interaction settings and on the limitations of such mechanisms. In addition, we can begin to specify the outlines of a new research agenda for future inquiry as the global move to computer-mediated interactions grows. Although many types of social and economic interaction are less amenable to computer mediation, the sheer efficiency and ease of such communication and transactions is generating intense interest across the social sciences as well as in engineering, business, and the field of communications.

The specific contributions to this volume cover three broad types of issues: first, theoretical and empirical analyses of the conditions under which trust problems can evolve and can be resolved through reputation mechanisms; second, comparisons of the nature and effects of different types of reputation systems on outcomes that matter (for example, price, repeat interactions or transactions, trustworthiness assessments, and the possibility of default or exploitation); and, third, field studies of ongoing exchange systems in which problems of trust and cooperation are paramount and the many ways in which such problems have been resolved or remain to be resolved.

One of the main agenda items for future inquiry is the extent to which the reputation mechanisms translate into strategies that work under specific conditions in other types of social and economic transactions. What can be learned about the organization of transactions and the social structures that support them from the types of studies reported here, and what are the limits of application outside the domain of the online world? Furthermore, what are the consequences socially, economically, and politically of the expansion of the types of interactions being mediated in the online world (for example, social support groups, the global market for services, spot transactions with their inherent problems of exploitation, social networking, and even political support for both good and bad causes)? What are the consequences for the global community when this type of social, political, and economic support transcends national boundaries? How do reputation mechanisms work to manage the integrity of such systems of contribution or transaction? What specific institutions will emerge to provide legitimate oversight and restitution for failed trust? How robust are the reputation mechanisms against deliberate manipulation? These are fairly large questions, but the bridge to this world has already been crossed, and it is important for social scientists to be at the forefront in investigating the potentially large consequences of the ongoing transformation in modes of social interaction and economic transactions. We hope this volume makes a significant contribution to this task.

In closing, we thank those who made this volume possible, in particular the Royal Dutch Academy of Arts and Sciences in Amsterdam and the University of Bielefeld, for hosting conferences on this topic from which some of the contributions to this volume derive, as well as the Russell Sage Foundation, for supporting the preparation of this volume for the Trust Series, coedited by Karen Cook, Russell Hardin, and Margaret Levi.

References

Axelrod, Robert M. 1984. *The Evolution of Cooperation*. New York: Basic Books.

Berg, Joyce, John Dickhaut, and Kevin McCabe. 1995. "Trust, Reciprocity, and Social History." *Games and Economic Behavior* 10(1): 122–42.

Buskens, Vincent. 2002. *Social Networks and Trust*. Boston: Kluwer.

Buskens, Vincent, and Werner Raub. 2002. "Embedded Trust: Control and Learning." In *Advances in Group Processes*, vol. 19, *Group Cohesion, Trust, and Solidarity*, edited by Shane Thye. Greenwich, Conn.: JAI Press.

Camerer, Colin F., and Keith Weigelt. 1988. "Experimental Tests of a Sequential Equilibrium Reputation Model." *Econometrica* 56(1): 1–36.

Coleman, James S. 1990. *Foundations of Social Theory*. Cambridge, Mass.: Belknap Press.

Dasgupta, Partha. 1988. "Trust as a Commodity." In *Trust: Making and Breaking Cooperative Relations*, edited by Diego Gambetta. Oxford: Blackwell Publishing.

Gibbons, Robert. 2001. "Trust in Social Structures: Hobbes and Coase Meet Repeated Games." In *Trust in Society*, edited by Karen S. Cook. New York: Russell Sage Foundation.

Granovetter, Mark S. 1985. "Economic Action and Social Structure: The Problem of Embeddedness." *American Journal of Sociology* 91(3): 481–510.

Greif, Avner. 1989. "Reputation and Coalitions in Medieval Trade: Evidence on the Maghribi Traders." *Journal of Economic History* 49(4): 857–82.

———. 2006. *Institutions and the Path to the Modern Economy: Lessons from Medieval Trade*. Cambridge: Cambridge University Press.

Hardin, Russell. 2002. *Trust and Trustworthiness*. New York: Russell Sage Foundation.

Klein, Daniel B. 1997. *Reputation: Studies in the Voluntary Elicitation of Good Conduct*. Ann Arbor: University of Michigan Press.

Kollock, Peter 1999. "The Production of Trust in Online Markets." In *Advances in Group Processes*, vol. 16, edited by Edward J. Lawler, Michael W. Macy, Shane Thye, and Henry A. Walker. Greenwich, Conn.: JAI Press.

Kreps, David M. 1990. "Corporate Culture and Economic Theory." In *Perspectives on Positive Political Economy*, edited by James E. Alt and Kenneth A. Shepsle. Cambridge: Cambridge University Press.

Raub, Werner, and Jeroen Weesie. 1990. "Reputation and Efficiency in Social Interactions: An Example of Network Effects." *American Journal of Sociology* 96(3): 626–54.

Resnick, Paul, and Richard Zeckhauser. 2002. "Trust among Strangers in Internet Transactions: Empirical Analysis of eBay's Reputation System." In *Advances in Applied Microeconomics*, vol. 11, *The Economics of the Internet and E-Commerce*, edited by Michael R. Baye. Amsterdam: Elsevier Science.

Snijders, Chris. 1996. *Trust and Commitments*. Amsterdam: Thesis Publishers.

Yamagishi, Toshio, and Midori Yamagishi. 1994. "Trust and Commitment in the United States and Japan." *Motivation and Emotion* 18(2): 129–66.

PART I

EFFECTS OF REPUTATION
SYSTEMS ON TRUST

Chapter 1

The Limits of Trust in Economic Transactions: Investigations of Perfect Reputation Systems

Gary E. Bolton and Axel Ockenfels

A s the Internet economy has grown, so too has the need for trust. A degree of trust is critical in virtually all economic relationships, Internet or otherwise. Every day we choose to trust plumbers, doctors, employers, employees, teachers, airlines, and others. The need for trust arises from the fact that we cannot contract on every move others make. And what we can contract on is often prohibitively costly to enforce. The anonymity of geographically dispersed Internet traders increases contracting difficulties: you may not be able to identify your eBay seller or verify the quality of the object being sold, let alone get your money back.[1]

The economic foundation of trust relationships is the reciprocity principle of tit-for-tat combined with reputation systems that store information on past performance (Greif 1993). Broadly speaking, there are two forms. *Direct* reciprocity applies to repeated relationships: 'I will trust you tomorrow if you are trustworthy with me today,' and is associated with bilateral reputation systems. *Indirect* reciprocal systems enforce trust when the relationship is one-shot by a more circuitous tit-for-tat: 'I will trust you tomorrow if you are trustworthy with a third party today,' and is associated with multilateral reputation systems. Internet markets tend to be anonymous places and feature a lot of one-time transactions. A study by Paul Resnick and Richard Zeckhauser, for example, found that a large majority of eBay trading encounters are one-shot (2002). As a result, Internet markets tend to lean heavily on multilateral systems to enforce trustworthiness (for a discussion of how community relationships influence the control mechanisms the community will accept, see chapter 9, this volume).

Take eBay's famous feedback forum, a kind of institutionalized gossip.[2] On eBay, after each encounter, buyers and sellers can evaluate each other by giving one another either a positive (+1), neutral (0) or negative (−1) feedback score, and maybe additional commentary. This feedback is publicly available and easy to access, so that each buyer can look at a seller's feedback history before he engages in bidding. The incentives for moral hazard are thus weakened by the feedback system: if traders punish sellers with negative feedback by refusing to buy from them or reducing the price they are willing to pay, then the threat of leaving negative feedback should discipline the seller.

In this chapter, we discuss our investigations of perfect reputation systems for indirect reciprocity. By *perfect*, we mean that the information about traders' past behavior circulating through the market is comprehensive and reliable. Of course, real world reputation systems are imperfect. By studying perfect reputation systems, however, we identify the maximal achievable benefit by market design improvements—absent from all kinds of institutional noise and incentive problems inherent to real world reputation systems. By the same token, we reveal how behavioral aspects may limit or assist the reputation system performance, and we get a clearer measure of the interplay of institutional and behavioral aspects on the effectiveness of reputation systems.

Studying perfect reputation systems is an important complement to field studies of feedback systems such as eBay's. One reason is that though most of the empirical literature observes that traders respond to reputation information, this observation in itself does not measure the virtues of reputation information. Evidence from eBay, for instance, shows that a seller's feedback profile may affect prices and the probability of sale (see Dellarocas et al. 2004; Dellarocas 2006; Resnick et al. 2006). The empirical results are mostly consistent with the theoretical expectation of buyers paying more to sellers with better reputations. It has also been observed that the impact of reputation ratings on buyer behavior tends to be stronger for riskier transactions and more expensive objects. This would seem to indicate that the reputation systems have at least some merit. But precisely how much is gained from these systems in terms of overall cooperation levels and efficiency gains remains unclear. We can get a sense of this measure by studying perfect systems under laboratory conditions. A second reason is that field studies have difficulties separating imperfect institutions and boundedly rational behavior. It may be that flawed systems work well because real-world traders cannot exploit the flaws as fully as theories assuming full rationality would suggest they do. Current studies are discovering changes in rules, procedures, and information aggregation that may well help generate more reliable information. Retaliatory feedback might be eliminated by not letting sellers evaluate buyers, as suggested by Werner Güth, Friederike Mengel, and Axel Ockenfels (2006), or by having a blind period in which trading partners can simultaneously leave feedback on each other, as suggested by Tobias Klein and colleagues (2007). Clever incentive schemes, based on economics (Miller, Resnick, and Zeckhauser 2005) or social psychology (Rashid et al. 2006), may overcome the public goods problem and promote full provision of all relevant feedback information. Modern authentication technologies or entry fees may also eliminate manipulative changes of online identities (see Friedman and Resnick 2001; Ockenfels 2003). But maybe the binding limitation for the effectiveness of reputation systems is not so much the institutional issues but rather the behavioral limitations. Studying perfect systems can cleanly expose these kinds of limitations.

It is also important to recognize that some of the pressing challenges that the imperfection of information in real-world systems creates have to do with strategic behavior (see also Bolton, Greiner, and Ockenfels 2008). One challenge for feedback systems such as eBay's is that feedback information must come from voluntary self-reporting of one's experiences with trading partners. Feedback is a public good, however; the costs of providing feedback are paid by the provider but the benefit goes only to other traders.[3] Furthermore, no trader can be excluded from using the information. As a result, economic theory suggests that feedback information will be underprovided. In fact, only about 50 to 70 percent of the transactions on eBay receive feedback (Resnick and Zeckhauser 2002; Bolton, Greiner, and Ockenfels 2008).[4] A second challenge is that feedback needs to be reliable to effectively deter fraudulent behavior. There are a variety of incentives to manipulate feedback, for example, to give good feedback to friends and bad feedback to competitors. A third major challenge is that negative feedback is often retaliated by additional negative feedback, creating incentives to not give negative feedback. It appears suspicious that less than half percent of the eBay feedback is negative (as observed by, among others, Resnick and Zeckhauser 2002). Further evidence for the limited reliability of eBay's feedback information comes from the observation that negative feedbacks are given late, in the last minute. On the other hand, positive feedback tends to be given earlier, to trigger a reciprocal response (for example, Klein et al. 2007; Bolton, Greiner, and Ockenfels 2008). As a consequence, the information value of feedback, if given at all, is likely to be something less than perfect.[5] A better understanding of the strategies that people pursue in a perfect, idealized system can help us identify and understand the strategies they pursue in more complex environments.

We study the scope and limitations of perfect reputation systems in thought experiments, using economic theory, and in laboratory experiments, exposing people to perfect systems. What we find, as we illustrate, is that economic theory tends to underestimate traders' intrinsic willingness to behave reciprocally, but at the same time to overestimate the effectiveness of extrinsic motivations induced by reputation institutions. One implication of our work is that understanding how social behavior can be sustained with the help of reputation mechanisms will require new understandings of how the institutional environment interacts with boundedly rational behavior.

Intrinsic Motivation: What Can Be Achieved Without a Reputation System?

Standard economic theory, based on a narrow definition of self-interest, implies that without external control and incentives, there is hardly any hope that trust and trustworthiness can emerge, but also that a perfect reputation system can create enough incentives to solve the problems. Our work suggests that economic theory is misleading on both counts. There can be trust without external enforcement, and there can be cooperation failure even with perfect reputation systems. Thus, when we attempt to measure the impact of the introduction of a perfect reputation system in a community of strangers, we need to carefully measure both how well the community does absent any external cooperation enforcement and how well it does with a perfect enforcement system. Although in reality neither environment exists, we can create both situations in the laboratory. For instance, we can create situations that are anonymous and truly one-shot for our subjects in the sense that none of the encounters are linked by flows of reputation information.

To make things simple and to abstract away from various complicating factors, we focus on a simple buyer-seller game featuring a trust problem typical of those that reputation systems are commonly used to mitigate. Figure 1.1 illustrates the moves in the buyer-seller encounter. Both the seller and the buyer are endowed with $35, which is the payoff when no trade takes place. The seller offers an item for sale at a price of $35 that has a value of $50 to the buyer. The seller's cost of providing the item is $20. If the buyer chooses to buy the item, he sends the seller his endowment of $35. The seller then has to decide whether to ship the item, or whether to keep both the money and the item. If the seller does not ship, he receives the price plus his endowment of $35 for a total of $70. If he ships, he receives the price minus the costs plus his endowment for a total of $50. If the buyer chooses not to buy the item, no trade occurs.

Figure 1.1   The Buyer-Seller Encounter

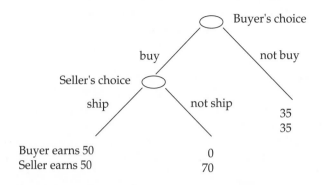

Buyer's choice

buy   not buy

Seller's choice

ship   not ship   35
35

Buyer earns 50   0
Seller earns 50   70

Source: Reprinted with permission from Bolton, Katok, and Ockenfels (2004a). Copyright 2004, the Institute for Operations Research and the Management Sciences, 7240 Parkway Drive, Suite 300, Hanover, Md. 21076, U.S.A.

At the heart of the game is a moral hazard problem that must be overcome if trades are to be successfully executed. With no common history or common future among traders that could give them the opportunity to reward or punish each other, and with no other kind of external (say, legal) enforcement, the seller can profit from not sending the item or sending poorer quality than promised. That is, the seller's pecuniary motive in the figure 1.1 game dictates that he keep the money along with his endowment. In this case, the buyer would lose his endowment and end up with nothing. Anticipating this moral hazard, buyers may not be willing to buy. As a consequence, trading that would make everyone better off would not take place. This is the essential trust dilemma that economic and social interactions—whether they be online or offline—need navigate.[6]

Economic theory presumes that under the given circumstance all rational sellers will fall to moral hazard, and consequently, all trustworthiness, and therefore trust, will vanish. However, the standard models assume that people are guided solely by pecuniary concerns. In reality, people care about other things as well. In fact, in trust games and related anonymous one-shot games (like the prisoner's dilemma game and the ultimatum game), psychologists, sociologists, experimental economists and others have identified several nonpecuniary motives that are important drivers of behavior in these situations. Most prominent in the recent economics literature are concerns for fairness (Fehr and Schmidt 1999; Bolton and Ockenfels 2000) and reciprocity (Rabin 1993; Dufwenberg and Kirchsteiger 2004). These social preference models assume that traders care about their monetary payoff but that some may also be concerned with the social impact of their behavior. Reciprocity models conjecture that people tend to be kind in response to kindness and unkind in response to unkindness, whereas fairness models posit that some individuals may have a preference for equitably sharing the efficiency gains from trade.[7]

We studied the game in figure 1.1 in a classroom experiment (Bolton, Katok, and Ockenfels 2004b). We found that 37 percent of the thirty sellers were willing to ship in anonymous one-shot encounters and that 27 percent of the buyers were willing to buy. Contrary to the predictions of standard theory, then, there is a nontrivial amount of trust and trustworthiness in anonymous one-shot encounters.[8] At the same time, room for improvement is substantial. On average, only about 10 percent of all encounters (= 0.27×0.37) end up in successful and efficient trade. Furthermore, this figure probably overestimates the power of intrinsic motivations to behave reciprocally in a dynamic setting. That is, in expected monetary terms, the probability of a trustworthy seller needs to be at least 70 percent to make buying in the trust game profitable. In our one-shot game, the probability was well below this threshold.

A natural hypothesis, then, is that if trust rests solely on behavioral propensities, trust will diminish over time. This hypothesis has been tested (Bolton, Katok, and Ockenfels 2004a). In our laboratory experiment, the market transactions take place over a series of thirty rounds. At the beginning of each round, a potential buyer is matched with a potential seller and they then play the trust game in figure 1.1. Each game is played with a different transaction partner and no information about trade outcomes leaks from one encounter to another one, so we call this experimental treatment the *strangers market*. All interaction was computer mediated and anonymous; subjects sat in cubicles in front of computers not knowing the true identity of their trading partners, capturing an important aspect of online trading. The rules, and that all rounds would be paid, were common knowledge. Observe that, absent reputation information, this market is essentially a sequence of one-shot games. Thus, because there is not enough intrinsic trustworthiness to make trust profitable in the nonrepeated one-shot game, we hypothesize that buyers quickly learn that cooperation does not pay out and that, subsequently, trading activities will collapse.

Figure 1.2 shows the average buying and shipping (conditioned on buying) behavior across rounds.

Aggregating over all rounds, trustworthiness is about the same as in the one-shot version of the trust game in figure 1.1. This reflects that the strangers market does not create additional incentives to be trustworthy compared to the one-shot game. On the buyer side, there is, on average, more trust in the strangers market than in the one-shot version of the

Figure 1.2   Strangers Treatment

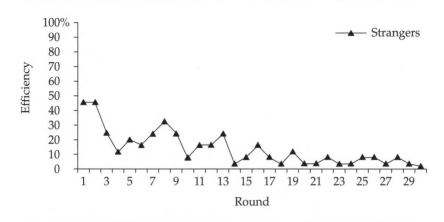

Source: Reprinted with permission from Bolton, Katok, and Ockenfels (2004a). Copyright 2004, the Institute for Operations Research and the Management Sciences, 7240 Parkway Drive, Suite 300, Hanover, Md. 21076, U.S.A.

game, possibly reflecting the hope that repeated action will support more cooperation. But the dynamics reveal that buyers respond to the fact that, on average, this expectation was disappointed: they start out by trusting quite a lot, but trust quickly collapses. In fact, the percentage of last round trust was only 0.04 percent, much less than in the one-shot game, indicating that buying in the one-shot game is mainly due to inexperience.

In sum, economic theory underestimates the degree of cooperation in one-shot encounters of anonymous traders; there is intrinsic trustworthiness. To the extent people cooperate, the need for a reputation system is diminished. However, in our setting there is not enough intrinsic motivation to stabilize positive reciprocity in an anonymous community without external enforcement. In this sense, economic theory is right: relying on solely intrinsic motivation will not, in the long run, lead to satisfactory cooperative behavior.

Extrinsic Motivation: What Is the Gain of Introducing a Perfect Reputation System?

Here we look at how well reputation systems provide an external enforcement device that may help overcome the cooperation problems in anonymous communities. A number of other external factors influence trust and trustworthiness. Elsewhere in this volume, Karen Cook and her colleagues discuss how, absent reputation information, competence and motivation can influence trust and trustworthiness (see chapter 7). Tapan Khopar and Paul Resnick discuss the influence of culture (see chapter 4).

From an economic theory perspective, the incentives created by reputation systems depend on the exact trading environment. Suppose, for the moment, that the buyer-seller encounter in figure 1.1 is played repeatedly, with an infinite time horizon, and so with no expectation of a stopping round of play. In such a setting, even if all traders are selfish and rational, equilibria exist in which the buyer always buys and the seller always ships. The equilibria can be supported by reciprocal trigger-strategies that call for a buyer, for instance, to trust as long as the seller has shipped when he or she has had opportunities to do so in the past. Once the seller defects, he will never be trusted again. If future payoffs are important enough, the seller has an incentive to be trustworthy all the time, and the buyer has an incentive to trust all the time (for example, Kandori 1992; Greif 1994). An interesting feature of this argument is that it is independent of whether the reputation system relies on direct or indirect reciprocity. The information available to the buyer about the seller is what is important; if the information is sufficient in quantity and accuracy, the buyer can act on it just as well if the information were generated elsewhere or if it were generated from the buyer's experience.

There are, however, in our context two problems with this kind of simple equilibrium. First, the trading horizon in online market platforms is typically finite. If either the buyer or the seller believes that there will be some upper limit to the number of items to be traded (so a finite horizon game), cooperation among selfish, rational traders will unravel (in the last round there is no trustworthiness, and so no trust and no trade, and for this reason no trade in the second to last round, and so on). Second, buying and shipping in the infinite game equilibrium does not capture trust and trustworthiness under conditions of uncertainty. Specifically, in the infinite game equilibrium, there is no uncertainty about each other's behavior because, in equilibrium, all sellers—not just some or most—have a material incentive to be trustworthy and ship.[9] In this sense, there is no risk of being exploited. Yet, in many cases, in real-world markets a buyer trusts in the sense that they decide to purchase knowing there is some chance of exploitation.

Because this chapter is concerned with trust (characterized by a risk of being exploited) in economic transactions (where traders typically trade a finite number of items), we think it more appropriate to study finitely repeated games. In models of these games, trust emerges when there is some, possibly small, amount of truly intrinsic trustworthiness within the seller population (Wilson 1985). That there is intrinsic trustworthiness has been demonstrated, for instance, in our experimental studies of the one-shot trust game of figure 1.1. In essence, in theory, the existence of some intrinsically trustworthy sellers gives all sellers an incentive to build a reputation as trustworthy, at least until toward the end of the game, at which point a good reputation is less valuable. Hence buyers can trust sellers, at least early on, because there is a high probability—albeit less than one in the last few rounds—that all sellers will act trustworthy. [10] It turns out that reputation building in this model, in the context of the buyer-seller encounter, is, as in the infinite horizon models, independent of whether the reputation system relies on direct or indirect reciprocity (Bolton and Ockenfels 2008), something we will come back to shortly.

Economic theory therefore suggests that, in principle, reputation mechanisms of the sort we describe in the introduction can solve many of the trust problems associated with economic transactions. All the various models, finite and infinite horizon alike, suggest that reliable information about past behavior is a necessary ingredient to the emergence of trust, because it allows buyers to avoid sellers who are known as fraudulent and to buy only from sellers who have proved trustworthy in the past. Conditioning trust on the seller's history creates incentives for sellers to build up a reputation for being trustworthy, at least when the end of the market is not too close and maintaining a good reputation is still valuable. A reputation of being trustworthy can be developed and sustained even by completely rational and selfish sellers—as long as the probability of being matched with intrinsically trustworthy sellers is strictly positive. We know from our experimental strangers market that intrinsic trustworthiness alone is not enough to sustain a trading platform that has no reputation system. So does a feedback system help promote trust and trustworthiness, as suggested by theory?

Gary Bolton, Elena Katok, and Axel Ockenfels compared the strangers market to a *reputation market*, played more than thirty rounds, in which, as before, a buyer never met the same seller more than once (2004a). However, in this market we introduced a reputation system that, similar to eBay's feedback forum, informs buyers about all past actions of their current seller (for related experimental work, see Duffy and Ochs 2003; Bohnet and Huck 2004). This feedback information is always shared and reliable, because it is not given by the buyers but by the experimenter, and sellers had no way to change their online identity. This way, the experiment studies the impact of feedback information on trading behavior when an ideal, frictionless reputation mechanism is available. And in the finite horizon theory, this should be enough information to enable trust and trustworthiness, and so successful trade.

Figure 1.3 shows the results of the reputation market experiment and compares with the strangers market results from figure 1.2. On average, there is significantly more buying (56 versus 37 percent; $p < .05$) and shipping (73 versus 39 percent; $p < .01$) in the reputation market than in

Figure 1.3   Reputation Market

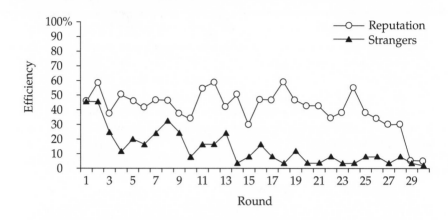

Source: Reprinted with permission from Bolton, Katok, and Ockenfels (2004a). Copyright 2004, the Institute for Operations Research and the Management Sciences, 7240 Parkway Drive, Suite 300, Hanover, Md. 21076, U.S.A.

the strangers market. In fact, the shipping probability is slightly higher than the threshold of 70 percent for trust being profitable. As a consequence, the trade dynamics also look quite different than in the strangers market; trading starts at about the same level as in the strangers market and remains stable until the very last rounds, when the strategic value of having a reputation for being trustworthy vanishes and virtually all cooperation collapses.

We conclude that introducing a perfect reputation system in a market with strangers has a strongly positive impact on trust, trustworthiness, and trading efficiency. Both buyers and sellers respond strategically to the information provided. At the same time, however, the experiment demonstrates the serious limits of perfect reputation systems in promoting cooperation. The realized surplus as a proportion of potential surplus is only 41 percent. The gain from introducing a perfect system into a strangers market, described earlier, as a proportion of the maximal potential gain is 41 − 14 = 27 percent, well below what would be expected theoretically (see Bolton and Ockenfels 2008). Obviously, trader behavior is different from what we expect from theory, in a way that limits the effectiveness of reputation systems.

What Behavior Limits the Effectiveness of Reputation Systems?

We have seen that even though reputation systems can build on intrinsic motivations to cooperate, their effectiveness is less than what can be ex-

Figure 1.4   Partners Market

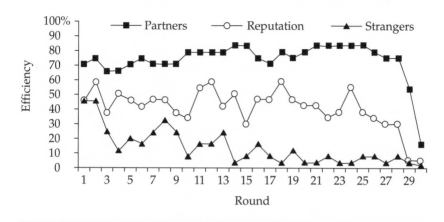

Source: Reprinted with permission from Bolton, Katok, and Ockenfels (2004a). Copyright 2004, the Institute for Operations Research and the Management Sciences, 7240 Parkway Drive, Suite 300, Hanover, Md. 21076, U.S.A.

pected from theory based on purely selfish traders. What is the source of these limitations?

Because the feedback system in the experiment is perfect with regard to the information it delivers, we need to look at departures from fully rational behavior for answers. Evidence in the data indicates that forward looking behavior is more limited than theory anticipates. Perhaps the strongest evidence for this is that out-of-equilibrium behavior is observed in the early rounds of play (see figure 1.4). For instance, the sellers' payoffs are strongly positively correlated with the overall number of shippings; the Spearman rank correlation is 0.504 ($p = .000$). Shipping early is not only trustworthy and fair, it also pays. However, many sellers have difficulty understanding the future benefits of being nice. About 40 percent of the sellers in the reputation market who receive an order in the first round of the market fail to ship.

Evidence also indicates that traders learn from looking back, a kind of learning the equilibrium model does not anticipate. For example, reputation market sellers are actually more inclined to ship in the middle rounds of the market than at the beginning. And in the strangers market, the 65 percent of buyers who start out trusting quickly learn that they should not. This behavior is consistent with low-rationality adaptive learning models that suggest that people come to strategic games with rough priors and adjust these priors according to the payoff reinforcement they get from experimenting with various strategies (see Erev and Roth 1998). Davide Barrera and Vincent Buskens, in the following chapter, present data that suggest that another form of learning by look-ing back, learning by imitation, is also important in games involving trust.

There is also additional evidence to suggest that bounded rationality is not the entire story for why reputation market trading performance falls short of what theory leads us to expect. Bolton and his colleagues also included a *partners market* (2004a). The only respect in which this market differed from the reputation market is that, in the partners mar-ket, the same buyer was matched with the same seller for the entire mar-ket. Recall that theory suggests that there should be no difference in the performance of the two markets: in both cases, buyers should be able to play tit-for-tat strategies to keep sellers trustworthy. Nevertheless, figure 1.4 demonstrates a substantial difference between them. Overall, trading (efficiency) levels in the partners markets, 74 percent, is significantly higher than in the reputation market ($p < 0.025$).

The amount of trading in the partners markets is still substantially less than perfect, indicating that bounded rationality explanations still apply. Still, trade efficiency is greater than in the reputation markets, which suggests that some other things beside bounded rationality are at play. We argue that the flow of information in the reputation markets creates information externalities in that, out of equilibrium, the incen-tives to invest in the two markets are different. Specifically, there is a public goods problem in the reputation market not present in the part-ners market. Buyers do not benefit from the reputation information they themselves produce. As a consequence, reputation market buyers under-invest in the production of reputation information relative to partners markets.[11] In this way, trust is an attribute of the system, not just the in-dividuals in it (for a demonstration of this point in a different market context, see chapter 3, this volume).

So boundedly rational trading is off the equilibrium path, and the re-sulting out-of-equilibrium incentives may in turn affect traders' behav-ior. A second observation in this regard is that reputation information, even in a system with comprehensive and reliable feedback information, need be interpreted as a noisy signal because the predictive value of rep-utation information suffers from the noise generated by the behavior of real traders. This has consequences in a number of ways (for evidence on the relationship between noisy signals in reputation and perceptions of fraud, see chapter 8, this volume). Also, we have experimentally shown in a recent paper that market competition tends to increase the effectiveness of reputation systems in environments with noisy behav-iors (Bolton, Loebbecke, and Ockenfels 2008). It does so because, with competition, buyers can discriminate between sellers on the basis of the reputation information provided by the reputation system, creating stronger incentives for sellers to behave consistently trustworthy over time. The experiments involved matching competition (each buyer gets to choose between two sellers and prices are fixed) and price competition (the two sellers compete on prices) to both the reputation and partners markets described earlier. Our experiments showed that seller competition in (perfect) reputation markets typically enhances trust and trustworthiness, and always increases total gains from trade. We also found that information about reputation trumps pricing in the sense that traders usually do not conduct business with someone having a bad reputation—not even for a substantial price discount. (Andreas Diekmann, Ben Jann, and David Wyder, in chapter 5 of this volume, find that buyers are willing to pay a higher price to sellers with good reputations.) Price competition thus does not significantly undermine the sellers' incentives to be trustworthy. Finally, we found that a reliable reputation system can largely reduce the advantage of partners markets over reputation markets in promoting trust and trustworthiness described earlier, if the market is competitive enough. One important overall conclusion from the study, then, is that in a world with noisy traders and well-functioning reputation systems, encouraging greater market competition may be a powerful tool for increasing cooperation and trade efficiency (Bolton, Loebbecke, and Ockenfels 2008).

Complex Reputation Measures

We have discussed markets where reputation is equivalent with (perfect) information about the sequence of a seller's shipping decisions. In theory, this measure is enough to sustain cooperation through indirect reciprocity. In fact, simple and stable cooperation in these market settings can theoretically be reached with just information about a seller's last shipping decision, because this information is all one needs to use tit-for-tat strategies. Here we look at markets that are more complex and, in theory, require more reputation information to produce cooperation.

We examine two types of complexities. One arises in markets where reputation must be built on multidimensional facets of the seller's history. When assessing a seller's trustworthiness, buyers need to take into account, for instance, technical and cultural communication problems, the possibility of incomplete or manipulative feedback, the reliability of the postal service, and so on. Even perfect reputation mechanisms, which deliver all relevant information to promote cooperative interaction, may become quite complex, so that real traders experience information overload.

A second type of complexity arises from information requirements in two-sided reputation systems, which are necessarily much more demanding than one-sided systems. For example, consider a system in which buyers rate sellers and sellers rate buyers to mitigate moral hazard incentives on both market sides.[12] Now suppose that a buyer receives reliable information that the seller did not send the object to the last buyer. Does this imply that the seller is not trustworthy? No. It could be that the seller did not ship because his or her last buyer never sent the payment. Let's think this one step further. Would it then be enough for our current buyer to know whether the current seller's last buyer paid? Again, the answer is no. Whether the last buyer's action can be interpreted as trustworthy depends on the history of play of his or her earlier transaction partners. In principle, the entire history of both trading partners as well as their trading partners, and their trading partners, and so on, may be required to construct a system that has enough information of the sort we tested in the one-way settings discussed earlier.

Clearly, this information is difficult to process, even when comprehensive and perfectly reliable. There is a way to avoid the processing problems, though. The relevant information can be captured in a single reputation rating, which does not directly reveal past behavior but rather evaluates these behaviors according to all traders' histories and with respect to a trading norm. This rating can, in theory, be easily processed. On the other hand, however, the information content is less comprehensible because of the rather complex information aggregation processes behind the rating.

Let us illustrate the issues with the help of the simple image scoring game (Nowak and Sigmund 1998). As with the markets we have already studied, the image scoring game conceives of the group interacting over a series of rounds. Again, in each round, people are paired off at random. One person in the pair, designated as the *mover*, is given the opportunity to give a favor to the other, designated as the *receiver*. These designations are assigned randomly, so over many rounds, each player is a mover about half the time and a receiver the other half. Giving a favor would cost the mover c and benefit the receiver $b > c > 0$. Figure 1.5 illustrates the situation.

The efficient outcome in this game, the outcome that maximizes the total social benefits, is for everyone to give when they are the mover. Although keeping maximizes short-run payoffs, reputation can help by providing the information necessary to reward those who give with giving and punishing those who do not with keeping. This kind of reciprocity is not unlike the trust game context we discussed in earlier sections. However, even though the game looks much simpler than the one presented in figure 1.1, the basic reputation issue is more complicated. To see why, consider the kind of reciprocity that works in the trust game markets based on the game in figure 1.1. The mover gives if he knows the receiver played give the last time as a mover, and keeps if the receiver last played keep. Suppose now that you are the mover matched

Figure 1.5   Mover Meets Receiver in Image Scoring Game

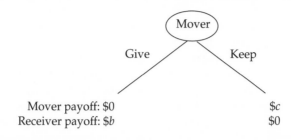

Mover payoff: $0 $c
Receiver payoff: $b $0

Source: Authors' compilation.

with someone who last played *keep* as a mover. If you play keep as the reciprocity strategy stipulates, then the next time you are the receiver, you can expect the mover to play keep on you (if others too play the reciprocity strategy). Consequently, you make more money playing *give* (lose c now, pays b later) than playing keep (gain c now, pays 0 later). The problem is that if enough people decide to give to keepers then it pays to be a keeper. And if it pays to have a bad reputation, then why have a good one?

So, this kind of first-order information about what the opponent did last time as a mover is, theoretically, not enough to stabilize cooperation. If we add second-order information, the receiver's reputation would include not only what he did last time as a mover, but also what the receiver he faced did last time as a mover. For example, the reputation might reveal that the receiver last played keep with a player who last played give. This amount of recursive information pushes the unraveling problem back by a step. To see this, consider a mover who, for the first time, encounters a receiver who played keep on a giver. To support his punishment, keeping on a keeper would have to be rewarded, meaning that there needs to be giving to someone who gives to a keeper—which is not consistent with self-interest because keeping on a keeper pays more. So now players would have to think two steps ahead and be confident others do so as well before cooperation would unravel.

Of course, thinking three steps ahead is still not enough. To stabilize cooperation in a population of rational traders, one would need the entire transaction histories of basically all traders. For this reason, some theorists have cautioned that indirect reciprocal systems might not be stable outside very small groups, where information demands are relatively modest.

Boundedly rational traders, however, often do not think many steps ahead (see earlier and, for example, Nagel 1995), and people's ability to do backwards induction is rather limited. In fact, in an experimental study of the image scoring game, we find that first-order information significantly increases cooperation rates above the level in a market without any reputation information (for details, see Bolton, Katok, and Ockenfels 2005).[13] Second-order information again significantly increases cooperation rates, reflecting that traders do some of the backward induction, but do not think through the whole problem. However, both markets with strangers matching perform dramatically worse than the corresponding partners market. Figure 1.6 illustrates the situation.

How can the gap of the effectiveness of reputation systems between partners and strangers matching markets be closed? We think it unlikely that higher-order information would help considerably, because second-order information is already difficult to communicate and to process. One way could be to aggregate all the relevant information into a single reputation score so that traders might then apply a simple reciprocity strategy in a way that cannot be cheated on (Kandori 1992).

In our experiment (Bolton, Katok, and Ockenfels 2005), we proposed the following reputation score along the following lines. We labeled each player in each round as a member of either the *matcher* club or the *nonmatcher* club according to the following rules. In the first round, everyone is a matcher. In every round after that, a player's label is updated: If the player gave to a matcher the last time he was mover, he is a matcher. If the player kept on a nonatcher, he is a matcher. If the player did anything else, he is a nonmatcher. Now consider a reciprocity strategy that stipulates giving to a matcher and keeping on a nonmatcher. If everyone follows this rule, then everyone will stay a matcher and there will be 100 percent cooperation. Moreover, you cannot benefit by cheating. If you keep on a matcher, you become a nonmatcher, which lines you up to be punished because the next time you are matched with a mover, he will keep on you. And punishment is now with impunity: keeping on a nonmatcher allows a mover to maintain matching status—he won't be punished for doing the right thing.

When all information is processed in this way, the reciprocal strategy yields stable cooperation—at least in theory. To our surprise, however, the experimental data does not confirm at all the prediction. The bar called *labels* in figure 1.6 shows the average giving rate in this setting. The information that should stabilize the cooperation rate in fact significantly reduces the cooperation rate compared to the other settings, which involve theoretically insufficient reputation information. It appears that real traders have difficulties with reputational reports that filter actions, and respond more favorably to reputational reports about recent past actions. The dilemma is that this information, when complete, cannot be processed by boundedly rational traders.

Figure 1.6   Giving Levels (Averaged over All Rounds)

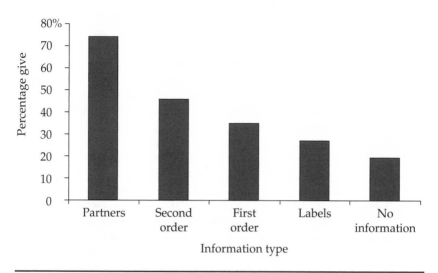

Source: Authors' compilation.

Conclusions

What we learn from the experimental and theoretical work is that it is the interplay of institutions with bounded rational behavior that drives the results. No doubt, institutions matter, but behavioral aspects of reputation-building matter as well. As a result, standard economic models based on full rationality and narrow self-interest tend to overestimate the difficulties of promoting trust in one-shot situations, and underestimate the difficulties in ongoing interaction in communities of strangers.

Because the laboratory reputation systems we study here are perfect, the limits of their effectiveness cannot be the result of institutional defects but must be due to behavioral defects. That is, the restraints that we observe are rooted in boundedly rational behavior. There are basically two types of noisiness in the behavior that significantly affect the functioning of the institutions. For one, bounded rationality can directly affect trust and trustworthiness though nonrational choices. Besides difficulties that arise when handling complex reputation measures, we observe that real traders have difficulties coping with reputation-building dynamics. Many traders fail to look forward enough and to fully take into account the future consequences of current behavior. Other behaviors are characterized by too much backward looking and simple, adaptive learning patterns. Second, noisy behavior moves the reputation-building dynamics off the equilibrium path and thus changes (out-of-equilibrium) incentives in ways that systematically affect strategic reputation-building. We observe, for instance, that noisy behavior creates information externalities so that the flow of reputation information through the community becomes critical to the effectiveness of reputation systems. Also, when trading dynamics are out of equilibrium, seller competition becomes a powerful support for reputation systems.

We think that only a combination of complementary field, laboratory, and thought experiments can reveal the full story behind reputation systems. Field studies strive for external validity and require a careful look at institutions. It can be difficult, if not impossible, however, to separate institutional from behavioral influences, to measure the impact of either aspect on the effectiveness of reputation systems, and to measure the overall impact of a reputation system (for an in-depth discussion of the limitations of field data and techniques that might be used to overcome them, see chapter 6, this volume). Thought experiments (for example, equilibrium theory) help us understand how behavior and institutions interact, reveal basic incentive structures, and allow generalizing from empirical observations. But it is risky not to complement thought experiments with data because it is known that theory can sometimes yield dramatically wrong conclusions, especially when it comes to social interaction (for example, Bolton and Ockenfels 2000). Thought experiments also tend to neglect institutional details, which can turn out to be critical, both in the equilibrium analysis and in reality (for example, Klemperer 2004). Laboratory experiments can separate and measure the different impacts and the interplay between institutional and behavioral influences. Combined with field and thought experiments, they are a powerful tool for analyzing the effectiveness of existing and newly designed reputation systems.

Gary Bolton gratefully acknowledges the support of the National Science Foundation. Axel Ockenfels gratefully acknowledges the support of the Deutsche Forschungsgemeinschaft. We are advising firms, including eBay, on reputation mechanism design and other market design issues; the views expressed are our own.

Notes

1. In this chapter, we deal with trust and trustworthiness in Internet marketplaces. For a taxonomy of information exchange systems, see chapter 10.
2. Although online auction transactions appear to be particularly vulnerable to fraud, the problems we report here exist in basically all reputation-based interaction. We consider eBay a convenient example because it allows re-

searchers to quantify some of the benefits and problems. We also note that eBay's feedback forum is only one part of a mix of (imperfect) policies and rules that interact to promote trade efficiency. Only a very few papers address this interaction. One is that of Werner Güth and his colleagues, who investigate the joint effectiveness of buyer insurance, which is part of eBay's so-called Purchase Protection Program, and eBay's feedback forum (Güth, Mengel, and Ockenfels 2006).

3. The cost of generating feedback includes the risk of trusting sellers, something we discuss later.

4. One of the main motives for giving feedback appears to be reciprocity (Dellarocas, Fan, and Wood 2004). That is, a trader's propensity to leave feedback is driven by the expectation that the trading partner reciprocates with positive feedback. This observation is remarkably in line with the literature in experimental economics on voluntary provision of public goods (see, for example, Ledyard 1995; Ockenfels and Weimann 1999).

5. Another potential source of noisy feedback information is fraudulent identity change. The costs of changing an online trader identity is often close to zero, implying that fraudulent sellers can exploit their buyers and then reappear with a clean record. If buyers are willing to buy only from a newbie, a seller with no record, if the object is offered at a lower price, compared to the price offered by a seller with a positive reputation record, then trust and trustworthy behavior can be sustained (Ockenfels 2003; see also Friedman and Resnick 2001).

6. We assume that the seller fixes the price. For example, Amazon.com permits sellers of used books and CDs to make offerings on its site, along with its own new goods offerings. A used goods seller posts on the market platform an offer that includes a description of the item and its condition, and a price at which he or she is willing to sell. A willing buyer sends the money to Amazon. On receiving the money, the seller is supposed to ship the item to the buyer. In addition, the moral hazards surrounding shipping and accurate representation of good quality are controlled by a feedback system not unlike the one we will introduce to our game. However, all arguments in this chapter hold equally if the price is endogenously determined, such as in eBay's auctions (in this case the auction winner is the buyer).

7. To be more specific, in our trust game, reciprocity models suggest that a seller ships because the buyer was so kind to buy, whereas fairness models suggest that the seller ships because otherwise the payoff distribution would be unfair (see also the discussion of motives like efficiency concerns and procedural fairness in related games in Bolton and Ockenfels 2008).

8. Payoffs, framing, and context may all affect the exact numbers. However, based on our extensive research with various payoff parameters, different framings, contexts, and experimental procedures (see reference list), we are confident that the qualitative results we discuss in this chapter are robust. One element we do not consider is buyer-seller verbal communication. For data suggesting that such communication can mitigate moral hazard, see chapter 11, this volume.

9. There are also more subtle equilibria in these models in which cooperation in any given round is uncertain, but this raises yet a third problem—that

there are many equilibria in these models with outcomes ranging from full cooperation to no cooperation. In our view, trust is not satisfactorily described as an equilibrium selection problem.

10. The mechanics of these equilibria are relatively complex, and we will not delve into them here (for a theoretical and experimental treatment within a trust game environment, see Bolton and Ockenfels 2008).

11. It turns out that there are no information externalities in the incomplete information model of reputation building on the equilibrium path of the buyer-seller encounter or in other market games such as Selten's chain store game (for a discussion and a formal experiment that shows that the phenomenon is more robust than theory suggests it should be, see Bolton and Ockenfels 2008).

12. This is much like eBay, where both transaction partners can rate each other. However, because eBay transactions are typically sequential (first buyers send money, then sellers ship the object), the moral hazard problem is mostly on the seller side.

13. Subjects were Penn State University students, mostly undergraduates from various fields of study, and were recruited by fliers posted around campus—in total, 192 participants. We ran two image scoring games for each information condition, each game with sixteen subjects playing for fourteen rounds. In each round, subjects were anonymously paired, interfacing with one another by computers. The value of a gift, B, was $1.25, and the cost of giving, C, was $0.75. Subjects knew that they would be in each role, mover or receiver, for half the trials (seven times), and roles would generally rotate between rounds.

References

Bohnet, Ing, and Steffen, Huck. 2004. "Repetition and Reputation: Implications for Trust and Trustworthiness When Institutions Change." *American Economic Review* 94(2): 362–66.

Bolton, Gary E., and Axel Ockenfels. 2000. "ERC: A Theory of Equity, Reciprocity and Competition." *American Economic Review* 90(1): 166–93.

———. 2008. "Information Value and Externalities in Reputation Building: An Experimental Study." Working paper. Cologne: University of Cologne.

Bolton, Gary E., Ben Greiner, and Axel Ockenfels. 2008. "Engineering Trust: Reciprocity in the Production of Reputation Information." Working paper no. 42. Cologne: University of Cologne.

Bolton, Gary E., Elena Katok, and Axel Ockenfels. 2004a. "How Effective Are Online Reputation Mechanisms? An Experimental Investigation." *Management Science* 50(11): 1587–602.

———. 2004b. "Trust among Internet Traders: A Behavioral Economics Approach." *Analyse & Kritik* 26(2): 185–202.

———. 2005. "Cooperation among Strangers with Limited Information about Reputation." *Journal of Public Economics* 89(8): 1457–68.

Bolton, Gary E., Claudia Loebbecke, and Axel Ockenfels. 2008. "How Social Reputation Networks Interact with Competition in Anonymous Online Trading: An Experimental Study." *Journal of Management Information Systems* 25(2): 145–69.

Dellarocas, Chrysanthos. 2003. "The Digitization of Word-of-Mouth: Promise and Challenges of Online Reputation Mechanisms." *Management Science* 49(10): 1407–424.

———. 2006. "Reputation Mechanisms." In *Handbook on Economics and Information Systems*, edited by Terrence Hendershott. Amsterdam: Elsevier Science.

Dellarocas, Chrysanthos, Ming Fan, and Charles Wood. 2004. "Self-Interest, Reciprocity, and Participation in Online Reputation Systems." MIT Sloan School of Management working paper no. 4500-04. Cambridge, Mass.: Massachusetts Institute of Technology.

Duffy, John, and Jack Ochs. 2003. "Cooperative Behavior and the Frequency of Social Interaction." Working paper no. 274. Pittsburgh: University of Pittsburgh.

Dufwenberg, Martin, and Georg Kirchsteiger. 2004. "A Theory of Sequential Reciprocity." *Games and Economic Behavior* 47(2): 268–98.

Erev, Ido, and Alvin E. Roth. 1998. "Predicting How People Play Games: Reinforcement Learning in Experimental Games with Unique, Mixed Strategy Equilibria." *American Economic Review* 88(4): 848–81.

Fehr, Ernst, and Klaus M. Schmidt. 1999. "A Theory of Fairness, Competition, and Cooperation." *Quarterly Journal of Economics* 114(4): 817–68.

Friedman, Eric J., and Paul Resnick 2001. "The Social Cost of Cheap Pseudonyms." *Journal of Economics and Management Strategy* 10(2): 173–99.

Greif, Avner 1993. "Contract Enforceability and Economic Institutions in Early Trade: The Maghribi Traders' Coalition." *American Economic Review* 83(3): 525–48.

———. 1994. "Cultural Beliefs and the Organization of Society: A Historical and Theoretical Reflection on Collectivist and Individualist Societies." *Journal of Political Economy* 102(5): 912–50.

Güth, Werner, Friederike Mengel, and Axel Ockenfels. 2007. "An Evolutionary Analysis of Buyer Insurance and Seller Reputation in Online Markets." *Theory and Decision* 63(3): 265–82.

Kandori, Michihiro. 1992. "Social Norms and Community Enforcement." *Review of Economic Studies* 59(1): 63–80.

Klein, Tobias J., Christian Lambertz, Giancarlo Spagnolo, and Konrad O. Stahl. 2007. "Reputation Building in Anonymous Markets: Evidence from eBay." Working paper. Mannheim: University of Mannheim.

Klemperer, Paul. 2004. *Auctions: Theory and Practice*. Princeton, N.J.: Princeton University Press.

Ledyard, John O. 1995. "Public Goods: A Survey of Experimental Research." In *Handbook of Experimental Economics*, edited by John H. Kagel and Alvin E. Roth. Princeton, N.J.: Princeton University Press.

Miller, Nolan, Paul Resnick, and Richard Zeckhauser. 2005. "Eliciting Honest Feedback: The Peer Prediction Method." *Management Science* 51(9): 1359–73.

Nagel, Rosemarie. 1995. "Unraveling in Guessing Games: An Experimental Study." *American Economic Review* 85(5): 1313–26.

Nowak, Marin A., and Karl Sigmund. 1998. "Evolution of Indirect Reciprocity by Image Scoring." *Nature* 393(June 11): 573–77.

Ockenfels, Axel. 2003. "Reputationsmechanismen auf Internet-Marktplattformen." *Zeitschrift für Betriebswirtschaft* 73(3): 295–315.

Ockenfels, Axel, and Joachim Weimann. 1999. "Types and Patterns: An Experimental East-West-German Comparison of Cooperation and Solidarity." *Journal of Public Economics* 71(2): 275–87.

Rabin, Matthew. 1993. "Incorporating Fairness into Game Theory and Economics." *American Economic Review* 83(5): 1281–302.

Rashid, Al Mamunur, Kimberly Ling, Regina D. Tassone, Paul Resnick, Robert Kraut, and John Riedl. 2006. "Motivating Participation by Displaying the Value of Contribution." In *Proceedings of the SIGCHI Conference on Human Factors in Computing Systems 2006,* edited by Rebecca Grinter, Thomas Rodden, Paul Aoki, Ed Cutrell, Robin Jeffries, and Gary Olson. New York: ACM.

Resnick, Paul, and Richard Zeckhauser 2002. "Trust Among Strangers in Internet Transactions: Empirical Analysis of eBay's Reputation System." In *Advances in Applied Microeconomics,* vol. 11, *The Economics of Internet and E-commerce,* edited by Michael R. Baye. Amsterdam: Elsevier Science.

Resnick, Paul, Richard Zeckhauser, John Swanson, and Kate Lockwood. 2006. "The Value of Reputation on eBay: A Controlled Experiment." *Experimental Economics* 9(2): 79–101.

Wilson, Robert B. 1985. "Reputations in Games and Markets." In *Game-Theoretic Models of Bargaining,* edited by Alvin E. Roth. Cambridge: Cambridge University Press.

Chapter 2

Third-Party Effects

DAVIDE BARRERA AND VINCENT BUSKENS

IMAGINE THAT you have decided on a financial investment, for example, for a private pension, and you have to choose among several companies offering similar services. Imagine also that you do not have much experience with this type of investment. You could investigate the past performances of all companies and compare them, but this would take considerable time, especially if there are many of them. You could ask a friend who made a similar investment about her experience, but this provides information on only one company. You could choose by reputation, simply picking the most well-known company, but companies with the most successful marketing strategy do not always offer the best products. Malicious companies might invest your money in a risky manner, making large profits themselves if things go well, and you end up with the costs if the investment goes wrong.

Typically, these problems are not, in markets with asymmetric information between buyer and seller, solved by market forces (Akerlof 1970). To make your choice even more complex, the success of your investment will also depend on chance. For example, if you are planning a long-term investment, the behavior of financial markets is hard to predict over longer periods. Therefore, part of the information you are able to gather might be hard to interpret; for example, the failure of a specific investment might have been caused by a bad financial advisor, but it could also have simply been due to adverse contingencies. Starting such an investment represents a typical trust problem, whereby trustworthy investors invest money in such a way that it is both in their own and in the consumer's interest. Untrustworthy investors invest only to maximize their own short-term profits without taking the consumer's interests into account.

Such a setting can be analyzed applying existing theories on the effects of reputation and information in trust problems. Here we focus on an actor's (Ego) decision to trust her partner (Alter) based on the relevant information available to her.[1] Specifically, the goal of this chapter is to provide empirical evidence for the types of mechanisms influencing trusting behavior in settings with network embeddedness. Given existing theories about these effects, we investigate the conditions under which these effects operate. Moreover, interpreting information about a partner's behavior can be more or less difficult depending on uncertainties in the setting. We therefore also explore the relation between available information and uncertainty in trust problems.

Experimental research on conditions that affect actors' decisions to trust and reciprocate in one-shot games—that is, abstract representations of single encounters between strangers—is already substantial (see Berg, Dickhaut, and McCabe 1995; Snijders 1996; Snijders and Keren 2001; Camerer 2003, 83–100). However, most trust problems in real life differ from such abstract situations in many ways. First, in most trust problems, there is a positive probability that the same actors will meet in the future—*dyadic embeddedness*—and face a similar trust problem again. Second, actors are embedded in a social structure characterized by social relations, ethical norms, laws, institutions, and so on—*network and institutional embeddedness* (Granovetter 1985; Raub and Weesie 2000). Because we want to study the effects of information, we focus on a situation in which pairs of actors repeatedly face trust problems and are embedded in a network of relations from which they obtain information, but we neglect institutional aspects such as laws and norms. Several institutional aspects of online information exchange systems are discussed elsewhere in this volume (see chapters 10 and 11).

The effects of dyadic and network embeddedness on trust problems have been theorized, and existing models identify two types of mechanisms—*learning* and *control* (Buskens 2002; Buskens and Raub 2002). Both mechanisms are related to reputation in the literature. Learning refers to the extent to which Ego can learn about unknown characteristics of Alter that affect Alter's behavior in the trust situation. Learning in that sense is closely related to what David Kreps and Robert Wilson called reputation (1982). Control indicates the extent to which Ego can sanction or reward Alter by spreading information about Alter's behavior, and is more related to reputation in the sense that Werner Raub and Jeroen Weesie use it (1990). Other forms of social control are discussed elsewhere in this volume (see chapter 9). These mechanisms are explained in more detail in the theory section. To avoid confusing between the learning and control mechanism, we minimize the use of the term reputation from here on.

This chapter addresses two limitations in the existing literature. First, existing theories often make rather strong assumptions about actors' computational abilities, and neglect the possibility that actors apply simpler heuristics such as imitation, or are influenced by the outcomes obtained by relevant others through a mechanism of social comparison.

Second, empirical research on trust problems in situations characterized by network embeddedness is often unable to distinguish between different mechanisms that determine trust in embedded settings (see, for example, Buskens 2002; Buskens and Raub 2002, 2008). In experimental research, some studies have focused on trust problems with dyadic embeddedness (Gautschi 2000; Cochard, Nguyen Van, and Willinger 2004). Others have included a certain degree of network embeddedness (Güth et al. 2001; Duwfenberg et al. 2001; Buchan, Croson, and Dawes 2002; Bolton, Katok, and Ockenfels 2004, 2005). Furthermore, experimental studies on reputation systems—such as those used on eBay—effectively implement network embeddedness by making information about previous transactions available to all users (see chapters 1, 3, and 4, this volume). However, only one other recent working paper has described an experiment that also disentangles learning and control effects for dyadic as well as network embeddedness, but it did not include imitation and social comparison effects (Buskens, Raub, and van der Veer 2009). In other types of empirical research, it is mostly even more difficult to disentangle different mechanisms of embeddedness. Still, for example, at least two studies have found effects of third-party information on trust among colleagues (Burt and Knez 1995; Barrera and van de Bunt 2009). Also in studies on reputation systems such as the one used on eBay, researchers have found effects of third-party information on trust. For example, evidence indicates that buyers are willing to pay more for a product of a seller if that seller has more positive evaluations of previous buyers (see chapters 5 and 6, this volume).

We present a laboratory experiment designed to disentangle effects of various types of information stemming from dyadic and network embeddedness. More precisely, this experiment represents an empirical test in which relative complex arguments to trust, such as learning and control effects, are compared with other simpler heuristics, such as imitation or social comparison. In this experiment, groups of actors embedded in small networks play a repeated investment game and exchange information concerning their own behavior as well as their partner's behavior in the game (Berg, Dickhaut, and McCabe 1995). The manipulation of information exchange resembles the experiment conducted by Güth and his colleagues (2001): Egos know exactly what happened to other Egos in some conditions and they know only the choices of the other Egos, but not the related choices of the Alters in other conditions. We also vary uncertainty in the sense that the choices of Alters are ambiguous for Egos in some conditions (for a similar manipulation, see

Coricelli, Morales, and Mahlstedt 2006). We first deal with theories and hypotheses.

Theories and Hypotheses

We consider trust problems as interactions involving two interdependent actors. In correspondence with James Coleman (1990, chapter 5), a trust problem is defined by four characteristics: Ego has the possibility to place some resources at the disposal of Alter, who has the possibility to honor or abuse trust. Ego prefers to place trust if Alter honors trust, but regrets placing trust if Alter abuses it. There is no binding agreement that protects Ego from the possibility that Alter abuses trust. There is a time lag between Ego's and Alter's decisions.

This definition is consistent with the game-theoretic formalizations of the trust game (Camerer and Weigelt 1988; Dasgupta 1988; Kreps 1990) and the investment game (Berg, Dickhaut, and McCabe 1995; for a replication of the original experiment, see also Ortmann, Fitzgerald, and Boeing 2000). These two games differ in the following way. In the trust game, trust and trustworthiness are represented by dichotomous choices—trust versus no trust, honor trust versus abuse trust—and the investment game exhibits some continuity both in the choice of placing trust and in the choice of honoring or abusing trust. Because this continuity implies that we can distinguish not only between whether or not Ego trusts Alter, but also the extent to which she trusts him, we use the investment game in our theoretical analysis as well as in our experiment.

In the investment game, the two players start with initial endowments E_1 and E_2. Ego has the possibility to send all, some, or none of her endowment to Alter. The amount of money that she decides to send, say S_1 ($0 \leq S_1 \leq E_1$), is then multiplied by a factor m (with $m > 1$) by the experimenter. Alter receives an amount equal to m times the amount S_1 sent by Ego. The parameter m can be interpreted as the returns Alter makes on Ego's investment. Subsequently, Alter can decide to send back to Ego all, some, or none of the money he has received. The amount returned by Alter is denoted R_2 ($0 \leq R_2 \leq mS_1$). After Ego and Alter have concluded their task, Ego earns $P_1 = E_1 - S_1 + R_2$ and Alter earns $P_2 = E_2 + mS_1 - R_2$.

The One-Shot Game

Assuming complete information, standard forward-looking rationality, and selfish actors who are interested only in their own payoffs, the one-shot investment game has a straightforward subgame-perfect equilibrium: Alter maximizes his payoff by returning nothing to Ego (that is, choosing $R_2 = 0$). Therefore, Ego, who anticipates this behavior from Alter, maximizes her payoff by sending nothing to Alter in the first place (that is, choosing $S_1 = 0$).[2] Therefore, *send nothing* and *return nothing* are the equilibrium choices, and the payoffs in equilibrium are E_1 and E_2. This outcome is Pareto-suboptimal, because both actors would prefer any outcome yielded in a situation in which trust is to some extent placed and honored, $E_1 - S_1 + R_2$ and $E_2 + mS_1 - R_2$, with $S_1 > 0$ and $R_2 > S_1$. The pie that the actors divide reaches its maximum when Ego sends everything $(S_1 = E_1)$, which means that Pareto improvements are always possible if $S_1 < E_1$. Ego gains from trusting Alter if Alter returns more than he received $(R_2 > S_1)$, but, once S_1 has been chosen, Alter's decision resembles the move of the dictator in the dictator game: he decides how to split the pie of size mS_1. Given Ego's decision, all possible outcomes are Pareto non-comparable, since whatever Alter returns goes directly to Ego.

Learning Through Dyadic Embeddedness

Dyadic embeddedness refers to a situation in which two actors repeatedly play an investment game together. Thus, Ego has the possibility of learning about the trustworthiness of Alter. Learning models typically assume that actors do not look ahead, but they rather change their behavior adaptively according to the experiences they had in the past. Different types of learning mechanisms can be distinguished (for an overview of such models, see Camerer 2003, chapter 6). The most widely applied families of learning models are *belief learning* and *reinforcement learning*.

Reinforcement learning models are based on the payoffs actors received in previous games: the higher the payoff obtained by a given decision, the more likely it is that a player will make that decision again. Reinforcement models are straightforwardly applicable to the investment game because a heuristic of the type that rewards trustworthiness and punishes abuse seems particularly realistic for the investment game given the continuity of the possible moves in the game. This heuristic, in fact, implies that Ego compares the amount received in previous games with the amount sent in previous games. The more satisfied she is with the amount she receives back, the more she will send in the next game, whereas if she is unsatisfied with the amount she receives back, she will in the next game decrease the amount she sends. This reinforcement could depend on both the payoff earned in the previous game (that is, $E_1 - S_1 + R_2$), and on the proportion returned by Alter (that is, R_2/mS_1).[3] Therefore, assuming that subjects' learning in an investment game can be mislabeled as reinforcement learning, we expect the following effect of learning from dyadic embeddedness.

Hypothesis 1 (dyadic learning). The higher the amount earned by Ego (proportion returned by Alter) in previous games, the more Ego sends in the present game.

Control Through Dyadic Embeddedness

If we assume a finitely repeated game and complete information, standard game theory predicts that Alter will send nothing back in the last game (because $E_2 + mS_1 > E_2 + mS_1 - R_2$, for any $S_1, R_2 > 0$) and Ego will then send nothing in the last game, anticipating the behavior of Alter. Knowing that he has nothing to lose in the last game, Alter will not return anything in the last but one game and accordingly, Ego will send nothing as well. This argument, known as *backward induction*, unravels the whole game back until the first stage, making any trust impossible (for a prominent application, see Selten 1978). However, in their articles on sequential equilibrium, David Kreps and his colleagues (1982) and Kreps and Robert Wilson (1982) have shown that assuming incomplete information in the sense of John Harsanyi (1967–1968), cooperation can be sustained in the first games of a finitely repeated prisoner's dilemma. Similarly, this argument can be applied to a finitely repeated investment game.

Assuming that some Alters exist who do not have an incentive to abuse trust—for example, because they are in some sense altruistic— and that Ego is uncertain about her partner's incentives and will update her beliefs about Alter after obtaining information about him, Ego will send a positive amount in the first game, hoping to be playing with a nonselfish Alter. Thus, although a nonselfish Alter will not abuse trust anyway, even a selfish Alter will return an amount $R_2 \geq S_1$, to build a trustworthy reputation, if he is aware of Ego's uncertainty. Note that, according to Kreps and Wilson's model, even a very small proportion of altruistic Alters in the population is enough to support a cooperative equilibrium in the early rounds of the repeated game. Only when the repeated game approaches its end, a selfish Alter will abuse trust because he has nothing to lose in future interactions.[4] Consequently, Ego will send positive amounts in the early periods of the game because she knows that even a selfish Alter will return positive amounts. The model predicts that toward the end of the game the incentives to honor trust for selfish Alters become too small. Thus, Alters start to abuse trust, and Egos start to withhold trust. As soon as trust has been abused once or trust has been withheld once, there will be no more trust. Empirically, it is regularly observed in experiments with finitely repeated games that only in the very last periods do trust and trustworthiness rates decrease dramatically (see, for example, Selten and Stoecker 1986; Camerer and Weigelt 1988). This leads to the following two hypotheses on dyadic control effects.

Hypothesis 2a (dyadic control). The higher the number of periods remaining in the repeated game, the higher the amount that Ego is willing to send.

Hypothesis 2b (end-game effect). The amount sent by Ego decreases to a larger extent in the last few periods than in earlier periods of the repeated game.

Learning Through Network Embeddedness

The situation just analyzed represents a repeated interaction between two isolated actors. However, most transactions in real life take place between actors embedded in a social structure. In particular, other actors could have some kind of relation with Ego, Alter, or both. Therefore, we now relax the assumption of isolated actors introducing social networks in the game. We start by adding one other actor. Imagine two Egos playing a finitely repeated investment game with the same Alter. Moreover, these two Egos can exchange information about their interactions with Alter. Although learning models are widely applied in sociology to study the behavior of groups in social dilemma situations (for example, Heckathorn 1996; Macy and Skvoretz 1998; Flache and Macy 2002), learning models have not yet been applied to study the investment game. However, some effects of a common past have been observed in an experimental study using the investment game (Barrera 2007).

If two Egos play a repeated investment game and can exchange information with each other, every Ego obtains additional information from which she can learn, namely, information concerning games played by the other Ego with Alter. Assuming that this is a game of incomplete information, the additional information concerning games played by Alter with another Ego can reveal to Ego what kind of player Alter is. Therefore, Ego's decision is expected to be influenced by this information.

Now, we introduce additional complexity. Imagine more than one Alter in the network—for example, two Alters, each playing a repeated investment game with two Egos. Moreover, we assume that every Ego can receive information from another Ego playing with the same Alter or from another Ego playing with another Alter. Information concerning another Alter can be relevant if we assume that it affects Ego's idea about the population of Alters as a whole. Positive information about any Alter can then increase Ego's expectation that "her" Alter is trustworthy as well.[5] For example, if Ego is informed that another Alter has been returning a high proportion of what he receives to another Ego, Ego will raise her estimate of her Alter's propensity to return a high proportion, and she will be more inclined to send a higher amount to her Alter.

Davide Barrera and Vincent Buskens found some evidence for effects of this type of information using a vignette experiment (2007). As for dyadic learning, information Ego used to adjust her expectations about her Alter's behavior can include the proportion returned by any Alter to another Ego or the amount earned by this other Ego. This leads to the following two hypotheses concerning Ego using information about her Alter playing with another Ego and information about another Alter playing with another Ego, respectively.

Hypothesis 3a (network learning). Assuming that Ego receives information concerning previous game or games played by her Alter with another Ego, the higher the proportion returned by her Alter to another Ego (amount earned by another Ego) in the past, the more Ego sends to her Alter in the present game.

Hypothesis 3b (network learning). Assuming that Ego receives information concerning previous game or games played by another Alter with another Ego, the higher the proportion returned by another Alter to another Ego (amount earned by another Ego) in the past, the more Ego sends to her Alter in the present game.

Imitation

One of the other possible effects of information stemming from network embeddedness is imitation. Imitation is usually considered a form of learning that plays an important role in socialization processes (for example, Bandura and Walters 1963, chapter 2). In interactions resembling social dilemmas, imitation could be viewed as a parsimonious way to achieve the optimal decision, especially in settings where information is scarce (see Hedström 1998). Some imitation models have been proposed by economists, but apply to rather specific situations in which it is assumed that actors are fully informed about the past (for example, Pingle 1995; Pingle and Day 1996; Schlag 1998). In these models, actors make their decisions after receiving some information about the actions chosen by others and the outcomes obtained by them. However, the latter information might not always be available. For example, in an investment game, Ego could be informed about the choice of another Ego, but may be unaware of Alter's response in that game (for practical examples of such trust situations, see Barrera 2008). We restrict the term *imitation* to situations in which available information does not include the outcomes obtained by others, but only their behavior. Conversely, we use the label *learning* for decisions based on full information that includes the outcomes obtained by others.

In the investment game, we could imagine a situation in which two Alters play a finitely repeated investment game with two Egos each, just like before, but now Egos receive only information concerning the amount sent by other Egos. If an Ego receives information that another

Ego has repeatedly sent high amounts for some games to her Alter, she could infer from this information that her Alter is returning high amounts to this other Ego; if this were not the case, this other Ego would stop sending anything to Alter. Therefore, we expect that also such partial information will influence Ego's decision, particularly if full information concerning Alter's behavior is not available. As for hypothesis 3b, if Ego's trusting decision is based on her estimates of the tendency to honor trust of a population of Alters, her decision could be influenced also by information concerning the behavior of another Ego in interaction with another Alter. This leads to the following two hypotheses.

Hypothesis 4a (imitation). Assuming that Ego is informed about games played by her Alter with another Ego, the more another Ego has sent to her Alter in previous games, the more Ego sends to her Alter in the present game.

Hypothesis 4b (imitation). Assuming that Ego is informed about games played by another Alter with another Ego, the more another Ego has sent to another Alter in previous games, the more Ego sends to her Alter in the present game.

Social Comparison

To account for deviations from standard rationality—such as cooperation in a one-shot prisoner's dilemma or trust game and contribution in public good type of games—observed in a number of experiments, some scholars have developed models that release the assumption of purely selfish behavior, substituting it with the assumption of partly altruistic behavior.[6] These models assume that subjects are not only interested in their own outcomes, but also, to some extent, in the outcomes obtained by the other player. Thus, in these models, the utility function incorporates different types of nonstandard preferences, such as *fairness* (Rabin 1993) and *equity* or *inequality-aversion* (Fehr and Schmidt 1999; Bolton and Ockenfels 2000).

Rabin's fairness model assumes that actors behave nicely toward those who have been nice to them, and retaliate toward those who have harmed them. Ernst Fehr and Klaus Schmidt proposed a model in which actors care about their own outcomes as well as about the difference between their own outcomes and those of others (1999). According to this model, actors dislike receiving lower payoffs (envy), but also, to a smaller extent, higher payoffs (guilt). Finally, in the model Gary Bolton and Axel Ockenfels proposed, individual utility depends on both an actor's payoffs and his or her relative share (2000). Individuals prefer to receive a relative payoff equal to the average earned by all other players. These models are applied to settings in which actors are assumed to compare their outcomes with those of their interaction partners, but are not designed for comparisons within a network of actors who do not directly interact with each other. In particular, if actors are embedded in a network, they might compare their outcomes with those of others who occupy similar positions instead of with those of their interaction partners. Although these social comparison effects are not the main focus of this chapter, we pay attention to the most obvious effect, envy. Egos will sanction Alter if they feel treated unfairly compared to other Egos. More specifically, Ego will decrease the amount she sends if she sees that either her Alter or another Alter returns a larger proportion of the received amount to another Ego than the focal Ego obtains herself.

Hypothesis 5a (envy). The higher the (positive) difference between the proportion returned by her Alter to another Ego and the proportion returned to Ego in previous games, the less Ego sends to her Alter in the present game.

Hypothesis 5b (envy). The higher the (positive) difference between the proportion returned by another Alter to another Ego and the proportion returned by her Alter to Ego in previous games, the less Ego sends to her Alter in the present game.

Control Through Network Embeddedness

As for dyadic embeddedness, control effects have been theorized for network embeddedness. Vincent Buskens and Jeroen Weesie developed a model for a repeated trust game with a network of Egos (2000; see also Buskens 2002, chapter 3). This game-theoretic model predicts control effects through network embeddedness, but it applies to an infinitely repeated game. Buskens applied Kreps and Wilson's finitely repeated prisoner's dilemma model to a finitely repeated trust game and extended the original model by including an *exit* and a *voice* option for Ego (Buskens 2003; Kreps and Wilson 1982). In the voice model, two Egos can inform each other about the behavior of Alter in previous interactions. This model assumes, as in Kreps and Wilson, incomplete information and predicts that Ego's decision to place trust increases with the frequency at which the two Egos can inform each other.

Looking at the embedded investment game and assuming that Egos have incomplete information—that is, that some Alters do not have an incentive to abuse trust—and that any abuse of trust is type-revealing, Buskens showed that Egos' possibility to inform each other about the behavior of Alter makes Alter more trustworthy than if Egos play with Alter individually (2003). Thus, though Alters without incentive to abuse trust will not abuse trust anyway, other Alters will mimic this behavior longer than they will if they play with one Ego, to maintain a positive reputation. Therefore, the effect of the expected duration of the game (hypothesis 1a) should be stronger if Egos can inform each other, because a longer future implies that Ego has the possibility to punish her Alter for abusing trust not only by withholding trust herself in future games, but also by informing other Egos and thus further damaging her Alter's reputation. This argument is summarized in the following hypothesis.

> *Hypothesis 6 (network control).* The more Ego is able to inform other Egos, who are also playing with her Alter, about her Alter's behavior, the stronger the positive effect of the remaining number of periods in the repeated game is on the amount sent by Ego.

Uncertainty

In a trust problem like the one described by the investment game, Ego might be uncertain about the meaning of the amount that Alter returns. Reconsider again the example in which Ego asks Alter to invest her money. Ego might be uncertain about the actual profit Alter has made in a certain period. Even if Alter is a good investor, he might be luckier at some times than at other times. If, in such a situation, Ego is not able to observe how successful Alter was, Alter could simply return a small amount to Ego and claim that he did not make a large profit, while he actually did. In terms of the investment game, this implies that Ego is uncertain about the multiplier m with which the amount sent by Ego is multiplied. Assuming that Ego is uncertain about how much an Alter received, information about Alter's behavior becomes more difficult for Ego to interpret. A low return could be due to a low return on the investment rather than to an abuse of trust. Because information is more difficult to interpret under this kind of uncertainty, all effects of Alter's past behavior on trust are expected to become weaker.

> *Hypothesis 7a (dyadic learning under uncertainty).* If Ego is uncertain about returns on investment made by her Alter, the effect of her Alter's past behavior in interactions with Ego on Ego's trusting decision is smaller.

> *Hypothesis 7b (network learning under uncertainty).* If Ego is uncertain about returns on investment made by any Alter, the effect of this Alter's past behavior in interactions with *other* Egos on Ego's trusting decision is smaller.

> *Hypothesis 7c (envy under uncertainty).* If Ego is uncertain whether or not another Alter, who is interacting with another Ego, has the same returns on his investment as her Alter, the effect of the difference between the amount returned to another Ego and the amount returned to Ego is smaller.[7]

Method

The constituent game in the experiment is the investment game described earlier (Berg, Dickhaut, and McCabe 1995). The experiment is designed to investigate the effects of dyadic and network embeddedness on Ego's decision in more or less uncertain conditions. Three features are therefore manipulated: the structure of the information network, the amount of information carried by network ties and Ego's uncertainty about the returns on investment. Dyadic embeddedness is also implemented in the experiment because all subjects play three finitely repeated investment games, each with one partner.

The structure of the information network is manipulated in three different ways—corresponding to the three finitely repeated investment games, which we refer to as *supergames*—as illustrated in figure 2.1. Each supergame consists of fifteen periods. Each network consists of six subjects, four Egos and two Alters. In every period, each Alter plays the investment game with two Egos simultaneously. Which Alter plays with which Egos is indicated with straight lines in figure 2.1. Egos are variously connected with each other, and a connection between two actors, denoted by a dotted line, indicates an exchange of information between them. Information available to one node is automatically transmitted to all other nodes with whom the focal node is connected by a dotted line.

The software takes care of the transmission of information through the network, which is provided to the subjects in history boxes displayed on the computer screens.[8] History boxes are windows at the lower part of the screen and provide subjects with information about previous games. Thus, when a game is played at time t_n, information about all games previously played from t_1 until t_{n-1} is available to the subjects in their history boxes. Alters are not connected, and their history boxes show only outcomes of their past transactions. We are more specific about the content of the history boxes when we describe how we manipulated information.

In the first supergame, every Ego receives information from another Ego who is playing with the same Alter. We refer to this other Ego as Ego 2 and to the Alter who is playing with Ego 2 as well as with the focal Ego as Alter 1. A tie connecting Ego and Ego 2 provides Ego with information about interactions involving Alter 1 and Ego 2. Thus, Ego can use this tie to learn or make inferences about the trustworthiness of Alter 1. In the second supergame, every Ego receives information from another Ego who is playing with another Alter. Hereafter, we refer to this Ego as Ego 3 and to the Alter who is playing with Ego 3 as Alter 2. Through this tie to Ego 3, Ego can learn or make inferences about Alter 2 who is interacting with Ego 3, but does not obtain information about Alter 1 other than from her own interactions. In the third supergame,

Figure 2.1   Experimental Networks

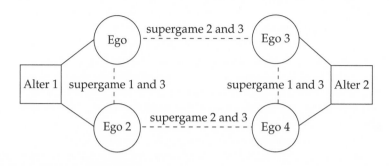

Source: Authors' compilation.

every Ego receives information from two other Egos, one (Ego 2) playing with her Alter (Alter 1) and the other (Ego 3) playing with another
Alter (Alter 2). Thus the structure of the information network varies
within subjects: every participant plays three supergames of fifteen
games each, one for every network type, in a fixed order: in the first supergame she has a tie to Ego 2 only; in the second supergame she has a
tie to Ego 3 only; and in the third supergame she has two ties, one to
Ego 2 and one to Ego 3. This design is used to analyze how subjects
process information coming from different sources. The order of the
three parts of the experiment is kept constant for every subject to provide subjects with the same sequence such that they have similar
amounts of experiences in each of the supergames.

The amount of information carried by the ties between Egos is also
manipulated: information can be full or partial. If a tie carries full information, subjects at both ends receive information about both the amount
sent by the other Ego and the amount returned by the related Alter for
every game previously played. By contrast, if a tie carries only partial information, subjects at both ends receive information only about the
amount sent by the other Ego, but not about the amount returned by the
related Alter.

In practice, the manipulation was implemented through the information subjects obtained in their history boxes at the screen. For example,
assume that Ego in figure 2.1 has a tie to Ego 2 carrying partial information and a tie to Ego 3 carrying full information. In this case, her history
box displays the amount sent by herself to Alter 1 and the amount returned by Alter 1 to herself for all games previously played (this information is always available for all players in all experimental conditions).

In addition, the history box shows the amount sent by Ego 2 to Alter 1 (but not the amount returned by Alter 1 to Ego 2), the amount sent by Ego 3 to Alter 2, and the amount returned by Alter 2 to Ego 3 for all games previously played.

The amount of information carried by ties varies both between and within subjects. A given tie of any given actor does not change from full to partial information or vice versa between supergames, but actors may have one tie carrying full information and one partial information. Therefore, the tie to Ego 2 in the third supergame carries the same information as the tie to Ego 2 in the first supergame. Similarly, the tie to Ego 3 in the third supergame carries the same information as the tie to Ego 3 in the second supergame. Hence, four information conditions are possible: full information on both ties (FF), partial information on both ties (PP), full information on the tie to Ego 2 and partial on the tie to Ego 3 (FP), and vice versa (PF). Note that the positions of the four Egos within one network are symmetrical with respect to the information they receive through their ties.

Finally, uncertainty is implemented by means of the multiplier m: in the treatment without uncertainty $m = 3$ for all Alters (C), while in the treatment with uncertainty $m = 2$ or 4, with probability .50 each, for all Alters (U).[9] Uncertainty varies only between subjects. In the condition with uncertainty, the value of the multiplier is chosen independently for the two Alters at the beginning of every period, and the Alters are informed about the value of m before the Egos make their choices.[10] The value of the multiplier of a given Alter for a given period applies to the amount of points sent by both Egos playing with this particular Alter. The Egos do not find out what the value of m is either during or after the game. However, occasionally the choice of Alter may reveal the value of m; for example, if, in a game with uncertainty, Alter returns a value $R_2 > 2S_1$, Ego can infer that the value of m for this period was 4.

Combining the four information conditions with the two possible conditions for uncertainty (C and U) yields eight possible experimental conditions. The eight conditions with the number of subjects that participated in each condition are summarized in table 2.1. All information concerning network embeddedness, amount of information transmitted, and uncertainty is common knowledge: all players have the same information, and everybody knows that everybody has the same information.

Each session of the experiment had eighteen subjects, except for one session in which only twelve subjects participated. The experiment runs as follow: the participants are divided in groups of six subjects, and every participant is randomly assigned a role, Ego or Alter. Each group consists of four Egos and two Alters. Subjects keep the same role throughout the experiment. The experiment consists of three supergames.

Table 2.1 Experimental Conditions

	FFC (N = 36)	FFU (N = 36)	PPC (N = 36)	PPU (N = 36)	FPC (N = 36)	FPU (N = 30)	PFC (N = 36)	PFU (N = 36)
Tie to Ego with *her* Alter	Full	Full	Partial	Partial	Full	Full	Partial	Partial
Tie to Ego with *another* Alter	Full	Full	Partial	Partial	Partial	Partial	Full	Full
Multiplier m	3	2 or 4	3	2 or 4	3	2 or 4	3	2 or 4

Source: Authors' compilation.
Note: Number of subjects per condition in parentheses.

During each supergame, two Egos are anonymously matched with one Alter, and play the investment game with him fifteen times. Therefore, each Ego plays one investment game every period, whereas each Alter plays two games per period, one with each Ego.

Before the beginning of the first supergame, subjects run through a tutorial in which they have to answer some questions on whether they understand the stage game. If they give wrong answers they receive feedback on what the correct answer is and why it is correct. They are allowed to ask questions to the experimenter if they would still not understand the instructions. They then play an investment game against the computer two times to learn how the game works. They know that they play these two periods against the computer, that the answers are preprogrammed, and that this is only to practice without actual payment.

After these practice rounds, all subjects are assigned to a group of six; they do not know who the other subjects in their group are. Then, the first supergame starts. At the beginning of every period, all players receive an initial endowment of 10 points (1 point = .01 euro). All Egos have the possibility to send all, some, or none of their points to their Alter. They are instructed that the points they receive are completely at their disposal, and they can freely decide whether they want to send something to their Alter and, if so, how much. The amount of points that they decide to send is then multiplied by a factor m by the experimenter, where $m = 3$ in the condition without uncertainty and $m = 2$ or 4 in the condition with uncertainty. The Alters receive an amount equal to m times the amount sent by the Egos. The Alters can decide to send back to Egos all, some, or none of the points they have received. Obviously, the Egos have to decide first, and the Alters must wait until all the Egos have entered their decisions. After a subject has made a choice, a waiting screen appears on her monitor instructing him or her to wait until all other subjects have entered their decisions. When all the Egos have completed their task the Alters have to decide how much they want to return to each of their two Egos separately. The two decisions that Alters have to make in every period appear simultaneously on their screen, and the game does not proceed until every Alter has entered both decisions. After all subjects have completed a period, the computer displays their earnings, and the history boxes are updated.

The history boxes of the Alters contain information about the period number, the amount of money received from each of the two Egos, and the amount returned to each of the two Egos. The history boxes of Egos contain the period number, the amount of money sent and returned, and information about the other Egos with whom they are tied. The information displayed in the history boxes of both Ego and Alter is reported for all periods previously played and remains available to the subject until the end of the supergame.

After all tasks have been completed and the history boxes have been updated, a new period starts. After fifteen periods, the supergame ends and subjects move on to the next supergame. The Egos are always matched to a different Alter in every supergame, and they are (partially) embedded with new Egos.[11]

Statistical Model

The dependent variable we want to predict in the analyses is how much does subject i trust his or her partner at time t, operationalized as the amount sent by subject i at time t, say y_{it}. We assume that y_{it} can be described as a linear function of the predictors x, which have been discussed in the theory section. However, we take into account the panel structure of the data, namely, that we have multiple observations per subjects. Therefore, we estimate the model

$$y_{it} = x_{it}\beta + v_i + \varepsilon_{it}$$

where v_i is the random effect at the subject level and ε_{it} is the random effect at the observation level. Both random effects are assumed to be normally distributed, to be independent from each other, and to have a mean equal to zero. The vector x_{it} of predictors includes variables for learning, imitation, envy, and control.

The dependent variable is measured by the amount of points, varying between 0 and 10, a subject sends to the partner. Theoretically, the latent dependent variable trust is a continuous property of subjects. Therefore, we assume that our measurement of trust can be interpreted as an interval measurement for the actual trust level. For example, if a subject sends one point, it implies that his or her trust level corresponds with sending some value between .5 and 1.5 points. Similarly, the intervals are determined for sending 2 to 9 points. Because a subject cannot send more than 10 points, sending 10 points indicates only that a subject wants to send something larger than 9.5. Therefore, the upper bound of the interval for sending 10 points is set to infinity. Defining the appropriate interval of trust levels related to sending nothing is even more difficult. We assume that there are many different levels of distrust that all lead to sending nothing, implying that we set the lower bound of the interval around 0 at minus infinity.[12] Regression models in which the observed values represent intervals are called *interval regression models*. We estimated a panel version of this type of model using the xtintreg command in Stata 8.2 (Stata Corporation 2003, 108–14).

In principle, adding only a random effect at the subject level is not enough to account for all interdependencies in the data. Two additional random effects accounting for the clustering of the observations that belong to the same triad—in supergame one and three—and of the observations that belong to the same experimental network—in supergame two and three—should be added to the statistical model because the choices of subjects in the same network are interdependent. However, we did not have statistical tools in which we could estimate interval regression models with three additional random effects. Alternatively, we estimated standard linear multilevel regression models with multiple random effects. These analyses showed that adding more random effects than only the subject-level effect led to only very marginal changes. However, when we compared the standard linear model with the interval regression model, both with a random effect at the subject level, some—though not many—of the somewhat weaker results changed in the analyses. For this reason, we decided to present the results obtained with the interval regression model because this model is theoretically more appropriate given the distribution of our dependent variable. Still, we will be carefully interpreting results that are only just significant at the 5 percent level.

Independent Variables

For dyadic learning (hypothesis 1), we looked both at the amount earned in the past and at the proportion returned by Alter 1 in the past. The amount earned by Ego in previous periods is operationalized by taking a discounted sum of the difference between the amount sent in previous periods and the amount returned in previous periods. Assuming that recent experiences are more important, experiences are discounted by a weight w_1 ($0 \leq w_1 \leq 1$) for each period they are further in the past. Thus, at time t,

$$\text{amount earned}_t = \sum_{i=1}^{t-1} w_1^{t-i-1}(E_{1i} - S_{1i} + R_{2i}),$$

where S_{1i} and R_{2i} are the amounts sent and returned at time i. Similarly, the proportion returned by Alter 1 in the past is operationalized by adding the proportion returned by Alter 1 in all previous periods, discounted by a weight w_2 ($0 \leq w_2 \leq 1$). Thus, at time t,

$$\text{proportion returned}_t = \sum_{i=1}^{t-1} w_2^{t-i-1} \frac{R_{2i}}{mS_{1i}}.$$

Under uncertainty, we also computed proportion returned assuming $m = 3$ because in this case m is equal to 2 or 4, both with probability .50. Moreover, we include in the analyses one variable for the amount sent by Ego in the past. This variable captures the individual propensity to trust and to stick to past decisions. This variable is operationalized by adding the proportion sent by the subject in all previous periods discounted by a weight w_3 ($0 \leq w_3 \leq 1$).[13] Thus, at time t,

$$\text{proportion sent}_t = \sum_{i=1}^{t-1} w_3^{t-i-1} \frac{S_{1i}}{10}.$$

Dyadic control (hypothesis 2a) is operationalized simply by taking the number of periods still to go before the end of the supergame, whereas for the end-game effect (hypothesis 2b) we use a dummy variable that has a value of 1 in the last period of a supergame and 0 otherwise. More complicated operationalizations for end-game effects did not improve the model. The variables for network learning (hypotheses 3a and 3b) are constructed in a similar way as the variables for dyadic learning. We took a discounted sum (w_4, $0 \leq w_4 \leq 1$) of the proportion returned from Alter 1 to Ego 2 for hypothesis 3a and a discounted sum (w_5, $0 \leq w_5 \leq 1$) of the proportion returned from Alter 2 to Ego 3 for hypothesis 3b.[14] For imitation, assuming that subjects react to observed behavior of other Egos when the behavior observed differs from their own behavior, we took a discounted sum of the difference between the amount sent by the subject and the amount sent by Ego 2 in previous games for hypothesis 4a. Thus at time t,

$$\text{Difference in proportion sent}_t = \sum_{i=1}^{t-1} w_4^{t-i-1} \frac{S_{1i}^{\text{Ego 2}} - S_{1i}^{\text{Ego}}}{10},$$

where S_{1i}^{Ego2} is the amount sent by Ego 2 at time i and S_{1i}^{Ego} is the amount sent by the focal subject at time i. For hypothesis 4b, we took the same difference with respect to Ego 3, discounted by w_5.[15] For social comparison (envy, hypothesis 5a), we took a discounted difference between the proportion returned from Alter 1 to Ego 2 and the proportion returned from Alter 1 to the subject in previous periods. Thus, at time t,

$$\text{envy}_t = \sum_{i=1}^{t-1} w_4^{t-i-1} \max[0, \frac{R_{2i}^{\text{Ego 2}}}{mS_{1i}^{\text{Ego 2}}} - \frac{R_{2i}^{\text{Ego}}}{mS_{1i}^{\text{Ego}}}].$$

where the superscript indicates who received or sent the indicated amount, and m is equal to 3.[16] Similarly, we looked at the same difference with respect to Ego 3 in interaction with Alter 2, discounted by w_5 for hypothesis 5b.[17] For network control, we constructed an interaction term between the number of periods remaining before the end of the supergame and a dummy variable taking the value one when the tie to Ego 2 carries full information. We operationalized network control in this way because the effect described in the theory and hypotheses section only applies if Egos can exchange full information. If Egos receive only partial information, the advantage of such exchange as derived by Buskens (2003) disappears. Uncertainty is included in the analyses as a dummy taking the value one in the experimental conditions with uncertainty and zero otherwise.

At the end of the experiment, subjects filled in a short questionnaire concerning some individual characteristics, such as gender, age, field of study, and number of friends participating in the same session. Moreover, we included a set of eighteen items on trusting attitude mainly adopted from Toshio Yamagishi and Midori Yamagishi (1994) and from Lawrence Wrightsmann (1974), and a set of items measuring the responsiveness of the subject to third-party information, based on William Bearden, Richard Netemeyer, and Jesse Teel's (1989) scale of susceptibility to personal influence. Both the items measuring trust and those measuring susceptibility to interpersonal influence were entered in a factor analysis, and in both cases two factors were found and the standardized scores were used as scales.

Results

In this experiment, 282 subjects participated and each of the eight experimental conditions was implemented twice, each time with three networks of six subjects each, except in one case, when we only had two networks of six subjects. Because we focus on the behavior of the Egos, only two-thirds of the subjects are included in the analyses, and all the Alters are excluded. Every subject participated in three supergames of fifteen games each. Thus, the total number of observations is $45 \times 188 = 8460$ choices made by subjects in the role of Ego.[18]

Most trust is placed in the conditions in which there is full information between Egos who are playing with the same Alter. In the first supergame, subjects sent on average over fifteen periods 6.44 points if they obtained only partial information from Ego 2, while they sent 7.21 points if they obtained full information (see left part of figure 2.2). This difference is significant ($p = .020$). In the third supergame, the average amount sent with partial and full information between Ego and Ego 2 is 6.42 and 7.35 points, respectively (see the left part of figure 2.3). This difference is also significant ($p = .018$). There is hardly any difference between certainty and uncertainty conditions depending on the amount of information that is carried by the tie between Ego and Ego 2. However, in the right parts of figures 2.2 and 2.3, we see that under uncertainty, subjects sent more points if information from Ego 3 was partial than if information from Ego 3 was full. This difference is significant in the second supergame ($p = .007$), but not in the third supergame ($p = .12$).

To analyze the dynamics and take into account the clustering of subjects within networks, we run also interval regression models with a random term for subjects, as explained in the methods section. To compare the experimental conditions, we include dummy variables for the main effects of uncertainty and information conditions concerning the relevant ties as well as interaction effects between uncertainty and information conditions. These analyses confirm that information about Ego 2 has a positive effect on trust in the first as well as the third supergame, and that information about Ego 3 has a negative effect on trust in the second supergame under uncertainty. In the third supergame the level of trust seems, under uncertainty, to be slightly lower for full than for partial information about Ego 3 likewise, but this difference is not statistically significant. We will pay more attention to this unexpected negative effect of information about Ego 3 when we analyze the dynamics in more detail in the following subsection.

Figures 2.2 and 2.3 also show that trust declines over time. Although this reduction seems to depend on the conditions, we did not find interaction effects between conditions and the number of periods to be

Figure 2.2   Average Sent per Period in First and Second Supergame

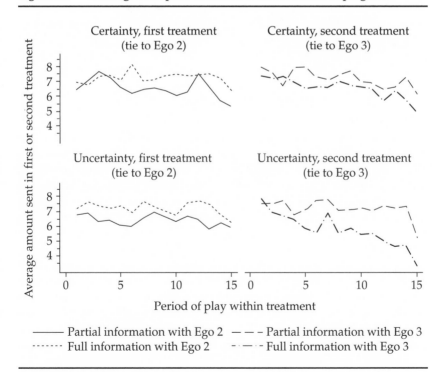

Period of play within treatment

——— Partial information with Ego 2   — — – Partial information with Ego 3
------- Full information with Ego 2   – · — · · Full information with Ego 3

Source: Authors' compilation.

Figure 2.3   Average Sent per Period in Third Supergame

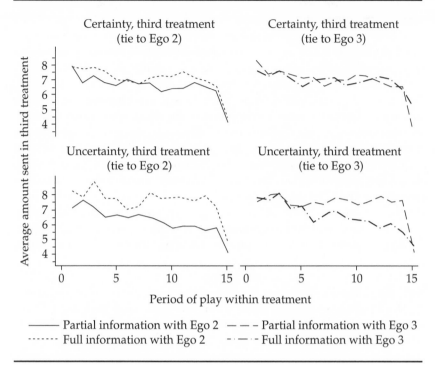

Source: Authors' compilation.

played, on the amount sent to Alter. The end-game effect can be observed by the strong decline in trust in the last period of the second and third supergame. It seems that subjects need some experience to realize that trust can easily be abused in the last period and that they could have been more cautious in the first supergame. Additional descriptive information on the results of the experiment, including separate tables and graphs for each experimental condition, can be found in Barrera (2005, chapter 3).

Tests of the Hypotheses

Because different subsets of mechanisms are applicable in each supergame and because there might be spillover effects between supergames, the three supergames are analyzed separately. For every supergame, two models are presented. Model 1 includes only main effects, and model 2 includes main effects as well as the interaction terms with uncertainty. In the first supergame, Ego has a tie to Ego 2 but not to Ego 3 and vice versa in the second supergame. In the third supergame, both ties are present. Therefore, all variables related to Ego 2 are included in the analyses of the first and third supergame but not in the second, and all variables related to Ego 3 are included in the analyses of the second and the third supergame, but not in the first.

For all variables referring to past experience, it seems reasonable to assume that more recent experiences have a stronger effect on current decisions than experiences from longer ago. Therefore, a discount parameter was applied to all past variables as explained in the operationalizations. The discount parameters were estimated iteratively, and the values of the parameters that gave the best fit, based on the log-likelihood of the models, were chosen. Nine variables referring to past experience are included in the analyses: three for Ego's own past (amount sent in previous periods, points earned in previous periods, and proportion returned by Alter 1 in previous periods), three for Ego 2's past (proportion returned by Alter 1 in previous periods, difference between the amount sent by Ego 2 and the amount sent by Ego, and difference between the proportion returned to Ego 2 and the proportion returned to Ego), and the same three variables for Ego 3 in games played with Alter 2. We used three weights for own past, one for each variable, but we used only one weight for Ego 2's past and one for Ego 3's past. Initially, we tried also different values for different types of past with respect to the third parties, but whatever combination we tried, the conclusion was always the same: only third-party experiences from the last period matter for Ego's current decision. Thus, the weights related to Ego 2 and Ego 3's pasts are equal to zero. This is in line with the results of Vincent Buskens, Werner Raub, and Joris van der Veer in a similar experiment on the trust game (2008).

Also for amount earned by Ego in the past, the discount parameter w_1 is estimated to be zero. The proportion returned to Ego seems longest, because for that parameter w_2 is estimated at .9. Finally, the estimated discount parameter for amount sent by Ego w_3 is .5. These discount parameters were estimated independently for all three supergames, and the estimations proved rather consistent. Therefore, the same values of the discount parameters were fixed for all analyses. We were not able to estimate simultaneously the discount parameters and the random-effects interval regression model. For this reason, we do not have confidence interval for the estimations of the discount parameters, and the standard errors in the analyses presented here are conditioned on the assumption that the discount parameters indeed equal the estimated value.[19]

Analyses of all three supergames are displayed in table 2.2. The first three variables are two dummies for whether the information carried by the tie to Ego 2 or Ego 3 is full and one dummy for uncertainty. We could have added also interactions between these dummies to control even further for differences in conditions. We added only these because they are used in interaction with other variables, but we did not want to make the model more complex than necessary, given that none of the controls for conditions are significant after introducing variables for the substantive mechanisms for which we developed the hypotheses discussed in the theory section. Thus we are able to explain the differences identified earlier with our theoretical mechanisms.

We added a dummy variable for the first period to control for how subjects start the game. This variable is positive and significant in all models, showing that Egos, on average, start investing relatively much of their initial endowment. The next variable in the model is *Ego's past sending behavior*, which accounts for individual propensity to stick to one's own trust decisions. This variable is strongly significant in all analyses, implying that subjects' own past decisions determine their current choices to a considerable degree. Hypotheses 1a and 1b on *dyadic learning* are consistently supported in all models. Amount earned in the past as well as proportion returned in the past have a strong positive effect on Ego's trusting decision. Hypotheses 2a and 2b on *dyadic control* are also consistently supported. The end-game effect (last round) is not significant in the two models referring to the first supergame, but it becomes increasingly significant in the two following supergames. This can be seen also in figures 2.2 and 2.3. This result indicates that subjects' experience in the first supergame that trust is likely to be abused in the last round, and therefore they become more careful in last rounds of subsequent supergames. Summarizing, we find strong and consistent support for all the hypotheses at the dyadic level. These results are also robust for all alternative model specifications.

Now, we turn to the network effects. Only two times an effect of *network learning* is weakly significant throughout the analyses shown in table 2.2. Therefore, hypotheses 3a and 3b are not supported. Actors learn neither from the behavior of Alter with respect to Ego 2 nor from the behavior of another Alter with Ego 3. It is especially surprising that the behavior of Alter with Ego 2 is not affecting Ego's behavior, given that she is playing with this Alter herself and given that full information about the behavior of Alter with Ego 2 leads to more trust on average.

Imitation is the effect of the behavior of other Egos in the past on Ego's decision in the present. We included this variable twice to control separately for the effects of behavior of other Egos when information about the related Alter's returning decisions was available (full information) and when it was not available (partial information). This distinction is important because for subjects who receive only partial information from other Egos, imitation is the only way to adapt their behavior, whereas subjects who receive full information can be affected by the behavior of Alter as well.

The variables for imitation are constructed using an interaction term of the imitation variable—as explained earlier in the discussion on the independent variables—once with a dummy with value 1 if information was full, and once with a dummy with value 1 if information was partial. Both these variables are strongly significant, which means that actors imitate both when information is partial and when information is full. Therefore, hypothesis 4a is supported in both supergames with information about Ego 2. The combination of the effects of network learning and imitation under full information gives an indication about the extent to which Egos actually learn or just imitate what Ego 2 does. In both supergames involving Ego 2, imitation is much more important than learning. If either learning or imitation is added as explanatory variable in the analysis, learning is at best marginally significant, whereas the imitation effects are always strongly significant independent of which model specification we choose.

Hypothesis 4b is not supported. In the second supergame, the results show some weak support for the hypothesis that Egos imitate Ego 3 only when information concerning the behavior of Alter 2 is not available (partial information); otherwise they ignore it. Apparently, Egos do not become more or less trustful toward their own partner from observing Ego 3 interacting with Alter 2. We do not have an explanation for the negative imitation effect related to Ego 3 under full information in the third supergame. Both effects related to imitating Ego 3 are significant only at the 5 percent level and depend on the model specification. Therefore, we can conclude only that evidence that Egos take the choices of Ego 3 into account in their decisions is scant.

Concerning envy, we find mixed results. Hypothesis 5a is supported in the first supergame, but not in the third supergame, though this effect is in the expected direction. The strong negative effect in the first supergame implies that if Alter 1 returned more to Ego 2 than to Ego in the past, Ego punishes him by sending significantly less in the current period. Again, the much weaker effect in the third supergame might be caused by the increased complexity, which decreases subjects' concern with this rather subtle effect. Concerning envy toward an Ego 3 who is playing with Alter 2, we particularly expect an effect under certainty, because under uncertainty returns to Ego 3 are difficult to evaluate for Ego, given that the multiplier of Alter 2 can be different from the multiplier of her Alter. In the second supergame, we find no effects of envy toward Ego 3. However, in the third supergame, there is a negative effect for envy toward Ego 3 under certainty, and the interaction effect with uncertainty shows that this effect does not exist under uncertainty. One problem with testing the hypotheses with respect to envy is that we can

Table 2.2   Random-Effects Interval Regression

Hyp.	Variables	Expected Sign	First Supergame (Ego 2)		Second Supergame (Ego 3)		Third Supergame (Ego 2 and Ego 3)	
			Model 1	Model 2	Model 1	Model 2	Model 1	Model 2
	Full information with Ego 2		0.40	0.40			0.41	0.41
	Full information with Ego 3				−0.63	−0.65	−0.68	−0.68
	Uncertainty		0.30	0.03	−0.19	0.09	0.23	0.51
	First round		3.70**	3.69**	5.68**	5.69**	5.97**	5.89**
	Ego's past trustfulness		3.16**	3.15**	3.72**	3.73**	3.93**	3.85**
1	Dyadic learning 1 (amount earned)	+	0.24**	0.24**	0.33**	0.33**	0.43**	0.43**
1	Dyadic learning 2 (proportion returned)	+	0.71**	0.64**	2.38**	2.53**	1.62**	1.63**
2a	Dyadic control	+	0.22**	0.22**	0.51**	0.51**	0.41**	0.42**
2b	Last round	−	−0.53	−0.53	−1.48**	−1.48**	−3.83**	−3.80**
3a	Network learning (Ego 2)	+	1.30*	1.10			−0.61	−0.04
3b	Network learning (Ego 3)	+			0.26	0.09	1.24	2.12*
4a	Imitation (Ego 2) × full information	+	1.11**	1.11**			2.40**	2.32**
4a	Imitation (Ego 2) × partial information	+	1.33**	1.33**			1.29**	1.30**

4b	Imitation (Ego 3) × full information	+			0.01	−0.01	−1.12*	−1.06*
4b	Imitation (Ego 3) × partial information	+		−3.32**	0.74*	0.76*	−0.43	−0.43
5a	Envy (Ego 2)	−	−3.31**				−0.75	−0.74
5b	Envy (Ego 3)	−					−2.06	−3.96*
6	Network control	+	−0.02	−0.02	−0.03	0.01	0.05	0.04
7a	Dyadic learning 2 × uncertainty	−		0.15		−0.29		0.07
7b	Network learning (Ego 2) × uncertainty	−		0.48				−1.26
7b	Network learning (Ego 3) × uncertainty	−				0.27		−2.11
7c	Envy (Ego 3) × uncertainty	+				−0.04		3.97*
	Constant		0.31	0.46	−3.56**	−3.71**	−2.58**	−2.72**
	Standard deviation of subject level random effect		1.65	1.66	1.78	1.76	2.15	2.18
	Standard deviation of residual		3.60	3.60	4.58	4.58	4.56	4.55
	Log likelihood		−4943.4	−4942.9	−4369.7	−4369.1	−4080.1	−4077.9
	Number of observations		2700	2700	2700	2700	2700	2700
	Number of subjects		180	180	180	180	180	180

Source: Authors' compilation.

Note: One-sided significance for effects for which hypotheses are indicated in the table and two-sided significance for the other variables.

** $p < .01$, * $p < .05$

only test them in a meaningful way if Alters provide Egos with a reason to be envious. We know that Alters tend to behave consistently toward the two Egos with whom they are playing, and this consistency increases in later supergames. Therefore, Egos do not often have reasons to be envious of Ego 2, especially in the third supergame. By contrast, because the two Alters are not informed about each other's behavior, one could expect more possibilities for envy between the focal Ego and Ego 3.

Network control is not significant; thus hypothesis 6 is not supported. Theoretically, another effect of network control might be hypothesized, namely that the end-game effect occurs later under full information than under partial information. However, this alternative formulation of network control is also not supported. This might be because the end-game effect starts already very late in all conditions. We do not have a final explanation for the lack of evidence for network control. Certainly, network control is not a straightforward effect for Egos because it requires that Egos place themselves in the shoes of Alter and anticipate that Alter takes into account that information about his behavior will spread through the network, affecting his reputation and hence his final profit. Although we do not analyze in detail Alters' behavior in this chapter, we do observe that the reason for Egos to place more trust under full than under partial information is that Alters return larger amounts in this experimental condition. Therefore, although Egos do not anticipate this effect on Alters' behavior, Alters actually behave as if they care about their reputation under full information. The positive effect of information from Ego 2 on Egos' behavior results indirectly, mainly through learning from their experiences with Alter and by imitating Ego 2. Buskens, Raub, and van der Veer provided additional evidence in another experiment in which they indeed found a network control effect for Alters, but again not for Egos (2008).

Finally, *uncertainty* does not seem to affect dyadic and network learning effects. Uncertainty has no effect on imitation because imitation is not based on the returns of an Alter anyway, so it is not affected by whether Ego knows how much an Alter can return. All interactions with dyadic and network learning are not significant. Hence hypotheses 7a and 7b are not supported. Only in the third supergame do we find the clear and well-interpretable interaction with envy, which we discussed earlier. Thus we find some support for hypothesis 7c.

In preliminary analyses, we included variables accounting for individual attributes in these models: namely, gender, age, number of friends participating in the same experimental session, field of study, measurements for an intrinsic tendency to trust, and of the scale measuring susceptibility to interpersonal influence. Because of a random assignment of subjects to conditions, it is unlikely that individual characteristics influence the results of our analyses. Still, to exclude even further that these results are codetermined by individual characteristics, we ran several analyses to investigate main and interaction effects of subject characteristics. None of the substantive findings depend on whether the variables for individual characteristics are included. Moreover, the main effects for individual characteristics are rather unstable. The only consistent finding is that economists trust less than students from other disciplines, in this case primarily sociology and psychology. Even the items that should measure trust did not affect the extent to which subjects trust others. However, given the relatively small number of subjects in the experiment and the limited variation in some of these variables, it is not surprising that we hardly found significant individual differences (for more on the effects of individual characteristics, see Barrera 2005, chapter 3).

Conclusion and Discussion

In this chapter, different effects of third-party information on trust are compared. A trust problem is defined and operationalized by means of the investment game. Hypotheses are tested in a laboratory experiment in which subjects play a repeated investment game and simultaneously exchange information about the games played. Two types of embeddedness are discussed: dyadic embeddedness, referring to the situation in which two actors play the investment game repeatedly with each other, and network embeddedness, referring to the situation in which two actors play the investment game while being part of a network of actors that exchange experiences about their past interactions. Existing theories stress the importance of mechanisms such as learning, control, imitation, and social comparison. The experiment allowed us to test hypotheses reflecting all of these mechanisms in a controlled environment. Moreover, because effects of information are expected to be particularly important under uncertainty, uncertainty was manipulated together with information conditions. The analyses focused on actors' trusting behavior, and the other actor's trustworthiness was used as one of the predictors for trusting behavior.

The effects of dyadic embeddedness on trust are strong and consistent in all experimental conditions. Egos are particularly influenced by their own experience with their Alter (dyadic learning) and by the length of the expected future with their Alter (dyadic control). For network embeddedness, not all predicted effects are supported. We found strong support for imitation of behavior of other Egos playing with the same Alter as the focal Ego.

The most striking result from this experiment is that the Egos adapt their behavior in the direction of the behavior of another Ego playing with the same Alter, though this adaptation does not seem to be influenced by the amount Alter returned to the other Ego. In other words, Egos imitate other Egos rather than learning whether Alter should be trusted by observing Alter's behavior toward these other Egos. Thus the increase in the level of trust observed under full information is caused by a chain of mechanisms: Alters return higher amounts in this experimental condition, supposedly because they are concerned about their reputation; consequently, through a mechanism of dyadic learning, Egos' trust in Alter increases; finally, Egos' trust in Alter is reinforced by observing the behavior of the other Ego through a mechanism of imitation. By contrast, Egos are hardly influenced by the behavior of other Egos involved with another Alter. This seems to contradict earlier findings in which Egos' choices were found to be affected by information about other Alters (see Barrera and Buskens 2007). However, in the experiment presented by Barrera and Buskens, Egos had either information about their Alter or about another Alter (2007). Our experiment shows that if Egos have a combination of both types of information, information about another Alter becomes largely irrelevant.

Another new result in the context of investment games is that we found some support for effects of social comparison. In the network configuration characterized by only one tie between two Egos playing with the same Alter, the focal Ego punished her Alter if Alter treated the other Ego better than herself. Conversely, in another network configuration in which every Ego had two ties—one to another Ego playing with the same Alter and one to another Ego playing with another Alter—Egos reacted by punishing their Alter when they saw that the other Alter was being more generous than their own Alter. Finally, there was neither support for network control nor for mitigation of learning and social comparison effects by uncertainty.

To summarize, this chapter provides new and complementary evidence for learning and control mechanisms on trust (see Buskens and Raub 2002, 2008). Although Buskens and Raub provided evidence for learning and control effects from a survey on IT transactions and two vignette experiments (2004), here we find similar evidence in a laboratory experiment. Moreover, this experiment provided possibilities to distinguish between learning, control, imitation, and social comparison, whereas the earlier studies focused on learning and control only. Especially challenging is the strong support found for imitation effects, as opposed to the weak support found for a real learning mechanism. It seems to indicate that our subjects preferred to opt for more parsimonious heuristics rather than thoroughly evaluate all the information available to them. Although this might be due to the complexity of our experimental design, it induces the theoretical question whether it is possible to predict under which conditions learning or imitation is the more prevalent mechanism.

We chose to use the investment game to obtain a more fine-grained measurement of trust compared to the standard trust game in which actors can only choose between trusting Alter or not. The disadvantage is that, in the investment game, the behavior of Alter is more difficult to interpret. For example, a low return might simply indicate that Alter is untrustworthy, but it might also be a sign of Alter's disappointment in an offensively low investment of Ego. In addition, as our analyses show, multiple mechanisms, including imitation and envy, might lead Ego to increase or decrease the amount sent, and these mechanisms depend mainly on Ego's interpretation of Alter's motives. However, the behavior of Alter remains still largely uninvestigated. Preliminary analysis of our data show that Alters return a higher proportion of the amount received if the multiplication factor is lower and a slightly higher proportion if there is full information exchange between the two Egos with whom a given Alter is playing. In addition, Alters are strongly affected by the end-game effect and return less in the last or even in the last two periods. More detailed analyses of Alters' behavior would require new theory development on how Alters adapt their choices depending on their experiences with the Egos, but this exceeds the scope of this chapter. Furthermore, given the difficulties related to the complexity of the investment game, a comparison of our results with results of standard trust games played in the same setting could be rather informative (for results based on the standard trust game, including analyses of Alters' behavior, see Buskens, Raub, and van der Veer 2008).

Finally, the results presented here support a range of mechanisms operating simultaneously, whereas the predictions are derived from different theoretical arguments rather than an integrated theoretical model. Building such an integrated model is a challenge for future research, and the outcomes of this study provide useful information on the importance of certain assumptions related to the importance of third-party information such a model should include. More specifically, such a model should include forward-looking arguments related to control, backward-looking arguments on learning and imitation, and even sideward-looking arguments on social comparison and other-regarding preferences (compare Macy and Flache 1995; Flache 1996).

Notes

1. For reader friendliness, we refer to Ego using female pronouns and to Alter using male pronouns.
2. Empirically, trust in one-shot interactions is not impossible, but if information from third parties is not available, actors can assess Alter's trustworthiness only on the basis of other informational cues, different from reputation (see chapter 7, this volume).

3. Other effects due to the amounts returned by Alter are possible if Ego interprets such returns in a different way. For example, a low return following a low investment could simply mean an abuse of trust, but could also be interpreted as disdain caused by an offensively low investment.

4. Strictly speaking, the sequential equilibrium of David Kreps and his colleagues also includes a learning mechanism (1982). However, we discussed this model because it applies forward-looking rationality, whereas the learning models discussed earlier apply backward-looking rationality.

5. To prevent confusing between which Alter is meant, we refer to the Alter playing with the focal Ego as "her Alter" and the other Alter as "another" or "the other Alter" whenever this seems necessary.

6. Experimental evidence does indicate that some actors do indeed have altruistic preferences. James Cox combined an investment game and a dictator game to show that cooperation in the one-shot investment game can be attributed partly to a reciprocity norm governing the behavior of Alters, on which Egos anticipate, and partly to altruistic preferences observed in a non-trivial number of subjects (2004). Conversely, for an experimental study on conditions facilitating the observation of self-regarding preferences, see Elisabeth Hoffmann and her colleagues (1994).

7. As illustrated in the method section, the returns on investment m are always the same for parallel interactions with the same Alter. This hypothesis can therefore only be tested for envy toward an Ego involved with another Alter. We formulate this hypothesis in terms of amount returned rather than proportion returned because the proportion is unknown if m is unknown.

8. The experiment was programmed and conducted with the software z-Tree (Fischbacher 2007).

9. Martin Duwfenberg and his colleagues (2001) manipulated uncertainty in a similar way, but in their experiment m was private information held by Ego and not by Alter. In other words, they treated m as a property of Ego.

10. This way of manipulating m is consistent with the interpretation that the multiplier represents exogenous circumstances affecting the return of an investment such as good or bad luck, and is independent of Alter's goodwill or competence.

11. The complete instructions of the experiment are available from the authors.

12. We compared our analysis with plausible other implementations such as setting the lower bound related to sending 0 at 0. Also we compared the analysis with alternatives such as a tobit regression in which we consider only sending 10 as a left-censored observation and ordinary random-effects regression considering the amount sent as an interval variable. All these alternative analyses substantially led to the same conclusions, though significance levels might slightly vary.

13. We also estimated a model with the same discount parameter w for all three variables operationalizing own past, but the model with three different weights fitted the data better.

14. Clearly, we could include two parallel effects as we did for dyadic learning, adding a variable related to the amount earned by the other Ego. However, the two effects can be disentangled for the dyadic effects be-

cause we have more observations and the effects are stronger. We run into colinearity problems if we try to disentangle these effects for third-party information. Therefore, we restrict ourselves here to the stronger effect, because substantially these two effects represent the same mechanism anyway. Moreover, the proportion returned by Alter 2 to Ego 3 seems a better operationalization for network learning because this information is more easily accessible to Ego since it requires fewer calculations.

15. We use the same discount parameters w_4 and w_5 for all variables operationalizing information concerning Ego 2 and Ego 3, respectively. A justification for this is detailed in the results discussion.

16. For all variables constructed with the proportion returned by Alter 1 or Alter 2 in previous periods, we assumed $m = 3$ in the experimental conditions with uncertainty.

17. The effects of guilt could also be tested by looking at how Egos react when they are treated better than other Egos. However, preliminary analyses showed that actors only reacted when they were treated worse than other Egos, but did not care if they were treated better. Therefore, we include only envy in the analyses displayed here.

18. Eight times an undergraduate student subject was replaced by a stand-in, mostly a Ph.D. student. We excluded the choices of the Ph.D. students from the analyses because some of the Ph.D. students have specific knowledge about the scope of the experiment. Still, excluding these subjects did not significantly affect the results of our analyses.

19. We realize that this is a second aspect that compromises our standard errors. We were able to do the simultaneous estimation for simpler models. In these models, the standard errors became only marginally larger, but still we interpret effects that are significant only at the 5 percent level with caution.

References

Akerlof, George A. 1970. "The Market for 'Lemons': Quality Uncertainty and the Market Mechanism." *Quarterly Journal of Economics* 89(3): 488–500.

Bandura, Albert, and Richard H. Walters. 1963. *Social Learning and Personality Development.* New York: Holt, Reinhart and Winston.

Barrera, Davide. 2005. *Trust in Embedded Settings.* Veenendaal, the Netherlands: Universal Press.

———. 2007. "The Impact of Negotiated Exchange on Trust and Trustworthiness." *Social Networks* 29(4): 508–26.

———. 2008. "The Social Mechanisms of Trust." *Sociologica* 2(September-October): DOI: 10.2383/27728.

Barrera, Davide, and Vincent Buskens. 2007. "Imitation and Learning: A Vignette Experiment." *International Sociology* 22(3): 366–95.

Barrera, Davide, and Gerhard G. van de Bunt. 2009. "Learning to Trust: Networks Effects Through Time." Forthcoming in *European Sociological Review* DOI:10.1093/esr/jcn078.

Bearden, William O., Richard G. Netemeyer, and Jesse E. Teel. 1989. "Measurement of Consumer Susceptibility to Interpersonal Influence." *Journal of Consumer Research* 15(4): 473–81.

Berg, Joyce E., John Dickhaut, and Kevin McCabe. 1995. "Trust, Reciprocity, and Social History." *Games and Economic Behavior* 10(1): 122–42.

Bolton, Gary E., Elena Katok, and Axel Ockenfels. 2004. "How Effective Are Electronic Reputation Mechanisms? An Experimental Investigation." *Management Science* 50(11): 1587–602.

———. 2005. "Cooperation among Strangers with Limited Information about Reputation." *Journal of Public Economics* 89(8): 1457–68.

Bolton, Gary E., and Axel Ockenfels. 2000. "ERC: A Theory of Equity, Reciprocity, and Competition." *American Economic Review* 90(1): 166–93.

Buchan, Nancy R., Rachel T. A. Croson, and Robyn M. Dawes. 2002. "Swift Neighbors and Persistent Strangers: A Cross Cultural Investigation of Trust and Reciprocity in Social Exchange." *American Journal of Sociology* 108(1): 168–206.

Burt, Ronald S., and Marc Knez. 1995. "Kind of Third-Party Effects on Trust." *Rationality and Society* 7(1): 1–36.

Buskens, Vincent. 2002. *Trust and Social Networks*. Boston, Mass.: Kluwer.

———. 2003. "Trust in Triads: Effects of Exit, Control, and Learning." *Games and Economic Behavior* 42(2): 235–52.

Buskens, Vincent, and Werner Raub. 2002. "Embedded Trust: Control and Learning." *Advances in Group Processes* 19(2002): 167–202.

———. 2004. "Soziale Mechanismen rationalen Vertrauens: Eine Theoretische Skizze und Resultate aus Empirische Studien." In *Rational-Choice-Theorie in den Sozialwissenschaften: Anwendungen und Probleme*, edited by Andreas Diekmann and Thomas Voss. Oldenbourg: Scientia Nova.

———. 2008. "Rational Choice Research on Social Dilemmas." In *Handbook of Rational Choice Social Research*, edited by Rafael P. M. Wittek, Tom A. B. Snijders, and Victor Nee. New York: Russell Sage Foundation.

Buskens, Vincent, and Jeroen Weesie. 2000. "Cooperation via Social Networks." *Analyse & Kritik* 22(1): 4–74.

Buskens, Vincent, Werner Raub, and Joris van der Veer. 2008. "Trust in Triads: An Experimental Study." Working paper. Utrecht: Utrecht University.

Camerer, Colin F. 2003. *Behavioral Game Theory*. Princeton, N.J.: Princeton University Press.

Camerer, Colin F., and Keith Weigelt. 1988. "Experimental Tests of a Sequential Equilibrium Reputation Model." *Econometrica* 56(1): 1–36.

Cochard, Francois, Nguyen Van Phu, and Marc Willinger. 2004. "Trusting Behavior in a Repeated Investment Game." *Journal of Economic Behavior and Organization* 55(1): 31–44.

Coleman, James S. 1990. *Foundations of Social Theory*. Cambridge, Mass.: Belknap Press.

Coricelli, Giorgio, Louis G. Morales, and Amelie Mahlstedt. 2006. "The Investment Game with Asymmetric Information." *Metroeconomica* 57(1): 13–30.

Cox, James C. 2004. "How to Identify Trust and Reciprocity." *Games and Economic Behavior* 46(2): 260–81.

Dasgupta, Partha. 1988. "Trust as a Commodity." In *Trust: Making and Breaking Cooperative Relations*, edited by Diego Gambetta. Oxford: Blackwell Publishing.

Duwfenberg, Martin, Uri Gneezy, Werner Güth, and Eric van Damme. 2001. "Direct versus Indirect Reciprocity: An Experiment." *Homo Oeconomicus* 18(1): 19–30.

Fehr, Ernst, and Klaus M. Schmidt. 1999. "A Theory of Fairness, Competition, and Cooperation." *Quarterly Journal of Economics* 114(3): 817–68.

Fischbacher, Urs. 2007. "z-Tree - Zurich Toolbox for Readymade Economic Experiments: Experimenter's Manual." *Experimental Economics* 10(2): 171–78.

Flache, Andreas. 1996. *The Double Edge of Networks: An Analysis of the Effect of Informal Networks on Cooperation in Social Dilemmas*. Amsterdam: Thesis Publishers.

Flache, Andreas, and Michael W. Macy. 2002. "Stochastic Collusion and the Power Law of Learning: A General Reinforcement Learning Model of Cooperation." *Journal of Conflict Resolution* 46(5): 629–53.

Gautschi, Thomas. 2000. "History Effects in Social Dilemma Situations." *Rationality and Society* 12(2): 131–62.

Granovetter, Marc S. 1985. "Economic Action and Social Structure: The Problem of Embeddedness." *American Journal of Sociology* 91(3): 481–510.

Güth, Werner, Manfred Königstein, Nadège Marchand, and Klaus Nehring. 2001. "Trust and Reciprocity in the Investment Game with Indirect Reward." *Homo Oeconomicus* 18:241–62.

Harsanyi, John C. 1967–1968. "Games with Incomplete Information Played by 'Bayesian' Players," I-III. *Management Science* 14(3): 159–182, 320–334, 486–502.

Heckathorn, Douglas D. 1996. "The Dynamics and Dilemmas of Collective Action." *American Sociological Review* 61(2): 250–77.

Hedström, Peter. 1998. "Rational Imitation." In *Social Mechanism: An Analytical Approach to Social Theory*, edited by Peter Hedström and Richard Swedberg. Cambridge: Cambridge University Press.

Hoffmann, Elisabeth, Kevin McCabe, Keith Shachat, and Vernon Smith. 1994. "Preferences, Property Rights, and Anonymity in Bargaining Games." *Games and Economic Behavior* 7(3): 346–80.

Kreps, David M. 1990. "Corporate Culture and Economic Theory." In *Perspective on Positive Political Economy*, edited by James Alt and Kenneth Shepsle. Cambridge: Cambridge University Press.

Kreps, David M., Paul R. Milgrom, John Roberts, and Robert B. Wilson. 1982. "Rational Cooperation in the Finitely Repeated Prisoners` Dilemma." *Journal of Economic Theory* 27(2): 245–52.

Kreps, David M., and Robert B. Wilson. 1982. "Reputation and Imperfect Information." *Journal of Economic Theory* 27(2): 253–79.

Macy, Michael W., and Andreas Flache. 1995. "Beyond Rationality in Models of Choice." *Annual Review of Sociology* 21: 73–91.

Macy, Michael W., and John Skvoretz. 1998. "The Evolution of Trust and Cooperation between Strangers: A Computational Model." *American Sociological Review* 63(5): 638–60.

Ortmann, Andreas, John Fitzgerald, and Carl Boeing. 2000. "Trust, Reciprocity, and Social History: A Re-Examination." *Experimental Economics* 3(1): 81–100.

Pingle, Mark. 1995. "Imitation versus Rationality: An Experimental Perspective on Decision Making." *Journal of Socio-Economics* 24(2): 281–316.

Pingle, Mark, and Richard H. Day. 1996. "Modes of Economizing Behavior: Experimental Evidence." *Journal of Economic Behavior and Organization* 29(2): 191–209.

Rabin, Matthew. 1993. "Incorporating Fairness into Game Theory and Economics." *American Economic Review* 83(5): 1281–302.

Raub, Werner, and Jeroen Weesie. 1990. "Reputation and Efficiency in Social Interactions: An Example of Network Effects." *American Journal of Sociology* 96(3): 626–54.

———. 2000. "The Management of Matches: A Research Program in Durable Social Relations." *The Netherlands Journal of Social Science* 36(1): 71–88.

Schlag, Karl. 1998. "Why Imitate, and If So, How? A Bounded Rational Approach to Multi-Armed Bandits." *Journal of Economic Theory* 78(1): 130–56.

Selten, Reinhard. 1978. "The Chain Store Paradox." *Theory and Decision* 9(1): 127–59.

Selten, Reinhard, and Rolf Stoecker. 1986. "End Behavior in Sequences of Finite Prisoner's Dilemma Supergames." *Journal of Economic Behavior and Organization* 7(1): 47–70.

Snijders, Chris. 1996. *Trust and Commitments*. Amsterdam: Thesis Publishers.

Snijders, Chris, and Gideon Keren. 2001. "Do You Trust? Whom Do You Trust? When Do You Trust?" In *Advances in Group Processes*, vol. 18, edited by Shane R. Thye, Edward J. Lawler, Michael W. Macy, and Henry A. Walker.

Stata Corporation. 2003. *Stata Cross-Sectional Time-Series Reference Manual Release 8*. College Station, Tex.: Stata Press.

Wrightsmann, Lawrence S. 1974. *Assumption about Human Nature: A Social Psychological Analysis*. Monterey, Calif.: Brooks/Cole.

Yamagishi, Toshio, and Midori Yamagishi. 1994. "Trust and Commitment in the United States and Japan." *Motivation and Emotion* 18(2): 129–66.

Chapter 3

Solving the Lemons Problem with Reputation

TOSHIO YAMAGISHI, MASAFUMI MATSUDA, NORIAKI
YOSHIKAI, HIROYUKI TAKAHASHI, AND YUKIHIRO USUI

IN THIS chapter we ask whether reputation can be successfully used to provide a solution to the *lemons problem*. This is a potential threat to traders who conduct trades without institutional mechanisms for enforcing contracts. In a classic paper on the market for lemons, George Akerof argued that asymmetry of information, which existed in the used car market in the days when buyers did not have an easy access to research the complete maintenance and accident history of a particular vehicle easily, could drive honest traders and high quality goods out of the market, resulting in a market where lemons or fraudulent commodities prevail (1970). Akerof examined the used car market as an example of a market for lemons. In the used car market of his day, only sellers had access to complete information about problems with the cars they were selling, and most consumers were incapable of discerning any problems. Contemporary online traders, such as visitors to Internet auction sites, face the same problem. Individuals who purchase a product online may learn about the quality (or condition) of the item only after they have paid for it. In the worst scenario, the item never arrives and the buyer cannot track down the seller. Thus online traders face greater risk than traders in offline brick and mortar businesses (Friedman and Resnick 2001; Houser and Wooders 2006; Kollock 1999; Resnick and Zeckhauser 2002; Resnick et al. 2000; Standifird 2001). The high level of information asymmetry in online trading creates a situation ripe for fraud, embezzlement, and the lemons problem. However, students of Internet auctions report that relatively few frauds are observed in Internet trades (Kollock 1999; Resnick and Zeckhauser 2002; Resnick et al. 2000).[1] Scholars studying online trades have found that the reputation system created endogenously keeps the level of fraud low and lemons from pervading the marketplace.

Before discussing the role of reputation as a solution to the problem of lemons, however, let us briefly present the distinction between bilateral and multilateral reputation. An individual can learn about a trading partner through direct experience or from someone who has had direct experience. We use *bilateral reputation* to refer to the former and restrict the use of the term *reputation* to the latter, which is often called *multilateral reputation*. According to Robert Wilson's definition, a reputation is a "characteristic or attribute ascribed to one person . . . by another" (1985, 27–28). Similarly, according to Stephen Standifird, "reputation is defined as the current assessment of an entity's desirability as established by some external person or group of persons" (2001, 281). In our terminology, a reputation is a characteristic or attribute ascribed to a person (and believed to be useful in predicting that person's future behavior) by a third party. When a person ascribes a characteristic or attribute to another based on experience with that person, we call it *experience-based information*. Sharing experience-based information with someone else produces a reputation.

The Roles of Reputation

A reputation-based solution to the problem of lemons is found in Avner Greif's analysis of the Maghribi coalition (1989). Maghribi traders of the eleventh century who conducted business across the Mediterranean operated in highly uncertain environments in which they could not directly observe the quality of the commodities they traded. They also faced a high level of information asymmetry in dealing with their agents. Such asymmetry is known to produce a market for lemons, especially when there are no institutional arrangements to prevent such a market from developing. Because the merchants have no way of determining whether their agents are being honest or cheating them, it is in the agents' best interest to cheat the merchants unless a high premium, paid to the agent, gives the agent enough incentive to continue to be the agent for that merchant. Because the merchants know this and because the premium to induce agents to behave honestly is often very high, it is in the merchants' best interest to not hire rational agents. Had the merchants refrained from doing so, extended trading activities across the Mediterranean might not have existed. Through a thorough reading of archival records of Maghribi merchant trades, Greif concluded that a unique institution called the *coalition* provided a solution to the problems that arose from the asymmetry (1989, 1993). He further argued that the key to the success of the coalition in curtailing opportunistic behavior and promoting trust among traders was that reputations were shared within the coalition. Developing a system to share experienced-based information among a group of traders and making that information a public reputation provides a solution to the problem of lemons in a market characterized by information asymmetry. This solution, however, works only insofar as the reduction in the expected future profit caused by the reputation of a dishonest trader exceeds the immediate profit derived from the dishonest behavior. Greif argued that the closed nature of the coalition among Maghribi traders was essential to the success of the reputation system. An agent who behaves dishonestly to a member acquires a reputation for dishonesty, and is excluded from the coalition and thus from future opportunities to trade with any coalition member. Exclusion from the coalition and future opportunities to trade with coalition members works as a deterrent to dishonest trades for the agent only to the degree that he has no alternative trading partners outside the coalition. When the coalition members are the only possible trading partners, exclusion from the coalition means no future trading opportunities. In such a situation, exclusion is a powerful deterrent. By contrast, when the agent who cheats a patron merchant and is shunned from trading with other coalition members can trade with noncoalition members and make an equivalent profit there, exclusion based on reputation will have no disciplinary effect.

The requirement of closed boundaries for reputation to function as a deterrent is not likely to be met in online trade. The effectiveness of a negative reputation system to control the lemons problem is expected to be compromised to the extent that dishonest traders have alternative markets to move into without paying exit and entrance costs. Contemporary online traders face a market that differs significantly from the one Maghribi traders faced in the eleventh century. Most important, the online market has no closed boundaries and thus exclusion from the market is impracticable. Although online markets try to establish boundaries, online traders can assume many identities and create many pseudonyms. They can change these as needed and come back to the same market under a different identity. This flexibility is expected to deprive the market of any real disciplinary power against traders based on reputation. Furthermore, researchers of Internet auction sites find another potential problem. That is, fear of retaliation prevents online traders from submitting negative evaluations of their trading experience (see Resnick and Zeckhauser 2002). Thus using a reputation system as *the* solution to the online market lemons problem seems to be a hopeless endeavor.

The reality, however, is much brighter than theoretically predicted (Kollock 1999; Resnick and Zeckhauser 2002). Reported frauds on the

Internet are relatively infrequent compared to the predicted level, and the reason for the low rate has been attributed to the reputation system used in online markets. Many researchers claim that the disadvantages of online markets for reputation are well offset by the sheer quantity of quickly and cheaply accumulated and disseminated reputation information (see Kollock 1999; Resnick and Zeckhauser 2002; Resnick et al. 2006; Standifird 2001). Specifically, observers point out that the rapid development of information technology makes the cost of sharing information very low (Avery, Resnick, and Zeckhauser 1999; Kollock 1999; Resnick and Zeckhauser 2002). They claim that the vast quantity of information offsets the corresponding lack of quality and reliability. The studies that examined the effects of reputation on auctioning in eBay, one of the largest Internet auctioning sites, in some cases report a small price premium of reputation—that those who have acquired a highly positive rating score (good reputation) enjoy an advantage in the price for which they sell their goods. Further, those with a negative reputation score are effectively punished when they receive a low bid (which translates to a low selling price) in the auction (Eaton 2002; Houser and Wooders 2006; Lucking-Reiley et al. 2007; Resnick and Zeckhauser 2002; Standifird 2001; Resnick et al. 2006). In chapter 6 of this volume, Chris Snijders and Jeroen Weesie argue that the positive effect of reputation in the studies of eBay is largely underestimated, given that actual sales price and the probability of successful sales are affected by many uncontrolled factors other than the buyer's willingness to pay extra.

Peter Kollock, however, proposed another explanation (1999). He makes a distinction between two types of reputation systems: a positive system and a negative. A positive system evaluates traders only in the positive direction. A new entrant receives a neutral reputation of zero, the lowest possible level given that all evaluations are positive. A negative reputation system, by contrast, evaluates only in the negative direction. A new entrant receives a neutral reputation of zero, which is by the same reasoning the highest level. Kollock asserted that traders who have acquired a negative reputation have an incentive to change their identity and re-enter the market with a fresh reputation score of zero. Under such a system, therefore, reputation does not accumulate. On the other hand, traders under the positive system have incentives to maintain their reputation because a positive reputation is a valuable asset. The freedom to change identities in online trades seems to make boundaries of the market meaningless. However, the freedom to change identities does not affect the effectiveness of the positive system given that traders voluntarily keep their brand name once they have acquired a good reputation. The fear of exclusion loses its disciplinary power on online traders, but incentives for online traders to maintain positive reputations remain. Chrysanthos Dellarocas provided a formal model in which he claimed that requiring newcomers to start with the lowest level of a reputation score is helpful to prevent negative effects of cheap pseudonyms (2003; Friedman and Resnick 2001).

Building on Internet auction researchers' claims that the lemons problem in online trades occurs less often than predicted, we articulate that the reason is found in the role of a reputation system (Kollock 1999; Resnick and Zeckhauser 2002; Resnick et al. 2000). Through a series of experiments, we examine whether reputation provides a solution even in a market in which excluding dishonest traders is difficult. Further, if reputation does help us solve the lemons problem, we examine whether the type of reputation system (positive or negative) makes a difference.

Basic Features

To address the question, we use a laboratory version of online trades characterized with information asymmetry. Despite the problem of external validity that plagues experimental studies in the social sciences, the merit of experimental studies is invaluable in addressing the research questions of this study because the critical variables—such as the true quality of the commodities produced and sold in the market, and thus the level of cheating involved in trades—is almost impossible to assess in real trading data outside the laboratory. By contrast, in the experiment presented, we know the exact level of dishonesty in selling commodities and in evaluating the seller. Paul Resnick and his colleagues conducted a clever field experiment in which they could and did successfully manipulate the seller's reputation score, but could not manipulate the level of seller cheating (2006). Laboratory experiments are the only methodology that allows us to precisely manipulate and measure these critical but otherwise unobservable variables.

The experiment was conducted in Japan with Japanese participants using Japanese yen as incentives. In this experimental market, all players (that is, voluntary participants) take on two roles: the buyer's role and the seller's role. As a seller, each player produces a commodity (an abstract commodity without any substance) by expending some cost, ranging from ¥10 to ¥100 per commodity, in increments of ¥10.[2] The quality level of the produced commodity is determined by the amount of money the seller has expended for its production. For simplicity, the quality level is expressed in terms of how much the seller has spent for its production, from 10 to 100 in whole integers. For example, a commodity with a quality level of 70 has cost the seller ¥70 to produce. The commodity produced by a seller is then put on the market for sale with a price set by the seller. At the same time, the seller announces the quality of the commodity—that is, how much was spent for its production. The advertised quality level may or may not reflect the true quality. For example, a seller who has spent ¥30 to produce a commodity may put it on the market at ¥100 with an announcement that its quality level is 80 (though its true level is 30). Any other player, acting as a buyer, can purchase the commodity for that price. Once a buyer purchases the commodity, it disappears from the market. That is, each commodity can be purchased by only one buyer.

Each player may purchase any of the commodities in the market. The information available to a buyer is the price and the advertised quality of the commodity. For the buyer, each commodity is worth 1.5 times its true quality level. The difference between the value to the buyer and the purchase price becomes the profit (or loss) for the buyer. In the example of a trade in which a buyer pays ¥100 for a commodity with a true quality level of ¥30, the buyer loses ¥55 because the commodity is only worth ¥45 (1.5 times its true quality of 30). The buyer, that is, paid ¥100 for something worth only ¥45.

Asymmetry of information about the quality of the commodity trades in this market is obvious. The true quality of the commodity is known only to the seller, as in Akerof's used car market (1970). The buyer learns the quality of the commodity only after he has paid for it. There is no way the buyer can retract the money paid for a fraudulent commodity.

As mentioned, each player takes on the role of a seller as well as that of a buyer. She can act as a buyer at any time. On the other hand, she can act as a producer-seller only occasionally. Specifically, each player is provided with a production opportunity every fifty seconds with a random variation in the range of plus and minus fifteen seconds. Once a production opportunity is provided, a player is given ¥100 from the experimenter as an endowment and then decides how much of it to invest in the production of a commodity (in increments of ¥10). A player is required to produce one and only one commodity per production opportunity. As explained, how much is spent for the production of a commodity determines the quality level of the commodity produced. The remaining amount of the endowment (¥100 minus the amount invested in the production of a commodity) is for the player to keep. In addition to the price and the advertised quality of the commodity, each commodity for sale on the market may come with other information, depending on the experimental conditions, that is, the identity or reputation of the seller.

Hypotheses

We examine the following set of hypotheses concerning the effect of reputation (and a player's identity) as a solution to the lemons problem. The term *experimental market* refers to the market characterized with information asymmetry as outlined.

Hypothesis 1. In the experimental market we create in the laboratory, in which players cannot be identified and contracts cannot be enforced, the quality of the goods sold will be reduced to the lowest level.

Experimental economists examining principal-agent relations have found that agents exhibit the predicted opportunistic behavior in the absence of a continued relationship between specific principals and agents (DeJong, Forsythe, and Lundholm 1985; Fehr, Gachter, and Kirchsteiger 1997). The effort level of the agent in the relationship, however, is not—as expected by the rational choice model of the agent—reduced to zero. For example, Ernst Fehr, Simon Gachter, and Georg Kirchsteiger examined an experimental labor market in which principals (firms) hire agents (workers) at a wage level w set by the principal (1997). The principal, in turn, expects an effort level e from his agent. The agent who receives the wage w can then freely choose the level of e that he actually performs. That is, the contract between the principal and the agent about the level of e for w cannot be enforced. In this situation, the agent who cares only about his own welfare should exert zero level of effort. In contrast to this zero effort prediction, Fehr and his colleagues' experiment did not find that the agents exerted a zero level of effort in such a situation (1997). Similar experiments by Douglas DeJong and his colleagues (DeJong, Forsythe, and Lundholm 1985; DeJong et al. 1985) also fail to confirm the zero effort prediction by rational choice models of behavior.

According to Fehr and his colleagues, reciprocity explains the failure of the zero effort prediction (Fehr and Gachter 2000; Fehr, Gachter, and Kirchsteiger 1997). This may be true in the context of an exchange of wage and effort. In the experimental online market we create in our laboratory, however, reciprocity is expected to play a minimal role. The economic transactions of selling and buying are less likely to activate the norm of reciprocity than the exchange of labor for wages. Thus we expect that the pure market for lemons will result in our experimental market in which players cannot be identified by each other and no reputation of the traders is provided.

Hypothesis 2. The buyer's ability to identify sellers and to remember the sellers' past behavior will improve the quality level of the goods sold in the market.

Players can accumulate experience-based information when they can be clearly identified, so that players can avoid interacting with known cheaters. The players' ability to identify sellers will discourage sellers from cheating buyers and losing future customers. We thus predict that if the players can be identified, the lemons problem will be alleviated.

Hypothesis 3. Reputation—that is, information obtained from other players—will improve the quality level of the goods sold in the market.

A study of principal-agent (firm-worker) relations examined the effect of sharing experience-based information on the effort level exerted by the workers in the experimental labor market they created in their laboratory (DeJong et al. 1985). The researchers found a positive effect of information sharing. In their experiment, however, information-sharing and experience-based information were manipulated simultaneously such that the effects of the two could not be separated. We examine the role of reputation independent of the role of experience-based information in our experiment.

The following two hypotheses address the effect of identity change on the effectiveness of reputation systems in alleviating the lemons problem in online markets.

Hypothesis 4. When players are permitted to freely change their identities, the quality level of the goods sold in the market will be reduced.

Hypothesis 5. The detrimental effect of the option for identity change predicted in hypothesis 4 will be stronger in a negative reputation system than in a positive or mixed reputation system.

Online traders can have as many identities or handling names as they wish, and they can change these identities as often as they wish. An online trader who has accumulated negative reputations can shake them off by assuming a new identity with a new e-mail address and thus pretend to be another person. As a result, the effectiveness of reputation as a solution to the problem of lemons can be greatly undermined in online trading. Furthermore, the problem of unstable identities is expected to be especially serious with respect to negative reputations. As Peter Kollock suggested, positive reputations are free from this problem because online traders have incentives to maintain the positive reputation that accompanies their identity (1999). Having a positive reputation is a valuable asset, and traders who have acquired a positive reputation will not want to voluntarily change their identities.

Experiment 1: Effect of Identity and Reputation

We conducted the first experiment to examine the first three hypotheses. Because explaining the manipulations of the condition we used requires knowledge of the details of the experimental design, let us first review the computer screen the participant faced.

Figure 3.1 presents an example of how the market looks on a player's

Figure 3.1   Image of Computer Screen of Identity Condition of Experiment 1

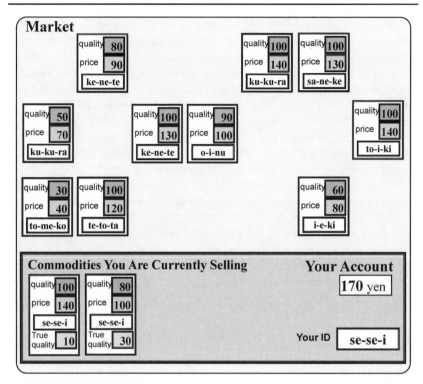

Source: Authors' compilation.
Note: All characters are translated from Japanese.

computer screen. The screen is divided into an upper section and a lower section. The upper section displays commodities placed for sale by other players. The lower section displays those the player has produced and placed for sale. Information related to the player's personal account is also displayed. In the example shown in figure 3.1, the other players have placed ten commodities on the market. Each box in the upper section represents a commodity. In the box in the lower-left corner, for example, the seller-producer to-me-ko sells a commodity for ¥40, advertising its quality level to be ¥30. Note that the identity of the producer-seller is provided in this example, but this is not always the case. Note also that the original screen is written in Japanese, not English. The player's identity is expressed in three randomly assigned Japanese characters. Because the commodities the player has produced do not appear for that player, each player's screen is unique. Furthermore, the boxes in the upper section are periodically shifted so that it is difficult to keep track of all of the commodities on the market in the condition in which identities are not stable.

The lower section of the display in figure 3.1 indicates that this player, se-se-i, is currently selling two commodities represented by the two boxes shown. To produce the commodity displayed in the box on the far left side, this player spent ¥10. She advertises its quality level as 100, and is selling it for ¥140. If someone purchases it, the seller, se-se-i, makes a profit of ¥130. She spent only ¥10 to produce the commodity but she will sell it for ¥140. The buyer who purchases this commodity loses ¥125 because the item is worth only ¥15 (1.5 times its true quality level of 10). The box to the right of the first box represents another commodity the player is selling. The far right corner displays the identity of this player, se-se-i, and her current financial situation. According to the information displayed, this player has made a profit of ¥170 so far.

Another feature of this experimental market, common to all experimental conditions, is that a commodity placed on the market remains there for five minutes only. A commodity that has not been sold within the five minutes disappears from the market, and the producer-seller cannot recover the cost spent for its production. This option was introduced to the current experiment to avoid overcrowding the market with too many commodities.

Conditions

The research design includes the following three conditions:

- Anonymity. In the anonymity condition, the commodities placed on the market have no identity markers. Buyers are unable to find out who the seller of a particular commodity is. In such a purely anonymous market, which offers no possibility of intentionally repeating transactions between a particular seller and a particular buyer, we predict that sellers will come to sell only the lowest quality goods (hypothesis 1). Even honest sellers are likely to sell only the lowest quality goods because, given the possibility of lemons, buyers will dare pay only the price for the lowest quality goods. The comparison of the quality level of the commodities produced in this market with the theoretically predicted level of 10 (that is, the lowest possible quality level) serves as a test of the first hypothesis. Because only the lowest quality of commodities are produced and traded, participants in this condition fail to achieve the benefit of trading commodities of high quality. When a seller produces a commodity with the quality level of 100, he and the buyer of that commodity share the extra value of ¥50 provided by the experimenter. When a seller produces a commodity with the quality level of 10, the extra value they share is only ¥5. Sellers and buyers forgo opportunities to enjoy a larger value to share when only the lowest quality commodities are produced and sold.

- Identity. The second condition is one in which commodities placed on the market come with identity markers (one of forty-eight Japanese characters).[3] In this condition, buyers can use experience-based information about sellers' known behavior. Buyers will avoid purchasing commodities from sellers with whom they have had sour experiences, and will prefer to buy from sellers who have sold them profitable commodities. Thus we predict that giving players a permanent identity will improve the market and reduce the likelihood of lemons to a certain degree (hypothesis 2). Comparing the average quality level of the goods sold in this condition with that in the anonymity condition serves as the test for the second hypothesis.

- Reputation. To assess the effect of reputation, the last condition, independent of the effect of experience-based information (available in the identity condition), the unique identities (Japanese characters) of the sellers are not attached to the commodities placed on the market. Instead, only the reputation information of the sellers is attached. Reputation information is formulated as follows. Each buyer evaluates the seller from whom she buys a commodity. Evaluation is made by assigning a number between -2 and $+2$ (-2 = very bad, -1 = bad, 0 = neutral, $+1$ = good, $+2$ = very good) to the seller from whom the buyer has just purchased a commodity. Buyers can choose any one number regardless of the quality of the commodity purchased. The sum of evaluation scores a seller has accumulated becomes her overall evaluation score. Each commodity placed on the market for sale by a seller comes with a signal indicating the overall evaluation score of the seller at the time she put the product up for sale. Because providing an exact evaluation score for each seller makes it possible for buyers to identify a seller by his evaluation score, an evaluation score for the seller is translated into a shade of a particular color. Specifically, each box representing a commodity is colored either blue (positive) or red (negative). The shade of blue or red reflects the absolute value of the total score. The screen is flushed periodically, and the locations of the commodities on the display change places randomly each time. Thus it is impossible for the players to identify the producer-seller of a commodity, and yet it is possible for them to determine how other buyers evaluate the producer-seller of each product on the market.

If buyers honestly reveal their evaluations, the quality label expressed as the color of the box will provide at least a partial solution to the lemons problem. Buyers will avoid commodities sold by sellers with a negative reputation (in red) and seek commodities sold by sellers with a positive reputation (in blue). The buyers' response to the reputation information will exert discipline on the seller. The sellers who want to earn good reputations for successfully selling their commodities have to behave in a way that does not offend the buyer. The comparison of this condition with the anonymity condition serves as a test of the third hypothesis, in which we predicted that reputation (information obtained from other players) will improve the quality level of the goods sold in the market.

Procedure

From a participant pool of about 1,500 students at a major university in Japan, fourteen individuals—ten males and four females—were recruited to participate in the experiment. Monetary incentives were emphasized, and no class credit was offered. The experiment was run in two groups, each of which consisted of seven participants. Each group participated in six experimental sessions. The first three sessions lasted forty-five minutes each, and the last three lasted twenty minutes each. In total, the experiment lasted an entire afternoon, approximately five hours. Participants were paid the amount they earned in the experiment. The most any one participant earned was ¥8,965 (about $80), and the least any one participant earned was ¥910 (about $8). The average pay was ¥5,597. Each of the forty-five-minute sessions was assigned to one of the three conditions. We added the twenty-minute sessions to learn how the experience of the first three sessions would affect the participants' behavior. Each of the twenty-minute sessions was assigned to one of the three conditions as well. Participants were not told how long each session would last. The order of presentation of the three conditions was randomized for each group. A rest period of ten minutes was provided between sessions.

The experiment was conducted in a laboratory consisting of eight small rooms. Each room was equipped with a computer that was connected by LAN to a host computer controlled by the experimenter. On arrival at the laboratory, each participant was escorted to her or his individual room. All instructions were presented on the computer screen. The production and purchasing decisions made by the participant were entered into the participant's computer with a click of a mouse. In each session, participants were allowed to produce commodities as many times as possible for the first two minutes. That is, during the first two minutes of the session, a new production opportunity was given to the participant as soon as she or he finished producing a commodity. The experiment was conducted this way to provide the market with enough commodities with which to start. After the two minutes, a production opportunity was provided to the participant every fifty seconds with a random variation within the range of plus or minus fifteen seconds.

Findings

Figure 3.2 presents the average level of quality of the commodities produced and placed on the market during both the forty-five-minute and the twenty-minute session. Each session is broken into time blocks lasting five minutes each. The main effect of the condition in a condition (a repeated factor) × time block (a repeated factor) ANOVA on the forty-five-minute session indicates a significant main effect of the conditions, $F(2, 39) = 16.73$, $p < .0001$. The main effect of the time block, $F(8, 312) = 2.05$, $p < .05$, and the conditions × time block interaction, $F(16, 312) = 4.34$, $p < .0001$, were also significant.[4] As shown in the figure, both the main effect of the time block and the interaction effect reflect the downward trend of the average quality of the commodity that occurred only in the anonymity condition. A post hoc analysis of mean quality levels in the three conditions, using a Tukey's studentized range test, indicates that the mean quality level of the anonymity condition (29.65) is significantly different from the mean quality level of the other two conditions (70.76 in the identity condition and 71.07 in the reputation condition). The mean quality levels of the identity condition and the reputation condition were not significantly different from one another. A similar analysis was conducted on the twenty-minute sessions, and similar results were obtained. As in the forty-five-minute session, there was a significant difference between the mean quality level in the anonymity condition (16.52) and the mean quality level in the other two conditions (67.51 in the identity condition and 76.89 in the reputation condition). These results support hypotheses 2 and 3.

The first hypothesis is also supported by the data. The average quality level of the commodities in the anonymity condition approached the theoretically predicted lowest quality of 10 in both the first forty-five-minute session and the second twenty-minute session. The average quality during the last time block (11.96) of the forty-five-minute session is only very slightly above 10, and not significantly different from 10, $t(13) = 1.69$, ns. In the twenty-minute session, this equilibrium was reached more quickly. The average quality level was not significantly different from 10 in the third time block (10.94, $t(13) = 1.46$, ns) and the fourth time block (10.29, $t(13) = 1.00$, ns). These results confirm the first hypothesis.

In addition to confirming all three hypotheses, the data also provide

Figure 3.2   Average Quality Level of Produced Commodities in Experiment 1

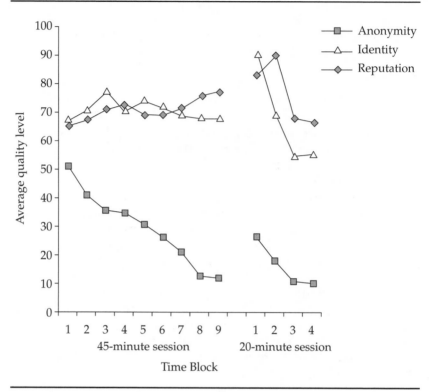

Source: Authors' compilation.

further interesting findings. Figure 3.3 shows the average fraudulence level—the difference between the advertised quality and the true quality—in the three conditions. For example, a commodity advertised as having a quality level of 80 but having a true quality of 30 receives a fraudulence score of 50 (80 − 30). The fraudulence level was much higher in the anonymity condition than in the other two conditions. In the ANOVA of the fraudulence level for the forty-five-minute session, the main effect of the conditions was significant, $F(2, 39) = 5.36$, $p < .01$. The main effect of the time block, $F(8, 312) = 1.93$, $p < .06$, and the conditions × time blocks interaction effect, $F(16, 312) = 1.56$, $p < .08$, were marginally significant. For the twenty-minute session, the main effect of the conditions was significant, $F(2, 39) = 3.61$, $p < .01$, and so were the main effect of the time blocks, $F(3, 117) = 2.93$, $p < .05$, and the interaction effect, $F(6, 117) = 4.74$, $p < .001$. [5]

Figure 3.3   Level of Dishonesty in Experiment 1

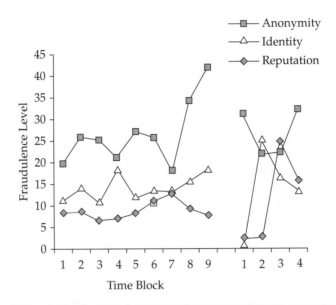

Source: Authors' compilation.

We also examined how accurately buyers reported their experience with the sellers from whom they made purchases. For this analysis, we calculated a correlation for each participant between the fraudulence scores of the commodities purchased and the evaluation scores given to the sellers of those commodities. To avoid confusion, we reversed the sign of the correlation, so that high scores reflect honest evaluations and low scores reflect dishonest evaluations. We call this inverse of the correlation the *index of honest evaluation*. The average index score of honest evaluation in the reputation condition was .67 ($p < .0001$) in the forty-five-minute session and .73 ($p < .0001$) in the twenty-minute session. These results indicate that the participants in this experiment reported their personal experience-based information to be shared with others fairly accurately.

In conclusion, the results of the first experiment replicate the findings of Bolton and his colleagues (reported in chapter 1, this volume) about the effects of reputation and provide support to the first three hypotheses presented earlier in this chapter. The market for lemons did emerge in the anonymity condition as the quality of the goods in this condition was reduced to the lowest level (hypothesis 1). Moreover, being able to identify the sellers by name (hypothesis 2) and having reputation information about the sellers (hypothesis 3) increased the quality of the goods sold on the market, thereby alleviating the problem of lemons. The additional findings regarding fraud and the honest evaluation of the sellers merely confirm these findings. Fraud occurred less often in the identity and reputation conditions than it did in the anonymity condition. In addition, honest evaluations by the buyers of the sellers were made in the reputation condition to help ensure the success of this system.

Experiment 2: Stability of Reputation

The second experiment was conducted to test the fourth and the fifth hypotheses. In the fourth hypothesis, we predict that when players are permitted to freely change their identities, the quality level of the goods sold in the market will be reduced. We also tested whether the direction of reputation—negative, positive, or mixed—makes a difference. We predict in the fifth hypothesis that the detrimental effect of identity change will be more serious in the negative reputation system than in the positive or mixed reputation system.

We manipulated three types of the reputation system as follows. Under the negative system, evaluation scores have only three levels, 0 for neutral, −1 for bad, and −2 for very bad. Such a negative scale would make reputation completely useless when traders can freely change their identities, because those who earn negative reputation scores soon change their identities and enter the market under new identities with a reputation score of 0. If this happens, practically everyone will have a reputation score of 0, which is equivalent to providing no reputation. Under the positive reputation system, evaluation scores have three levels: 0 for neutral, 1 for good, and 2 for very good. We predict that the positive effect of reputation will be stronger here. Because even a slightly positive reputation is better than having none, anyone who has earned a positive evaluation score should be motivated to maintain it. The incentive to maintain a positive reputation will discourage a seller from changing identities. The players who have earned high reputation scores will be strongly motivated to maintain their current identity. Thus the detrimental effect found in the condition where players can freely change their identities will be weaker in a positive reputation system. Finally, players in the mixed reputation system in which evaluation scores take on either positive or negative values will want to cancel negative reputations, on the one hand, and yet maintain positive reputations, on the other. Thus the detrimental effect of identity change is predicted to be similar to that in the positive reputation system, and not as strong as in the negative reputation condition.

To test the fourth hypothesis, we compare the results of the second experiment with the results of the first. In the second experiment, both the identity and the reputation of the seller are provided, that is, the commodity placed on the market by a seller has the identity label of the seller and the reputation color. The seller chooses her or his identity as a combination of three Japanese characters at any time during the experiment. Because both identity and reputation have positive effects on the quality levels of the commodities in the first experiment, we predict that the average quality level in the second experiment will be at least as high as the average quality level in the identity or the reputation condition in the first experiment if the freedom of changing identities has no effect. The comparison of the average quality of the commodities sold in the mixed-reputation condition of the second experiment with those in the identity and the reputation conditions in the first experiment tests the fourth hypothesis. The comparison of the average quality of the commodities sold in all three conditions tests the fifth hypothesis.

Procedure

A total of sixty-six college students—forty males and twenty-six females—drawn from the same subject pool as in the first experiment participated in the second experiment. Twenty participants were assigned to the positive reputation condition in three groups, twelve were assigned to the negative reputation condition in two groups, and thirty-four were assigned to the mixed reputation condition in five groups. The experimental session was not repeated. That is, each participant experienced only one forty-five-minute session and was paid the amount she or he earned in that session. Participants started with an identity character set—a combination of three Japanese characters—and were then allowed to assume a new identity at any moment of the experiment. When they assumed a new identity, they started over with a reputation score of zero. In the positive reputation condition, participants assigned a positive evaluation score (0 for neutral, 1 for good, 2 for very good) to the seller every time they purchased a commodity. In the negative reputation condition, participants assigned a negative evaluation score (0 for neutral, –1 for bad, –2 for very bad), and in the mixed reputation condition they assigned either a negative or a positive evaluation score ranging from –2 to 2. The average payment was ¥798, with the maximum at ¥3,195 and the minimum at ¥300.

Findings

The average quality level of commodities produced and sold (divided into nine time blocks) is presented in figure 3.4. As predicted by the fifth hypothesis, the average quality level was lowest in the negative reputa-

Figure 3.4   Average Quality in Experiment 2 Versus Experiment 1

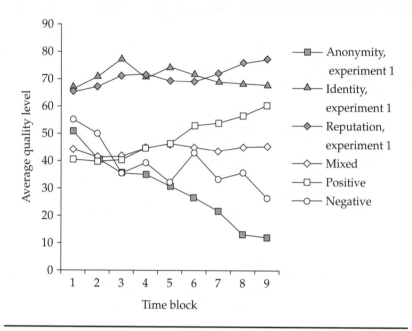

Source: Authors' compilation.

tion condition and highest in the positive reputation condition. Neither the main effect of the conditions in the condition x trial block ANOVA of the average quality ($F(2, 59) = 0.72$, *ns*) nor of the trial block ($F(8, 472) = 1.65$, *ns*) were significant. On the other hand, the condition x block interaction was highly significant ($F(16, 472) = 5.05$, $p < .0001$). The interaction effect indicates that the predicted differences in the average quality gradually emerged over time; the effect of the conditions reached the significance level in the last trial block ($F(2, 59) = 5.07$, $p < .01$). These results provide general support for the fifth hypothesis.

Hypothesis 4 asserts that the average quality level in the second experiment should fall in between the anonymity condition and the identity or the reputation condition of the first experiment. The results in figure 3.4 show that this is in fact the case. Table 3.1 reports the overall average quality of the commodities and the average quality during the last five minutes in the three conditions of the second experiment. The table also reports the same means for the three conditions of the first experiment as well as the statistical differences of the means in the second experiment from each of the three conditions of the first experiment.

Table 3.1   Average Quality in Experiments 1 and 2

Experiment	Condition	Overall Average	Last Five Minutes
1	Anonymity	29.65 (21.95) [iiii, rrrr]	11.96 (4.33) [iiii, rrrr]
1	Identity	70.76 (25.28) [aaaa]	67.89 (30.53) [aaaa]
1	Reputation	71.07 (17.44) [aaaa]	77.31 (18.82) [aaaa]
2	Mixed reputation	44.10 (19.94) [a, ii, rrrr]	45.31 (27.12) [aaaa, i, rrr]
2	Positive reputation	48.46 (22.02) [a, ii, rr]	60.28 (36.22) [aaaa]
2	Negative reputation	38.94 (20.60) [iiii, rrrr]	26.39 (17.62) [aa, iii, rrr]

Source: Authors' compilation.
Notes: Difference from anonymity, a < .05, aa < .01, aaa < .001, aaaa < .0001
Difference from identity, i < .05, ii < .01, iii < .001, iiii < .0001
Difference from reputation, r < .05, rr < .01, rrr < .001, rrrr < .0001

From the table, it is clear that the average quality level in all three conditions of the second experiment was higher than that in the anonymity condition of the first experiment. That is, reputation had at least some effect in alleviating the lemons problem even when identity change was allowed. At the same time, the average quality level in the three conditions in the second experiment was generally lower than that in the identity condition or the reputation condition of the first experiment. This finding indicates that the effect of reputation or identity alone, with no identity change, is stronger than the effect of reputation and identity, with identity changes. Specifically, as predicted by the fourth hypothesis, the average quality in the mixed reputation condition was substantially lower than the average quality in the reputation condition of the first experiment.

The average index of honest evaluation (see the first experiment) was .57 in the mixed reputation condition, .41 in the positive reputation condition, and .66 in the negative reputation condition. All of these figures are significantly greater than 0, $p < .0001$. This suggests that the weaker effect of reputation observed in the second experiment is not due to the participants' unwillingness to honestly and accurately report their evaluations of the sellers.

On average, participants changed their identities 1.75 times in the positive reputation condition, 7.00 times in the mixed reputation condition, and 10.17 times in the negative reputation condition. These differences were highly significant ($F(2, 63) = 4.39$, $p < .05$). The correlation between the frequency of identity changes and reputation was negative in the positive reputation condition ($r = -.56$, $p < .05$) and the mixed reputation condition ($r = -.41$, $p < .05$). The correlation between frequency of identity changes and reputation was positive, though not significant ($r = .41$, *ns*) in the negative reputation condition. These results suggest that those who acquired high reputation scores maintained their brand names in the positive and mixed reputation conditions, whereas those who acquired bad reputations and changed their identities frequently maintained their reputation at close to the highest level, 0, in the negative reputation condition. The correlation between the fraudulence level of the participants and the frequency of identity changes was positive in all three conditions ($r = .40$, $p < .08$ in the positive, $r = .88$, $p < .0001$ in the mixed, and $r = .88$, $p < .001$ in the negative reputation conditions). These figures confirm our expectation that it is mostly dishonest sellers with negative reputations who change their identities.

Did Honesty or Dishonesty Pay?

Previous research based on the analysis of actual Internet auction data consistently indicates a price premium of reputation (Eaton 2002; Houser and Wooders 2006; Lucking-Reiley et al. 2007; Resnick et al. 2006; Resnick and Zeckhauser 2002; Standifird 2001). We examined whether reputation had a positive effect on the gross earnings of the sellers in these two experiments. For this purpose, the gross earnings of the seller were regressed on her or his cumulative reputation at the end of the experiment, controlling for group differences using a dummy variable for the group. The effect of the final reputation on the overall gross earnings from sales was positive in all conditions except in the negative reputation condition of the second experiment ($b = 40.14$, $p < .01$ in the reputation condition of the first experiment (forty-five-minute session); $b = 24.53$, $p < .05$ in the mixed reputation condition; $b = 52.14$, $p < .0001$ in the positive reputation condition; $b = -163.12$, ns in the negative reputation condition). In the negative reputation condition, the range of reputation is extremely small because the traders changed their identities often, and thus reputation did not play a positive role in that condition. In this regression analysis and in the regression analyses presented below, group differences were controlled with dummy variables.

The benefit of the experimental study is in its capability for examining whether the price advantage of reputation translates into profit advantage. On the one hand, sellers can accumulate a good reputation by selling high quality goods at honest prices. By doing so, they can take advantage of the price premium derived from their reputation. On the other hand, the honest sellers forgo opportunities to exploit buyers by selling lemons. In the analysis of actual auction data, it is impossible to determine whether honesty is the best strategy because the researcher has no access to how lucrative sales of lemons are. We therefore decided to examine whether good reputation translates into good profit. For this purpose, we use a regression analysis in which the amount of the seller's profits (gross overall income from sales minus the overall cost of production) is regressed on her or his final reputation. The regression coefficient of reputation on seller's profit is positive ($b = 8.88$, ns) in the reputation condition of the first experiment (forty-five-minute session), in the positive reputation condition ($b = 14.55$, $p < .001$) of the second experiment, but not in the mixed reputation condition ($b = -10.01$, $t(27) = 1.58$, ns) or the negative reputation condition ($b = -2.73$, $t(11) = 0.05$, ns). In short, it is only in the positive reputation condition of the second experiment that acquiring a good reputation helped sellers earn more profit.

This poses an interesting question. On the one hand, introducing reputation improved the overall level of the commodities produced and sold in the experimental market over the anonymity condition. This resulted in a tremendous difference in the overall profit participants made. Participants in the anonymity condition in fact lost an average of ¥371 in the forty-five-minute session and ¥288 in the twenty-minute session, whereas those in the other conditions made positive profits. Even the average quality levels in the negative or mixed reputation conditions of the second experiment, in which acquiring good reputations were not individually profitable strategies, were substantially and significantly higher than that in the anonymity condition. This contrast between the system-level advantage of the reputation and the individual-level advantage of having good reputations suggests that the effect of a reputation system is a system-level phenomenon rather than an aggregation of individual-level effects. We come back to this issue in the general discussion.

Experiment 3: Mock Auction

The results of the two experiments provide clear support to all five hypotheses on the role of reputation as a solution to the lemons problem. However, the small n (the total number of participants was eighty: fourteen in the first experiment and sixty-six in the second) and the small group size (between six and eight) used in the experiments pose serious concerns about the external validity of the findings. Especially problematic is the small group size, given that the small group size may inflate the effect of member identification and experience-based information. When the group is small, each player can keep a detailed history of her trades with each of the other players. In a larger group, in which it is difficult for each player to keep track of her trading history, member identification may not play as important of a role. The difference between the first and the second experiments attibutable to the option to change identities may therefore not be as pronounced as in the current experiment. Furthermore, the small number of groups in each condition made it impossible to use groups as the unit of analysis to take care of the interdependent nature of the data within groups.

Facing the potential limitations of the first and the second experiments, we decided to conduct a third experiment, the purpose of which is to replicate the first two using more participants and larger experimental groups (markets). We also decided to run the third experiment more realistically than the first two. For these purposes, we set up a mock auction site similar to real auction sites such as eBay on the Internet and solicited participants from the general public. A total of 781 active participants played the simulated auctioning game in twenty-nine groups.

Features

We set up an online auction site and recruited participants. The site was designed to simulate the basic features of the real auction sites such as eBay. Each experimental session lasted for twelve to fourteen days rather than forty-five minutes in the first two experiments. The major difference between our site and the real ones is found in the nature of the traded goods. In this experiment, as in the first two, only one kind of abstract commodity was traded. At real sites, various concrete goods are traded. The quality level of the commodity was known only to the producer-seller, as before, and the buyer was informed of the quality only after payment was made. Information asymmetry thus characterized trades in the third experiment as they did in the first two experiments.

Participants   Public notice about the experiment was made at a national newspaper and a high-traffic website, not our own. Paid advertisements were placed on another high-volume site. Those who were interested were encouraged to visit the recruitment site. Potential participants who visited the recruitment site were further encouraged to indicate their willingness to participate in our study and provide us with information about them such as their names, addresses, telephone numbers, and basic demographic characteristics. They were promised monetary rewards for their participation. However, in offering these rewards, we did not specify the manner in which the points they earned in the experiment would be converted to yen. About 1,500 people registered. Those who registered were informed that they would be contacted by a postcard a few days before the start of the experiment.

The experiment was run in twenty-nine groups, each consisting of twenty to fifty initial participants. Initial participants are those who received a postcard notifying them of the start of their experimental session. Some never actually participated in the experiment. Among those who logged on at least once, a few did not actively take part in the experiment, that is, they did not return after their initial log-in. We decided to use data only from the active participants, those who logged in and produced commodities more than five times during the twelve to four-teen days, which left 781 active participants in our data set.

Procedure   When a participant received a postcard notifying the start of her experimental session, a practice session was ready. For a few days before the experiment actually started, participants were encouraged to visit the practice session site and get familiarized with the operation of the auction site. They were informed that the experiment would last more than ten days, and they would be informed a day in advance of the end of the experiment. They could log on to their group site any time of the day during the course of the experiment. As in the first two experiments, each participant played the role of both producer-seller and buyer.

As a producer-seller, each participant received a gold bar worth 50 points once every four hours, or six gold bars per day. When a participant logged in and found one or more gold bars, she or he could use each bar to produce one (and only one) commodity. Participants could produce as many commodities as the number of gold bars at hand. The quality of the commodity produced was determined by how many points the producer invested in production (in intervals of 5 points), as in the first two experiments. Twice (rather than 1.5 times as in the first two experiments) the number of points the producer invested for the production of a commodity was defined as the quality of the commodity which is the value of the commodity to the buyer. For example, when a producer invested 30 points in the production of a commodity, its qual-ity level was 60. That is, the buyer who purchased it received 60 points from the experimenter and the 60 points were put in the buyer's vault. The points the producer did not invest were automatically put in the producer's vault. The producer could also put all 50 points in her or his vault if she or he did not want to produce a commodity.

A producer who decided how many of the 50 points to invest in the production of a commodity also decided on the advertising quality level, between 10 and 100 (in intervals of 10). When a producer made these two decisions, the commodity was placed on the auction site. On the auction site, each commodity was displayed, depending on the ex-perimental condition, with its advertised quality level, the identity of the seller, and/or the reputation score of the seller. To discourage collu-sion among participants, the identities were jumbled in such a way that the same seller's identity appeared as a different identity on each of the other participants' screens.

A commodity placed on the auction site stayed there for twenty-two to twenty-six hours. Exactly when the auction ended was randomly de-termined within this range. This was designed to minimize the effect of the few participants who sat up all night and made the highest bid at the last moment. From testing, we learned that a few such extremely serious participants deprived other participants of chances of successful bidding and thus discouraged them from actively participating in the experiment. Participants could make as many bids to as many commodities on the auction site, though the total amount of their bids could not exceed the total points in their vaults. Buyers could make bids only at a higher price than the current highest bidding price. A commodity was purchased at the end of the auction by the highest bidder. The highest bidder paid his bidding price to the seller and received points worth its true quality level from the experimenter. The price was paid from the buyer's vault, and the payment from the experimenter went into the buyer's vault.

Buyers assigned evaluation scores as in the first two experiments. However, the evaluation score was displayed as numbers instead of colors. The range of the evaluation score was −2 and +2 in the mixed reputation conditions and −2 and 0 in the negative reputation conditions. The evaluation score of the seller in the third experiment was the cumulative average or cumulative sum of the scores.[6] We did not replicate the positive reputation conditions, because the critical factor was in the presence of the positive rather than the negative component.

The following six conditions were used:

- Anonymity. This is equivalent to the anonymity condition in the first experiment. No information about the seller's identity or reputation was provided about the commodities placed on the auction site. A total of twenty-eight active participants were run in two groups.

- Fixed identity (FID). This is equivalent to the identity condition of the first experiment. Only the seller's identity was provided and was fixed for the duration of the experiment. A total of 107 active participants were run in four groups.

- Mixed reputation (No-Mix). This is equivalent to the reputation condition of the first experiment. Only the reputation score of the seller of a particular commodity was displayed. The identity of the seller was not. The range of the evaluation score assigned by the buyer was between −2 and +2. A total of 110 active participants were run in four groups.

- Fixed ID and mixed reputation (F-Mix). This is a new condition. Both the seller's identity and reputation were provided and stay fixed throughout the experiment. The buyer was assigned an evaluation score between −2 and +2. The average quality level of the commodities is expected to be the highest in this condition. A total of 367 participants were run in thirteen groups. We originally divided this condition into two conditions. That is, we allowed 254 participants in nine groups to change their identities only once. We suspected that giving sellers who have acquired bad reputations a chance to repent and start a new life might boost the overall level of honesty. Because the difference between those who did not have such a chance and those with one chance in the average quality level was small and insignificant (73.11 with one chance versus 70.82 without a chance, $t(365) = 1.13$, ns), we decided to pool the two conditions.

- Variable ID and mixed reputation (V-Mix). This is equivalent to the mixed reputation condition of the second experiment. The sellers' identities and reputations were displayed, but the sellers could change their identities at any time. When the seller changed identity, a new reputation score of 0 was assigned. A total of 113 participants were run in four groups.

- Variable ID and negative reputation (V-Neg). This is equivalent to the negative-reputation condition of the second experiment. It is similar to the V-Mix condition except that the range of the reputation was only in the negative direction; the range was –2 and 0. A total of fifty-six participants were run in two groups.

Findings

Because the experiment ended in twelve days in some groups, and the participants were notified of the end of the experiment twenty-four hours beforehand, reputation may lose its disciplinary power during the last day of the experiment. To eliminate the end-of-the-game effect, we decided to analyze data from the first eleven days of the experiment. The average levels of quality over the first eleven days are shown in figure 3.5.

The similarity between figure 3.5 and figures 3.2 and 3.4 are striking. Especially striking is the decline in quality in the anonymity condition in all three experiments. The average quality level steadily declined over the eleven days of the experiment toward the lowest quality level of 10. Three hundred and forty-four commodities were produced and placed on auction during the tenth and the eleventh days, and 93.3 percent of them were of the lowest quality of 10. It took about ten days for the quality level to reach the near bottom level in the third experiment, but only forty minutes or so in the first experiment. Despite the differences in the experimental design and the time the quality took to get to the bottom, the similarity in the declining pattern in the two experiments is apparent. The first hypothesis is thus clearly supported. That is, in the absence of experience-based information or reputation, the lemons problem comes to pervade the market sooner or later.

The second hypothesis is also clearly supported. The average quality

Figure 3.5   Average Quality over Eleven Days

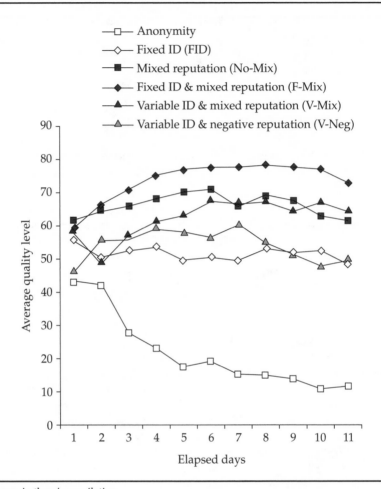

level in the FID condition (51.57, *sd* = 28.05) was higher than that in the anonymity condition (22.03, *sd* = 12.15), and the difference was highly significant ($t(104) = 8.31$, $p < .0001$). This difference is statistically significant even when group means instead of individual responses are used as the unit of analysis ($t(4) = 4.47$, $p < .05$).

The third hypothesis also receives a clear support. The average quality level in the No-Mix condition (64.95, *sd* = 17.27) was significantly greater than that in the anonymity condition ($t(58) = 15.19$, $p < .0001$, at the individual level; $t(13) = 12.43$, $p < .0001$ at the group level). Furthermore, even the higher level of quality in F-Mix indicates that the success of reputation as a solution to the lemons problem is more pronounced when reputation is combined with fixed identity. The average quality level in F-Mix condition (72.40, sd = 17.96) was higher than the same average in FID condition ($t(132)$ = 7.26, $p < .0001$, at the individual level; $t(6)$ = 3.74, $p < .01$, at the group level) or No-Mix condition ($t(475)$ = 3.85, $p < .0001$, at the individual level; $t(14)$ = 2.47, $p < .05$, at the group level). Combining identity and reputation, or experience-based information and reputation, provides a more powerful solution to the lemons problem than using identity or reputation separately.

Finally, reputation provided a partial solution to the lemons problem even when participants can freely change their identities. The average quality level in V-Mix condition (64.83, sd = 19.36) was significantly higher than in the anonymity condition ($t(65)$ = 14.60, $p < .0001$, at the individual level; $t(4)$ = 10.71, $p < .001$, at the group level), and so was the average quality in V-Neg condition (56.57, sd = 18.00; $t(75)$ = 10.39, $p < .0001$, at the individual level; $t(2)$ = 8.76, $p < .05$, at the group level). As predicted by the fourth hypothesis, the average quality level in V-Mix (64.83, sd = 19.36) was lower than that in F-Mix ($t(478)$ = 3.85, $p < .0001$, at the individual level; $t(15)$ = 2.32, $p < .05$, at the group level).

Finally, the detrimental effect of changing identities was more pronounced in the negative reputation system than in the mixed reputation system, as predicted by the fifth hypothesis. That is, the average quality level in V-Neg (56.57) was lower than that in V-Mix (64.83; $t(167)$ = 2.67, $p < .0001$, at the individual level; $t(4)$ = 2.04, ns, at the group level). Although the group level difference did not reach significance, it did when the average quality level during the last five days (day seven through day eleven) was compared ($t(4)$ = 2.86, $p < .05$). Thus, it is safe to conclude that the results support the fifth hypothesis.

In addition to providing support to the hypotheses, the results of the third experiment show that the average level of fraud (that is, the difference between the advertised level of quality and the true quality) was the highest in the anonymity condition (22.01), followed by FID (16.78). The average fraud level was negative in the three conditions involving mixed reputation (−6.45 in No-Mix, −4.03 in the F-Mix, and −1.43 in the V-Mix). The negative average fraud levels in these conditions seem to indicate that sellers in these conditions intended to positively impress buyers by surprising them with a commodity with better than their advertised quality. The average fraud level was positive (8.57) in V-Neg. The mean fraud levels shown are all significantly different than 0, except the mean in V-Mix either at the individual level or the group level.

What was the price premium of having a good reputation? We address this question using within-participant regressions. In this analysis, we first regressed the highest bidding price the seller received for the commodity on the reputation score that accompanied the commodity. We ran this regression for each participant using each commodity produced as the unit of analysis. The commodities that were produced in the first three days were excluded from this analysis because the sellers had not earned stable reputations in the early days of the experiment. We also excluded participants who maintained about the same level of evaluation scores throughout the experiment (with the within-individual standard deviation of evaluation less than .15) or those who received evaluations less than ten times during the fourth through the eleventh day from this analysis, leaving 409 in our data set. We then took the average of the individual regression coefficients. The average regression coefficient was 13.35 ($sd = 21.25$) in No-Mix, 9.82 ($sd = 30.48$) in F-Mix, 13.99 ($sd = 27.74$) in V-Mix, and 21.27 ($sd = 20.52$) in V-Neg. All of these values are significantly greater than 0, at .001. These results indicate that sellers commanded higher prices for their commodities when their reputation was high than when it was low. We then examined whether the price premium existed at the individual level—whether those who earned good reputations commanded higher prices on average than those who earned bad reputations. For this purpose, we regressed the average successful sales price on the seller's average reputation score while controlling for the group differences using dummy variables. The regression coefficient was positive in all four conditions involving reputation ($b = 4.33$, $t(106) = 2.51$, $p < .05$, in No-Mix; $b = 7.75$, $t(353) = 8.07$, $p < .0001$, in F-Mix; $b = 8.74$, $t(110) = 5.85$, $p < .0001$, in V-Mix; $b = 5.02$, $t(54) = 2.26$, $p < .05$, in V-Neg). These results show that the price premium exists at the individual level as well—that the sellers who had high reputation scores were able to sell their commodities at a higher price than those with low reputation scores.

We then examined whether sellers with better reputations earned more profit. The advantage of acquiring a good reputation does not necessarily mean that behaving honestly to accumulate good reputations is a better strategy than taking advantage of the information asymmetry and selling lemons. This is because sellers must give up the opportunities to sell lemons and make large profits to acquire a good reputation. We thus examined how sellers' reputations are related to their profits. As in the analysis of price premium, we first conducted a series of within-individual regression analyses. The results show that the average individual regression coefficient was positive in all conditions (11.10, $sd = 19.38$, in No-Mix; 7.75, $sd = 27.75$, in F-Mix; 12.00, $sd = 23.14$, in V-Mix; 11.05, $sd = 30.47$, in V-Neg, all significant at .0001 except in V-Neg), indicating that when sellers have good reputations, they earn better profits. We then repeated the same analysis with between-individual regressions. When the seller's total profit was regressed on the seller's reputation while controlling for group differences using dummy variables, the individual-level regression coefficient was positive in F-Mix ($b = 261.70$, $t(353) = 4.67$, $p < .0001$) and V-Mix ($b = 116.32$, $t(110) = 1.38$, ns), whereas it was negative in No-Mix ($b = -106.72$, $t(106) = 1.07$, ns) and V-Neg ($b =$

392.13, $t(54) = 2.38$, $p < .05$. These results indicate that earning a good reputation pays off—that is, sellers with more positive reputations made more profits than those with more negative reputations—only in F-Mix. The within-individual regression coefficient of reputation on profit represents the immediate effect of reputation on profit, whereas the between-individual regression coefficient includes the cost of earning good reputations in the form of forgone opportunities to exploit buyers.

We finally examined in a more straightforward manner whether selling lemons is a more profitable strategy for the seller than conducting honest trades. For this purpose, we regressed profit on fraud level both at the within-individual level and the between-individual level.[7] The average regression coefficient of the fraud level on profit in the within-individual regression was positive in all six conditions (.20, $sd = .26$, in the anonymity condition; .31, $sd = .54$, in FID; .55, $sd = .42$, in No-Mix; .52, $sd = .53$, in F-Mix; .48, $sd = .54$, in V-Mix; .43, $sd = .61$, in V-Neg). All of these coefficients were significant at 0.01. Sellers could make up to a half point more profit by overstating the quality of the commodity by one point. These results indicate that selling lemons is more profitable than trading honestly in the short run (within-individual effect). This short-term advantage may be mitigated, though, by the fact that sellers of lemons receive bad reputations. The between-individual regression controlling for group differences shows that the effect of the fraud level on profit is positive—that is, dishonesty pays—in the anonymity condition ($b = 5.82$, $p < .07$), No-Mix ($b = 15.49$, $p < .001$), V-Mix ($b = 5.53$, ns), and V-Neg ($b = 22.38$, $p < .0001$). The same effect is negative—that is, honesty pays—in FID ($b = -3.63$, ns) and F-Mix ($b = -3.07$, ns), though the effects are not significant. In none of the five conditions did honesty significantly pay off monetarily.

The overall picture emerging from this series of analyses is, first, that dishonesty or selling lemons at a cost of earning a bad reputation is financially a better strategy than honestly trading commodities and receiving a good reputation when sellers had no identities or could freely change their identities (that is, No-Mix, V-Mix, and V-Neg). When the seller's identity was fixed (that is, FID and F-Mix), the advantage of dishonest trades is not as clear. Either way, however, earning good reputations does not provide the seller enough of an incentive for honest behavior. This finding is particularly interesting and puzzling in the face of the other finding, that introducing a reputation system alleviates the lemons problem in all three experiments.

Discussion

All five hypotheses in this study received consistent support from the three experiments. Considering the differences in the experimental settings and the subject populations, the consistency is impressive. The messages we receive from the three experiments presented in this chapter are clear. First, information asymmetry drives the experimental market among anonymous traders into a lemons market in which only the lowest quality goods prevail. In this market, opportunities to achieve better profits from trading high quality goods are forgone. Second, either experience-based information or reputation about other traders alleviates the lemons problem. Third, the power of reputation as a solution to the problem of lemons is substantially reduced when traders can freely change their identities and recreate their reputations. Fourth, the negative reputation system is more vulnerable to identity changes than the positive or the mixed reputation systems.

In an effort to design better reputation systems to resolve the lemons problem, our findings concerning the positive, negative, and mixed reputation systems provide valuable insights. Previous research on Internet auction sites have pointed out stronger effects of negative reputations than that of positive reputations (for example, Eaton 2002; Houser and Wooders 2006; Lucking-Reiley et al. 2007; Resnick and Zeckhauser 2002; Standifird 2001). Standifird attributed the stronger effect of negative reputation to the gain-loss asymmetry in subjective utility (2001; Kahneman and Tversky 1979). At the same time, negative reputations are used rarely. For example, Resnick and Zeckhauser concluded, based on 36,233 randomly chosen transactions in eBay, that less than 1 percent of ratings submitted by buyers are negative (2002). According to them, fear of retaliation as well as a courtesy helps explain why Internet traders use more-effective negative reputations less often than less-effective positive reputations. Internet traders provide positive evaluations to their trading partners to elicit similar positive reputations from them. They also refrain from providing negative evaluations to their trading partners to avoid retaliatory negative evaluations from them. Dellarocas suggested that the paucity of negative ratings in eBay reflects an actual lack of dissatisfying experiences because the reputation system helps eBay traders achieve an equilibrium in which cheating rarely occurs (2003). The results of the current experiments, however, suggest a different reason. Specifically, negative reputations may be more effective than positive reputations in the short run, but can be less effective in the long run. In the second experiment, the average quality of commodities was higher in the negative reputation condition than in the positive reputation condition in the first time block. This initial strong effect of negative reputation may reflect the strong aversion of negative outcomes that Standifird suggested (2001). The advantage of the negative reputation system, however, did not last long. The average quality in the negative reputation condition in fact soon plummeted, whereas the average quality in the positive reputation condition steadily improved. The positive effect of the negative reputation system was short lived because it was neutralized by frequent identity changes. The positive effect of positive reputations, on the other hand, may take time to be realized, but is cumulative. In part, such a situation occurs because identity changes are rare in the positive reputation system. A similar pattern was observed in the third experiment, though not as pronounced as in the second, between the negative reputation and the mixed-reputation conditions. The differential long-term effects of positive and negative reputation systems, in addition to the psychological factors Resnick and Zeckhauser discussed (2002), may be behind the differential frequencies of the two types of reputations.

These findings have important implications on the roles of positive reputation and negative reputation in the two types of social relations we discussed in the introduction. The success of the Maghribi coalition, according to Greif's analysis, lies in the fear of exclusion (1989, 1993). A Maghribi coalition member balances the immediate profit of behaving dishonestly with the risk of being excluded from the coalition (and from future profit) once his dishonesty is detected and his reputation of dishonesty spreads among coalition members. Thus, it was predominantly negative reputation that was critical to the success of the coalition. Greif further argued that the success of negative reputation requires closure of the coalition. Exclusion from a market matters only when it is closed to nonmembers. This issue speaks to why negative reputation was not particularly effective in curtailing the lemons problem when traders could freely change their identities. Those individuals who have acquired bad reputations and are excluded or shunned by the other members can freely re-enter the same market under a new identity. The central characteristic of online trading—that is, its openness—thus prevents negative reputation from exerting its power. The openness of online trading, on the other hand, promotes positive reputation as an effective way to curtail the lemons problem.

To understand why positive reputation is useful in online trading, we need to realize that there are two functions of reputation: exclusion and inclusion. The power of negative reputations is based on the principle of exclusion. Negative reputations exclude dishonest traders from the market. The power of positive reputations, in contrast, is based on the principle of inclusion. Positive reputations are not effective for excluding dishonest traders from the market. However, positive reputations are useful in attracting potential trading partners. Attracting new partners is not central to a closed market because the membership of the market is limited. Establishing a good reputation in the Maghribi coalition does not help a Maghribi trader expand his deals beyond the boundaries of the coalition. In sharp contrast, the number of potential trading partners is unlimited in an open market or in online trading. Therefore, the merit of obtaining good reputations in an open market is also unlimited. Established brand names are much more valuable, in this sense, in open markets than in closed markets.

An unexpected finding from our experiments concerns the discrepancy between the system-level effect of reputation and the individual-level effect of reputation. A strong group-level effect of having a reputation system was observed in all three experiments. That is, the average quality level of the commodities was much higher when some form of reputation is involved. And yet honest sellers with good reputations did not enjoy a high profit advantage. Commodities sold by sellers with a good reputation commanded a higher price. This result supports the conventional economist's logic that "in equilibrium, a good reputation must command a price premium" (Resnick et al. 2006, 82). However, sellers had to pay costs to acquire a good reputation in the form of forgone opportunities to exploit buyers with lemons. Honest sellers failed to earn significantly more profits than dishonest sellers, that is, those who sold commodities at a high fraud level, in all conditions of all three experiments. The price premium does not provide enough of a monetary incentive to behave honestly, because it often does not outweigh the forgone profits from selling lemons. What is noteworthy is that the introduction of a reputation system had a substantial positive effect on the overall quality level of goods in the market even when there was no monetary incentive for the sellers to behave honestly.

The discrepancy between the system-level effect and the individual-level effect of reputation poses an interesting question about the economist's view that aggregation of individuals' rational behavior sustains equilibrium. On careful examination of the Internet auction practices, however, this kind of equilibrium is found to be untenable in the online marketplace because individual sellers have no way to find out about the price premium of maintaining good reputations, as Michael Macy discussed in the First International Symposium of Online Reputation held at MIT in April of 2003. One way the sellers find out about the price premium of reputation is to read journal articles and conference papers. The findings concerning price premium so far have been scarce and are not consistent (for a review, see chapter 6, this volume; see also Resnick et al. 2006). Another way for the sellers to learn is to experiment for themselves, behaving honestly and dishonestly under different pseudonyms. After doing so, they can then choose the optimum level of honesty and reputation. However, as discovered in the analysis of the third experiment, price advantage does not translate directly into profit advantage. When the cost of earning and maintaining good reputations is taken into account, sellers in the third experiment often did not enjoy better profits from behaving honestly. These considerations strongly suggest that the strong group-level effect of reputation in that condition is not an aggregation of individual sellers' rational decisions.

If the group-level effect of reputation observed in our experiments in the absence of individual-level advantage is not an aggregation of individuals' rational decisions, what explains it? Macy suggested the belief shared by the market participants that reputations do work. The key point here is that, as discussed, those who believe in the sanctioning power of reputation have no opportunity to personally experience the validity of the belief. The belief thus can be maintained among market participants, and whether having good or bad reputations actually affects their profit is irrelevant. The trend over time of the fraud level in the reputation condition shown in figure 3.3 further supports the claim that the group-level effect of reputation was based on existing beliefs rather than experience. The average level of fraud as well as the average quality level of commodities produced for sale in the market stayed at about the same level throughout the experimental session. Even in the positive reputation condition of the second experiment and F-Mix in the third experiment in which an upward change in the average quality of the commodities are observed, the relative gain in the quality is relatively small in relation to the difference from the anonymity condition. The effect of having a reputation system existed from the beginning of the experiment.

The tentative conclusion of this discussion that the group-level effect of reputation is maintained by an unchallenged belief requires further careful examination because its implication is so weighty. Especially important is the fact that the equilibrium is not sustained by individuals' rational and self-interested considerations, the implication of which is that once the belief is found to be groundless, the positive effect of having a reputation system may evaporate quickly. People may have acquired the belief that reputation functions as a strong and powerful deterrent against fraudulent behavior in the rather traditional, closed social environment, and apply the belief without carefully assessing its validity. If so, the role of reputation in a more open social environment represented by the Internet auction market is on precarious ground. This is a good topic for future research to examine, because knowledge about the effectiveness of the reputation system can be clearly manipulated in the experiment. Furthermore, and more important, we should look for a design of a reputation system that furthers the advantage of honest behavior. The positive reputation system provides a design starting point, but it is still an open field to explore, possibly with experimental methodology.

In conclusion, we started with the assertion that the closed nature of the coalition was a critical condition for the negative reputation system to control the lemons problem among Maghribi traders (Greif 1989). Based on our findings, we propose that the lack of a closed market among online traders, which appears at first grant to be a formidable problem, may actually be a blessing. To realize why positive reputations, rather than negative reputations, are effective in resolving the lemons problem in the experimental market we designed as well as in the real Internet auction sites (compare Kollock 1999), we must turn to the principle of inclusion rather than the principle of exclusion. Put differently, although the principle of exclusion has been the central one adhered to when examining the effect of reputations in markets, we find that the effect of reputations in open markets is best understood using the principle of inclusion. Having said this, we need to draw the reader's attention to the cultural differences Tapan Khopkar and Paul Resnick find in chapter 4 of this volume. These conclusions are based on the findings of a series of experiments conducted in Japan with Japanese participants known to be low in trust and trustworthiness (Buchan, Croson, and Dawes 2002; Takahashi et al. 2008), and thus there is a possibility that the findings in these experiments may not generalize in their entirety beyond this limited cultural group. As Khopkar and Resnick note, how institutional arrangements interact with cultural norms and culturally endorsed strategies is worthy of further, more systematic studies.

Notes

1. Although the Federal Trade Commission reports that the number of consumer complaints about Internet auctions have exploded from 107 in 1997 to 10,700 in 1999 (Federal Trade Commission press release, February 14, 2000), the number is relatively small compared to the sheer volume of trades conducted online. According to a projection cited in a Reuters news release, January 31, 2001, 42 million P2P transactions were made online in 2000.
2. The exchange rate for \$1 was roughly ¥100 at the time the experiment was conducted.
3. The number of letters was increased to three in the second and the third experiments.
4. The data could be treated in a more sophisticated way by treating the results of the previous period as inputs for the current period (and by assuming that the errors are likely to correlate over time). What remains unclear, given the setup of our experiment and our analyses, is how likely it is that such diverging patterns are determined by perhaps coincidental choices in the first rounds of the experiment.
5. In this analysis, time block was treated as a nominal variable and not as a covariate because we did not have a theoretical basis to predict that time would have a consistently increasing or decreasing effect on the quality of the commodities.
6. We used both cumulative average and cumulative sum of evaluation scores to examine whether the two methods make any difference. We found no significant difference in the average quality of goods. We thus decided to pool data from the two presentation methods.
7. Two hundred and fifty-four participants who consistently received similar

evaluation scores—that is, those whose within-individual standard deviation of the fraudulence level is less than 5—and those who sold commodities fewer than ten times are excluded from this analysis, leaving 527 participants in the data set.

References

Akerof, George A. 1970. "The Market for Lemons: Quality Uncertainty and the Market Mechanisms." *Quarterly Journal of Economics* 84(3): 488–500.

Avery, Chris, Paul Resnick, and Richard Zeckhauser. 1999. "The Market for Evaluation." *American Economic Review* 89(3): 564–84.

Buchan, Nancy, Rachel Croson, and Robyn Dawes. 2002. "Swift Neighbors and Persistent Strangers: A Cross-Cultural Investigation of Trust and Reciprocity in Social Exchange." *American Journal of Sociology* 108(1): 168–206.

DeJong, Douglas V., Robert Forsythe, and Russell J. Lundholm. 1985. "Ripoffs, Lemons, and Reputation Formation in Agency Relationships: A Laboratory Market Study." *Journal of Finance* 40(3): 809–20.

DeJong, Douglas V., Robert Forsythe, and Russell J. Lundholm, and Wilfred C. Uecker. 1985. "A Laboratory Investigation of the Moral Hazard Problem in an Agency Relationship." *Journal of Accounting Research* 23(3): 81–120.

Dellarocas, Chrysanthos. 2003. "Efficiency and Robustness of Binary Feedback Mechanisms in Trading Environments with Moral Hazard." MIT Sloan School of Management working paper 4297–03. Cambridge, Mass.: Massachusetts Institute of Technology.

Eaton, David H. 2002. "Valuing Information: Evidence from Guitar Auctions in eBay." Department of Economics and Finance working paper 0201. Murray, Ky.: Murray State University. Available at: http://databases.si.umich.edu/reputations/bib/papers/eatonpaper.pdf (accessed April 5, 2009).

Fehr, Ernst, and Simon Gachter. 2000. "Fairness and Retaliation:The Economics of Reciprocity." *Journal of Economic Perspective* 14(3): 159–81.

Fehr, Ernst, Simon Gachter, and Georg Kirchsteiger. 1997. "Reciprocity as a Contract Enforcement Device: Experimental Evidence." *Econometrica* 65(4): 833–60.

Friedman, Eric J., and Paul Resnick. 2001. "The Social Cost of Cheap Pseudonyms." *Journal of Economic and Management Strategies* 10(2): 173–99.

Greif, Avner. 1989. "Reputation and Coalitions in Medieval Trade: Evidence on the Maghribi Traders." *Journal of Economic History* 49(4): 857–82.

———. 1993. "Contract Enforceability and Economic Institutions in Early Trade: The Maghribi Traders Coalition." *American Economic Review* 83(3): 525–48.

Houser, Daniel, and John Wooders. 2006. "Reputation in Auctions: Theory and Evidence from eBay." *Journal of Economics and Management Strategy* 15(2): 353–69.

Kahneman, Daniel, and Amos Tversky. 1979. "Prospect Theory: An Analysis of Decisions under Risk." *Econometrica* 47(3): 263–91.

Kollock, Peter. 1999. "The Production of Trust in Online Markets." In *Advances in Group Processes*, vol. 16, edited by Edward J. Lawler, Shane R. Thye, Michael W. Macy, and Henry A. Walker. Greenwich, Conn.: JAI Press.

Lucking-Reiley, David, Doug Bryan, Naghi Prasad, and Danie Reeves. 2007. "Pennies from eBay: The Determinants of Price in Online Auctions." *Journal of Industrial Economics* 55(2): 223–33.

Resnick, Paul, and Richard Zeckhauser. 2002. "Trust among Strangers in Internet Transactions: Empirical Analysis of eBay Reputation System." In *Advances in Applied Microeconomics*, vol. 11, *The Economics of Internet and e-Commerce*, edited by Michael R. Baye. Amsterdam: Elsevier Science.

Resnick, Paul, Richard Zeckhauser, Eric Friedman, and Ko Kuwabara. 2000. "Reputation Systems: Facilitating Trust in Internet Interactions." *Communications of ACM* 43(1): 45–48.

Resnick, Paul, Richard Zeckhauser, John Swanson, and Kate Lockwood. 2006. "The Value of Reputation on eBay: A Controlled Experiment." *Experimental Economics* 9(2): 79–101.

Standifird, Stephen S. 2001. "Reputation and E-commerce: eBay Auctions and the Asymmetrical Impact of Positive and Negative Ratings." *Journal of Management* 27(3): 279–95.

Takahashi, Chisato, Toshio Yamagishi, James H. Liu, Feixue Wang, Yicheng Lin, and Szihsien Yu. 2008. "The Intercultural Trust Paradigm: Studying Joint Cultural Interaction and Social Exchange in Real Time over the Internet." *International Journal of Intercultural Relations* 32(3): 215–28.

Wilson, Robert B. 1985. "Reputations in Games and Markets." In *Game-Theoretic Models of Bargaining*, edited by Alvin E. Roth. Cambridge: Cambridge University Press.

Chapter 4

In the Eye of the Beholder: Culture, Trust, and Reputation Systems

Tapan Khopkar and Paul Resnick

A REPUTATION SYSTEM collects, aggregates, and distributes information about people's past behavior. Little is known about cross-cultural differences in how people interpret information from reputation systems and adjust their strategic behavior. This chapter presents the first experimental evidence about such cross-cultural differences. In the process, we also shed light on the question of whether apparent cross-cultural differences in trust are merely a rational response to differences in trustworthiness.

The purpose of a reputation system is to enable trust and encourage trustworthiness in situations of social uncertainty. Denise Rousseau and her colleagues defined trust as "a psychological state comprising the intention to accept vulnerability based on positive expectations of the intentions or behavior of another" (1998, 395). Diego Gambetta defined it as the confident expectation that the other party will perform the transaction according to the trustor's expectations (1988). According to James Coleman, situations of trust are a subclass of situations that involve risk, where the risk one takes depends on the performance by another actor (1994). Coleman's functional definition is most appropriate for the conditions of our experiment, where we measure trusting behavior without attempting to ascribe psychological states to the actors: we describe an actor as trusting if she voluntarily accepts vulnerability to the choice her transaction partner will make. Similarly, we describe an actor as trustworthy if he would act in a way that benefits the trustor, when the trustor puts herself in a vulnerable position.

Social uncertainty exists for an actor when her interaction partner has an incentive to act in a way that imposes a cost on her, and she does not have enough information to predict the partner's intentions (Yamagishi and Yamagishi 1994). Clearly, if an interaction partner has an incentive not to be trustworthy, a decision to trust involves a greater risk, and hence will be undertaken less frequently. In those cases where the interaction partner is trustworthy, a lack of trust prevents a mutually beneficial transaction, to the detriment of both parties. Thus, trust is sometimes considered a form of social capital because it enables wealth-generating interactions to take place that might otherwise be missed (Fukuyama 1995; Putnam 1994).

According to Peter Kollock, high social uncertainty promotes committed partnerships, which result in repeated interactions between particular trading partners (1994). Repeated interaction between trading partners enables trust in two ways. First, each person can use evidence from past interactions to assess the partner's character. Second, the expectation of future interactions creates a strategic incentive for good behavior in the present, what Robert Axelrod poetically described as the shadow of the future (1984). Anticipating the strategic effect on the trustee of the shadow of the future, it may become rational to trust an interaction partner in the present.

Not all of the potentially beneficial transactions, however, are between partners who will transact repeatedly. For example, one study of the electronic marketplace eBay found that 89 percent of buyer-seller pairs conducted just one transaction during a five-month period, and just 18 percent of the transactions were between partners who had previously conducted a transaction (Resnick and Zeckhauser 2002). To facilitate transactions among strangers, a different source of trust is needed, where trust is not based on long-term committed partnerships.

Culture and Trust

One source of trust without committed partnerships is broad cultural norms. Edward Hall and Mildred Hall defined culture as a system for creating, sending, storing and processing information (1990). Geert Hofstede considered culture as "the collective programming of the mind that distinguishes the members of one group from another" (2001, 9). To study the similarity and differences between national cultures, Hofstede conducted a survey of matched samples of IBM employees from more than fifty countries, along with a series of follow-up studies on other samples. Based on this empirical research, Hofstede proposed a framework of five independent dimensions of national culture. Each of these dimensions, he claimed, deals with a basic problem with which all societies have to cope, and to which their approaches vary.

Hofstede's cultural dimensions are power distance, uncertainty avoidance, individualism versus collectivism, masculinity versus femininity, and long-term versus short-term orientation. A detailed description of these is beyond the scope of this research. We focus mainly on the cultural dimension of individualism versus collectivism. We are interested in this dimension because it is considered to have an impact on economic behavior and trust in particular.

The cultural dimension individualism versus collectivism is related to the integration of individuals into groups. Individualism describes a culture in which people are connected by loose ties and are expected to look after themselves and their immediate families. Collectivism describes a culture in which individuals are connected by strong ties and are integrated into strong, cohesive groups that pervade most of their activities. In general, countries in Europe and North America are high on individualism, whereas countries in Asia, South America, and Africa are high on collectivism (Hofstede 2001).

Toshio Yamagishi and various colleagues have argued that in a collectivist culture people respond to social uncertainty by forming committed, long-standing groups that are mostly closed to outsiders (Yamagishi 1988; Yamagishi, Cook, and Motoki 1998). Trustworthy behavior is expected within groups but is not extended to out-group individuals. In essence, the shadow of the future created by repeated interactions with a single partner covers all members of the in-group, even those with whom a particular person may interact rarely. In individualist cultures, on the other hand, people exhibit a more generalized trust; trustworthy behavior is expected most of the time, even from strangers. In this sense, individualistic cultures might be better described as universalist (Yamagishi, Jin, and Miller 1998).

Differences in generalized trust across cultures are well documented. Social surveys like the World Values Survey have reported significant variability in generalized trust across nations based on responses of carefully chosen samples of respondents. The World Values Survey asks respondents a series of questions concerning trust in various political and social institutions, as well as general questions such as, "Generally speaking, would you say that most people can be trusted or that you can't be too careful in dealing with people?"

Although the surveys report differences in trust for a large number of cultures using attitudinal measures, Edward Glaeser and his colleagues demonstrated that such attitudinal measures can diverge from behavioral measures taken from actual trust decisions (2000). Several smaller studies compare trusting and trustworthy behavior, typically in experimental settings using games such as the prisoner's dilemma game or the trust game.

Nahoko Hayashi and his colleagues reported findings from Motoki Watabe and his colleagues, who studied differences in trust among Japa-

nese and American subjects using a one-shot prisoner's dilemma game
(Hayashi et al. 1999; Watabe et al. 1996). Both studies found Japanese
subjects to be significantly less trusting than the American subjects.
Nancy Buchan, Rachel Croson, and Robyn Dawes compared the behavior of subjects from the United States, China, Japan, and Korea in a mod-
ified version of the trust game that elicits trust and trustworthiness in a
group setting (2002). They reported significant differences in the levels
of trust and trustworthiness across cultures. They found that the Americans and Chinese were more trusting, compared to the Japanese and Koreans, and that the Chinese and Koreans revealed themselves to be more
trustworthy than either of the other two groups. Marc Wilinger and his
colleagues compared the behavior of French and German subjects in a
one-shot trust game and found the German subjects more trusting but as
trustworthy as the French subjects (2003). Abigail Barr had subjects from
Zimbabwean villages participate in a one-shot trust game and found
significantly less trust among subjects from villages where long-standing ties between families were disturbed by resettlement (2004).

Reputation Systems in Electronic Marketplaces

The convergence of computer and telecommunication technologies led
to the explosive growth of the Internet during the 1990s and brought
about a revolution in the business world. Electronic marketplaces like
eBay brought together "hundreds of thousands of businesses and millions of individual customers" by providing a platform for interaction
and trading (Bakos 1997, 1676). Sulin Ba and Paul Pavlou argued that
the revolutionary feature of electronic markets is that they enable trading partners to exchange goods and services without ever meeting one
another (2002). Of course, the strangers who act as trading partners may
not be trustworthy.

By matching strangers for potentially beneficial trades, electronic
markets enhance the need for generalized trust. Many electronic marketplaces use a reputation system to enable trust. A reputation system
can gather information about participants' past behavior, both objective
data such as the number of transactions and their value, and subjective
feedback from interaction partners. For example, following each transaction, eBay allows both the buyer and seller to submit a multiple-
choice rating (positive, neutral, negative) and a one-line review of the
trading partner. Both the individual reviews and summary counts of the
number of ratings of each type are visible to potential future trading
partners.

Just as repeated transactions in a committed long-term partnership
yield information about who has been trustworthy and thus create an

incentive to be trustworthy, a reputation system provides similar information and incentives even for one-time interactions. A buyer can examine the past feedback profile of a seller he has not purchased from before, and decide not to buy or to offer a lower price to compensate for the possibility that the seller will not be trustworthy. For the seller, the expectation that her feedback profile will be visible to future buyers creates an incentive to be trustworthy. When a reputation system is in place, the future casts a shadow even if the seller does not expect any further interactions with that particular buyer.

Observational and experimental evidence indicates that many buyers use seller reputation profiles as a signal of trustworthiness and adjust their bidding behavior accordingly. Paul Resnick and his colleagues described a controlled experiment in which an established seller profile led to 8.1 percent more revenue for sales of similar items (matched pairs), and also summarize results from many cross-sectional observational studies of eBay sales (2006). Because reputations affect buyer behavior, and hence future seller profits, sellers do indeed have some incentive to behave in a trustworthy manner if they are to get positive feedback ratings.

In controlled laboratory settings as well, reputation systems have an effect. Toshio Yamagishi and his colleagues found that, in a multiple round principal-agent game, in the reputation condition subjects expended more in the production phase and were more honest in advertising the produced quality (see chapter 3, this volume). Gary Bolton and his colleagues compared three experimental markets: partners, strangers, and reputation. In the partners market, the same pair interacted with each other repeatedly, but in the strangers and the reputation markets, the subjects were matched up randomly in each round (Bolton, Katok, and Ockenfels 2004; see also chapter 1, this volume). In the reputation condition, the trustors had access to information about the trustee's past behavior, but no information was available in the strangers market. The reputation market had significantly higher trust and trustworthiness than the strangers market, but fared poorly on both counts compared to the partners market. Bolton and his colleagues also found that in the reputation market the trustor's own experience affected his or her trust, in addition to the effect of information about the trustee's reputation. In particular, the authors found that previous experience of being cheated (by another trustee) diminished trust significantly.

The literature leaves two questions unanswered that we attempt to answer here. First, do reputation systems eliminate the behavioral differences in trust and trustworthiness that are known to exist between individualistic and collectivist cultures? Second, if such differences persist, are the differences in trust merely a response to differences in trustworthiness of interaction partners in a particular setting, or are there additional differences in how people from different cultures assess comparable reputation profiles?

Experimental Design

We investigated these questions in a laboratory setting. Student subjects from an individualist culture (the United States) and from a more collectivist culture (India) played a sequence of trust games against randomly matched subjects from their own culture. Subsequently, subjects assessed the trustworthiness of a set of eBay seller profiles.

Trust Game

Twelve subjects arrived for each experimental session. Six were randomly assigned to the role of seller, the other six to the role of buyer. Once assigned, they maintained their roles throughout the trust game.

In each of fifteen rounds, a seller and a buyer were randomly matched to play a simultaneous-move trust game. It is conventional to use a sequential-move trust game, where the buyer first decides whether to buy and the seller decides whether to ship only when the buyer chooses to buy. For reasons explained below, our experiment used a simultaneous-move game instead. The seller committed to a shipping strategy, a decision about whether she would ship if the buyer chose to buy. In the event that the buyer did not buy, the seller's decision had no impact on the outcome. The strategies and the payoffs (in experimental currency) in the game are depicted in table 4.1. The number of rounds was announced in advance to permit the endgame effects to be observed and to maintain experimental control (Bolton, Katok, and Ockenfels 2004).

The chapter appendix includes screenshots (see figures 4A.2 to 4A.5) illustrating the information presented to subjects and the form of their responses. Before choosing a buy or ship action, each buyer was asked to predict the action of his or her partner. This provides a subjective assessment of risk, to complement the behavioral measure taken from their actions.

To aid in trust assessments, each buyer saw a reputation profile of the seller she was matched with. The seller's profile included the total number of positive and negative feedbacks and a round-by-round history. For those rounds where the seller's partner chose to buy, the history showed that the seller received positive feedback if she shipped the item, and negative feedback if she did not. For those rounds where the seller's partner chose not to buy, the seller's action was not revealed in his subsequent reputation profile; the entry for those rounds simply identified the product as not sold. Note that reputation profiles automatically and accurately recorded a seller's history—there were no considerations of strategic feedback reporting as might occur in a system where buyers choose whether to leave feedback. Sellers received no in-

Table 4.1   Simultaneous Move Trust Game

		Seller	
		Ship	Not Ship
Buyer	Buy	50, 50	0, 70
	Not buy		35, 35

Source: Authors' compilation.

formation about the buyer's history, so could not predict the buyer's action based on the buyer's history. Sellers were reminded, however, that the buyer was looking at the seller's history.

After each round, buyers and sellers were told how many points they earned. Those points came from two sources. First, each subject received a payoff for the transaction outcome, according to table 4.1. Second, each received a payoff based on the accuracy of their prediction about their partner's action. Subjects were rewarded according to a proper scoring rule, detailed in the appendix, so that a buyer maximized the expected payoff by reporting his true beliefs about the probability that the seller would ship. Because sellers chose shipping strategies contingent on buyer actions, it was possible to evaluate the accuracy of a buyer's prediction of the seller's action even when the buyer did not buy. This was the reason for implementing a simultaneous move game rather than a sequential game.

eBay Profile Assessment

After fifteen rounds of the game, the experiment was over. The subjects answered a short demographic questionnaire. They then completed a second task. Each subject was asked to assess twelve eBay feedback profiles. Subjects were reminded that on eBay not every transaction results in feedback, so the percentage of positive feedback received might be higher or lower than the actual percentage of happy customers. For each profile, the subject was asked to state a probability that the seller with the stated profile would complete a transaction as agreed in a timely manner. The subject was also asked to give a brief textual explanation for why they chose the particular number. The subjects were given fifteen minutes to complete the questionnaire.

Experimental Protocol

There were seven sessions in all, and twelve subjects in each session. For logistical reasons, we conducted all our experiments in the United States. All subjects were undergraduate or graduate students at the University of Michigan. In four sessions, all the subjects were born in the United States and had lived there for most of their lives. For three sessions, subjects were born in India and had lived most of their lives in India. When recruiting Indian subjects, we wanted subjects who had little exposure to cultures outside India. We conducted six sessions of our experiment in the first month of the fall 2006 semester; 63 percent of our Indian subjects were incoming students who had only been outside India for about a month. To get enough subjects we also included some students who had been in the United States for up to eighteen months. U.S. subjects were similarly restricted to those who had not spent more than eighteen months outside the United States. Although we tried to make our subjects as similar as possible, there were other demographic differences between the groups.[1] Twenty-seven of the initial thirty-six U.S. subjects were female, but twenty-seven of the thirty-six Indian subjects were male. Most of the Indian subjects (twenty-five of thirty-six) were graduate students, and almost all of the U.S. subjects (thirty-one of thirty-six) were undergraduates. A reviewer of an early draft of this chapter raised a concern that the effects we attribute to culture were in fact due to the differences between graduate and undergraduate students. To check for this possibility, in May 2007 we conducted an additional session with only U.S. graduate students. Three of the twelve subjects in the additional session were male, and nine were female. Data from all seven sessions are pooled in the analysis.[2]

The total time for each session was between forty-five and sixty minutes. Subjects, on average, earned $20.51 for their participation, which included a $3.00 show-up fee and $10.00 for completing the eBay profile assessments. The experiments were conducted at the Institute for Social Research at the University of Michigan in September 2006 and one session in May 2007. The experiment was programmed and conducted with the software z-Tree (Fischbacher 2007). The chapter appendix provides more details of the experimental protocol, including screenshots from the software used to implement the trust game.

Results

The first research question was whether the presence of a reputation system is enough to erase differences between cultures in the level of trust and trustworthiness exhibited in a trust game. The answer is a clear no.

In the context of the trust game, trust refers to a buyer choosing to buy from a seller, and trustworthiness refers to a seller choosing to ship. For this analysis, we aggregate the decisions made across all sessions in all the rounds.

As seen in table 4.2, aggregate levels of trust and trustworthiness are higher in the U.S. group than in the Indian group. There is a high correla-

Table 4.2   **Aggregate Trust and Trustworthiness**

	United States	India
Percentage of choosing buy (aggregate trust)	77%	56%
Percentage of choosing ship (aggregate trustworthiness)	74%	49%
Total decisions	360	270

Source: Authors' compilation.

tion between levels of trust and trustworthiness, as would be expected. The aggregate differences between the two groups are statistically significant using a two-sample Wilcoxon rank-sum test (p-value < .01).

The round-by-round trading patterns in the two cultures can be seen in the plots of trust in figure 4.1, perceived trustworthiness in figure 4.2, and actual trustworthiness in figure 4.3. As before, trust is defined as the percentage of buyers who chose to buy, and trustworthiness is the percentage of sellers who chose to ship. Perceived trustworthiness is the buyers' assessment of the probability that the seller will ship in that round. In all three figures, data for a trading period have been aggre-

Figure 4.1   **Trust: Proportion of Buyers Choosing to Buy**

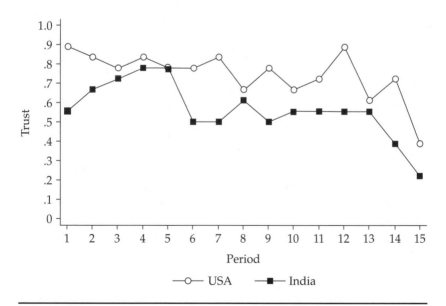

Source: Authors' compilation.

Figure 4.2   Buyer Predictions of Seller Trustworthiness

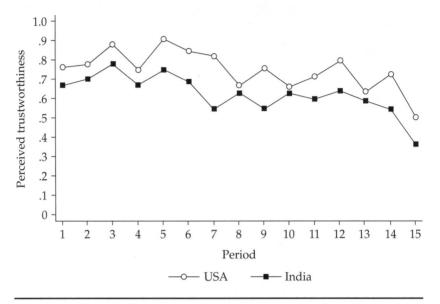

Source: Authors' compilation.

gated, within a culture, across all subjects and hence all experimental sessions.

There are both similarities and differences between the trading patterns of the two groups. The U.S. sessions start with fairly high levels of trust and trustworthiness and remain fairly high for the first twelve rounds. Average trust in the U.S. sessions for those rounds is 0.80, and average trustworthiness is 0.81. On the other hand, the Indian sessions begin with fairly low levels of trust, which increases until the fifth round, and then dips sharply following a drop in trustworthiness in the fifth period. The average trust in the first twelve rounds in the Indian sessions is 0.6, and the corresponding average trustworthiness is 0.56. For both groups, there is a drop-off in trust and trustworthiness in the last few rounds, which can be attributed to the end-game effect—subjects realize that a reputation will have little importance in the future as the game draws to a close.

The logistic regression reported in model 1 in table 4.3 confirms statistically, at an individual level of analysis, the differences in trustworthiness between the two groups of subjects. The outcome variable is the sellers' decision to ship or not ship. A dummy variable codes for the last

Figure 4.3   Trustworthiness: Proportion of Sellers Choosing to Ship

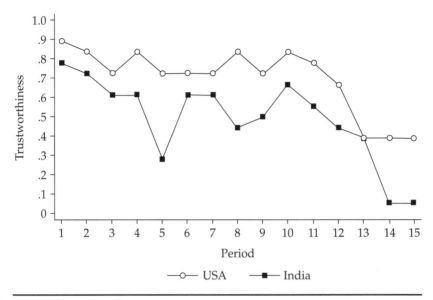

Source: Authors' compilation.

three rounds, to capture the endgame effect, and an ordinal variable codes the round number for the first twelve rounds. Sellers are significantly less likely to ship in the last three rounds, and trustworthiness declines slightly during the first twelve rounds.

Similarly, the logistic regression in model 2 of table 4.4 statistically confirms the difference in trust between the two groups. Indians trust (buy) less compared to their U.S. counterparts, and in the experiment are also less trustworthy than the U.S. subjects.

The models include random effects for the individual subjects to account for the correlated errors introduced by repeated measures from the same subjects. Versions of the models with fixed effects for the sessions showed no significant effects for the sessions within each culture, so we have ignored session effects in the remainder of the analysis.

Our second research question was whether the differences in trust between the two groups reflect a difference in broad outlook, or whether they can be explained by differences in the local environment of the experiment. We answer this question in two stages.

First, we consider whether the trust differences can be explained as a purely rational response to differences in trustworthiness of the interaction partners. If this were the case, then Indian and U.S. subjects, when

Table 4.3   Logistic Regression for Seller's Ship Decision

Outcome: Seller Ships	Model 1
Culture	−2.306
0 for United States, 1 for India	(3.08)*
Periodforreg	−0.096
Period for the first twelve periods	(2.59)*
Last3	−3.224
Dummy variable indicating the last three rounds	(7.93)*
Gender	0.195
0 = male, 1 = female	−0.36
Grad	0.514
0 = undergrad, 1 = gradaute	−1.25
Constant	2.656
	(4.15)*
Observations	630
Number of uniqID	42

Source: Authors' compilation.
Note: Absolute value of z-statistics in parentheses.
$^+ p < 0.10$, $^{**} p < 0.05$, $^* p < 0.01$

paired with partners having the same reputation histories, ought to make the same trust decisions. In the experiment, the Indian and U.S. subjects did not have partners with the same reputation histories. The sellers' profiles can be statistically controlled, however.

Model 3 in table 4.4 adds two independent variables—one for the number of positive feedbacks in the seller's profile and one for the number of negative feedbacks in the seller's profile. There is a high degree of multicolinearity between these variables and the period number, so we drop the period number from the model.[3] The model also includes inter-action terms between culture and the new independent variables to account for the fact that Indians may be affected differently by the sellers' feedback profiles. As expected, the more rounds in which a seller was trustworthy, the more the buyer trusts; the more rounds in which a seller failed to ship, the less the buyer trusts. Even controlling for the seller's history, however, there is a significant difference between Indian and U.S. subjects in their trust decisions. For example, when faced with a seller who has four positive and two negative feedbacks before the last three rounds, the model predicts that a U.S. subject will buy (trust) 72.25 percent of the time, and that an Indian subject will do so 58.78 percent of

Table 4.4   Buyer's Buy Decision

Buyer Decision: Buy or Not Buy	Model 2	Model 3	Model 4
Culture	–1.162	–1.111	–1.186
0 = United States, 1 = India	(3.79)*	(2.47)**	(2.09)**
Period	0.03		
Period for first twelve periods	–1.33		
Grad	0.734	0.305	0.058
0 = undergrad, 1 = graduate	(2.67)*	–1	–0.14
Gender	0.336	0.327	0.333
0 = male, 1 = female	–1.13	–0.98	–0.75
PartnerPlus		0.147	0.305
Seller's past positive feedback		(2.87)*	(3.20)*
PartnerMinus		–0.731	–0.469
Seller's past negative feedback		(6.47)*	(2.76)*
Culture × PartnerPlus		0.079	–0.021
Interaction of culture and PartnerPlus		–1.2	–0.2
Culture × PartnerMinus		0.215	0.109
Interaction of culture and PartnerMinus		–1.38	–0.46
Last3		–0.96	–0.653
Dummy variable indicating last three periods		(2.77)*	(1.72)+
ExperiencePlus			–0.136
Previous good experience			–1.2
ExperienceMinus			–0.725
Previous bad experience			(2.75)*
Culture × ExperiencePlus			0.153
Interaction of culture and ExperiencePlus			–0.97
Culture × ExperienceMinus			0.255
Interaction of culture and ExperienceMinus			–0.83
Constant	0.71	1.447	1.877
	(2.42)**	(3.74)*	(3.66)*
Observations	630	630	630
Number of uniqID	42	42	42

Source: Authors' compilation.
Note: Absolute value of z-statistics in parentheses.
$^+ p < 0.10$, ** $p < 0.05$, * $p < 0.01$

the time. The interaction effects between culture and the partner's past feedback profile are not statistically significant.

The work of Gary Bolton and his colleagues suggests that a buyer's history in an experiment may influence her trust decisions (Bolton, Katok, and Ockenfels 2004). The adage "once burned, twice shy" may influence a buyer even when she is paired with a different seller than the one who cheated her in the past. Even if both U.S. and Indian subjects respond to getting cheated by sellers in the same way, that more Indian subjects were cheated during the experiment might explain the differences in their trust decisions, without invoking some larger cultural difference in how they make trust decisions.

Model 4 in table 4.4 adds two additional covariates to the logistic regression. ExperiencePLUS counts the number of previous rounds where the buyer bought and the seller shipped. ExperienceMINUS counts the number of previous rounds where the buyer bought but the seller did not ship. Finally, to assess whether Indian and U.S. subjects responded differently to being cheated, we included the interaction terms culture × ExperiencePLUS and culture × ExperienceMINUS.

The results indicate that buyers are indeed influenced in their trust decisions by their own history of good treatment, even though that treatment came mostly from sellers other than the one they are currently matched with. There was not a significant effect from the number of previous transactions that went well. The interaction terms of culture and own experience did not have a significant effect on the buyer's buy decision. Controlling for all these factors, however, a difference between the two groups remains, and is significant only at the .05 level. Thus, there is some difference between U.S. and Indian buyers in making trust decisions that is not explained by their different experiences with sellers in the experiment. Apparently, different levels of trust between the two cultures are not simply a response to the trustworthiness of their immediate environments.

A similar pattern of results holds in regression models predicting the buyers' direct assessments of seller trustworthiness rather than the buyers' decisions to buy. The outcome variable here is the probability buyers assign to the event that a particular seller will ship. Models 5 through 7 in table 4.5 have the same independent variables as models 2 through 4. Because buyers' assessments of those probabilities are naturally linked to their buying decisions, it is not surprising that the signs on all the coefficients are the same. In these models, however, some of the coefficients are not statistically significant.

Results from the subjects' assessments of eBay profiles also confirm a cultural difference in risk assessments. In these tasks, subjects had no information about whether their trust decisions were correct, and thus there was no impact of personal experience. Table 4.6 shows the results

Table 4.5   Buyer's Assessment of Seller's Probability of Shipping

Buyer's Belief of Seller Trustworthiness	Model 5	Model 6	Model 7
Culture	−0.151	−0.135	−0.136
0 = United States, 1 = India	(3.20)*	(2.58)*	(2.75)*
Period	0.005		
Period for first twelve periods	(1.73)+		
Grad	0.1	0.024	−0.004
0 = undergrad, 1 = graduate	(2.41)**	−0.68	−0.13
Gender	0.064	0.05	0.039
0 = male, 1 = female	−1.41	−1.28	−1.17
PartnerPlus		0.018	0.02
Seller's past positive feedback		(4.01)*	(2.36)**
PartnerMinus		−0.102	−0.099
Seller's past negative feedback		(9.28)*	(6.14)*
Culture × PartnerPlus		0.01	0.012
Interaction of culture and PartnerPlus		−1.55	−1.08
Culture × PartnerMinus		0.045	0.059
Interaction of culture and PartnerMinus		(2.87)*	(2.51)**
Last3		−0.122	−0.109
Dummy variable indicating last three periods		(3.51)*	(2.99)*
ExperiencePlus			0
Previous good experience			−0.02
ExperienceMinus			−0.019
Previous bad experience			−0.9
Culture × ExperiencePlus			0.021
Interaction of culture and ExperiencePlus			−1.36
Culture × ExperienceMinus			−0.047
Interaction of culture and ExperienceMinus			−1.64
Constant	0.667	0.761	0.78
	(14.80)*	(17.54)*	(19.88)*
Observations	630	630	630
Number of uniqID	42	42	42

Source: Authors' compilation.
Note: Absolute value of z-statistics in parentheses.
+ $p < 0.10$, ** $p < 0.05$, * $p < 0.01$

Table 4.6   Probability Assessment

Stated Probability of Shipping	Model 8	Model 9
Perc	0.005	0.005
Percentage of Positive Feedback	(29.14)*	(18.80)*
Culture	–0.041	–0.071
0 = United States, 1 = India	(2.42)**	(2.01)**
Gender	–0.003	–0.023
0 = male, 1 = female	–0.22	–0.94
Grad	0.007	0.033
0 = undergrad, 1 = graduate	–0.44	–1.25
ExperiencePlus		–0.003
Previous good experience		–0.59
ExperienceMinus		0.007
Previous bad experience		–0.73
Constant	0.45	0.468
	(21.95)*	(8.27)*
Observations	1008	504
Number of uniqID	84	42

Source: Authors' compilation.
Note: Absolute value of z-statistics in parentheses.
$^+ p < 0.10$, $^{**} p < 0.05$, $^* p < 0.01$

of a regression model predicting the probability that the subject will assign to a profile, controlling for percentage of positive feedbacks in the profile. To be sure that experiences in the previous trust experiment were not directly carrying over to their assessments of the eBay profiles, model 9 includes a control for the number of times the subject was cheated by a seller during the experiment. Consistent with the findings in the experiment, the Indian subjects assigned lower probabilities of good seller behavior than the U.S. subjects did—about 4 percent lower on average. For a seller with no previous feedback, the American subjects assessed the likelihood of trustworthy behavior to be 51.9 percent, and the Indian subjects assessed it to be 41.8 percent.

Discussion

The presence of a reputation system appeared to increase trust and trustworthiness for both Indian and U.S. subjects. Buyers assigned higher probabilities of good behavior to sellers with better feedback profiles and were more willing to risk transacting with them. Moreover, in the last few rounds, when the potential future benefits of a good reputation no longer cast a long shadow, trust and trustworthiness declined markedly. This suggests that the higher levels of trust and trustworthiness before the last few rounds were due in part to the presence of the reputation system. However, for the two cultures in our experiment, the reputation system did not eliminate the differences in trust and trustworthiness between the two cultures. Trust and trustworthiness both were consistently lower among Indian subjects than U.S. subjects throughout the experiment. It is not clear why a difference in trustworthiness between the cultures remained in spite of the incentives created by the reputation system. It could be that, due to cultural norms or less strategic analysis, some or all U.S. subjects were more trustworthy than they would have been were they merely optimizing their payoffs in response to the difference in expected future revenues from having a good reputation. In the last round, for example, when the future value of a reputation was 0, 40 percent of U.S. sellers were trustworthy anyway, whereas fewer than 10 percent of Indian sellers were. It is possible, however, that the lower trustworthiness in the Indian sessions was in part a rational response by the sellers to the lower trust. Because of the lower trust, a good reputation is less valuable for an Indian seller than for an American seller. Based on the data available, we cannot further tease apart these effects; further experimentation is needed.

Buyers assessing the risk of interacting with a particular seller can incorporate three types of information: their personal prior beliefs about the trustworthiness of people in general, information about the characteristics or history of actions of people in the current interaction environment, and information about the characteristics and history of actions of the current interaction partner. Do people from different cultures differ in their personal prior beliefs, reflecting differences among cultures in generalized trust? Do they differ in how they incorporate information about their immediate environments?

In the experiment, U.S. and Indian buyers actually operated in different environments. Sessions were culturally homogeneous, so U.S. buyers were paired with U.S. sellers and Indian buyers with Indian sellers. Subjects could easily assess the cultural makeup of the subject pool because they saw each other across the room. Thus it is not possible to isolate with certainty the sources of differences in buyer trust between the two subject pools.

Even so, the results suggest a difference in generalized trust between the two populations. First, in the first round, before subjects had received any information about the trustworthiness of their partners, U.S. subjects were more trusting than their Indian counterparts. Second, in the assessment of eBay profiles for new sellers with no previous feedback, U.S. subjects were more trusting.[4] Third, regression models provided statistical controls for information about the pool of participants (the subject's history of treatment by sellers in previous rounds) and about the current interaction partner (the seller's history). The regression models indicate that buyers with similar information were less trusting if they came from the Indian subject pool.

Future experiments could eliminate differences in the local environment, and thus isolate the effects of differences between subjects in generalized trust. For example, both U.S. and Indian buyers could be paired with the same pool of sellers (U.S., Indian, or mixed).

Our results were less clear about cultural differences in how subjects interpret information about the pool of interaction partners and about particular interaction partners. The only interaction term that was statistically significant showed that Indian subjects were less affected than U.S. subjects by negative feedback in their partners' profiles. This effect was significant only in the analysis of the buyers' beliefs about seller trustworthiness, not in the trust decisions. On the other hand, in assessing eBay feedback profiles, Indian subjects imposed a greater penalty on new sellers who had no previous feedback. Further research is needed to better understand cultural differences in how people incorporate information about a local environment and about individual participants in it.

One caveat in interpreting the results is that the U.S. sessions had a larger percentage of female subjects. We have statistically controlled at the individual level for gender, and found no significant differences in trust or trustworthiness. It is possible, however, that the percentage of female subjects has an effect at the session level, affecting both male and female participants equally, so that it does not show up at the individual level of analysis. We did not conduct enough sessions with variability in gender balance among them to conduct a multilevel analysis. Thus, we cannot rule out the possibility that some of the effects we attribute to culture may be due to differences in gender balance between different experimental sessions.

Another possibility is that the differences in trust and trustworthiness arise out of an income effect. At the time of our experiment, a majority (63 percent) of our Indian subjects had been in the United States for less than a month. It is plausible that they considered the earnings from the experiment to be higher stakes than the American subjects. Previous experimental research has found significant reduction in trust as the stakes increase (Johansson-Stenman, Mahmud, and Martinsson 2005). With our current data, we cannot rule out the possibility that income effect was a driving factor in our results. To eliminate this confound, we would recommend that if logistically feasible, future researchers should conduct experiments in the subjects' native country and design the experiment taking into account the purchasing power of the local currencies (Henrich, Boyd, and Fehr 2001).

One more caveat in interpreting the results is that the trust game in our experiment was a simultaneous move game, instead of the classic sequential game. Kevin McCabe, Vernon Smith, and Michael LePore showed that this distinction affects behavior (2000). They found higher levels of cooperation in a sequential move game than in a simultaneous move game. This raises the possibility that the sequentiality of the game affects the Indian subjects differently than the Americans. We are not aware of research that examines such cross-cultural differences. Whether Indians would be more trusting and trustworthy in a sequential environment is a question for future research.

One other potential limitation is that we provided incentives both for correct reports of beliefs about a seller's actions, and for the buyer's choice of action to trust or not. Given the payoff structures, a subject maximized expected payoffs by reporting beliefs honestly and buying whenever he believed the seller would ship with probability greater than .7. It is possible, however, that some risk-averse subjects chose to hedge their bets. For example, a subject could report low confidence in the seller's trustworthiness yet still buy, reasoning that either the belief or the action was bound to be correct and be compensated. In fact, when subjects reported beliefs below .7, in 30 percent of the cases they bought anyway. When they reported beliefs above .7, in 10 percent of the cases they did not buy. Overall, reported beliefs were not consistent with actions for Indian subjects in 19 percent of cases and for U.S. subjects in 15 percent. Some of the inconsistencies may reflect errors in calculating that the optimal cutoff was .7. Others may reflect rational risk spreading. If subjects did hedge their bets, it would result in incorrect measurement of either the attitudinal or behavioral measure of trust, or both. Most likely, the additional noise would simply make it harder to detect culture differences in trust, and we found similar patterns for both measures of trust. Still, a replication of this study with an experimental protocol that does not provide rewards for belief reports could rule out this potential confound.

Further research is also needed to replicate this study and test it across other cultures. We have attributed the observed differences between Indian and U.S. subjects to a cultural difference along the individualist-collectivist dimension. Tests with other individualist and collectivist cultures are needed to determine whether this attribution is correct, or whether some other dimension of difference between the United States and India is the root cause.

Conclusion

A better understanding of the interaction between culture and the impact of reputation could have important implications for the design of reputation systems. If culture primarily affects the beliefs people have about the trustworthiness of partners without established feedback profiles, then it may be valuable to provide information about the general level of trustworthiness of people with such profiles. For example, eBay could indicate the percentage of all sellers who received a positive feedback on their first transaction. If there are also cultural differences in the interpretation of long-term feedback profiles, then a different approach is needed to teach people how to interpret these profiles. Similarly, if sellers in some cultures are not accounting appropriately for the effect of bad feedback on their future interactions, it may be helpful to make the effect salient in some manner.

Through experimental investigation, we found that reputation systems do not eliminate cross-culture differences in trust and trustworthiness in a situation of social uncertainty. Many important questions remain, however. Do cultural factors merely affect the initial interactions in an environment and then those initial interactions affect later interactions? Or do larger cultural norms continue to exert an influence on behavior beyond the effect of the norms and expectations created within an online marketplace or community? Research opportunities are vast, with important implications for the design of systems.

Appendix

Experimental Instructions

The printed instructions handed to the subjects are reproduced here.

Introduction   This is a study intended to provide insight into certain features of decision processes. There are two parts of this study. In part I, you will participate in a game with other participants in the room. Part II of the study is a questionnaire.

In part I you will play a game that gives you an opportunity to earn cash. If you make good decisions you may earn a considerable amount of money. Decisions and payments are confidential: No one will be told your actions or the amount of money you make. At the end of the session, you will be paid your earnings plus a $3 show-up fee. In part II you will be given 20 minutes to answer questions from a questionnaire. Completing the questionnaire earns you an additional $10.

Part I
PROCEDURES AND PAYOFFS   You and the other participants in the room are the players in the game. Half of the players are randomly assigned to play the role of "buyers," whereas the other half play "sellers."

You will maintain the same role throughout the experiment.

In each round, each player is randomly matched with another player to trade a (fictional) commodity. The buyer chooses to either buy or not buy. At the same time, the seller chooses whether she will ship or not ship if the buyer decides to buy from her. If the buyer chooses not buy, both players receive 35 points. If the buyer chooses to buy and the seller chooses to

Figure 4A.1   Payoffs

Seller Buyer	Ship	Not Ship
Buy	50, 50	0, 70
Not Buy	35, 35	

Source: Authors' compilation.

ship, each player receives 50 points. If the buyer chooses to buy and the seller chooses to not ship, the buyer gets 0 points and the seller gets 70 points. Figure 4A.1 illustrates the payoffs for different outcomes.

The exchange rate in the game is 1 dollar per 100 points.

- In each cell, the first number is the buyer's payoff, and the second number is the seller's payoff

- After both players have made their decision, the computer reveals your match's decision and your payoff for the current round. The computer also records the seller's ship decision automatically, and reveals it in the form of a feedback in the rounds where the buyer chooses to buy.

- If the buyer chooses to buy, and the seller chooses to ship, the seller will get a positive feedback for this round. If the buyer chooses to buy and the seller chooses to not ship, the seller will get a negative feedback. If the buyer chooses to not buy in this round, the seller will not get any feedback for this round.

INFORMATION   Throughout the game, you will be able to view the information about your transaction history on the left side of the screen. The information about your current match will be displayed on the right side of the screen.

Each player can view his or her total earnings in the session. The following set of information about a seller will be available to herself and her current match:

- The number of items sold (the number of times the buyer chose to buy from her).

- The number of positive and negative feedbacks.

- For each round, a seller can see whether she sold the item, her shipping decision, and the points earned in the round. A buyer can see a round-by-round history of the seller with whom he is currently matched: for each round, whether that seller sold an item (that is, whether the buyer chose to buy from her), and if so, the feedback for that round.

The following set of information about a buyer will be available only to himself:

- The number of times buying.
- For each round in the current session, a buyer can see whether he bought an item, whether the item was shipped to him, and the points earned in the round.

Note that sellers do not have any information about a buyer's previous actions.

Predicting your current match's choice   At the beginning of each round, before you make your choice of buy/not buy or ship/not ship, you will be given an opportunity to earn additional money by predicting the choice of your match.

If you are a seller, you will be asked to predict a probability (from 0 to 1) that the buyer will choose to buy from you. On the other hand if you are a buyer you will be asked to predict the probability that the seller will choose to ship. At the end of each round, we will compare your prediction with the choice actually made by your match. You will earn additional points between 0 to 10 for your prediction. You can maximize your payoff by stating your true belief about what you think your match will do. The payoffs for prediction are calculated as follows.

Suppose you are a buyer, and you predict that your match will choose ship with a probability of 0.9.

Now, suppose your match actually chooses ship. In that case your payoff will be: Prediction Payoff when seller chooses ship

$$= 10 - 10 \times (1 - \text{Predicted Probability of ship})2$$
$$= 10 - 10 \times (1 - 0.9)2 = 10 - 10 \times (0.1)2 = 9.9$$

If your match actually chooses not ship, your payoff will be: Prediction Payoff when seller chooses not ship

$$= 10 - 10 \times (\text{Predicted Probability of ship})2 = 10 - 10 \times (0.9)2 = 10 - 8.1 = 1.9$$

Suppose you are a seller, and you predict that your match will choose buy with a probability 0.75.

Now, suppose your match actually chooses buy. In that case your payoff will be: Prediction Payoff when buyer chooses buy

$$= 10 - 10 \times (1 - \text{Predicted Probability of buy})2$$
$$= 10 - 10 \times (1 - 0.75)2 = 10 - 10 \times (0.25)2 = 9.375$$

If your match actually chooses not buy, your payoff will be: Prediction Payoff when buyer chooses not buy

$$= 10 - 10 \times (\text{Predicted Probability of buy})2$$
$$= 10 - 10 \times (0.75)2 = 10 - 5.625 = 4.375$$

Note that your prediction payoff does not affect or depend on your payoff in the actual game. The prediction payoff depends only on how accurately you are able to predict your match's choice. At the end of each round you will be able to see your prediction payoff for that round. This is true even when the buyer chooses not buy. In that case, the seller's ship decision is not revealed to the buyer, but the buyer and the sellers still earn points for the accuracy of their predictions.

Since your prediction is made before you know what your match will choose, the best thing you can do to maximize the expected size of your prediction payoff is to simply state your true beliefs about what you think your match will do. Any other prediction will decrease the amount you can expect to earn as a prediction payoff.

The consent form explains your rights as a subject as well as the rules of confidentiality that will be adhered to regarding your participation.

Screenshots

Figure 4A.2   Buyer Screen: Prediction Task

Source: Authors' compilation.

Figure 4A.3   Buyer Screen: Trading Task

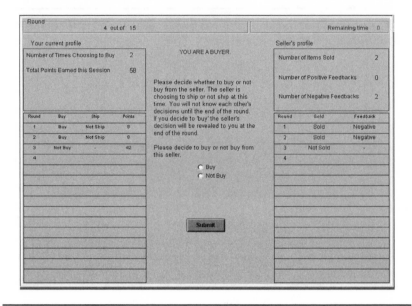

Source: Authors' compilation.

Figure 4A.4   Seller Screen: Prediction Task

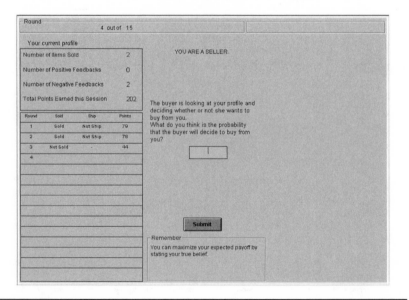

Source: Authors' compilation.

Figure 4A.5   Seller Screen: Trading Task

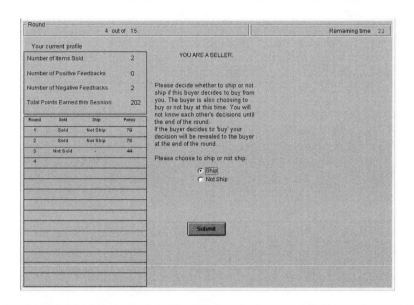

Source: Authors' compilation.

Notes

1. We tested for the effect of academic status and gender as covariates and found that the effects were not significant.
2. Results using only the first six sessions were similar to those with the full seven sessions; the addition of the seventh session more definitively rules out graduate student status as a confound.
3. There is not perfect colinearity because a seller does not get any feedback for a round in which the buyer chose not to buy.
4. This could reflect previous experiences of the subjects with eBay in the United States versus eBay in India, rather than a difference in general propensity to trust strangers.

References

Axelrod, Robert M. 1984. *The Evolution of Cooperation*. New York: Basic Books.
Ba, Sulin, and Paul Pavlou. 2002. "Evidence of the Effect of Trust Building Technology in Electronic Markets: Price Premiums and Buyer Behavior." *MIS Quarterly* 26(3): 243–68.

Bakos, Yannis J. 1997. "Reducing Buyer Search Costs: Implications for Electronic Marketplace." *Management Science* 43(12): 1676–1692.

Barr, Abigail. 2004. "Trust and Expected Trustworthiness: Experimental Evidence from Zimbabwean Villages." In *Foundations of Human Sociality: Economic Experiments and Ethnographic Evidence from Fifteen Small-Scale Societies*, edited by Joseph Henrich, Robert Boyd, Samuel Bowles, Colin Camerer, and Ernst Gintis. Oxford: Oxford University Press.

Bolton, Gary E., Elena Katok, and Axel Ockenfels. 2004. "How Effective Are Electronic Reputation Mechanisms? An Experimental Investigation." *Management Science* 50(11): 1587–602.

Buchan, Nancy, Rachel Croson, and Robyn Dawes. 2002. "Swift Neighbors and Persistent Strangers: A Cross-Cultural Investigation of Trust and Reciprocity in Social Exchange." *American Journal of Sociology* 108(1): 168–206.

Coleman, James S. 1994. *Foundations of Social Theory*. Cambridge, Mass.: Harvard University Press.

Fischbacher, Urs. 1999. "z-Tree: Zurich Toolbox for Ready-Made Economic Experiments." *Experimental Economics* 10(2): 171–178.

Fukuyama, Francis. 1995. *Trust: Social Virtues and the Creation of Prosperity*. New York: Free Press.

Gambetta, Diego. 1998. *Trust: Making and Breaking Cooperative Relations*. New York: Blackwell Publishers.

Glaeser, Edward L., David I. Laibson, José A. Schneinkman, and Christine L. Soutter. 2000. "Measuring Trust." *Quarterly Journal of Economics* 115(3): 811–46.

Hall, Edward T., and Mildred Reed Hall. 1990. *Understanding Cultural Differences*. Boston: Intercultural Press.

Hayashi, Nahoko, Elinor Ostrom, James Walker, and Toshio Yamagishi. 1999. "Reciprocity, Trust, and the Sense of Control: A Cross-Societal Study." *Rationality and Society* 11(1): 27–46.

Henrich, Joseph, Robert Boyd, and Ernst Fehr. 2001. "In Search of Homo Economicus: Behavioral Experiments in 15 Small-Scale Societies." *The American Economic Review* 91(2): 73–78.

Hofstede, Geert. 2001. *Culture's Consequences: International Differences in Work-Related Values*. Newbury Park, Calif.: Sage Publications.

Johansson-Stenman, Olof, Minhaj Mahmud, and Peter Martinsson. 2005. "Does Stake Size Matter in Trust Games?" *Economics Letters* 88(3): 365–69.

Kollock, Peter. 1994. "The Emergence of Exchange Structures: An Experimental Study of Uncertainty, Commitment, and Trust." *American Journal of Sociology* 100(2): 313–45.

McCabe, Kevin A., Vernon L. Smith, and Michael LePore. 2000. "Intentionality Detection and 'Mindreading': Why Does Game Form Matter?" *Proceedings of the National Academy of Sciences* 97(8): 4404–9.

Putnam, Robert D. 1994. *Making Democracy Work: Civic Traditions in Modern Italy*. Princeton, N.J.: Princeton University Press.

Resnick, Paul, and Richard Zeckhauser. 2002. "Trust among Strangers in Internet Transactions: Empirical Analysis of eBay's Reputation System." In *Advances in Applied Microeconomics*, vol. 11, *The Economics of Internet and e-Commerce*, edited by Michael R. Baye. Amsterdam: Elsevier Science.

Resnick, Paul, Richard Zeckhauser, John Swanson, and Kate Lockwood. 2006. "The Value of Reputation on eBay: A Controlled Experiment." *Experimental Economics* 9(2): 79–101.

Rousseau, Denise M., Sim B. Sitkin, Ronald S. Burt, and Colin Camerer. 1998. "Not So Different after All: A Cross-Discipline View of Trust." *The Academy of Management Review* 23(3): 393–404.

Watabe, Motoki, Shigeru Terai, Nahoko Hayashi, and Toshio Yamagishi. 1996. "Cooperation in the One-Shot Prisoner's Dilemma Based on Expectations of Reciprocity." *Japanese Journal of Experimental Social Psychology* 36(2): 183–96.

Willinger, Marc, Claudia Keser, Christopher Lohmann, and Jean-Claude Usunier. 2003. "A Comparison of Trust and Reciprocity between France and Germany: Experimental Investigation Based on the Investment Game." *Journal of Economic Psychology* 24(4): 447–66.

Yamagishi, Toshio. 1988. "The Provision of a Sanctioning System in the United States and Japan." *Social Psychology Quarterly* 51(1): 32–42.

Yamagishi, Toshio, Karen S. Cook, and Watabe Motoki. 1998. "Uncertainty, Trust and Commitment Formation in the United States and Japan." *American Journal of Sociology* 104(1): 165–94.

Yamagishi, Toshio, Nobuhito Jin, and Allan S. Miller. 1998. "In-Group Bias and the Culture of Collectivism." *Asian Journal of Social Psychology* 1(3): 315–28.

Yamagishi, Toshio, and Midori Yamagishi. 1994. "Trust and Commitment in the United States and Japan." *Motivation and Emotion* 18(2): 129–66.

PART II

FIELD STUDIES ON THE REPUTATION PREMIUM

Chapter 5

Trust and Reputation in Internet Auctions

ANDREAS DIEKMANN, BEN JANN, AND DAVID WYDER

CONOMIC EXCHANGE between anonymous actors is risky for all interacting parties. Whether in barter or in sale against cash, in a bilateral exchange situation both actors have to choose between
being more or less cooperative or acting fraudulently. A seller, for example, needs to decide whether to deliver at all, to deliver good quality, or
to deliver bad quality, and a buyer may choose to evade, reduce, or
delay the payment. It is well known that such cooperation problems can
be solved by repeated interactions if the shadow of the future, that is,
the expectation and valuation of future transactions, is sufficiently large
(Axelrod 1984; for a survey, see Diekmann und Lindenberg 2001). However, no such temporal embeddedness occurs in single transactions
(Raub and Weesie 2000). Hence it is likely that both actors behave unco-
operatively. Internet auctions, characterized by anonymity and nonrepe-
tition of transaction, closely correspond to this type of interaction. Sellers and buyers may adopt virtual identities, that is, they may act under
fictitious names and fake addresses, and it is evident that to realize mutually satisfactory exchanges a basic trust problem must be overcome.[1]
In terms of game theory, an Internet auction with simultaneous transaction corresponds to the ideal type of a single one-shot prisoner's
dilemma. If, however, the actors fulfill their obligations sequentially
such that the second actor can condition his move on the action of the
first, a sequential prisoner's dilemma or trust game is played.

A single exchange between anonymous actors is a precarious situation and gives reason for the prediction that both parties will strongly
tend toward fraudulent behavior without intervention by a central au-

thority. Therefore, one would expect cheating in Internet transactions and unstable markets that collapse rapidly or fail to emerge despite demand.

Contrary to expectation, several Internet auction platforms such as eBay, QXL ricardo (now Tradus), or Amazon have been successful for years. Apparently, these markets do not erode due to lack of mutual trust. Furthermore, cheating in Internet auctions seems to be relatively rare. Peter Kollock mentioned early figures by eBay according to which only twenty-seven cases of fraud have been reported out of 2 million auctions between May and August 1997 (1999). The National Fraud Information Center/Internet Fraud Watch (NFIC/IFW), a project of the National Consumers League of the United States, is concerned with registering cases of Internet fraud and forwarding them to the appropriate law enforcement agencies. According to the Internet Fraud Statistics of the NFIC/IFW, the majority of all registered cases of Internet fraud around the time of our study occurred in Internet auctions.[2] The average monetary loss per Internet auction fraud victim amounted to between $300 and $400. Even if the NFIC/IFW statistics underestimate the actual crime rate, risk of fraud is relatively low given the millions of transactions handled by auction platforms such as eBay and Tradus.[3]

The reason for the success of these Internet markets is a simple institutional rule. Both actors participating in a transaction, buyer and seller, are advised to rate each other after the deal has been completed. That is, the actors may valuate the other party's business conduct by assigning marks and verbal statements, and these assessments are open to anyone who is interested. Thus a potential buyer can browse a seller's list of received ratings from previous transactions before placing a bid. To simplify matters, auction platforms usually also provide summary reputation indices based on the single ratings. In the time we collected our data, ricardo.ch declared the average number of stars and the number of transactions on which this average measure was based. Additionally, separate statistics for positive (four or five stars), neutral (three stars), and negative (one or two stars) assessments were provided for the most recent transactions (figure 5.1). Although the rating process is reciprocal, that is, seller and buyer can both submit a rating in a given transaction, the assessments given to sellers seem to be more important, because bidders may pick sellers by their reputation, but sellers may not choose buyers.

Trust in exchange situations arises from learning from past behavior of the contracting partner and from control, that is, the possibility to impose sanctions in the case of uncooperative behavior (Buskens and Raub 2004). From the viewpoint of the buyer, both elements, learning and control, are inherent components of the rating procedure. Moreover, a high participation rate in the feedback system and perfect transparency

Figure 5.1   Rating of Internet Auctions

General profile ★★★★ (104)

Member since Saturday, December 2, 2000.	Summary of recent comments		
		Past 7 days	Past month	Past 6 month

	Past 7 days	Past month	Past 6 month
Positive	1	2	43
Neutral	0	0	3
Negative	0	0	5
Total	**1**	**2**	**51**

89 positive comments from **80** user(s).

5 neutral comments from **5** user(s).

10 negative comments from **10** user(s).

Positive comment samples

From	Rating	Comment
Inscher	★★★★	Everything went normal and the item is okay
Manu01	★★★★★	honest business partner with fair prices would buy again at any time
Webshuttle	★★★★★	Since falsified tickets were circulating and the action was stopped, soundgard refunded the money without discussion. Very friendly and good consulting.
Haemmi	★★★★★	Fast and trouble-free :)

Negative comment samples

From	Rating	Comment
Pdf	★	Slow delivery, wrong accessories kit sent, correct accessories kit not sent until 2 reclamations, hang up on me.
Xanimalex	★	did not receive the tickets
Drago7	★	Did not receive any reply to my mails, unfortunately, nor have I ever found the product in the letter box.
Rspm	★★	It has not been delivered completely until reclamation at Ricardo. Did not respond to my e-mails.

Source: Authors' compilation and translation based on screenshots from Ricardo.ch.

compose a reputation mechanism that not only generates trust on the side of potential bidders, but also makes investments in reputation worthwhile for sellers. For if a positive rating facilitates future business, the actors have a strong incentive to acquire good reputation. Positive reputation may be gained only through cooperative behavior, however. Thus the dynamics of reputation simultaneously launch a dynamic process of cooperation. Honesty is in fact the best policy and—at least if willing to stay in business—even the most unscrupulous character is forced by these institutional constraints to invest in reputation and behave cooperatively. The rating mechanism introduces the future into single-shot games because the current behavior of an actor will influence future behavior of the market participants. Hence the feedback system may be seen as a substitute for repeated interactions (for similar arguments, see Dasgupta 1988; chapter 1, this volume).

Reputation Mechanisms and Cooperation

Reputation systems, nota bene, are not an invention of the Internet era. That said, the technical capabilities of the Internet make it possible to implement the reputation principle simply and elegantly and to establish stable, efficient, and fraud-proof markets. Avner Greif, in an informative historical economic study, described the Maghreb traders in the eleventh century who conducted their extensive trading activities in the Mediterranean area through representing agents (1989, 1993). A principal-agent problem existed for the traders (principals) because the representatives (agents) had practically uncontrollable opportunities to engage in fraud. Nonetheless, in general, the representatives acted cooperatively. The explanation for the compliance of the agents is that the traders formed a coalition through which they were able to exchange information about the activities of the agents. "Within the coalition an internal information-transmission system served to balance asymmetric information and a reputation mechanism was used to ensure proper conduct" (Greif 1989, 881). The result of disingenuous business conduct of an agent was that no trader of the coalition would commission the agent ever again. In addition, agents and traders were often swapping roles and a deceitful agent would no longer have been accepted to join the coalition of traders. In sum, the reputation mechanism set up by the Maghreb traders made a substantial contribution to solving the cooperation problem (see also Homann and Suchanek 2000).

Apart from reputation per se, reliable methods to indicate and verify reputation are also critical to successful business. This is an aspect Max Weber emphasized in his 1920 study, "The Protestant Sects and the Spirit of Capitalism," describing various personal observations related to the apparent creditworthiness of members of Protestant sects. On a railroad journey during his America travels in 1904, for example, Weber sat next to a traveling salesman whose business was selling iron letters for tombstones. The businessman told him, "Sir, for my part everybody may believe or not believe as he pleases; but if I saw a farmer or a businessman not belonging to any church at all, I wouldn't trust him with fifty cents" (2002, 128). A German-born nose-and-throat specialist in Ohio was puzzled by his first patient, who emphasized that he was a member of a Baptist Church. The doctor, who later reported the incident to Weber, was informed by an American colleague "that the patient's statement of his church membership was merely to say: 'Don't worry about the fees'" (129). After attending a baptism ceremony of a Baptist congregation, Weber learned that

> "once being baptized he will get the patronage of the whole region and he will outcompete everybody." Further questions of "why" and "by what means" led to the following conclusion: Admission to the local Baptist congregation follows only upon the most careful "probation" and after closest inquiries into conduct going back to early childhood (Disorderly conduct? Frequenting taverns? Dance? Theatre? Card Playing? Untimely meeting of liability? Other Frivolities?) The congregation still adhered strictly to the religious tradition. Admission to the congregation is recognized as an absolute guarantee of the moral qualities of a gentleman, especially of those qualities required in business matters. Baptism secures to the individual the deposits of the whole region and unlimited credit without any competition. He is a "made man." (129–30; see also Voss 1998)

Several aspects are critical in creating a reputation. First, the sect chooses its members after careful inquiries and gives them—in Weber's words—"a certificate of moral qualification and especially of business morals" (2002, 130). Second, admission of a new member occurs by ballot, that is, by vote of the sect members. Third, the acquisition of reputation is supposed to be forgery-proof, so that impostors have no chance. And, fourth, it is advantageous that the reputation can easily be disclosed.

A secular variant of these elements can be found in Internet auctions. The qualification certificate corresponds to the rating outcome, which is generated by vote, that is, by the customers' assessments. Furthermore, the mechanism is relatively forgery-proof, because a good reputation can be achieved only through cooperative behavior. As noted, the values of the ratings and especially their frequencies are visible to all interested users. Thus simple institutional regulations generate reputation, which rests on the judgments of many interactive partners, appears to be more or less unforgeable, and is perfectly transparent; thus the rules establish ideal conditions for a functioning market.

The relation between reputation and cooperation has been analyzed theoretically in various case studies, as well as in studies using formal modeling (see, for example, Akerlof 1970; Granovetter 1985; Coleman 1990; Raub and Weesie 1990; Greif 1993; Hägg and Göran 1994; Voss 1998; Ziegler 1998; Kollock 1999; Abell and Reyniers 2000). On the other hand, at the time we started our research, relatively few studies existed in which a systematic attempt was made to evaluate the implications of reputation mechanisms on an empirical basis. Internet auctions provide an excellent resource to study the effects of reputation and to test hypotheses about reputation mechanisms. Other types of hypotheses, for example, about how the temporal distribution of bids depends on auction rules (for example, last-minute bidding) or about the determination of minimum bids, may be tested effectively as well (Roth and Ockenfels 2002; Bajari and Hortaçsu 2003). Unlike population surveys, Internet auctions are like field experiments in which the researcher observes the results. Contrary to questionnaire data, the auction data are process-produced, nonreactive, and reflect realities without distortion. Although some of the available Internet auction studies report on the degree and development of reputation (for example, Kollock 1999; Brinkmann and Seifert 2001), the focus of this chapter lies in the analysis of the effects of the reputation mechanism on auction prices and the choice of payment modes.[4]

The term *investment in reputation* is not meant only figuratively. Reputation really generates its returns. On the one hand, it paves the way for future business, on the other, enhanced auction prices, a sort of a reputation surcharge, can be realized. If reputation is high, the bidder's risk of getting exploited is reduced and a bidder will therefore be willing to pay more. In a way, the surcharge is like a premium for risk coverage against being defrauded.

Early empirical evidence supporting the hypothesis of a reputation premium is provided by David Lucking-Reiley and his colleagues (2007), Cynthia McDonald and Carlos Slawson (2002), and Daniel Houser and John Wooders (2006), based on analyses of eBay auctions data. In the second two studies, auctions of homogeneous goods have been examined (451 auctions of Harley-Davidson Barbie dolls in factory packaging and 94 auctions of Pentium III 500 processors, respectively) so that differences in product characteristics should not play a role (see also Melnik and Alm 2002). Lucking-Reily and his colleagues, on the other hand, estimated the effect of reputation based on a random sample of 461 auctions of U.S. Indian head pennies of varying quality (2007). They found a weak price effect for positive reputation and a strong effect for negative reputation, but no significant effect for the eBay summary reputation index, which takes into account both positive and negative ratings. However, because the varying quality of the traded coins in the analyzed auctions opens the door for confounding effects, this study's results are probably less reliable than the results of the two other studies. Lucking-Reiley and his colleagues themselves classified their analysis as explorative (2007).[5]

Looking out for sellers with good reputation, a buyer can reduce the risk of becoming a victim of a fraudulent seller. But how can sellers protect themselves against cheating buyers? The buyer's reputation does not give a hold here because, usually, offerers cannot choose buyers. Sellers, however, have the power to set the payment and delivery mode.

Depending on the payment mode, the risks in business between anonymous actors are divided differently between the actors. In spot transactions, where goods are exchanged against cash simultaneously, the risks are distributed symmetrically (figure 5.2). By contrast, if payment is due in advance or as cash on mail delivery (figure 5.3) or on account (figure 5.4), the risks are divided unevenly between the interacting partners. In terms of game theory, the symmetric payment mode (figure 5.2) corresponds to a prisoner's dilemma, the asymmetric types (figures 5.3 and 5.4) correspond to a sequential prisoner's dilemma, in which the second player gets to know the choice of the first player before making his own decision.[6] The second player, that is, has the second-mover advantage. For example, imagine a customer who receives

Figure 5.2   Symmetric Payment Mode (Goods Against Money)

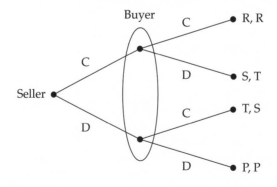

Source: Authors' compilation.
Notes: C = Cooperation. The seller delivers good quality; the buyer makes the payment promptly.
D = Defection. The seller delivers poor quality; the buyer does not make the payment, diminishes or delays it.
Payoffs: T > R > P > S (for example, T = 5, R = 3, P = 1, S = 0; only the order of the utility values matters). The oval marks the information set. The buyer has to make his own choice without knowing the decision of the seller. This game corresponds to the symmetric prisoner's dilemma.

Figure 5.3   Asymmetric Payment Mode in Favor of Seller (Pay in Advance or COD)

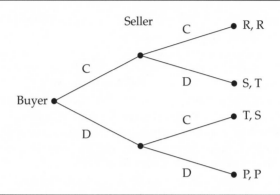

Source: Authors' compilation.
Notes: C = The buyer makes the prepayment; the seller delivers good quality.
D = The buyer does not make the agreed payment; the seller delivers poor quality or does not deliver.
This game is a sequential prisoner's dilemma. If the game ends with payoff (P, P) after the buyer played D, it corresponds to the trust game (Dasgupta 1988; Kreps 1990).

the product, inspects it, and only then decides whether to pay the bill. The situation illustrated in figure 5.3 is asymmetric in favor of the seller (the customer cannot inspect the product before paying if cash is due on delivery). In figure 5.4, on the other hand, the seller bears the risk of

Figure 5.4   Asymmetric Payment Mode in Favor of Buyer (Delivery on Account)

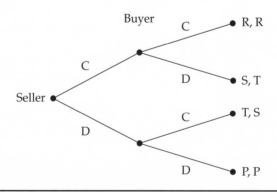

Source: Authors' compilation.
Notes: C = The seller delivers good quality; the buyer endeavors to pay the bill promptly.
D = The seller does not deliver or delivers poor quality; the buyer does not make the payment, or either diminishes or delays it.

payment. Which payment modes are chosen in Internet auctions? Because it is risky for a buyer to engage in an asymmetric game in favor of the seller, it may be assumed that a buyer will not be willing to accept cash on mail delivery and, in particular, payment in advance unless the seller has a good reputation.

Data

To examine comparable transactions we chose a homogeneous good that is traded relatively frequently and is not too inexpensive, so that the threat of being cheated is salient. Mobile phones of a specific make and type ideally fulfill these criteria. In autumn 2001, Nokia released a new cell phone with the type designation Nokia 8310. The retail price was approximately 700 Swiss francs (CHF). Between October 2001 and January 2002, we kept track of all auctions on the e-commerce platform ricardo.ch in which a new and unlocked Nokia 8310 without phone company contract was offered. Overall, our master sample consisted of 204 auctions. However, sellers could draw back an offer as long as no bids had been placed and, in addition, the auction house reserved the right to cancel an auction if irregularities occurred, which happened in ten cases. Furthermore, extensive reinspection of the data material and the stored screen shots revealed that in six cases the offered cell phone was not really new but only in as good as new condition, that in one case the offer also included some older model, and that two auctions had been recorded twice. Furthermore, eight auctions turned out to be not comparable to the other auctions because multiple items were offered. The auction rules for multiple offers were such that if, say, five cell phones were offered, then the top five bidders each received one piece. Finally, five cases had to be dropped because documentation was incomplete. This left us with a net sample of 172 auctions.[7]

QXL ricardo plc (now Tradus) is one of the leading providers of auction platforms in Europe. The vendues proceed in the manner of an English auction, that is, the auction is open and the highest bid wins (for a description of different auction formats, see Lucking-Reiley 2000). This winning bid equals the net selling price, not including shipping and handling, of the auctioned item. Sellers and bidders have to register before participating in an auction. The confirmation of the registration, which includes the access code for offering and bidding, is sent to the specified postal address. If one plans to cheat, one may, of course, set up a temporary address and suspend it after receiving the access code. The nonrecurring registration is valid for all future auctions and, according to our investigations, changes of the postal address are not verified. By the time an auction ends, a legal contract exists between the seller and the buyer, who placed the highest bid. The auction house collects from the seller a fee amounting to a small percentage of the selling price (4 percent for deals below 1000 CHF at the time of our study). Seller and buyer have the possibility to rate each other after the transaction and also submit verbal comments. At the time of our study, one to five stars could be assigned: one and two stars corresponded to a negative rating, three stars were neutral, and four or five stars indicated a positive assessment.[8] As mentioned, the ratings and the verbal comments are accessible by anyone interested.

The seller sets the duration of the auction, a starting bid, and the smallest increment between bids (the minimum selling price is the starting bid plus one minimum bid increment). Furthermore, the seller also specifies the payment mode and indicates the shipping costs to be paid by the buyer in addition to his bid. These characteristics are exogenous, that is, they do not change during the course of an auction, though there is one important exception. Sometimes, sellers specify a buy-it-now price at which the good can be purchased immediately. A buyer placing a bid in this height wins the auction right away and cannot be outbid anymore. In such cases the duration of the auction is shortened ex post (for theoretical reflections on buy prices in auctions, see Reynolds and Wooders 2009).

Apart from the mentioned auction attributes, we also recorded the seller's reputation as the average number of stars and the total number of ratings (measured at the beginning of the auction), the description of the offered product, and some characteristics of the auction process. The latter include calendar time, the value of the winning bid (net auction price), and the number of bids.

Results

As in various other studies, our sample includes numerous positive ratings: a positive rating seems to be the rule, a negative rating the exception (see Kollock 1999; Brinkmann and Seifert 2001). The number of positive ratings therefore seems to be the real signal for reputation, rather than the average degree of the ratings. We first give an account of the distribution of reputation, then estimate the effect of reputation on the minimum price, the likelihood of successful selling, and the selling price, and then provide results concerning payment modes.

Distribution of Reputation

In forty-two of our 172 auctions the seller appeared as a first-time seller, that is, no rating was available. In 125 of the remaining 130 auctions (96 percent), the ratings of the seller were positive on average (four or five stars) and in only five cases did the seller have a negative or neutral reputation (one to three stars). The very high fraction of positive judgments indicates that the reputation mechanism functions well and most of the sellers behave cooperatively. Even though no control group from an Internet auction platform without rating system is available, it seems very unlikely that the cooperation rate would have reached such a high level without the institution of the rating mechanism. In experiments with the one-time prisoner's dilemma game, for example, the cooperation rates are found to reach at most 50 percent (Rapoport and Chammah 1965; Ledyard 1995).

A positive rating as the rule does not mean, however, that the offerers would be indistinguishable with respect to their reputation. In fact, high variance exists in the number of ratings. With a range from 0 to 102, a median of 5, and a mean of 10.8 (neglecting the five cases with nonpositive reputation), the distribution is markedly right-skewed. Because almost all sellers are either newcomers without reputation or have been judged positively on average, the assumption is evident that the number of ratings makes the difference and therefore should be considered as the real sign for reputation.

In addition, the number of positive assessments represents a relatively reliable and forgery-proof signal. No doubt it is possible to change identity on the Internet; a fraudulent seller with a bad reputation may just change his name. The seller then, however, must start over again with no reputation. Possibly, one could fake reputation by means of fictitious transaction with stooges. The required effort, however, is considerable and costly, because, for each fake rating, some percentage of the transaction volume has to be paid in real terms to the auction platform. Of course, it would be imaginable that a swindler acquires a high reputation index by numerous little sham deals to be able to claim advance payment for an expensive good and then, after receiving the money, vanish, never to be seen again. Apparently, though, the expenses for such an enterprise seem to be disproportionate to the potential profit, as such cases of fraud occur relatively seldom. If they were to appear more frequently, it would possibly be wise to adjust the reputation index. For example, the single assessments could be weighted by the volume of the associated deal; acquiring fictitious reputation would then be considerably more expensive.

In the analyses that follow, the five cases with nonpositive average ratings are disregarded. The number of observations is thus reduced to 167 auctions. The definitions of the variables and descriptive statistics of the sample are provided in table 5.1. Because we exclude the few cases with nonpositive average assessments, the degree of a seller's reputation can be measured simply as the total number of ratings. The reputation index is 0 if a seller has not yet been rated.

Table 5.1   Descriptive Statistics

Variable	Minimum	Maximum	Mean	SD	Number of Cases
Reputation (number of ratings)	0	102	10.84	19.80	167
Starting bid	0	756	487.53	221.22	167
Starting bid > 0	0.5	756	515.30	193.24	158
Buy-it-now price	450	800	621.46	89.07	103
Shipping costs	0	28	16.78	5.77	167
Minimum bid increment	0.5	50	6.30	7.48	167
Number of supplementary accessories [a]	0	3	0.13	0.47	167
Calendar time at the start of the auction (in days; centered)	−61.32	56.33	0.00	31.65	167
Duration of the auction in days	0	15	5.76	4.49	167
Number of bids	0	65	5.99	11.53	167
Successful selling (0/1)	0	1	0.50		167
Net auction price	450	800	531.08	59.55	84
Gross auction price (incl. shipping costs)	460	800	545.53	58.14	84

Source: Authors' compilation.
Note: Currency is Swiss francs (CHF). SD is standard deviation.
[a] Reinspection of the raw data material (analyses of the product descriptions, in particular) revealed that the traded goods were not always purely homogeneous. In some cases the offer included accessories which were not part of the original Nokia 8310 distribution (namely, one or more additional covers, an additional battery, a leather sheath, an additional standard charger, a desktop stand, or a vehicle charger).

Starting Bid

The starting bid is fixed by the seller before the start of the auction. Nearly all offerers (158 of 167, or 95 percent) made use of this option. Sellers with high reputation probably have better chances to get away with a high starting price. Thus, it may be expected that the number of ratings brings about an increase in the minimum bid. The correlation between minimum price and the number of ratings is very low ($r = .034$), however, and not significant. But, as noted, the distribution of the number of ratings is heavily right-skewed. It may be assumed that whether a seller has eighty or ninety ratings will not make as much a difference as an increase from zero to ten positive assessments. Differences at the beginning of the scale are weighted more strongly if the correlation is calculated between the logarithm of the number of ratings and the minimum price. This yields a moderate but still insignificant correlation coefficient of $r = .158$ ($p = .139$).[9] Discrimination between the forty-two sellers without rating and the group of 125 offerers with at least one assessment reveals that offerers without reputation specified a minimum bid of 401 CHF on average (median 420), and sellers with reputation one of 517 CHF (median 600). Although quite substantial, the difference is not significant ($p = .120$). Altogether our data give only very weak evidence for a possible association between reputation and the determination of the starting bid.

Successful Selling

If no potential customer places a bid in an auction, the product cannot be sold. This happened quite frequently in our data. According to the numbers in table 5.1, only 50 percent of the auctions in our sample (eighty-four of 167) resulted in a sale. Obviously, the successful completion of a deal strongly depends on the value of the lower price limit. In some auctions, for example, the starting bid was higher than the official retail price of the product. Although some customers seem for some reason to be willing to fork out more than the retail price, a strong negative effect of the minimum price on the success of an auction must be assumed. Reputation, in contrast, should increase the chances of a sale. Table 5.2 displays the estimation results of logistic regression models.

As expected, the probability of sale is strongly influenced by the minimum price, and calendar time also has a considerable effect. Evidently, the Nokia 8310 rapidly lost attractiveness during the four months of our observation window.[10] The duration of the auction, the minimum bid increment, and the number of supplementary accessories did not seem to have any effect. The variable number of ratings shows the expected sign; however, a two-sided test with an error probability of .05 reveals that the coefficient is not significant ($p = .122$ in model 1). The effect of the logarithm of the number of ratings, which may be used as alternative measure for reputation, is also not significant (or only slightly significant in a one-sided test, model 3). Note, however, that the estimation of alternative specifications with the gross minimum price (starting bid plus minimum bid increment plus shipping costs) as an explanatory variable yield significant results for reputation ($p = .007$ in model 2 and $p = .046$ in model 4). In sum, the data give slight support to the hypothesis that the reputation of the seller promotes the chances of a successful sale.

Price Premium for Reputation

What is the effect of the seller's reputation on the selling price of the mobile phones? We estimate the reputation effect using linear regression on the basis of the eighty-four completed transactions.[11] Controls in the regression equation are the shipping costs, the minimum price, the mini-

Table 5.2   Reputation and Successful Selling

	Models with Absolute Number of Ratings		Models with Log Number of Ratings	
	Model 1	Model 2	Model 3	Model 4
Reputation (number of ratings)	0.022	0.033**	0.546+	0.668*
	(1.55)	(2.68)	(1.69)	(2.00)
Starting bid	–0.069**		–0.074**	
	(–4.15)		(–4.03)	
Minimum bid increment	0.064		0.061	
	(0.82)		(0.74)	
Shipping costs	–0.234+		–0.278*	
	(–1.80)		(–2.07)	
Gross minimum price (starting bid + minimum bid increment + shipping costs)		–0.056**		–0.054**
		–(3.77)		(–4.53)
Duration of auction in days	–0.068	–0.085	–0.058	–0.078
	(–0.63)	(–0.66)	(–0.54)	(–0.58)
Number of supplementary accessories	0.006	0.862	0.081	0.508
	(0.00)	(0.94)	(0.05)	(0.55)
Calendar time	–0.074**	–0.055*	–0.070*	–0.042*
	(–2.59)	(–2.32)	(–2.34)	(–1.96)
Constant	40.12**	31.24**	42.62**	29.87**
	(3.94)	(3.56)	(3.76)	(4.22)
McFadden R^2	0.853	0.836	0.855	0.834
Number of cases	167	167	167	167

Source: Authors' compilation.
Notes: Logistic regression of whether the good has been successfully sold (= 1) or not (maximum likelihood estimation of the effects on the log-odds). z-statistics in parentheses (adjusted for clustering on sellers; see note 9). Models with log number of ratings: Reputation = ln(number of ratings + 1). $+ p < 0.1$, $* p < 0.05$, $** p < 0.01$ (two-sided)

mum bid increment, the duration of the auction, the number of bids, the number of supplementary accessories, and calendar time (parabolic). Theoretically, the shipping costs should have a coefficient of minus one: higher shipping costs would be compensated by a corresponding reduction of the highest bid, and the gross price paid by the buyer would remain unchanged. In practice, however, it is possible that the shipping costs are psychologically underrated or overvalued, even though they are known. For the minimum price, the minimum bid increment, the duration of the auction, the number of bids, and the number of supplementary accessories, we expect all positive effects, that is, these variables should likely increase the selling price. In the course of calendar

Table 5.3   Reputation Effect on Auction Price

	Models with Absolute Number of Ratings		Models with Log Number of Ratings	
	Model 1	Model 2	Model 3	Model 4
Reputation (number of ratings)	0.455**	0.667**	9.132**	11.961**
	(3.26)	(4.81)	(3.35)	(3.69)
Starting bid	0.035	−0.022	0.038	−0.017
	(1.09)	(−0.62)	(1.26)	(−0.46)
Minimum bid increment	2.441**	1.732+	2.672**	1.967*
	(3.01)	(1.96)	(3.39)	(2.33)
Shipping costs	−1.883**	−1.839*	−2.604**	−2.723**
	(−2.90)	(−2.29)	(−3.68)	(−3.43)
Duration of auction in days	−2.409*	−4.159**	−2.594**	−4.355**
	(−2.51)	(−4.58)	(−2.84)	(−4.75)
Number of bids	0.729	0.127	0.873	0.274
	(1.11)	(0.22)	(1.38)	(0.47)
Number of supplementary accessories	27.486**	22.409**	27.046**	21.914**
	(3.32)	(2.65)	(3.39)	(2.63)
Calendar time	−0.858**	−0.736**	−0.827**	−0.700**
	(−6.25)	(−5.64)	(−6.25)	(−5.21)
Calendar time squared	0.011**	0.011*	0.011**	0.011*
	(3.21)	(2.29)	(3.42)	(2.35)
Constant	513.77**	564.15**	511.99**	562.80**
	(32.53)	(26.97)	(31.15)	(25.53)
R^2 / McFadden R^2	0.679	0.099	0.689	0.102
Number of cases	84	167	84	167

Source: Authors' compilation.
Notes: OLS regression (models 1 and 3) and censored-normal regression (models 2 and 4) of net auction price (excluding shipping costs). t/z-statistics in parentheses (adjusted for clustering on sellers; see note 9). Models with log number of ratings: Reputation = ln(number of ratings + 1).
+ $p < 0.1$, * $p < 0.05$, ** $p < 0.01$ (two-sided)

time, on the other hand, prices should fall with declining rates. The regression estimates are displayed in table 5.3 (model 1).

Contrary to our expectations, the minimum price and the number of bids have no significant effects on the selling price, and the duration of the auction is even negatively related to the auction outcome. The other variables—reputation, in particular—have significant effects in the anticipated direction. Shipping costs, however, seem to be slightly overweighted. Each extra franc demanded for shipping costs results in an average reduction of the net auction price by almost 2 CHF. Excessive shipping costs appear to harm the seller and, paradoxically, favor the buyer. Sellers seem therefore well advised to charge relatively low shipping costs, and buyers to place their bids in auctions in which high fees are appointed for shipment.[12]

The minimum bid increment stipulated by the seller also has a clear price effect. If the required increment between bids is enlarged by 1 CHF, the selling price raises by approximately 2.5 CHF on average. Buyers should thus be cautious if the minimum bid increment is rather large and they are about to decide whether to outbid an amount near their personal threshold of pain (reservation price).[13]

Note that our regression results may be inappropriate for two reasons. First, we considered only the (possibly selective) subsample of successful auctions because a selling price does not exist for the other cases. Second, we neglected the fact that in some auctions there is an upper bound for the highest bid, the buy-it-now price. The first issue introduces left censoring, that is, censoring from below, as illustrated in panel A in figure 5.5. No data points are possible in the shaded area of the plot because the selling price has to exceed the starting bid. Unsuccessful auctions may be treated as left-censored at the value of the minimum price, which is equal to the starting bid plus one minimum bid increment. There are eighty-three such cases, indicated by crosses in the plot.

The second issue, the buy-it-now price, introduces right censoring, that is, censoring from above, because no bid will exceed this upper limit (panel B in figure 5.5). A buy-it-now price was specified in 103 auctions and was reached in twenty-five cases (indicated by triangles). Both censoring mechanisms can cause standard regression estimates to be biased. We, therefore, replicate our analysis using a censored-normal regression model (a generalized tobit model) with known but varying lower and upper bounds (compare Maddala 1983; Amemiya 1985, 360; Breen 1996).[14] The results of the tobit regressions, models 2 and 4 in table 5.3, are quite similar to the results of the standard models except that the strong effect of the minimum bid increment collapses to a insignificant level[15] and the effect of the duration of the auction is more pronounced.[16]

Let us now get back to our main question: does reputation positively influence the selling price? The results shown in table 5.3 clearly support the existence of such a relationship. In the models with the absolute number of ratings and where the logarithm of ratings is used, a positive and significant reputation effect can be observed. Similar and even slightly more pronounced results are obtained if the censoring of the dependent variable is taken into account. Sellers with higher reputation get higher prices; customers seem to be willing to reward sellers who have a good record. This is not necessarily so because customers appreciate a seller's virtuousness, it is because cooperative behavior in the past signals that a seller will most likely not act opportunistically to keep his good reputation intact and turn it into hard cash also in future transactions.

Figure 5.5   Left- and Right-Censoring of Selling Price

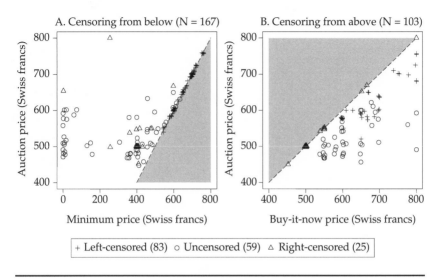

A. Censoring from below (N = 167)   B. Censoring from above (N = 103)

| + Left-censored (83)   o Uncensored (59)   △ Right-censored (25) |

Source: Authors' compilation.

Modes of Payment

According to the auction rules, the highest bid determines the winner of the auction and the final selling price. But, of course, buyers can also act opportunistically. In the case of delivery on account, for example, the seller makes a one-sided leap of faith, which can be exploited by the buyer by refraining from payment. However, a seller can protect himself against cheating buyers by setting the payment mode. He can decide whether the transaction should be symmetric, asymmetric with the seller as the first player (the trustor), or asymmetric with the buyer as trustor (see figures 5.2, 5.3, and 5.4). So how does the empirical distribution of the various payment modes look like?

Naturally, sellers try to opt for an asymmetric game in their own favor with only a few exceptions. In our data, payment in advance or cash-on-mail delivery are chosen in 95 percent of all cases (see table 5.4). The other extreme, a sequential prisoner's dilemma with the seller in the weak position of the trustor and the buyer in the strong position of the trustee, appears in only one of 167 cases.

Taken on its own, the power to set the rules of the game is not yet an explanation for the distribution seen in table 5.4. Buyers could go on

Table 5.4   Modes of Payment

Mode of Payment	Count	Percent	Symmetry- Asymmetry	Ranking of Asymmetry in Favor of Seller	Mean (Median) Reputation
Payment in advance	42	25.1	Asymmetric in favor of seller	4	22.12 (6.0)
Cash on mail delivery	116	69.4	Asymmetric in favor of seller	3	7.25 (5.0)
Cash on pickup	6	3.6	Symmetric	2	1.67 (0.0)
Cash on delivery in person	2	1.2	Symmetric	1	—
Mail delivery on account	1	0.6	Asymmetric in favor of buyer	0	—
Credit card	0	0.0	—	—	—
Total	167	100.0			

Source: Authors' compilation.

strike or choose sellers with better payment conditions, so that a seller could benefit from offering transaction modes in favor of the buyer. The reason the sellers are so uncompromising in their choice of the payment mode is that even though buyers can choose sellers, sellers cannot choose buyers. The seller is committed, regardless of the buyer's reputation, to accept the highest bid and complete the transaction with that buyer. The power to choose the business partner, an asymmetry in favor of the buyer, is counteracted by the power to set the payment conditions, an asymmetry in favor of the seller. Buyers overcome the trust problem by choosing sellers according to reputation; sellers solve the trust problem by choosing an adequate payment method.

Good reputation probably also helps a seller to enforce a payment mode in his own interest. As shown in table 5.4, the average value of reputation corresponds to the ranking of the chosen payment method with respect to the asymmetry in favor of the seller. To analyze the relation between reputation and choice of payment mode in more detail, we additionally report logistic regression estimates in which we discriminate payment in advance, which favors the seller most, against any of the other methods.

The results shown in table 5.5 reveal that reputation, at least in the logarithmic form, has a significant effect on the choice of the payment method. The higher the reputation, the more likely a seller requests payment in advance. Apparently, offerers with high reputation can afford to

Table 5.5   Reputation Effect on Payment in Advance

	Model with Absolute Number of Ratings	Model with Log Number of Ratings
Reputation (number of ratings)	0.038	0.556*
	(1.54)	(2.38)
Starting bid	−0.001	−0.002
	(−0.81)	(−1.12)
Minimum bid increment	0.031	0.038
	(0.81)	(0.91)
Shipping costs	−0.253**	−0.290**
	(−3.84)	(−4.24)
Duration of auction in days	−0.074	−0.084
	(−1.26)	(−1.43)
Number of supplementary accessories	−1.269	−1.336
	(−1.64)	(−1.59)
Calendar time	−0.003	−0.002
	(−0.30)	(−0.26)
Constant	3.333**	3.558**
	(3.00)	(3.04)
McFadden R^2	0.325	0.325
Number of cases	167	167

Source: Authors' compilation.
Notes: Logistic regression of payment in advance (= 1) (maximum likelihood estimation of the effects on the log-odds). z-statistics in parentheses (adjusted for clustering on sellers; see note 9). Model with log number of ratings: Reputation = ln(number of ratings + 1).
* $p < 0.05$, ** $p < 0.01$ (two-sided)

stipulate payment conditions that are strongly in their own interest, and buyers seem to be more likely to accept the risk associated with an unfavorable payment method if the risk is counterbalanced by a good seller reputation. Hence good reputation gives sellers a competitive edge not only in terms of selling price but also with regard to payment method. This is yet another incentive for offerers to invest in reputation.[17]

Summary and Discussion

The empirical evidence in this study clearly supports the hypothesis that, in single exchange situations between unknown and anonymously operating actors, reputation may cause a high degree of cooperation and promote a well-running market. By rewarding cooperative behavior in the long run, reputation creates order. Whereas Robert Axelrod's simulations suggest that the evolution of cooperation can succeed under the conditions of the repeated prisoner's dilemma (1984), it is shown here that social order is also possible under the condition of reputation, without the need for sanctioning interventions by an external authority. Reputation is an effective substitute for the lack of repeated interactions between the same actors. A simple institutional setting, that is, the assessment of the sellers by the buyers and the absolute transparency of the results, creates incentives for cooperative behavior, as demonstrated by the empirical findings on the effects of reputation. The empirical results can be summarized into four points:

- A predominant share of the transactions are rated positively. Negative reputation is the exception, and positive reputation is the rule.[18] At the same time, a high degree of cooperation and, therefore, a smooth functioning of the market is observable.

- Sellers have incentives to invest in reputation. Customers interpret reputation as a signal for a reduced transaction risk and are willing to pay a fee for it, similar to an insurance premium. According to the regression estimates, reputation has a positive effect on the selling price. In line with many other studies, a reputation premium is empirically detectable.

- Reputation seems to influence the determination of the starting price and the success of an auction, and has an effect on the choice of the payment mode. On average, offerers with high reputation seem to set higher starting bids, are more likely to successfully sell their goods, and can afford to request payment conditions that are strongly in their own favor.

- Sellers and buyers are in a situation characterized by information asymmetry. Buyers can address the trust problem by choosing a seller with better reputation, but must pay a premium for it. Sellers cannot use buyer reputation to solve the trust problem because they cannot choose buyers. Yet they have free choice of the rules of the game as far as the payment mode is concerned. The empirical finding is unambiguous: offerers almost exclusively choose asymmetric payment modes in their own favor to reduce the risk of being exploited. The risk is shifted, however, to the customers, who can secure themselves by selecting sellers by reputation.

Because the reputation system has proved valuable in Internet auctions, it seems reasonable to ask whether it could be transferred to other exchange situations outside the Internet. That more or less elaborate reputation mechanisms can exist in various settings is not only demonstrated by the introductory historical examples (Greif 1989, 1993; Weber 1920, 2002), but also becomes clear to any bank customer who applies for a loan and whose reputation is checked in the credit reports. Problems of trust with asymmetric information (Akerlof 1970) also exist in numerous other social situations—for example, when buying credence goods (Emons 1997), in recruiting university professors, when choosing dentists, lawyers, garages, courses of further education, plumbers, offerers of holiday apartments, secondhand car dealers, or marriage partners. Would it not be sensible in these situations as well to introduce the institution of an open reputation system according to the archetype of the Internet auctions? And how does this system compare to approaches such as Eco-Audit or product tests by consumer organizations, brand names, the rating of the credit-worthiness of enterprises, reputation systems in science (Gerhards 2002), or the evaluation of teaching and the ranking of universities?

Apparently there are miscellaneous, more or less institutionalized systems of reputation. Following a preliminary categorization, we can differentiate the following five types.[19] The first is informal reputation in social networks. For example, person A is recommended for a new job by person B. In this case, person B bestows reputation on A. Gossip in social networks can also be considered as an informal reputation system. The second type is more institutionalized forms of consumer ratings. Buyers and users assess products. Usually, the evaluators are a highly self-selective group. Here, too, institutionalized forms exist on the Internet—for example, the platforms Ciao.com and dooyoo.de, which encourage buyers to evaluate products and financially reward test reports. Similarly, but without financial incentives, at Amazon, readers review books. A typical element of these systems is that the evaluators' reports also get rated (readers can assign marks to the test reports and reviews), that is, there is a second layer of reputation on the meta level (see also Dworschak 2000). The assessments in these systems are transparent because they are accessible to anyone by a single click, but they are not forgery-proof. Involved parties, such as, say, the originator of a product, can submit an evaluation guided by self-interest (for example, using a pseudonym, authors can review their own books at Amazon). The third type is institutionalized expert ratings such as Eco-Audit or product tests by consumer organizations. The fourth is reputation based on brand names. Producers create distinctive products that are legally protected against imitation and are provided everywhere in the same quality. The fifth type is institutionalized and highly systematic reputation systems in Internet auctions, as described and analyzed in this study.

This last reputation system, which was the subject of our analysis, is highly effective in producing cooperation. However, it is also tied to narrowly defined conditions. It requires that sellers trade repeatedly, usually with changing partners (A), and that a buyer is able to quickly assess the seller's business conduct in an objective and reproducible manner (B). All or most transactions should be systematically rated (C). This requires that either there are incentives to provide ratings or that the costs are minimal. Finally, the ratings should be easily accessible by anyone interested (D). With respect to C and D, ubiquitous rating and transparency, the Internet provides ideal conditions.

The reputation system, however, will function less well if one or more of the mentioned conditions are violated. Additionally, Gary Bolton and Axel Ockenfels provide evidence in chapter 1 of this volume that even a perfect reputation system may only have limited effectiveness. Cooperation of dentists is often not immediately discernible to the customer. If causally attributable at all, the botch is possibly discovered not for years, when the expensive crown or filling has turned out to be more fugacious than expected. Similarly, toxic substances in edibles normally stay hidden to the consumer. This does not necessarily disqualify an increasing adoption of consumer ratings, because why shouldn't also doctors, dentists, lawyers, or university professors be evaluated by their customers? Furthermore, because transparency can be established easily and cost-efficiently on the Internet, such reputation systems could develop well. Additionally, if the quality of the cooperation, the good, or the service cannot be easily judged by the customer, as in the case of the toxic load of nourishments, reputation systems based on expert ratings should be helpful. Under which conditions and institutional regulations an effective cooperation-promoting reputation system emerges is a question that cannot be answered without a theory of reputation systems. Empirical analyses of existing reputation systems may contribute to that development.

Notes

1. Note that, usually, actors have to create an account at the auction platform and leave their postal address before participating in Internet auctions. It is not much of a problem, however, to sidestep this identification procedure using a temporary address.
2. Seventy-eight percent, or about 6,200 cases, in 2000, 70 percent or about 8,300 cases in 2001, 90 percent or about 28,000 cases in 2002 (see http://www.fraud.org/internet/intstat.htm, accessed February 18, 2004).
3. Likewise, a further institution, the Internet Fraud Complaint Center (IFCC), reported that the largest share of all complaints about fraudulent behavior came from Internet auctions—43 percent, or about 7,200 cases in 2001; and 46 percent, or about 22,000 cases in 2002 (see National White Collar Crime Center 2002, 2003). The IFCC estimated that less than 1 percent of all transactions on Internet auction sites resulted in fraud; according to the same report the most frequent Internet auction fraud items in the observed period were Beanies—soft toys, popular among collectors—followed by video consoles and games and tapes, laptop computers, cameras and cam-

corders, desktop computers, and jewelry (National White Collar Crime Center 2002). Furthermore, even if added up, the reported total money loss from Internet fraud—$6 million in 2001 and $15 million in 2002, according to NFIC/IFW, and $18 million in 2001, and $54 million in 2002, according to IFCC—amounted to only around .1 percent of the estimated U.S. e-commerce retail sales—$34.6 billion in 2001 and $43.5 billion in 2002, according to the U.S. Census (U.S. Bureau of the Census and U.S. Department of Commerce 2003).

4. This paper is based on a German language version published in the *Kölner Zeitschrift für Soziologie und Sozialpsychologie*, vol. 54: 674–93, 2002. Small errors in the data set were corrected. For example, almost new but used phones were deleted to include only homogeneous products. Moreover, in this version more refined statistical methods were applied. All data are from the Swiss auction platform ricardo.ch collected in the time span October 2001 to January 2002. The maximum number of positive ratings was 103, indicating that sellers' businesses were rather new. Therefore, this paper reports effects of the reputation system in the relatively new environment of ricardo.ch's auction platform. This specific feature of the sample might be an advantage compared to the analysis of today's auction data. We assume that the reputation system is of greater importance for newly established auction platforms than for platforms with a longer history. We would like to thank Debra Hevenstone, Andrea Hungerbühler, Wojtek Przepiorka, Thomas Voss, and Andreas Wald for helpful comments and suggestions.

5. Meanwhile, support for the reputation hypothesis is also provided by a series of other studies (see, for example, the surveys in Bajari and Hortaçsu 2004; Snijders and Zijdeman 2004; Resnick et al. 2006).

6. The sequential prisoner's dilemma is very similar to the trust game. Trust games end after the first player defects, whereas in a sequential prisoner's dilemma the second player may respond to the first player's defection by cooperation or defection (Dasgupta 1988; Kreps 1990; Snijders 1996; Gautschi 2002; on the notion of trust, also see Preisendörfer 1995).

7. The data, all 204 auctions, and documentation are freely downloadable for re-analysis from http://ideas.repec.org/p/ets/wpaper/1.html.

8. After we collected our data, QXL ricardo changed the system to *positive*, *neutral*, and *negative* ratings.

9. The data in our sample are clustered on sellers. The 167 auctions are from seventy-five unique sellers. Thus we report test statistics and p-values derived from cluster-correlation consistent variance estimators (see Rogers 1993; Williams 2000; White 1980).

10. One could also assume a decreasing absolute effect of calendar time and hence include a quadratic term in the logistic regression equation. However, the parabolic model did not prove to be superior.

11. The dependent variable is the net auction price in Swiss francs. Alternatively, one might consider using the logarithm of the selling price as the dependent variable and, therefore, estimate constant (semi-) elasticity models (as in, for example, Berger and Schmitt 2005). Apart from entailing rather odd interpretations for the effects of several of our covariates, the logarith-

mic models did not prove to outperform the linear models. We therefore report the results from the linear specifications.

12. Note, however, that in model 1 the coefficient for shipping costs does not significantly defer from –1 ($p = .180$, two-sided). It does, however, if the logarithm of the number of ratings is used as indicator for reputation (model 3; $p = .028$, two-sided).

13. Again, however, only in the logarithmic model is the coefficient significantly different from one. The two sided p-values are 0.081 and 0.039 for model 1 and model 3, respectively.

14. Note that the results of such a model depend on normality and homoskedasticity of the errors. Inspection of the data did not reveal any evidence for a strong departure from these assumptions.

15. Outlier diagnostics for the standard model indicate that the effect is quite unstable anyhow (Belsley, Kuh, and Welsch 1980; Fox 1991). It drops to around 1 to 1.5 CHF if outliers are excluded. The high effect of the minimum bid increment can be traced back, in essence, to one observation with a high minimum increment of 50 CHF and a phenomenal selling price of 800 CHF (see figure 5.3). The same results are obtained from the application of robust regression procedures (Berk 1990; Hamilton 1991).

16. The strong negative effect of the duration of the auction is quite puzzling. We believe that the effect is an artifact emanating from two mechanisms. First, the market value of the offered cell phones decreases in the course of an auction because of the general devaluation over calendar time. The shorter the duration of the auction, the smaller is the decrease in value. Thus, higher prices should be achieved in short auctions. Second, the duration of an auction is endogenous if the auction is prematurely terminated by a buy-it-now price. Taken together, these two aspects seem to produce the strong negative effect of the duration. At least, the effect disappears (that is, it is substantially smaller and no longer significant) if the twenty-five right-censored cases are discarded and calendar time is measured at the end of the auctions instead of the beginning.

17. An alternative explanation for the relation between reputation and the choice of payment method could be that there are some learning effects. Sellers with a high reputation score are also sellers that have a lot of experience in the market, and maybe it is just their experience that makes them opt for the more secure payment modes.

18. Note that, most likely, the ratings are positively biased to some degree. Because both the buyer and the seller can submit a rating, a buyer may fear retaliation and submit, say, a neutral instead of a negative rating (see chapters 1, 8, and 11, this volume; for an analysis of the feedback process in Internet auctions, see Dellarocas, Fan, and Wood 2004; Diekman et al. 2008).

19. For a thorough discussion of different ways for the provision of information on quality and trustworthiness in various settings, see also Daniel Klein's "Trust for Hire" (1997).

References

Akerlof, George A. 1970. "The Market for 'Lemons': Quality Uncertainty and the Market Mechanism." *Quarterly Journal of Economics* 89(3): 488–500.

Abell, Peter, and Diane Reyniers. 2000. "Generalised Reciprocity and Reputation in the Theory of Cooperation." *Analyse & Kritik* 22(1): 3–18.

Amemiya, Takeshi. 1985. *Advanced Econometrics*. Cambridge, Mass.: Harvard University Press.

Axelrod, Robert M. 1984. *The Evolution of Cooperation*. New York: Basic Books.

Bajari, Patrick, and Ali Hortaçsu. 2003. "The Winner's Curse, Reserve Prices, and Endogenous Entry: Empirical Insights from eBay Auctions." *RAND Journal of Economics* 34(2): 329–55.

———. 2004. "Economic Insights from Internet Auctions." *Journal of Economic Literature* 42(June): 457–86.

Belsley, David A., Edwin Kuh, and Roy E. Welsch. 1980. *Regression Diagnostics: Identifying Influential Data and Sources of Collinearity*. New York: John Wiley & Sons.

Berger, Roger, and Katharina Schmitt. 2005. "Vertrauen bei Internetauktionen und die Rolle von Reputation, Informationen, Treuhandangebot und Preisniveau." *Kölner Zeitschrift für Soziologie und Sozialpsychologie* 57(1): 86–111.

Berk, Richard A. 1990. "A Primer on Robust Regression." In *Modern Methods of Data Analysis*, edited by John Fox and J. Scott Long. Newbury Park, Calif.: Sage Publications.

Breen, Richard. 1996. *Regression Models. Censored, Sample Selected, or Truncated Data*. Newbury Park, Calif.: Sage Publications.

Brinkmann, Ulrich, and Matthias Seifert. 2001. "'Face to Interface': Zum Problem der Vertrauenskonstitution im Internet am Beispiel von elektronischen Auktionen." *Zeitschrift für Soziologie* 30(1): 23–47.

Buskens, Vincent, and Werner Raub. 2004. "Soziale Mechanismen rationalen Vertrauens: Eine theoretische Skizze und Resultate aus empirischen Studien." In *Rational-Choice-Theorie in den Sozialwissenschaften. Anwendungen und Probleme*, edited by Andreas Diekmann and Thomas Voss. München: Oldenbourg.

Coleman, James S. 1990. *Foundations of Social Theory*. Cambridge, Mass: Belknap Press.

Dasgupta, Partha. 1988. "Trust as a Commodity." In *Trust: Making and Breaking Cooperative Relations*, edited by Diego Gambetta. Oxford: Blackwell Publishing.

Dellarocas, Chrysanthos, Ming Fan, and Charles A. Wood. 2004. "Self-Interest, Reciprocity, and Participation in Online Reputation Systems." MIT Sloan School of Management working paper 4500–04. Cambridge, Mass.: Massachusetts Institute of Technology.

Diekmann, Andreas, Ben Jann, Wojtek Przepiorka, and Stefan Wehrli. 2008. "The Evolution of Cooperation on Anonymous Markets." ETH Zurich working paper. Zurich: Eidgenössische Technische Hochschule Zürich.

Diekmann, Andreas, and Siegwart Lindenberg. 2001. "Cooperation: Sociological Aspects." In *International Encyclopedia of the Social & Behavioral Sciences*, edited by Neil J. Smelser and Paul B. Baltes. Amsterdam: Elsevier Science.

Dworschak, Manfred. 2000. "Jahrmarkt der Meinungsfreude." *Der Spiegel* 39(September 25): 266–70.

Emons, Winand. 1997. "Credence Goods and Fraudulent Experts." *RAND Journal of Economics* 28(1): 107–19.

Fox, John. 1991. *Regression Diagnostics*. Newbury Park, Calif.: Sage Publications.

Gautschi, Thomas. 2002. *Trust and Exchange: Effects of Temporal Embeddedness and*

Network Embeddedness on Providing and Dividing a Surplus. Amsterdam: Thela Thesis.

Gerhards, Jürgen. 2002. "Reputation in der deutschen Soziologie – zwei getrennte Welten, Soziologie." *Forum der Deutschen Gesellschaft für Soziologie* 2(1): 19–33.

Granovetter, Mark S. 1985. "Economic Action and Social Structure: The Problem of Embeddedness." *American Journal of Sociology* 91(3): 481–510.

Greif, Avner. 1989. "Reputation and Coalitions in Medieval Trade: Evidence on the Mahgribi Traders." *Journal of Economic History* 49(4): 857–82.

————. 1993. "Contract Enforceability and Economic Institutions in Early Trade: The Maghribi Traders' Coalition." *American Economic Review* 83(3): 525–48.

Hägg, P., and T. Göran. 1994. "The Economics of Trust, Trust-Sensitive Contracts, and Regulation." *International Review of Law and Economics* 14(4): 437–51.

Hamilton, Lawrence C. 1991. "How Robust is Robust Regression?" *Stata Technical Bulletin* 1(2): 21–26.

Homann, Karl, and Andreas Suchanek. 2000. *Ökonomik. Eine Einführung.* Tübingen, Germany: Mohr Siebeck.

Houser, Daniel, and John Wooders. 2006. "Reputation in Auctions: Theory and Evidence from eBay." *Journal of Economics & Management Strategy* 15(2): 353–69.

Klein, Daniel B. 1997. "Trust for Hire: Voluntary Remedies for Quality and Safety." In *Reputation: Studies in the Voluntary Elicitation of Good Conduct.* Ann Arbor: University of Michigan Press.

Kollock, Peter. 1999. "The Production of Trust in Online Markets." In *Advances in Group Processes*, vol. 16, edited by Edward J. Lawler, Shane R. Thye, Michael W. Macy, and Henry A. Walker. Greenwich, Conn.: JAI Press.

Kreps, David M. 1990. "Corporate Culture and Economic Theory." In *Perspectives on Positive Political Economy*, edited by James E. Alt and Kenneth A. Shepsle. Cambridge: Cambridge University Press.

Ledyard, John O. 1995. "Public Goods: A Survey of Experimental Research." In *Handbook of Experimental Economics*, edited by John H. Kagel and Alvin E. Roth. Princeton, N.J.: Princeton University Press.

Lucking-Reiley, David. 2000. "Auctions on the Internet: What's Being Auctioned, and How?" *Journal of Industrial Economics* 48(2): 227– 52.

Lucking-Reiley, David, Doug Bryan, Naghi Prasad, and Danie Reeves. 2007. "Pennies from eBay: The Determinants of Price in Online Auctions." *Journal of Industrial Economics* 55(2): 223–33.

Maddala, G. S. 1983. *Limited Dependent and Qualitative Variables in Econometrics.* Cambridge: Cambridge University Press.

McDonald, Cynthia G., and V. Carlos Slawson Jr. 2002. "Reputation in an Internet Auction Market." *Economic Inquiry* 40(4): 633–50.

Melnick, Mikhail I., and James Alm. 2002. "Does a Seller's eCommerce Reputation Matter? Evidence from eBay Auctions." *The Journal of Industrial Economics* 50(3): 337–49.

National White Collar Crime Center. 2002. *IFCC 2001 Internet Fraud Report.* Glen Allen, Va.: National White Collar Crime Center. Available at: http://www.nw3c.org.

———. 2003. *IFCC 2002 Internet Fraud Report*. Glen Allen, Va.: National White Collar Crime Center. Available at: http://www.nw3c.org.

Preisendörfer, Peter. 1995. "Vertrauen als soziologische Kategorie: Möglichkeiten und Grenzen einer entscheidungstheoretischen Fundierung des Vertrauenskonzepts." *Zeitschrift für Soziologie* 24(4): 263–72.

Rapoport, Anatol, and Albert M. Chammah. 1965. *Prisoner's Dilemma: A Study of Conflict and Cooperation*. Ann Arbor: University of Michigan Press.

Raub, Werner, and Jeroen Weesie. 1990. "Reputation and Efficiency in Social Interactions: An Example of Network Effects." *American Journal of Sociology* 96(3): 626–54.

———. 2000. "The Management of Matches: A Research Program on Solidarity in Durable Relations." *The Netherlands Journal of Social Science* 36(1): 71–88.

Resnick, Paul, Richard Zeckhauser, John Swanson, and Kate Lockwood. 2006. "The Value of Reputation on eBay: A Controlled Experiment." *Experimental Economics* 9(2): 79–101.

Reynolds, Stanley S., and John Wooders. 2009. "Auctions with a Buy Price." *Economic Theory* 38(2009): 9–39.

Rogers, William H. 1993. "Regression Standard Errors in Clustered Samples." *Stata Technical Bulletin* 13(May): 19–23. Reprinted in Stata Technical Bulletin Reprints 3(13): 88–94.

Roth, Alvin E., and Axel Ockenfels. 2002. "Last-Minute Bidding and the Rules for Ending Second-Price Auctions: Evidence from eBay and Amazon Auctions on the Internet." *American Economic Review* 92(4): 1093–103.

Snijders, Chris. 1996. *Trust and Commitments*. Amsterdam: Thesis Publishers.

Snijders, Chris, and Richard Zijdeman. 2004. "Reputation and Internet Auctions: eBay and Beyond." *Analyse & Kritik* 26(1): 158–84.

U.S. Bureau of the Census and U.S. Department of Commerce. 2003. CB-03-177. Washington: U.S. Bureau of the Census. Available at: http://www.census.gov/mrts/www/data/pdf/03Q3.pdf.

Voss, Thomas. 1998. "Vertrauen in modernen Gesellschaften." In *Der Transformationsprozess*, edited by Regina Metze, Kurt Mühler, and Karl-Dieter Opp. Leipzig, Germany: Universitätsverlag.

Weber, Max. 1920. "Die protestantischen Sekten und der Geist des Kapitalismus." In *Gesammelte Aufsätze zur Religionssoziologie*. Tübingen, Germany: Mohr.

———. 2002. "The Protestant Sects and the Spirit of Capitalism," translated by Hans H. Gerth and C. Wright Mills. In *Max Weber, The Protestant Ethic and the Spirit of Capitalism*, 3d Roxbury edition. Los Angeles, Calif.: Roxbury Publishing.

White, Halbert. 1980. "A Heteroskedasticity-Consistent Covariance Matrix Estimator and a Direct Test for Heteroskedasticity." *Econometrica* 48(4): 817–30.

Williams, Rick L. 2000. "A Note on Robust Variance Estimation for Cluster-Correlated Data." *Biometrics* 56(3): 645–46.

Ziegler, Rolf. 1998. "Trust and the Reliability of Expectations." *Rationality and Society* 10(4): 427–50.

Chapter 6

Online Programming Markets

CHRIS SNIJDERS AND JEROEN WEESIE

MANY OF the mechanisms that exist offline and ensure that an interaction between people runs smoothly are not available in online interactions. A large shadow of the future cannot easily be guaranteed, for example: who knows whether you are going to deal with the people in this online help forum again, whether you will be buying from the same online reseller again. In addition, because the interacting partners can be geographically dispersed it is often impossible to sanction a partner who has misbehaved toward you, even if you manage to discover that individual's real world identity. In the absence of such mechanisms, interactions online tend to reduce to single-shot social dilemmas with high risk of opportunistic behavior and, as a result, a high risk of a possible breakdown in such potentially profitable interactions.[1]

Reputation systems, used by online auction sites such as eBay but also by other sites such as Amazon or Yahoo, provide one mechanism to potentially increase trust between interacting partners online. The lack of trust that can arise because of the online setting might be compensated for when both partners can judge the trustworthiness and capabilities of the other through their reputation. Many of us recognize such a reputation system in eBay. When you have bought or sold something on eBay, both buyer and seller get the opportunity to leave a feedback score (on eBay this is either a +1, 0, or –1) and a brief comment about the business partner. One's total score and the comments are made public and are available to all other buyers and sellers to see. The underlying idea is, of course, that buyers and sellers value their reputations, find it worthwhile to invest in them, and abstain from the opportunistic behavior (such as selling junk or refusing to pay) that they might otherwise be tempted to engage in. Although sites differ in the details of the reputation system they use, most of the larger sites that use reputation systems tend to follow a procedure similar to the one used by eBay.

Several studies have tried to assess whether reputation systems might work, and under what circumstances. Virtually all empirical studies focus on two dependent variables: the probability of sale and the selling price. Strangely enough, the empirical evidence in favor of reputation systems as a safeguard against opportunistic behavior is not that overwhelming. Some researchers have found no positive effects of a good reputation on probability of sale and selling price, and others have found statistically significant but substantially insignificant effects. Only a handful of researchers have found substantial effects in the expected direction—for instance, a positive correlation between the reputation score of a seller on eBay and the selling price of the product (which we cover briefly in the next section). This general lack of empirical support, combined with the current boom in online interaction, poses a tantalizing problem, part of which we hope to resolve in this chapter. As we argue, eBay data pose several problems to adequately testing effects of reputation when one considers probability of sale and selling price as the dependent variable. Moreover, what is critical but generally neglected is that arguments center on how much buyers would be willing to pay extra for a product from a seller with a good reputation, rather than on how much extra they might have to pay for that good. The latter depends on many often unmeasured factors, such as market conditions, which makes using the actual selling price as the dependent variable a poor proxy of what we should measure—the willingness to pay extra for an additional unit of reputation. We show that when you look in an online context where these problems of data quality and availability are less severe, the positive effect of reputation on the willingness to pay does indeed surface.

Reputation Scores on eBay

Most of the empirical work on the effects of reputation systems on sales in online interaction is based on eBay data. One reason for this is that eBay is by far the biggest auction site, representing 84 million active users and a gross volume of nearly $60 billion in 2007.[2] This suggests that whoever can understand eBay understands a large part of the financial online consumer world. Another reason is that eBay auction data are relatively easy to collect, either by hand or automatically through software that spiders the website. For the few who have never heard about eBay auctions: on eBay, the seller puts a product online for a specific amount of time (often seven days), and buyers can bid against one another for the product. The one with the highest bid gets the product and pays according to his bid. In fact, auctions allow several possibilities that seriously complicate the matter, such as private reserved prices (a minimum amount the seller wants to make), starting prices, and buy-it-now prices (prices for which the seller is willing to end the auction and sell immediately), but let us not consider these now, although they may have strong effects on probability of sale and selling price. As mentioned, after each transaction, buyer and seller get the possibility to leave a feedback score and a brief comment about the business partner. The number of (unique) positive evaluations minus the number of (unique) negative evaluations forms a person's public reputation score.

In most empirical applications, the data collected from eBay include as the dependent variable whether a seller sold the product and, if yes, at what price. Researchers vary considerably with respect to which operationalization of a seller's reputation they use: number of positive comments, number of negative comments, percentage of negative comments, and so on. They also vary with respect to which other characteristics they control for in their analyses: duration of auction, shipping costs, product characteristics, and so on. Most of the empirical papers use some form of regression analysis to analyze the data.

The most straightforward effects researchers aim to find—that a better reputation leads to a higher probability of sale and a higher selling price—are not always found. Some researchers even come up with highly unexpected results, such as a negative reputation having a positive effect on an auction's end price (Eaton 2002; Kauffman and Wood 2000). Chrysanthos Dellarocas has provided an overview (2003, 1412, table 2); many working papers on the topic are available from the Reputations Research Network.[3] In the majority of cases, the effect of the reputation score on selling price is positive, but the size of the effects is generally small. Several studies show no effect of the reputation score on price. Similar inconsistencies hold for negative reputation scores. They sometimes have a negative effect on the probability of sale and selling price, and when they do they are often larger than the effect of a positive reputation, but just as often we do not find any significant effects of negative reputation. It seems that the effects are stronger when the goods are less standardized, when, for example, they are secondhand rather than new, or complex rather than simple. This makes sense intuitively. More recent studies have reported relatively strong effects. For instance, Christian Grund and Oliver Gürtler found in an empirical analysis of DVD sales on eBay that there are substantial negative effects of the percentage of negative ratings on the selling price (2006). Cynthia McDonald and Carlos Slawson Jr. found a positive effect of reputation on selling price in the online sales of Barbie dolls (2002).

There are several reasons for the variation in results found in previous studies (see Lee, Im, and Lee 2000; Snijders and Zijdeman 2004).

First, there are differences with respect to the kind of product that is being sold in the auction data. Some studies consider only new products, others only used products. Some studies analyze several different products at the same time, whereas others analyze data about one kind of product. As Chris Snijders and Richard Zijdeman argued and demonstrated, data analysis on one kind of product can have an impact on the results in that statistically significant results are more likely when only one kind of product is analyzed (2004). In addition, it is likely that the higher the prices are and the more abundant the supply of sellers, the more a buyer will be inclined to use every bit of information he can get, including the reputation score of the seller. Another important factor that might lead to inconsistent results across studies lies in the way in which reputation is operationalized. Some studies consider the difference of (unique) positive minus (unique) negative ratings—which is what eBay reports as a person's reputation score—whereas others use the absolute number of negative ratings or the percentage of negative ratings as well, in some cases log- or otherwise transformed. Third, the way in which data were collected could contribute to the mixed results. Although some researchers control for variables related to product condition and others for those related to transactions like shipment costs and means of payment, still others control for few, if any, other possible intervening variables. Finally, as Paul Resnick and his colleagues have already pointed out, researchers have been using different statistical methods of analysis (2006).

Actually, another reason why using eBay data (or online data in general) is considered an attractive way of doing research is that, in principle, the researcher has pretty much the same data available as the eBay-user. One could therefore hope that, whatever the reasons are for the behavior of the buyer or seller, a large part of the information the buyer or seller can use as a basis for this behavior is in fact available to the researcher. In that sense, using online data has a natural place in between a standard lab experiment, where treatments are completely under the control of the experimenter, and the survey, where the researcher tries to measure anything that can be thought to cause or correlate with the behavior of the respondent. However, the analysis of eBay data, or data from an auction site with a similar setup, is not that straightforward, and the data are not as close to the underlying theory as one might expect from looking at research reports that use them.

The first thing to note about auction data that can be found on eBay is that they do not fully encompass the underlying arguments that should be involved according to auction theories. A typical person bidding on an item will choose his bid based on the value of the good to himself and on the expected maximum bid of other potential buyers. That is, to really statistically model the situation as close to the actual decision as possible, one needs to include how many other potential buyers the focal buyer expects in this particular auction, or in any case some kind of measure of the expected maximum of the other buyers' bids as experienced by the focal buyer. What makes the matter even more complicated is that it may very well be that a potential buyer can simultaneously consider similar auctions (that is, those for the same or a similar product), or can even decide to postpone buying until a similar auction comes along. Usually, such additional data are not available or are difficult to estimate on the basis of the data that are available online.

Other incompleteness issues concern the fact that giving feedback is voluntary, so that an analysis of reputation data should consider selectivity of the sample or assume it away. It is also possible to change identities or to create a high reputation score by engaging in numerous relatively small transactions. But even when we accept the incompleteness of the data and simply forget about such strategic and other arguments playing a role, the issue of the most appropriate mode of statistical analysis remains. First, because not all products are sold, there are reasons to model auction data using Heckman selection models: some factors influence whether the good gets sold, other and partly the same factors determine the selling price when the good is sold. Finding factors that determine one but not the other is difficult, which complicates estimating these models reliably. Because the selling price typically underestimates the value of the good to the buyer—the buyer might have been willing to pay more—there are also reasons to use tobit analysis or interval regression when the selling price is the dependent variable. However, in analyses with such truncated samples, the consequences of heteroskedasticity are severe (Hurd 1979), which implies, for instance, that one needs to be careful not to analyze vast quantities of auction data regarding many different products in a single analysis (see Snijders and Zijdeman 2004).

Thus, there are several reasons why simply running OLS analyses on auction data—even when you have thousands of data points—might not immediately reveal the actual underlying effects of reputation on auctions. Several attempts are being made to connect theoretical auction models and empirical data by making use of structural modeling. For example, Shanshan Wang, Wolfgang Jank, and Galit Shmueli used the bidding data to infer the distribution of other bids as assumed by the bidders (2004). Similarly, Raul Gonzalez, Kevin Hasker, and Robin Sickles estimated and controlled for the number of potential bidders for an auction (2004).[4]

Our attempt is different. At its core, the issue is whether a buyer values a positive reputation of a seller. That is, would a buyer be willing to pay more for the product when the seller has a better reputation score. This willingness to pay might depend on other factors, such as the condition of the product, shipping costs, or transaction costs such as whether payment through PayPal is possible. However, the selling price and the probability of sale depends on many other unmeasured factors, such as other buyers' willingness to pay for the product, the number of suppliers of similar goods, and other market conditions, such as the degree to which buyers and sellers have access to information about the market itself. Although we do not deny that probability of sale and selling price are interesting in their own right—what a good reputation is worth in the market place is certainly an important question—such analyses should not be confused with what the theory behind alleged effects of reputation is actually about. Of course, it would be possible to measure willingness to pay in an experimental setting. Doing so, however, would be throwing out the baby with the bathwater because one of the main advantages of eBay data—that they represent real rather than artificial transactions—would then be lost. To estimate willingness to pay from behavioral data, data should include the options an agent can choose and the attributes of these options. In our case, this implies that our data must at least contain the price and the reputation of all the options. If one has such data, the effect of reputation on willingness to pay can be estimated using the discrete choice approach (see, for example, McFadden 1974; Louviere, Hensher, and Swait 2000). Collecting such data is not feasible—or at least not easily accomplished—with eBay because the set of alternative options is not well defined and the information about which options have been considered by buyers is difficult to collect.[5] We therefore tried to find and analyze an online reputation system in which the typical disadvantages of eBay do not play a role, or at least to a much lesser extent. We found RentACoder.com. Our main hypothesis is that because the data provide a more seamless fit between data and underlying model, we will find a more pronounced positive effect of reputation on selling price there.

RentACoder.com

RentACoder.com is an Internet site where people can offer their programming jobs to programmers. The procedure runs as follows. First, a buyer puts a bid request online, describing the programming job in as much detail as possible, including a deadline for the project as a whole. This can range from designing a website, enhancing an algorithm, or creating a storefront, to coding scripts or parts of scripts in Perl, PHP, or some other programming or scripting language. The buyer also determines a rough price estimate: either very small (less than $100 dollars), small ($100 to $500), medium ($500 to $5,000), or large (greater than $5,000). Other options are open for fair offer and unsure of project price. For a fixed period, usually one or two weeks, programmers—called coders on the site—can respond to the bid request and mention the amount of money for which they would be willing and able to complete the job. All bids are visible to the buyer, but coders do not know the bids of other coders. During this phase, buyer and seller can communicate—about details of the job, for example—but in principle they can also haggle about the price. Coders can offer some general information about themselves, usually only about their capabilities and experience in programming ("I am an experienced programmer and am fluent in Visual Basic, C, and C++"). At any time, the buyer can decide to accept the bid of a particular coder and end the initial phase. As soon as the buyer has accepted a bid, the amount of money agreed upon is transferred to RentACoder. During the coding phase, the coder is obliged to provide weekly status reports about the progress of the coding job. When the coding has been completed, the source code and other deliverables are transferred to the buyer who then acknowledges that the job has been completed, after which RentACoder transfers the money to the coder. RentACoder profits because it keeps 15 percent of the agreed upon fee. RentACoder has been in business since 2001 and in the summer of 2006 hosted some 60,000 buyers and 155,000 coders from across the world.

Choosing Between Coders

As on eBay, coders on RentACoder have a reputation score, but the scoring mechanism is slightly different. At RentACoder, after a coding job has been completed, buyer and coder rate each other on a scale from 1 (horrible) to 10 (excellent). The name of the coder always shows his or her average rating directly beneath it, so that buyers get an idea about how satisfied previous buyers have been about this coder. In addition, information about all previous coding jobs of the coder is available, and a page with personal information about the coder. Figure 6.1 shows an example of the kind of information available per coder.

As can be seen from figure 6.1, the information about the coder includes the average rating (for PSergei this is 9.86), a quantile score comparing the coder with all other coders, sign-up date, number of jobs completed, number of jobs in progress, and several other characteristics. Two elements of the information deserve specific attention. The first is the number of arbitrations the coder has been involved in. Whenever buyers or coders are dissatisfied with the way in which an interaction proceeds, they can ask RentACoder to intervene. This typically occurs when a coder has delivered the code to the buyer, but the buyer is for some reason not satisfied with it. Because all communication between buyer and coder can (and should) run through the website, an arbitrator can make a reasonable estimate as to who is right and what should be done about it. As it appears, PSergei has been involved in ten such arbi-

Figure 6.1   Information about Coder as Displayed on RentACoder

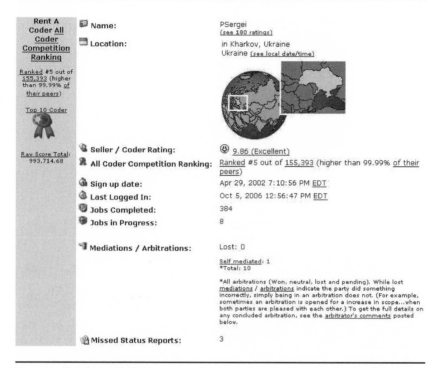

Source: Authors' compilation.

trations and has lost none of them. The second factor is the country of residence. This can be an important factor for a buyer. For many programming jobs, communicating about what is needed must be detailed and precise. It certainly helps considerably when a coder is fluent in English: the buyer can be more certain that the coder has understood the bid request and that when problems arise along the way, as they inevitably do, they will be solved more easily. It is also important because dealing with a coder in a time zone that makes quick back-and-forth e-mail communication impossible—the coder is typically asleep when the buyer is awake and vice versa—can be inconvenient. The kind of choice a buyer needs to make is presented in figure 6.2.

The programming job in figure 6.2 was a relatively small task. Still, the bids varied between $15 and $59. In this case the lowest bidder (firejump) did not get the job. Perhaps his relatively low rating made the buyer decide to choose the Net#Team offer that was $5 higher (see figure 6.2).

Figure 6.2   Example of Coders Bidding on Job

8/8/2006 8:46:48 AM	ozertsov	In Semenov, Russian Federation (see local date/time)	Not rated yet.	Ranked #69,926 out of 155,393 (higher than 55.00% of their peers).	View 1 message(s) / Reply	$50.00
8/8/2006 8:57:13 AM	Tirzar	In Unterföhring, Germany (see local date/time)	10 (Excellent) out of 3 ratings.	Ranked #8,651 out of 155,393 (higher than 94.43% of their peers).	View 1 message(s) / Reply	$59.00
8/8/2006 9:04:11 AM	firejump	In Odessa, Ukraine (see local date/time)	7.34 (Good) out of 47 ratings.	Ranked #155,047 out of 155,393 (higher than 0.22% of their peers).	View 1 message(s) / Reply	$15.00
8/8/2006 9:10:11 AM	xource	In City of Glasgow, United Kingdom (see local date/time)	8.93 (Superb) out of 16 ratings.	Ranked #5,888 out of 155,393 (higher than 96.21% of their peers).	View 1 message(s) / Reply	$50.00
8/8/2006 9:12:13 AM	Net#Team	In Timisoara, Romania (see local date/time)	8.63 (Superb) out of 11 ratings.	Ranked #7,621 out of 155,393 (higher than 95.09% of their peers).	View 15 message(s) / Reply	$20.00 was accepted (view)
8/8/2006 9:40:30 AM	Artis	In Donetsk, Ukraine (see local date/time)	9.78 (Excellent) out of 19 ratings.	Ranked #2,245 out of 155,393 (higher than 98.55% of their peers).	View 2 message(s) / Reply	$50.00

Source: Authors' compilation.

A mechanism as on RentACoder is not an auction in the same sense of the word as on eBay: the coder with the lowest bid need not get the job. However, the same underlying problems apply. The buyer is not sure whether the coder will deliver and cannot be sure about the quality of the work. Detailed demands mentioned in the bid request can be checked on delivery, of course. Whether a program can do what it is supposed to do is relatively easy to find out. However, if the coder is not able to change his code in a satisfactory way, the buyer is left empty-handed even though he will get his money back. In other cases, it might not be easy to check whether all demands of the bid request are met. For instance, how do you decide whether the coder has indeed designed a website that is "smooth and flashy," as suggested in the bid request? Often, several issues in a bid request must remain somewhat subjective, and whether the coder will be responsive to comments during and after the coding process remains to be seen. In addition, in programming it is often important that the coding is transparent so that the buyer can understand how it works and can adapt it if the need arises. Again, the competencies and willingness of the coder to provide clear coding are typically hard to establish beforehand. That puts buyers at RentACoder at a similar risk as buyers on eBay: you want to buy something but are not sure whether it will be delivered, and if it is, what condition the product will be in. One way to decrease the risk as a buyer is to stick to using coders with higher reputation scores.

Before describing the data in more detail, it is useful to realize that figure 6.2 shows that, indeed, the data from RentACoder allow statistical modeling closer to the actual decisions buyers are making. In the RentACoder transactions, we basically see all other options that would have been possible but did not materialize, which is what we need to estimate the willingness to pay for good reputation.

Descriptive Results

We analyze all public bid requests between May 14, 2001, and January 15, 2005.[6] During this time, a total of 30,742 completed transactions took place, and 10,710 buyers and 40,697 coders were active on the site. Table 6.1 shows the transactions per year, separately for all winning bids and for only those winning bids larger than $20. About 25 percent of the transactions ended with a winning bid smaller than $20 (see table 6.1). We exclude these from the analyses because it is likely that they deal with coding jobs so small that a serious comparison of bidders is not likely to occur and because the differences in bids will tend to be small.

We do not know how many bid requests received no bids (the data contains only those requests that were bid on). Closer inspection showed 922 excessive bids (that is, amounts larger than $50,000). We believe these are bogus and excluded them from the analysis. From those requests that did receive at least one bid, the average number is eleven, with a median of seven. Five percent received thirty-five bids or more (max=908). Of the 10,721 buyers who rented a coder at least once, 55 percent rented once, and 11 percent at least five times. On average, buyers have rented a coder (not necessarily the same one) about three times. A striking result is that 82 percent of the coders who have ever placed a bid have also never been chosen, which suggests that this is a buyer's market. Actually, there is a small minority of about 750 coders (about 2 percent) who have completed ten or more jobs. Together these 2 percent performed about 35 percent of the jobs. Table 6.2 gives an idea of the value of the winning bids. Many of the winning bids are smaller than $500.

One might think that the coder with the lowest bid is always chosen, but this is not the case. This can be seen by considering the cases in

Table 6.1   Transactions per Year

	Transactions		Transactions More Than $20	
	Number	Percentage	Number	Percentage
2001	1,426	4.6%	1,064	4.7%
2002	5,102	16.6	3,555	15.8
2003	10,071	32.8	7,337	32.6
2004	13,877	45.2	10,361	46.0
2005	266	0.8	189	0.8
Total	30,742	100.0	22,506	100.0

Source: Authors' compilation.

which the eventual winning bid is larger than $20, there are at least two bids (otherwise there is nothing to choose), and a unique minimum bid exists. We then find that minimum bids are chosen 28 percent of the time, and on average other bids only 8 percent of the time. We can conclude that to get the job it helps to have the lowest price, but the lowest price is certainly no guarantee. The strongest effect we find in these raw comparisons is when we compare a coder who has not done business with the buyer before with a coder who has. A coder who has done business with the buyer before has a 57 percent probability of being chosen; a coder who has not has a 3 percent probability.

Finally, we show the reputation ratings. On RentACoder, as mentioned, a reputation is a real number between 1 and 10, where 10 is high. The distribution of the reputation scores for coders when we consider all bid requests is present in figure 6.3. When we exclude the cases with winning bids smaller than $20, we get the distribution presented in figure 6.4.

As figure 6.3 shows, the bulk of the coders have a reputation of 6.5 or higher, so that differences are really between 6.5 and 10. We also see that restricting our analyses to winning bids larger than $20 removes many of the coders with dubious reputations.

Table 6.2   Percentages of Winning Bids

Winning bid < 20	27% (excluded from further analysis)
Winning bid ≥ 20 but < 100	44
Winning bid ≥ 100 but < 500	25
Winning bid ≥ 500 but < 5000	4
Winning bid ≥ 5000	0 (26 cases)

Source: Authors' compilation.

Figure 6.3   Distribution of Reputation Scores, All Bids

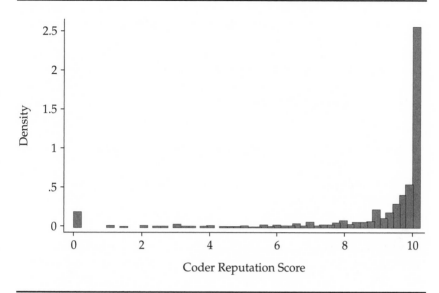

Source: Authors' compilation.

Figure 6.4   Distribution of Reputation Scores, Bids Higher than $20

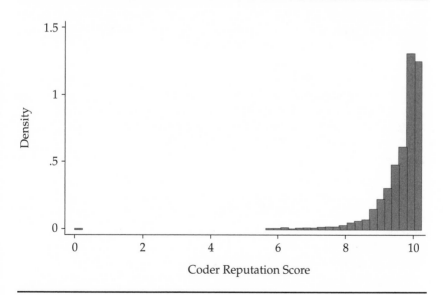

Source: Authors' compilation.

Analytical Strategy

We analyze the data using conditional logit modeling. That is, the dependent variable is whether a certain bid is chosen, and we therefore include the information of all bids, rather than only the selected ones, to estimate the value of reputation. The underlying model is equivalent to McFadden's choice model. In this model the assumption is that the latent attractiveness A_{ij} to buyer i of option j (in our case, the attractiveness to buyer i of a bid by coder j) can be written as a weighted average:

$$A_{ij} = c_{0i} + c_1 X_{1ij} + \ldots + c_p X_{pij} + \varepsilon_{ij}, j = 1, \ldots, n_i \text{ and } i = 1, \ldots, n,$$

where the attributes χ_{hij} ($h = 1, \ldots, p$) are characteristics of the bid (such as a bidder's reputation score or the asking price), ε_{ij} has an extreme-value distribution of the first type, and the attribute weights c are unknown coefficients. The buyer-specific intercept c_{0i} does not affect choice because it is constant within buyers and cannot be estimated from choice data. Note that the number n_i of alternatives of buyer i is allowed to vary with i. We then estimate the values c (the weights for the different attributes) from the data by maximum likelihood under the assumption that the buyer chooses the option with the highest value of A (McFadden 1974). As our predictors X_{ij} we use the variables in table 6.3. We distinguish between characteristics of the coder and characteristics of the coder-buyer combination. By definition of the choice model, buyer characteristics are not included. The analysis is within buyers, so any characteristic that is constant within buyers cannot add to the model as a main effect, but interactions of characteristics of the buyer with attributes of the alternatives are possible.

As an example, suppose we only consider $X_1 =$ <amount>, $X_2 =$ <# of past transactions>, and $X_3 =$ <reputation score> as attributes. Suppose we fitted the model and found estimates $c_1 = -1$, $c_2 = 2$, and $c_3 = 0.03$ for the attribute weights. The willingness to pay of buyers—the exchange rate of money to the attributes, so to speak—can then conveniently be written as:

$$WTP_i = c_{0i} + 2 <\text{\# past transactions} > + 0.03 < \text{reputation score} >$$

so that then, for each extra unit of reputation, the WTP would increase by 3 cents (irrespective of the unknown value c_{0i}). Note that in this example we used <amount> rather than <ln(amount)> for ease of exposition. With <ln(amount)> the WTP-expression takes the form:

$$WTP_i = \exp(c_{0i} + 2 <\text{\# past transactions} > + 0.03 < \text{reputation score} >)$$

Table 6.3   Overview of Variables

Dependent variable	
<Bid was chosen>	Whether bid was chosen (= 1) or not (= 0)
Coder characteristics	
<nr. of past transactions>	Number of past transactions by coder
<has a reputation>	Coder has a reputation (1 = yes)
<reputation score>	Public reputation score on RentACoder (0 to 10, equal to 0 if no score)
<ln(amount)>	The natural log of the amount that was bid (in U.S. dollars)
<length of bio>	Length of biographical information (measured in number of characters)
<coder jpg>	Coder has uploaded a photo or logo (1 = yes)
<country of residence>	Country dummies for the U.S., Romania, Canada, U.K., Pakistan, Russia, Ukraine, Australia (the countries of coders that occur most often)
<corruption index>	Corruption index 2004 of coder home country as indicated on Transparency International (www.transparency.org). Minimum value in the data is 1.5, maximum is 9.7, with a mean of 4.7. Higher is less corrupt
Characteristics of the (buyer, coder) pair	
<past business>	Whether or not buyer and coder have done business before (1 = yes)
<past business (n)>	How often buyer and coder have done business before (number)
<same country>	Buyer and coder are from the same country (1 = yes)

Source: Authors' compilation.

and this would imply that for each unit of reputation the *WTP* would increase by $(\exp(0.03) - 1) \times 100 = 3$ percent, again regardless of the value c_{0i}.

Analyses

The results of these analyses are presented in table 6.4. The models differ in the extent to which they use predictor variables, and with respect to the kinds of cases included.

Consider models A and B in table 6.4. We see that the probability of being chosen as a coder is higher for coders who posted low bids, coders who have done business with the buyer before (the more often, the better), coders with more experience, and coders who uploaded a photo or logo on their personal information page. We also sometimes see a small effect of the length of the biographical information. In the model, we represent a coder's reputation by two attributes: <has a reputation> and <reputation score>. Clearly, coders with higher reputations are preferred. In terms of the willingness to pay, as explained earlier, the results suggest that buyers are willing to pay 40 to 50 percent more for a coder with a reputation score one unit higher (most reputation scores run between about 7.6 and 10).

Models C, D, and E in table 6.4 are included to see how robust our results are for different kinds of coding jobs. Model C considers cases with a maximum bid between $20 and $100, model D at those with a maximum bid between $100 and $1,000, and model E at those with a maximum bid of more than $1,000. We find that the results with respect to reputation are consistent across the models in that the estimated effect is positive, significantly different from 0, and substantially similar. It seems that buyers engage in relatively high stakes interactions mainly with coders with which they have done business before: the effect of this variable is stronger in model E. Interestingly, when we added a dummy-variable <bid is the lowest bid> to the analysis of model B, it showed no statistically significant effect.

The results concerning country differences are interesting in their own right. Across all models except E, we can rank order the countries of the coders by attractiveness for the average buyer from most to least attractive: Romania, Ukraine, Australia, Canada, Russia, United Kingdom (the reference category with all others), India, United States, and Pakistan. These results strike us as somewhat counterintuitive, or at least as not easy to interpret, given that the analyses control for effects of the bidding amount, the reputation of the coder, and so on. Additional analyses trying to unravel what is going on here are necessary.

We ran separate analyses to further assess the stability of the results under different implementations of the analyses (not reported in detail in this chapter). The results appear to be extremely robust. For instance, we restricted the analysis to those cases with more than five (or ten or twenty) alternatives. We also estimated the model separately for bid requests on which all the bidding coders had not previously worked with the seller. None of these affect the substantial gist of our results: buyers are willing to pay a substantial amount for a coder with a high reputation. Now let us compare these results with the results when we analyze these data, as in most eBay research, by considering only the bids that were eventually accepted, hence disregarding the potential sales that could have occurred but did not. Table 6.5 shows the result of such analyses.

Our focus is, once again, on the effect of having a positive reputation. Table 6.5 shows that, though there still is a positive effect of reputation, its size has diminished dramatically to about 3.5 percent (recall the

Table 6.4   Probability of Being Chosen

	Model A	Model B	Model C	Model D	Model E
Ln(amount)	−0.7535***	−0.7626***	−0.3566***	−0.8612***	−1.3467***
Past business (dummy)	1.7203***	1.7378***	1.8814***	1.4004***	6.8926**
Past business (n)	0.1692*	0.1496*	0.0857	0.4819*	−2.3176
Number of past transactions	0.0153***	0.0147***	0.0125***	0.0159***	0.0257***
Coder has reputation score	−3.5882***	−3.1337***	−2.7130***	−2.9998***	−6.6255**
Mean rating of reputation (0 if no reputation)	0.4825***	0.4340***	0.3882***	0.4261***	0.7996***
Buyer and coder are from same country		0.4687***	0.4038***	0.5029***	0.7002*
Corruption index (higher=less corrupt) for coder country		0.0485***	0.0515***	0.0453**	0.0500
Length of bio coder		0.0232***	0.0121	0.0317**	0.0449
Coder uploaded jpg		0.2181***	0.2230***	0.2219***	0.2529
Coder from United States		−0.1536***	−0.1375	−0.1941*	−0.1750
Coder from India		−0.0864**	−0.1425**	−0.1356*	0.0384
Coder from Romania		0.2394***	0.1924***	0.2697***	0.3274
Coder from Canada		0.1637***	0.1222	0.0891	0.3105
Coder from United Kingdom		0.0413	0.0895	0.0895	0.3172
Coder from Pakistan		−0.4074***	−0.4015***	−0.4923***	−0.0331
Coder from Russia		0.0638	0.0502	−0.0151	0.5704
Coder from Ukraine		0.2262***	0.1924	0.2351*	0.2679
Coder from Australia		0.1753*	0.2964*	0.0839	−0.0758
Number of buyers	8,865	8,850	3,857	3,555	285
N	250,178	249,118	70,116	76,947	7,117
Pseudo-R^2	0.13	0.14	0.12	0.13	0.22

Source: Authors' compilation.
Notes: Conditional logistic regression of whether the coder has been chosen. Standard errors adjusted for clustering on buyer, ignoring clustering on coders.

Model A = all cases (and basic predictors)
Model B = all cases (and extended list of predictors)
Model C = cases with 20 < maximum bid ≤ 100
Model D = cases with 100 < maximum bid ≤ 1000
Model E = cases with maximum bid > 1000
* $p < 0.05$, ** $p < 0.01$, *** $p < 0.001$

Table 6.5   Amount Paid for Job

	Model A	Model B	Model C
Past business (dummy)	−0.1603***	−0.1607***	−0.1635***
Past business (n)	−0.0410	−0.0411	−0.0399
Number of past transactions	−0.0022***	−0.0027***	−0.0027***
Coder has reputation score	−0.2985*	−0.3018*	n.a.
Mean rating of reputation (0 if no reputation)	0.0342**	0.0342**	0.0367**
Buyer and coder are from same country		−0.0036	−0.0407
Corruption index (higher= less corrupt) for coder country		−0.0087	−0.0092
Length of bio coder		0.0001***	0.0001***
Coder uploaded jpg		0.0875***	0.0889***
Coder from United States		−0.0103	−0.0327
Coder from India		0.0440	0.0491
Coder from Romania		−0.0774**	−0.0826**
Coder from Canada		0.0007	−0.0061
Coder from United Kingdom		0.0035	−0.0055
Coder from Pakistan		−0.1007*	−0.0712
Coder from Russia		−0.0195	−0.0538
Coder from Ukraine		0.1929***	0.2121***
Coder from Australia		−0.1030	−0.0901
Constant	4.2621***	4.2173***	3.9060***
N	22,507	2,2451	16,456
R^2	0.01	0.02	0.02

Source: Authors' compilation.
Notes: OLS regression of the amount paid for the coding job. Standard errors adjusted for clustering on buyer, ignoring clustering on coders.
Model A = all cases (and basic predictors)
Model B = all cases (and extended list of predictors)
Model C = all cases where winning coder has a rating
* $p < 0.05$, ** $p < 0.01$, *** $p < 0.001$

greater than 40 percent in table 6.4). Apparently, even though buyers value reputation highly, the structure of the market—consider, for instance, the abundant supply of coders—is such that the net value of a high reputation is much smaller than what buyers would be willing to pay for it. In fact, this may very well be one of the main reasons the effects of reputation found in the empirical literature differ across analyses and are generally small. Such analyses can only consider what reputation is worth in the market (the amount you have to pay extra for a seller with a high reputation), which is not the same as the extent to which buyers value reputation (the amount a buyer would be willing to pay extra for a seller with a high reputation).

Conclusion and Discussion

The dominance of eBay as an auction site and the relatively easy avail-ability of eBay data for research have created the situation in which most empirical work about reputation mechanisms takes eBay as its focus. This has several disadvantages: the available data are not as close to the actual decision-making of the buyer as one might think, which makes es-timating the effect of reputation on probability of sale or on auction end price problematic. Our idea was that this might be the reason researchers find general inconsistencies in the empirical results—in particular, the lack of consistent support for a positive effect of reputation on both prob-ability of sale and end price. We examined whether a positive effect of reputation exists in online data where the data are much closer to the ac-tual decision-making by using data from the programmer's site, RentA-Coder. In this case, we do find strong support for a positive effect of a positive rating on the probability of being chosen as the preferred coder. Buyers value a positive reputation in this market.

An issue to highlight is that the analyses as presented here differ in im-portant ways from the kinds of analyses typically used when the data come from eBay (or another auction platform) in terms of what it is they estimate. In our analyses, we assume the underlying logic of McFadden's choice model and hence model the implicit attractiveness of a bid by a coder as perceived by the buyer. In this model, what we estimate is the ef-fect of reputation (and price, and so on) on the perceived attractiveness of the coder's bid. This allows us to infer and estimate a seller's preference. How much would a seller be willing to pay extra for a partner with a bet-ter reputation? This is fundamentally different from what is being calcu-lated in most other publications, where one uses the prices of the com-pleted eBay auctions and correlates them with the reputation score. In such cases, the researcher estimates what on average a buyer must pay extra to find a partner with a better reputation. Theoretical arguments about the positive effects of reputation are in essence about the prefer-ences of individuals over the reputation scores of others, what you would be willing to pay rather than what you have to pay. This makes using data from RentACoder a more appropriate test of the reputation mechanism. In any case, we show that the results strongly differ. Although buyers are willing to pay up to 40 percent extra for coders with good reputations, the market conditions are such that they have to pay only about 3 to 4 percent extra. Although our data are not necessarily representative for interac-tions on eBay, our results clearly show two important issues. First, one should clearly distinguish theoretically between the effect of reputation on the willingness to buy and on the selling price. These are different entities, and although reputation arguments are basically about the willingness to buy effect, they are usually tested with data on the selling price effect. Second, this discrepancy could be one of the main reasons the effects of reputation on selling price (or probability of sale) are so erratic and generally small. We find something similar in the RentACoder data: a high willingness to pay for reputation, but given the market, no need to do so.

Although our data allow estimating models that are closer to the real life decision-making of people, they are still far from perfect and suffer in part from the same problems as eBay data. For instance, we completely disregard strategic bidding by coders, who might anticipate how many other coders will participate. Coders might also offer extremely low bids to buyers with whom they have never done business, in the hope that the buyer will offer them more business after a successful first job. Nevertheless, our results do suggest that thus far the effect of reputation on trust between buyer and coder in an online environment may have been underestimated, and that incorporating market conditions in the analyses is likely to make the effect of reputation on trust more salient, as was the case in our data.

Notes

1. We gratefully acknowledge support by Ian Ippolito from RentACoder.com, who generously supplied us with the data for this project.
2. eBay Media Center, "About eBay,"available at: http://news.ebay.com/about.cfm, and "Fast Facts," available at: http://news.ebay.com/fastfacts.cfm (accessed January 2008).
3. Available at: http://databases.si.umich.edu/reputations (accessed January 2008).
4. Wang and his colleagues did not consider effects of seller's reputation score on price (2004). Gonzalez and his colleagues did find a nonlinear effect of feedback rating on price, without distinguishing between positive and negative feedback (2004).
5. With the cooperation of eBay, one could try to assess such information about buyers' search behavior to determine the set of options, but even then the strategic arguments with regard to, for instance, the number of potential other buyers, is unavailable.
6. It is also possible to arrange a private auction. That is, a buyer invites only a specific coder to bid on a bid request. Such cases are excluded from the analyses.

References

Dellarocas, Chrysanthos. 2003. "The Digitization of Word-of-Mouth: Promise and Challenges of Online Reputation Mechanisms." *Management Science* 40(10): 1407–24.

Eaton, David H. 2002. "Valuing Information: Evidence from Guitar Auctions on eBay." *Department of Economics and Finance* working paper 0201. Murray, Ky.: Murray State University. Available at: http://databases.si.umich.edu/reputa tions/bib/papers/eatonpaper.pdf (accessed April 5, 2009).

Gonzalez, Raul, Kevin Hasker, and Robin C. Sickles. 2004. "An Analysis of Strategic Behavior in eBay Auctions." Working paper. Houston, Tex.: Rice University. Available at: http://www.ruf.rice.edu/~rsickles/paper/auction.pdf.

Grund, Christian, and Oliver Gürtler. 2006. "The Effect of Reputation on Selling Prices in Auctions." *SFB/TR 15* discussion paper 114. Mannheim, Germany: Governance and the Efficiency of Economic Systems. Available at: http://www.gesy.uni-mannheim.de/dipa/114.pdf.

Hurd, Michael D. 1979. "Estimation in Truncated Samples When There Is Heteroscedasticity." *Journal of Econometrics* 11(2–3): 247–58.

Kauffman, Robert J., and Charles A. Wood 2000. "Running Up the Bid: Modeling Seller Opportunism in Internet Auctions." Paper presented at America's Conference on Information Systems. Long Beach, Calif. (August 10–13).

Lee, Zoonky, Il Im, and San Jun Lee. 2000. "The Effect of Negative Buyer Feedback on Prices in Internet Auction Markets." In *Proceedings of the 21st International Conference on Information Systems*. Brisbane, Australia: International Conference on Information Systems.

Louviere, Jordan J., David A. Hensher, and Joffre D. Swait. 2000. *Stated Choice Methods. Analysis and Application.* Cambridge: Cambridge University Press.

McDonald, Cynthia G., and V. Carlos Slawson Jr. 2002. "Reputation in an Internet Auction Market." *Economic Inquiry* 40(3): 633–50.

McFadden, Daniel. 1974. "Conditional Logit Analysis of Qualitative Choice Behaviour." In *Frontiers in Econometrics*, edited by Paul Zarembka. New York: Academic Press.

Resnick, Paul, Richard Zeckhauser, John Swanson, and Kate Lockwood. 2006. "The Value of Reputation on eBay: A Controlled Experiment." *Experimental Economics* 9(2): 79–101.

Snijders, Chris, and Richard Zijdeman. 2004. "Reputation and Internet Auctions: eBay and Beyond." *Analyse & Kritik* 26(1): 158–84.

Wang, Shanshan, Wolfgang Jank, and Galit Shmueli. 2008. "Explaining and Forecasting Online Auction Prices and Their Dynamics Using Functional Data Analysis." *Journal of Business and Economic Statistics* 26(2): 144–60.

PART III

ASSESSING TRUST AND REPUTATION ONLINE

Chapter 7

Assessing Trustworthiness in Providers

Karen S. Cook, Coye Cheshire,
Alexandra Gerbasi, and Brandy Aven

In this chapter, we examine the factors that individuals use when determining the trustworthiness of exchange partners who provide either goods or services in online environments. We argue that the competence and motivations of the exchange partner are two key bases of individuals' inferences about trustworthiness, particularly when no third-party or credible institutional devices are in place to reduce uncertainty and manage risk. However, we demonstrate that the effects of competence and motivation have different relative degrees of importance in online goods markets than in their service counterparts. We present the results of an exploratory study designed to examine how individuals assess the trustworthiness of others in online markets for goods and services.

Perhaps the main contributing factor to trust relations is the degree to which each party to the exchange views the other as trustworthy. In fact, the link between trust and trustworthiness is so strong that these terms are often confounded in the literature on trust (Hardin 2002; Cook, Hardin, and Levi 2006). The common argument that trust is good can only be true under circumstances in which it is warranted, that is, when the other party to the trust relation is trustworthy. The literature on trust, though varied, seems to converge on several key elements. First, it makes little sense to speak of trust when no uncertainty or risk is involved (Cook et al. 2005). Various types of exchange settings carry different levels of risk and uncertainty (see Molm 2003; Gerbasi 2008). As Carol Heimer has reminded us, risk and vulnerability are central in situations in which trust and trustworthiness play an active role (2001). Furthermore, the degree of uncertainty and risk in the setting often determines the nature of the mechanisms put in place to guard against defection, exploitation, or harm. When the stakes are high, we are unlikely to rely simply on trust relations. We are more likely to use institutional or organizational mechanisms to protect us against betrayal or harm (for a review of such mechanisms or devices that facilitate reliability and cooperation in the absence of trust, see Cook, Hardin, and Levi 2006). In settings where third-party enforcement or verification is not present, it takes time for the appropriate mechanisms to develop.

Relational Trust

Before we discuss how we go about assessing the trustworthiness of others under various conditions, we offer a specific relational definition of trust, building on the work of Russell Hardin (2002) and Karen Cook, Russell Hardin, and Margaret Levi (2006). In a two-party relationship, actor A is said to trust actor B when A views B to be trustworthy with respect to the matters at hand. To use the encapsulated interest view of trust, this means that A views B as trustworthy because B's interests encapsulate her own (Hardin 2002). That is, B is viewed by A as taking her interests to heart, and thus, as likely to act in ways that would not harm or take advantage of her. Although the term *interest* may seem out of place in discussions of trust relations, it is used here in the strong sense that when I trust you I believe that you have taken my interests as partly your own, significantly because you value our relation and its continuation. In the case of continued interaction, therefore, it is often in my interest to act trustworthy with respect to you.

To trust B, however, actor A must be able to make an assessment of B's likely trustworthiness with respect to her in particular situations and with respect to specific matters. We assume that it is rare that A would trust any actor with respect to everything at all times. In the next section, we briefly discuss how actors typically assess the trustworthiness of others in their social environments. Some individuals are more likely to be trusting than others (Rotter 1967, 1980), most likely as a result of their individual propensity for risk-taking, their lack of cautiousness, which varies across cultures as well as individuals (Weber, Hsee, and Sokolowska 1998; Hsee and Weber 1999), or because they have had primarily benign past experiences with new people in new situations.

There are also differences between those who are less cautious or more risk-taking and those who are not in their capacity to differentiate whom to trust from whom not to trust on the basis of specific cues. Toshio Yamagishi and his colleagues call this capacity social intelligence (2001; Yamagishi, Kikuchi, and Kosugi 1999). Because those who are less cautious interact with strangers more often, they are more likely to confirm their expectations concerning the other's trustworthiness more frequently, leading to greater opportunities for profitable interactions over time (Hayashi 1995). Those who are more cautious, on the other hand, typically end up with fewer beneficial transactions due to their lack of willingness to take risks on strangers (Orbell and Dawes 1993). These differences actually lead individuals to be better or worse at assessing the trustworthiness of their likely exchange partners and more or less likely to benefit from exchange under uncertainty.

Assessing Trustworthiness

A number of factors affect our judgments of trustworthiness. These factors include the nature of the situation, such as online or face to face, features of the object of the interaction, such as goods or services, and perceptions of the other party (or provider of the goods and services). If we view trust as *encapsulated interest,* the incentive for trustworthiness is built into the relationship itself if it is valued. The shadow of the future may be enough to ensure trustworthy behavior (Cook et al. 2005). However, it is difficult to determine whether people we come into contact with for the first time will be trustworthy in a particular interaction. If we enter a relationship with a stranger, typically we do so by first taking a minimal risk to gather more information through interaction before investing much in the relationship and eventually taking larger risks (Blau 1964/1986; Cook et al. 2005), especially if the interaction is initially computer mediated rather than face to face.

But how do we know when and with whom to take a risk of cooperating on initial encounter? Making inferences about another person is a general problem for both dimensions of assessing another's likely trustworthiness: competence and motivation. The traits that become salient for individuals who are assessing the trustworthiness of another person fall into two main categories. First, in judging others we tend to focus on cultural stereotypes or socially significant (socially valued) characteristics. Status characteristics such as age, gender, occupation, educational achievement, and race or ethnicity often form the basis for performance expectations and judgments about competence in specific situations, especially in task settings (see Ridgeway and Walker 1995). They may also form the basis of judgments about likely motivations to be trustworthy.

Available cultural stereotypes and schemas fill in for the details we are missing in our efforts to evaluate others. When we are under time pressure, we use stereotype-based inference strategies as cognitive shortcuts (Andersen, Klatzky, and Murray 1990). Under cognitive overload, we even prefer the use of stereotypes, tend to recall information that is consistent with our stereotypes (Macrae, Hewstone, and Griffiths

1993), and fail to process information that disproves them (Dijksterhuis and van Knippenberg 1996). We even generalize on the basis of such socially valued characteristics beyond the evidence at hand when making assessments of competence. Similarly, we often expect that others with these characteristics are more likely to be trustworthy, in the sense that they are competent to manage the matter at hand. It is much harder to evaluate motivations on the basis of these socially valued characteristics, though under some circumstances we do so.

Besides relying on stereotypes, we may make judgments of the trustworthiness of others by assuming that those who are similar to us are trustworthy and that those who are not similar to us are not. In many situations, similarity with respect to one or more statuses may be used "as a clue to probable similarity in opinion, attitude, ability or values" (Singer 1981, 78). Although we may not use these clues very often or when the risk is very great, in some settings such information suffices until better information can be obtained. In settings in which actors have other bases for their judgments of trustworthiness, similarity assessments may play only a minor role (McAllister 1995).

In addition to the presumption of high levels of trustworthiness in individuals with highly valued social characteristics and in similar others, Peter Wason and others have presented findings that support the argument that individuals often have a strong cognitive confirmation-seeking bias in their judgments of others (Wason 1960; Mitroff 1974; Good 1988, 40). Individuals seek evidence that confirms their actions, decisions, and judgments of others rather than weighing the evidence more carefully. This bias is an example of cognitive inertia (see, among others, Good 1988). Because a confirmation bias exists, reputations also can be self-enforcing.[1] Reputations are more likely to be confirmed than disproved even in the face of evidence to the contrary.

The greater likelihood for reputations to be confirmed than disconfirmed occurs because evidence that does not support the reputation, as it is initially perceived, is given less weight (Levin, Wasserman, and Kao 1993). For example, Carmen Huici and her colleagues found that the effect of information that disconfirmed an individual's original evaluation of a group had little impact (1996). In addition, Stephen Standifird studied the impact of reputation in e-commerce and investigated the importance of a trader's reputation on the final bidding price (2001). Although positive reputational ratings were found to be only mildly influential in determining the final bid price, negative reputational ratings were found to be highly influential and detrimental. Standifird thus found "strong evidence for the importance of reputation . . . and equally strong evidence concerning the *exaggerated influence of negative reputation*" (2001, 279, emphasis added). Thus good reputations can become tarnished, but a bad reputation is difficult to overcome.

The two main aspects of trustworthiness that individuals assess when making judgments are competence and motivation. Evaluations of both aspects should be part of every judgment of trustworthiness. However, individuals may focus on competence more than motivation in some cases, as noted, or they may focus mainly on motivation when competence is not particularly at issue. For example, when an individual relies on cultural stereotypes to assess the trustworthiness of another person, she may be focusing on competence, not motivation. Socially valued characteristics (race, age, gender) are often associated with beliefs about greater competence (Berger, Cohen, and Zelditch 1966, 1972), though this may not be objectively true (Balkwell 1994). In contrast, when an individual relies on the degree to which the other person is similar to her, she may be focusing on the motivation of the other party. Perhaps because actors tend to know their own motivations and feel as though these motivations are cooperative and benign, a similar person might be assumed to have similar motivations. Research on social cognition indicates that we frequently use cultural stereotypes as bases for judgments, especially as shortcuts to more complex forms of information processing, and that these judgments can be wrong because they overemphasize stereotypic characteristics of the actors involved. Individuals may even exploit this tendency for their own ends by mimicking traits or manipulating the situation to appear to be trustworthy (see especially Bacharach and Gambetta 2001).

A primary task in the design of social systems is the design of mechanisms for ensuring, reinforcing, and requiring the reliability or trustworthiness of the actors involved. This is also true in constructed social worlds, such as the Internet. We discuss a few of the mechanisms being developed in the world of online interactions to ensure such reliability and to aid in the assessment of the trustworthiness of those we interact with online.

Determinants of Trustworthiness

The problem of determining trustworthiness is a significant obstacle for developing interpersonal relationships, e-commerce transactions, and other forms of exchange in computer-mediated environments such as the Internet. Indeed, the question of how to build trust and encourage trustworthiness on the Internet has led to a substantial amount of research in academia and business. Much of the current empirical work on Internet trust and trustworthiness falls into one of three broad categories: website credibility from design and structure, interpersonal trust in computer-mediated environments, and online reputation systems as a mechanism for assessing trustworthiness. As one might expect, these three overlap and inform one another in a variety of ways. Furthermore, these areas are not necessarily exhaustive of the burgeoning research and literature on trust in online environments. Still, these categories are useful because they help us distinguish between some of the major areas of research in trust, trustworthiness, and computer-mediated interactions.

Website Design and Structure

The research on trustworthy website design and structure deals with the features, layout, and overall look of websites that promote or facilitate trust or perceptions of reliability. In this line of research, the concept of trust is more closely aligned with credibility and reliability of information rather than the relational forms of trust reviewed earlier. Understanding the factors that influence assessments of trust in websites and online systems is a multidisciplinary problem that links social science, computer science, and information science (Rieh and Danielson 2007).

Many individuals admit to making intuitive or emotional decisions based on their perceptions of a website (Karvonen 2000; Fogg 2003). The features of websites that actually promote perceptions of trustworthiness, however, are of great interest to researchers. A significant amount of this work is oriented toward issues that include ease of use (Gefen, Karahanna, and Straub 2003) and the navigational structure (Vance, Elie-Dit-Cosaque, and Straub 2008) of websites and online systems. Current research demonstrates that graphic, structure, content, and social-cue design are all essential in establishing the trustworthiness of a website (see Wang and Emurian 2005; Fogg 2003).

In a review of online trust issues in business-to-consumer transactions on the Internet, Ye Diana Wang and Henry Emurian described four characteristics of online trust in e-commerce (2005). First, the *truster* in this context is usually a consumer who is browsing an e-commerce website. Second, consumers must deal with larger degrees of uncertainty in online transactions than in analogous offline situations because the Internet environment leaves consumers open to both financial loss and potential privacy losses (see also Friedman, Kahn, and Howe 2000). Third, consumer trust leads to at least two specific actions: making a purchase and browsing additional website content. Thus, consumers who decide that a website is trustworthy will spend more time there and engage in financial transactions. Finally, Wang and Emurian argued that online trust is a subjective matter that varies between individuals (2005). In this last regard, online trust is no different from trust in offline interactions.

Intel Corporation and the Center for eBusiness at MIT conducted several experiments to examine trustworthiness as it relates to website design. The researchers examined several factors believed to be important in trust formation at an online business website. The most important aspects include privacy, security, error-free code, brand recognition, touch-

and-feel, available help, well-organized navigation, and the display of trust seals (Intel Corporation 2003).[2] The researchers used measurements of click-streams, that is, objective data about the content a given visitor views during a website visit. In addition, visitors elected to answer survey questions about their experience on the site. Among the many findings of this study, researchers found that third-party trust seals slightly increase user perception of the site's security, especially when the visitor is a novice. Furthermore, ease of navigation increases overall trust in the website. Using an adaptive experimental design on a commercial site, the researchers were able to reach thousands of individual users in a relatively short time compared to the dozens who might participate in a comparable lab study. Corporate and academic research groups such as the Intel-MIT collaboration and the Stanford Web Credibility Project continue to look at human motivations and design factors that influence credibility and trustworthiness as the delivery of online content evolves over time.[3]

Interpersonal Trust

The second primary area of research in online trust deals with interpersonal relationships. Early studies show that the development of trust in interpersonal environments is distinctly different from building trust in e-commerce settings (see, for example, Friedman, Kahn, and Howe 2000; Sproull and Kiesler 1991). Interpersonal communication environments may include, but are not limited to, online message boards (including forums and the USENET), e-mail discussions, and instant messaging systems.

One line of research investigates the effect of meeting individuals before interacting in online interactions. Not surprisingly, a face-to-face meeting before interacting in a computer-mediated social dilemma game helps promote trust (Rocco 1998). Furthermore, if individuals are given the opportunity to become acquainted with one another over a computer-mediated computer network, trust increases in text communication environments (Zheng et al. 2002). When analyzed separately, video, audio and face-to-face communication can lead to higher levels of trust than pure text chat. Additionally, video and audio communications are almost as good for building trust as face-to-face communication (Bos et al. 2002). As with many studies in this area, the findings suggest differences in assessments of trust between forms of mediated communication. However, the exact choice and use of communication technologies for the purpose of developing trust in real-world situations is a focal area for continuing research (see Riegelsberger, Sasse, and McCarthy 2007).

Jinjuan Feng, Jonathan Lazar, and Jennifer Preece investigated the role of empathetic accuracy in the construction of interpersonal trust in online environments (2004). Drawing on Ickes's definition, the researchers characterized empathetic accuracy as "the ability to accurately infer the specific content of other people's thoughts and feelings" (Ickes 1993; Feng, Lazar, and Preece 2004, 99). In addition, they examine the difference between supportive and nonsupportive response types. The researchers find that empathetic accuracy alone does not guarantee trust in these online environments. To establish trustworthiness in an online setting, an individual must correctly infer the feeling of others as well as provide supportive responses. One of the most intriguing findings from Feng, Lazar, and Preece's research is that individuals with higher levels of generalized trust may have more difficulty developing trust in online environments.[4] The reason for this discrepancy remains an open question for further investigation.

Another area of research examines how human warmth and social presence in Web interfaces can affect online trust. Khaled Hassanein and Milena Head varied the levels of socially rich text and visual design elements to investigate how they might affect the development of trust in online settings (2004). This empirical test shows that socially rich text and pictures on websites positively affect an individual's assessment of the website's trustworthiness.[5] This line of research draws links between the development of interpersonal trust as well as trust in website design and content. Individuals appear to identify and relate to content on the Internet when it triggers a social response. Thus building environments that evoke social presence may be an essential part of establishing trustworthiness in online environments.

Online Reputation Systems

The third major area of research in online trust deals with reputation systems in computer-mediated communication. As one of the first studies of online reputations, Peter Kollock's research identifies online Internet auctions as a convenient environment for the study of risk management when there is little or no access to third party enforcement. In many of these situations, no guarantees, warranties, or other third-party enforcement mechanisms are available (1999). Thus, endogenous reputation systems are a potential solution to the risks created in these online environments. In these cases, Kollock argued that risk is often the possibility of fraud, which is particularly common on auction sites.[6]

The type of reputation system used in a particular situation may affect the development of trust and trustworthiness in online exchange systems. Toshio Yamagishi and his colleagues examine in chapter 3 of this volume the role of experience-based (endogenous) and third-party (exogenous) reputation systems in online interactions. They also examine the advantages and disadvantages of both positive and negative reputation systems. When individuals have permanent identities, both experience-based and third-party reputation systems can help establish trustworthiness. However, the ability to switch identities, a common feature of most Internet environments, repeals the advantages of these reputation systems. Positive reputation systems appear to be more effective in open systems, which new participants can enter easily. On the other hand, negative reputation systems are more successful at establishing trustworthiness in closed systems, which new participants cannot easily access. Yamagishi and his colleagues demonstrate how these systems operate in a controlled laboratory experiment that emulates an online auction site.

Endogenous reputation systems have been cited as a way to determine trustworthiness in information asymmetric markets, such as the online market eBay (Kollock 1999; Snijders and Zijdeman 2004; chapters 3 and 5, this volume). In most cases, the term *reputation* has been used synonymously with *status*. Although they commonly converge in natural settings, however, reputation is conceptually distinct. For instance, a reputation is an evaluative measure, commonly associated with a normative valuation of past behavior (Wilson 1985). For example, we may describe a particular seller as always willing to go the extra mile for a buyer or being the most knowledgeable about the product. Status, on the other hand, is an ordinal ranking of actors based on resources and performance expectations, and not necessarily on past actions. Here we are concerned with the effect of reputations for trustworthiness.

Reputations help individuals overcome a lack of information about a potential partner. Information asymmetry occurs when one party, typically a seller, is privy to more information than another party, usually a buyer (Akerlof 1970). To guard against the risk of uncertainty in information asymmetric markets, actors may seek out signals that indicate partner trustworthiness or product quality (Kollock 1999; Podolny 1993). Michael Spence defined a signal as an observable indicator of quality that must meet two criteria (1973). First, the actor must be able to, at least in part, manipulate the signal. This ability is in contrast to other actor's characteristics that may be fixed, such as age or gender. Second, the difficulty of acquiring the indicator must be nonzero and inversely associated with the actor's quality grade (Spence 1973).

As stated, reputations represent information over which the individual has at least some control. Generally, reputations are empirical statements about past behavior with a predictive quality, such as, "this seller has always been honest in the past." In addition, reputations have different qualitative values, such as being honest or hardworking. This research focuses on reputations for trustworthiness because of its principal role in one-shot transactions. Assuming that others in the market believe that past behavior strongly indicates or predicts future behavior, a reputation for trustworthiness indicates to others that in future transactions the actor can be trusted (Fudenberg and Levine 1992; Kollock 1994; Wilson 1985). In short, for information asymmetric markets, reputation acts as a signal that reduces uncertainty in exchange.

Online interactions such as buying and selling on Internet auction sites can be conducted anonymously, which makes assessing trustworthiness problematic for both buyers and sellers. Various studies have investigated the effects of reputation systems, especially eBay's feedback system, as a source of information to determine the trustworthiness of online partners and as a mechanism to deter opportunistic behavior (Dellarocas 2003; Livingston and Evans 2005; Lucking-Reiley et al. 2007; Resnick and Zeckhauser 2002; Resnick et al. 2006). For the most part, this research has focused on buyers verifying the trustworthiness of sellers of products, such as guitars, vintage postcards and collectable cards (Eaton 2002; Lucking-Reiley et al. 2000; Resnick et al. 2006).

As researchers begin to disentangle the effects of reputation for online transactions, it becomes apparent that buyers on eBay and other online auction sites use complex decision-making processes in establishing seller trustworthiness. In general, an increasing positive reputation does have a measurable effect on increasing the item auction price and increases the likelihood of a sale (Eaton 2002; Lucking-Reiley et al. 2007; Resnick and Zeckhauser 2002). Paul Resnick and his colleagues also found that sellers with established reputations outperform new sellers; however, buyers do not simply look to a cumulative or overall score to determine the trustworthiness of online sellers (2006). David Lucking-Reiley and his colleagues found that buyers do not weigh negative and positive feedback equally and that negative feedback produced a greater effect on auction price than positive feedback (2007). Moreover, the research by Resnick and his colleagues showed that early negative points of one or two for a new seller did not dramatically affect buyers' willingness to pay (2006). In sum, these studies indicate that buyers use a sophisticated process to evaluate reputation information that researchers are just beginning to understand.

Exchange Partners in Goods and Services Markets

In many types of interaction situations, individuals must make a single, one-shot decision about whether to engage in an exchange or not with someone else. For example, an individual who wants to purchase a good or service through an online system must decide whether or not to risk sending money to a given seller without the aid of information from previous interactions. Thus, the problem is not about the construction of trust, because trust-building requires iterated interactions, but whether the individuals correctly assess the trustworthiness of the other person (Hardin 2003). Given that individuals cannot collect information about their partner through ongoing interactions, the assessment of trustworthiness must come from other information.

In one-shot decisions about trustworthiness in online settings, the nature of the object of exchange is an important factor. As our earlier discussion of research demonstrates, the relative risks involved in a given exchange—that is, value of the good, uncertainty about the quality of the good—are intimately tied to the possibility of trust. We argue that another key dimension is whether the object of exchange is part of a goods or a services market. Goods and services are often grouped as potential objects of exchange in offline as well as online environments. However, evidence is ample that individuals treat goods and services differently—not just because of variations in uncertainty, but because of the very nature of the relationship between the individual and the good or service.

One early effort to create a typology of exchange goods is resource exchange theory, which attempts to identify the structure of the exchange interactions between individuals by classifying the nature of resources exchanged (Foa and Foa 1974). These resources include a wide array of items such as love, services, money, goods, status, and information. This research focused on how these resources are exchanged in various patterns of rewards and punishments in interpersonal relationships. Uriel and Edna Foa's research focused on dyadic, reciprocal exchanges in an early attempt to investigate the importance of the nature of the specific resources, such as goods versus services, involved in exchange relationships (1974). They also studied the norms regarding the extent to which specific types of resources could be exchanged, such as money for goods but not for love, or status for information, and so on.

Physical goods are generally considered tangible and come with ownership rights (Hill 1999; Fuchs 1968; Sabolo 1975). Because of the transferability of ownership rights, physical goods can be exchanged from one owner to the next. Thus a good is an entity that exists independently from its owner and its identity is preserved across time. On the other hand, services are generally considered intangible and do not come with ownership rights (Fuchs 1968; Sabolo 1975). Many services consist of material changes in the persons or property of consumers, such as haircuts, surgery, house painting, website development, and so on. Because the services do not create entities, it is either extremely difficult or impossible to transfer ownership rights for the service.

A crucial distinction between goods and services is that services entail an implied relationship between two or more individuals, whereas goods do not necessarily. Services involve relationships between producers (service providers) and consumers (service recipients) because a service cannot, by definition, exist without both parties. The production of a service requires the agreement, cooperation, and possibly active participation of the consuming unit or units. Because services imply an interactive process and a relationship between the producer and the consumer, the motivation to work with a customer may be particularly important when an actor chooses a service provider rather than a provider of goods. We examine this potential difference in a later section.

Peter Mills and Dennis Mobert pointed out two characteristics of service operations that derive from the intangibility of the output from different service providers (1982). First, customers have few objective reference points when attempting to perceive the value of the services they use. The intangibility of services makes them elusive to both providers and consumers: services can be difficult to describe to new customers, and customers often find it challenging to express precisely what they expect from the service (Oliva and Sterman 2001). There may not be an agreed objective standard about the service to be delivered; the only criteria available to evaluate service quality are subjective comparisons of customers' expectations to their perceptions of the actual service delivered (Zeithaml, Parasuraman, and Berry 1990). To help ease the uncertainty that can arise from this discrepancy, service providers often try to socially construct value for the customer (Butler 1980).[7] For these reasons, the reduction of uncertainty through trust becomes increasingly necessary between the consumer and the service provider (Hasenfeld 1978). Reputation information about the service provider might be useful here, yet the ambiguity between what a consumer needs and what a given service provider offers makes it difficult to determine what kind of reputation information is beneficial in a given situation.

The second important issue is that the intangibility of services tends to put the burden on the service provider to make the relationships between customers and service providers satisfying to customers (Schneider 1991; Schneider, Parkington, and Buxton 1980). Mary Jo Bitner and her colleagues found that customers appreciate services that allow providers to adjust and adapt to the customer's needs (Bitner, Brown, and Meuter 2000). But how is the ability to adapt expressed to potential service consumers? Again, some kind of reputation information that a consumer can use when seeking a service provider seems like a logical answer. In the absence of comprehensive third-party reputation information that might meet all of a consumer's information needs, however, the burden falls on the service provider to supply relevant information to the consumer.

Given the many differences between goods and services, it is reasonable to believe that individuals are likely to use different information to assess the trustworthiness of goods versus service providers. Third-party reputations such as those found in online systems like eBay (chapters 3 and 5, this volume) and RentACoder (chapter 6) are good examples of online reputation systems that help consumers make informed decisions about the trustworthiness of goods and service providers, respectively. In many online systems of exchange, however, no third-party reputations are available. In online systems such as Craigslist, for example, sellers offer goods or services in a bulletin-board style setting without any structured reputation tracking system in place. In this kind of situation, consumers have extremely limited information when assessing the trustworthiness of sellers. Without built-in reputation systems, rating systems, or extensive context cues, how do individuals evaluate the trustworthiness of potential exchange partners in online one-shot interactions? To investigate this question, we turn to an exploratory study.

An Empirical Study of Assessments

Here we present some of the key findings from a study that examines how individuals assess the trustworthiness of those who provide goods and services in online environments without the aid of third-party reputation mechanisms. This study is a quasi-experimental survey distributed to undergraduates at a private university in the United States. Respondents rated, ranked, and made a single selection for the most trustworthy seller after reading various listings from online sellers of a good or service. The respondents also answered several general questions about assessing trustworthiness in online goods or service markets. Finally, respondents answered a few open-ended questions about how and why they made their choices.

Study Design

Sixty-four undergraduates signed up to take the short online survey about online sales. First, the respondents registered by completing a short questionnaire. One week later, the survey was distributed by e-mail. Thirty-three respondents were given the goods survey and thirty-one the services survey. In both surveys, respondents were asked to read four descriptions from sellers attempting to sell the same product or service, a camera valued at $1,500 or a web design service valued at $1,500. Using only the text descriptions given by each seller, the respondents were then asked to rate and rank the sellers in terms of their perceived trustworthiness. The descriptions varied according to the competence and motivations of the sellers. Because the object was a high-end camera and the service was web design services, competence was operationalized as established professional photographer or established web designer (high competence) and amateur photographer or amateur web designer (low competence). Motivation was operationalized as the degree to which the seller cares about the buyer's interests. Thus sellers with high motivation express an interest in working directly with the sellers to make a successful sale, and sellers with low motivation express an interest only in selling to the highest bidder. Together, the high and low conditions for competence and motivation created four possible combinations (or experimental conditions in a 2×2 fully crossed design). Table 7.1 presents a description of each of the four seller types in the goods and services surveys.

Assessing Online Sellers

To understand how individuals assess the trustworthiness of online sellers' descriptions in the absence of other information, we compared the respondents' selection of the seller that they believed was the most trustworthy. Figure 7.1 shows the mean choice of the most trustworthy seller, by survey type, either goods or services.

The proportions for the four seller types are significantly different within the goods survey ($x^2 = 16.1$, $p < .001$) and within the services survey ($x^2 = 26.7$, $p < .001$). The most apparent result from the mean responses shown in figure 7.1 is that the respondents in both survey types chose seller A (high competence and high motivation) as the most trustworthy seller, compared to the other possible choices. Specifically, 55 percent of the respondents in the goods survey and 61 percent of the respondents in the services survey chose seller A as the most trustworthy, as anticipated. On the other hand, only 12 percent of the respondents in the goods survey and 3.2 percent of the respondents in the services survey chose seller B (low competence and low motivation). The mean choices for neither seller A nor seller B differ significantly between the two survey types. In other words, respondents significantly chose seller A more than seller B in both the goods and services surveys, and did so at about the same levels. Respondents tended to select the high competence and high motivation seller as the most trustworthy. These findings generally support existing theory and research, which argues that both competence and motivation are related components that individuals use when assessing the trustworthiness of others.

Some important differences also occur between the remaining sellers and the two survey types. Twenty-one percent of the respondents in the goods survey and only 6.5 percent of those in the services survey chose seller C (high competence, low motivation) as the most trustworthy. This disparity (15 percent) is moderately significant ($x^2 = 2.9$, $p = .08$). Furthermore, 29 percent of the services survey respondents and only 12 percent of their goods survey counterparts chose seller D (low competence, high motivation) as the most trustworthy. This difference (17 percent) is also moderately significant ($x^2 = 2.82$, $p = .08$). Thus it appears

Table 7.1   Buyer Descriptions for Online Sales by Competence and Motivation

Manipulations	Goods Survey	Services Survey
High competence High motivation	I am selling a brand new Nikon D70 Camera. I am a professional photographer and I use this same camera in my own work. Please contact me directly if you are interested, I can work with you to make it a worthwhile purchase.	I am selling custom website photography and graphic design for your website. I am a professional graphic artist with my own firm. Please contact me directly if you are interested - I am open to discussing client needs before the service is purchased.
Low competence Low motivation	Hi, I have a Nikon D70 Camera for sale— brand new condition. I got it as a gift, and I really don't know much about photography. Best offer gets it.	Hi, I am offering custom web photography and graphic design. I recently switched careers and am beginning my own website design practice. Best offer gets it.
High competence Low motivation	I have a Nikon D70 Camera for sale. It is in brand-new condition. I am a professional photographer and I can say it is a great camera. I will sell to the highest bidder.	I am offering my services for custom website photography and design for your website. I run a professional website design firm. Please contact me after you successfully win the bid.
Low competence High motivation	Nikon D70 Camera for sale, brand new. I don't really take pictures that often so I don't need it. I would like to sell, so reply to me directly and we can work something out. Thanks.	Custom website photography and graphic design for sale. I am a new designer in the business. I would really like to develop my portfolio, so reply to me directly and we can discuss your requirements. I am sure we can work something out. Thanks.

Source: Authors' compilation.

Figure 7.1   Percentage Choice of Most Trustworthy Seller

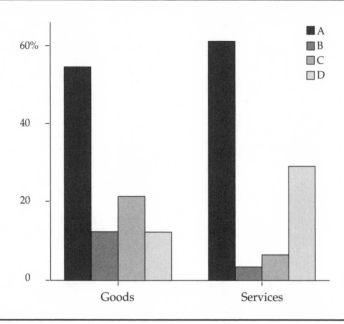

Source: Authors' compilation.
Notes: Seller A=high competence, high motivation; Seller B=low competence, low motivation; Seller C=high competence, low motivation; Seller D=low competence, high motivation.

that goods survey respondents tended to favor high competence but low motivation more so than services survey respondents did. Yet the inverse is also supported: services survey respondents tended to favor high motivation but low competence more so than goods survey respondents.

We also asked respondents in the two survey types to indicate how much they believed in their selection of the most trustworthy good or service provider by investing $0 to $5 in their choice. This investment money came from the original $10 participation payment. The participants were told that if they correctly identified the most trustworthy good or service provider, the experimenter would double their investment.[8] Thus, the investment amount is a good indicator of one's confidence in her choice. The average investment in the goods condition was $2.94 (SD 1.9) and $2.87 (SD 1.9) in the services condition. An ANOVA with the investment amount as the dependent variable and the survey version (goods or services) as the independent variable confirmed that the difference was not significant, $F (1, 62) = .02$, $p =$ ns. More important, there was no significant difference once we also controlled for the individual choice of the most trustworthy provider (A through D), as well as the interactions between choice and experimental condition. These results indicate that all participants were fairly confident in their choice, regardless of the condition or their selection of the most trustworthy provider.

The combined results from this study suggest that competence and motivation are indeed important to individuals who are attempting to assess the trustworthiness of online goods and service providers. In particular, sellers with both high competence and high motivation are more likely to be selected as the most trustworthy, especially over their counterparts with low competence and low motivation. Yet evidence that competence and motivation might work differently in some online goods versus service markets is also notable. Among respondents who selected sellers with differential levels of competence and motivation, high competence tended to be favored over motivation in the goods market and high motivation over competence in the services market. This reflects to some extent the relational aspect of the service market, as noted earlier.

Qualitative Responses and Decision-Making Processes

The respondents in both surveys provided open-ended responses to questions about how they chose the most trustworthy seller. To analyze these data, we first examined all the responses for common themes, reasoning, and explanations. Then we sorted the responses by survey type and selection of the most trustworthy seller (A through D). This procedure allowed us to compare the emergent themes to see whether any differences between relevant groups were consistent.

Responses to the Goods Survey

Among the respondents who participated in the online goods survey, we first examined those who chose seller C (high competence, low motivation). As the quantitative analysis shows, the goods respondents chose seller C more often than their services counterparts. If respondents were focusing on the competence of the seller as the most salient characteristic, we assume it should show up more often in their responses when they choose the high-competence seller (C or A). In fact, this was often clearly indicated when the respondents identified the seller as a professional photographer:

Goods, seller C: "I trust professional photographers, and the people who just wanted to sell their camera seemed less trustworthy because they gave a poor excuse for not needing the camera."

In some cases, the respondents inferred other information from the fact that seller C was a self-described professional. The competence of the seller, for example, was sometimes extended to how he or she may have taken care of the good (that is, the camera). Furthermore, the lack of motivation to directly work with the buyer was sometimes viewed as a positive attribute:

Goods, seller C: "He says he is a professional photographer so he probably has taken good care of the camera. Moreover, he is straightforward and says that the highest bidder will get the item, thus avoiding the hassle of having to bargain."

As the quantitative analysis demonstrates, seller A was chosen as the most trustworthy seller most often in both the goods and services surveys. Thus, an important question is what specific aspect or aspects of seller A was most important to respondents in the goods survey. That is, given that seller A's description includes high competence and high motivation, it would be interesting to know whether respondents focused on one or both of these features. Not surprisingly, many respondents in the goods survey who chose seller A tended to mention both competence and motivational factors:

Goods, seller A: "This seller sounded professional and knowledgeable. They also were willing to talk to the buyer and make a good deal rather than just selling the camera to the highest bidder."

Goods, seller A: "I picked my choice based on the fact that the seller said that they were a professional photographer and trusted this camera [sic]. Also the seller said they could work with the buyer in making the purchase, which added a sense of friendliness."

Goods, seller A: "A didn't seem to be an overly aggressive sell, but tried to make some claim of knowledge."

In fact, the most common response for those who chose seller A in the goods survey was some combination of competence and motivation. Although this is not surprising, given that the descriptions were designed to embody these two characteristics, that respondents who chose seller A in the goods survey tended to mention competence factors first was surprising. Furthermore, when individuals in the goods survey mentioned only one factor for seller A, it was almost always competence related:

Goods, seller A: "The one with the most experience. Most professional ad."

Goods, seller A: "He is a professional photographer."

Goods, seller A: "This seller seemed to have a lot of experience in the area, and would probably know more than the others, since he/she is a professional."

Responses to the Services Survey

In the quantitative analysis, we observed that respondents who took the services survey chose seller D (low competence, high motivation) more often than the respondents in the goods survey did. Just as we were interested in why individuals chose seller C in the goods survey, we wanted to investigate whether the respondents who chose seller D in the services survey would focus on motivational factors more than competence factors. In fact, the survey responses support this supposition:

Services, seller D: "This seller sounded the most personable; eager to offer his services not solely for his own profit."

Services, seller D: "The language of their ad: how sincere they actually sounded. Seller D used 'really' and seemed most willing to please the customer."

As with respondents in the goods survey, individuals in the services survey were more likely to choose seller A as the most trustworthy seller compared to the other sellers, and tended to mention both competence and motivation when they chose seller A. However, we also noticed an interesting detail: just as respondents in the survey on goods who chose seller A tended to mention competence factors first, respondents in the survey on services tended to mention motivational factors first. This difference consistently appeared throughout the open-ended responses:

Services, seller A: "The person was open to discussing the transaction before it took place. They also said they were a professional graphic/web designer, unlike two of the others, who were just starting out on this career."

Services, seller A: "A willingness to accommodate needs met before price set, one on one [sic] interaction. These things mean that there is no hiding behind corporate tape. When you're dealing with a real person you establish a relationship with them, which hopefully increases their trustworthiness."

> Services, seller A: "The most trustworthy to me was the one that put the client's needs before selling the product. The company did not seem pushy or nonchalant. This company was also not one that claimed to be new to the business, and therefore may have more practice."

It is important to note that just because a respondent mentions one characteristic before the other does not necessarily indicate that the first one mentioned is always the most important item. Still, we view this observation as a suggestive finding in the absence of alternative explanations. To be sure, in the actual text from the sellers (figure 7.1), the descriptions in both surveys always started with competence factors before motivational factors. Thus we can be relatively confident that the difference in observed order is at least not due to any operational difference in the descriptions provided in the two surveys.

Implications and Future Research

Our exploratory study has demonstrated that potential customers in online goods and service markets are likely to evaluate and view information that contributes to their capacity to evaluate two key aspects of reliability or trustworthiness of the vendor or supplier as important. These two dimensions include competence of the vendor to provide high quality goods and services, as well as their motivation to not take advantage of the customer. Both dimensions are hardest to communicate in an online world of exchange because there are no face-to-face cues or any history of interaction to reassure the first-time customer or consumer. Studying these first-time interactions, however, is important because they are often the key to the success of online goods and service markets. Appealing to complete strangers, such as new customers, is not an easy task in any type of market.

Our data suggest that though both key dimensions of perceived trustworthiness, competence and motivation, are central to consumer judgments, the relative importance of each dimension varies depending on the nature of the market. In particular, in markets for services it appears that information that offers cues about the motivation of the provider is more salient than information about competence. For goods markets, the reverse seems to be true. Thus the potential quality of the good is more important than information about the motivation of the provider, though clearly this is also relevant information, as indicated by the overall choice of the provider who meets both criteria as the most frequent selection by all subjects in the study.

An important limitation of our study is that it deals with the single domain of media production. Specifically, our fictional online sellers provide cameras and Web-photography services. We chose these two examples because they were comparable within the domain of media production, yet this choice also limits the generalizability of the exploratory findings. It is fair to assume that in other domains we might find different results. However, as we have argued throughout this chapter, such differences would most likely derive from alterations in the levels of uncertainty and risk in these domains, as opposed to substantive differences between the domains. Future research should investigate how assessments of trustworthiness differ across domains and, more important, identify the specific factors that may account for these differences.

Using these data as baseline, we intend to further investigate the relative importance of the types of cues that provide useful information for assessments of trustworthiness, especially to first-time customers. It is clear that variation in what is at stake in the transaction matters. The market for diamonds is very different from the market for cameras or even cars. Similarly, the market for professional legal and medical services is very different from the market for computer programming or auditing services. In many of these examples, the line between what is a good and what is a service is often blurred. Sometimes physical goods are fused with associated services, such as the retail market for diamonds, where value is often determined by the appraisal services before purchase. Additionally, some services, such as auto repair, imply the purchase and use of auto parts. It seems probable that the factors that influence how individuals assess the trustworthiness of online sellers are not stringently defined by just the goods versus service market dichotomy. Systematic study of these variations will help us sort out the relative importance and weights assigned to particular pieces of information in assessments of trustworthiness.

Varying the nature of the good or service and the risk involved in completing an exchange online will be important avenues for continued research. Future research should also include analysis of the effects of combined elements identified in previous research, including web design, type of information sources and content, and assessments of the providers of the goods or services—including reputation. Finally, developing new research tools for analyzing the information respondents find most useful in making judgments of trustworthiness will enable us to understand more fully how information contributes to decision-making in online markets for goods and services.

Notes

1. We discuss the role of reputations more fully later in the chapter.
2. Trust seals are brandings for third-party companies that ensure the trustworthiness of online content.
3. Available at: http://credibility.stanford.edu.

4. In this study, Julian Rotter's trust scale was used to measure generalized trust before the experimental manipulation (1967).

5. The outcome of online trust was measured with four Likert-scale questions about the honesty of the online vendor, the trustworthiness of the online vendor, how much the online vendor cares about customers, and whether the online vendor would likely provide good service.

6. Gary Bolton, Elena Katok, and Axel Ockenfels (2004) cited several examples of the rise of such fraud, including evidence from a U.S. Department of Justice survey (2002) and the National White Collar Crime Center and FBI report (2001).

7. Social psychological theory and research has also demonstrated that perceptual cues are often ambiguous (for example, Berger and Luckmann 1966; Festinger 1954). Like other similar environments, it is reasonable to assume that client perceptions are subject to several competing social influences in service markets.

8. Because there was no one most trustworthy good or service provider, all subjects received an equal bonus regardless of how much they invested or which provider they chose.

References

Akerlof, George A. 1970. "The Market for 'Lemons': Quality Uncertainty and the Market Mechanism." *Quarterly Journal of Economics* 89(3): 488–500.

Andersen, Susan M., Roberta L. Klatzky, and John Murray. 1990. "Traits and Social Stereotypes: Efficiency Differences in Social Information Processing." *Journal of Personality and Social Psychology* 59(2): 192–201.

Bacharach, Michael, and Diego Gambetta. 2001. "Trust in Signs." In *Trust in Society*, edited by Karen S. Cook. New York: Russell Sage Foundation.

Balkwell, James W. 1994. "Status." In *Group Processes: Sociological Analyses*, edited by Margaret Foschi and Edward J. Lawler. Chicago: Nelson-Hall Publishers.

Berger, Joseph, Bernard P. Cohen, and Morris Zelditch Jr. 1966. "Status Characteristics and Expectation States." In *Sociological Theories in Progress*, vol. 1, edited by Joseph Berger, Morris Zelditch Jr., and Bo Anderson. Boston: Houghton Mifflin.

———. 1972. "Status Characteristics and Social Interaction." *American Sociological Review* 37(3): 241–55.

Berger, Peter L., and Thomas Luckmann. 1966. *The Social Construction of Reality*. Garden City, N.Y.: Doubleday.

Bitner, Mary Jo, Stephen W. Brown, and Matthew L. Meuter. 2000. "Technology Infusion in Service Encounters." *Journal of the Academy of Marketing Science* 28(1): 138–49.

Blau, Peter M. 1964/1986. *Exchange and Power in Social Life*. New York: John Wiley & Sons.

Bolton, Gary E., Elena Katok, and Axel Ockenfels. 2004. "How Effective Are Electronic Reputation Mechanisms? An Experimental Investigation." *Management Science* 50(11): 1587–602.

Bos, Nathan, Judy Olson, Darren Gergle, Gary Olson, and Zach Wright. 2002.

"Effects of Four Computer-Mediated Communication Channels on Trust Development." In *Proceedings of the SIGCHI Conference on Human Factors in Computing Systems 2002: Changing Our World, Changing Ourselves*, edited by Dennis Wixon. New York: ACM.

Butler, Richard J. 1980. "User Satisfaction with a Service: An Approach from Power and Task Characteristics." *Journal of Management Studies* 17(1): 1–18.

Cook, Karen S., Russell Hardin, and Margaret Levi. 2006. *Cooperation without Trust*. New York: Russell Sage Foundation.

Cook, Karen S., Toshio Yamagishi, Coye Cheshire, Robin Cooper, M. Matsuda, and R. Mashima. 2005. "Trust Building via Risk Taking: A Cross-Societal Experiment." *Social Psychology Quarterly* 68(2): 121–42.

Dellarocas, Chrysanthos. 2003. "Efficiency and Robustness of Binary Online Feedback Mechanisms in Environments with Moral Hazard." Sloan School of Management working paper 4297–03. Cambridge, Mass.: Massachusetts Institute of Technology.

Dijksterhuis, Ap, and Ad van Kippenberg. 1996. "Trait Implications as a Moderator of Recall of Stereotype-Consistent and Stereotype-Inconsistent Behaviors." *Personality and Social Psychology Bulletin* 22(4): 425–32.

Eaton, David H. 2002. "Valuing Information: Evidence from Guitar Auctions on eBay." Department of Economics and Finance working paper 0201. Murray, Ky.: Murray State University. Available at: http://databases.si.umich.edu/reputations/bib/papers/eatonpaper.pdf (accessed April 5, 2009).

Feng, Jinjuan, Jonathan Lazar, and Jennifer Preece. 2004. "Interpersonal Trust and Empathy Online." *Behaviour and Information Technology* 23(2): 97–106.

Festinger, Leon. 1954. "A Theory of Social Comparison Processes." *Human Relations* 7(2): 117–40.

Foa, Uriel G., and Edna B. Foa. 1974. *Societal Structures of the Mind*. Springfield, Ill.: Thomas.

Fogg, B. J. 2003. "Prominence-Interpretation Theory: Explaining How People Assess Credibility Online." In *CHI '03 Extended Abstracts on Human Factors in Computing Systems*. New York: ACM.

Friedman, Batya, Peter Kahn, and Daniel Howe. 2000. "Trust Online." *Communications of the ACM* 43(12): 34–40.

Fuchs, Victor R. 1968. *The Service Economy*. New York: Columbia University Press.

Fudenberg, Drew, and David K. Levine. 1992. "Maintaining a Reputation When Strategies Are Imperfectly Observed." *Review of Economic Studies* 59(3): 561–79.

Gerbasi, Alexandra. 2008. *Attribution and Commitment in Different Types of Exchange*. Saarbrücken, Germany: VDM.

Gefen, David, Elena Karahanna, and Detmar W. Straub. 2003. "Trust and TAM in Online Shopping: An Integrated Model." *MIS Quarterly* 27(1): 51–90.

Good, David. 1988. "Individuals, Interpersonal Relations and Trust." In *Trust: Making and Breaking Cooperative Relations*, edited by Diego Gambetta. New York: Blackwell Publishers.

Hardin, Russell. 2002. *Trust and Trustworthiness*. New York: Russell Sage Foundation.

———. 2003. "Gaming Trust." In *Trust and Reciprocity: Interdisciplinary Lessons from Experimental Research*, edited by Elinor Ostrom and James Walker. New York: Russell Sage Foundation.

Hasenfeld, Yeheskel. 1978. "Client-Organization Relations: A Systems Perspective." In *The Management of Human Services*, edited by Rosemary C. Sarri and Yeheskel Hasenfeld. New York: Columbia University Press.

Hassanein, Khaled S., and Milena M. Head. 2004. "Building Online Trust through Socially Rich Web Interfaces." Presented to the Second Annual Conference on Privacy, Security, and Trust. Fredericton, New Brunswick, Canada (October 13–15).

Hayashi, Nahoko. 1995. "Emergence of Cooperation in One-Shot Prisoner's Dilemmas and the Role of Trust." *Japanese Journal of Psychology* 66(3): 184–90.

Heimer, Carol. 2001. "Solving the Problem of Trust." In *Trust in Society*, edited by Karen S. Cook. New York: Russell Sage Foundation.

Hill, Peter. 1999. "Tangibles, Intangibles and Services: A New Taxonomy for the Classification of Output." *Canadian Journal of Economics* 32(2): 426–47.

Hsee, Christopher K., and Elke U. Weber. 1999. "Cross-National Differences in Risk Preference and Lay Preferences." *Journal of Behavioral Decision Making* 12(2): 165–79.

Huici, Carmen, Maria Ros, Mercedes Carmon, Jose Ignacio Cano, and Jose Francisco Morales. 1996. "Stereotypic Trait Disconfirmation and the Positive-Negative Asymmetry." *Journal of Social Psychology* 136(3): 277–89.

Ickes, William. 1993. "Empathic Accuracy." *Journal of Personality* 61(4): 587–610.

Intel Corporation. 2003. "Building Trust on the Internet." Paper presented to the Center for eBusiness, MIT. Cambridge, Mass. (December).

Karvonen, Kristina. 2000. "The Beauty of Simplicity." In *Proceedings of the ACM 2000 Conference on Universal Usability*, edited by John Thomas. New York: ACM.

Kollock, Peter. 1994. "The Emergence of Exchange Structures: An Experimental Study of Uncertainty, Commitment, and Trust." *American Journal of Sociology* 100(2): 313–45.

———. 1999. "The Production of Trust in Online Markets." In *Advances in Group Processes*, vol. 16, edited by Edward J. Lawler, Shane R. Thye, Michael W. Macy, and Henry A. Walker. Greenwich, Conn.: JAI Press.

Levin, Irwin P., Edward A. Wasserman, and Shu-fang Kao. 1993. "Multiple Methods for Examining Biased Information Use in Contingency Judgments." *Organizational Behavior & Human Decision Processes* 55(2): 228–50.

Livingston, Jeffrey A., and William N. Evans. 2005. "Do Bidders in Internet Auctions Trust Sellers? A Structural Model of Bidder Behavior on eBay." *Review of Economics and Statistics* 87(3): 453–65.

Lucking-Reiley, David, Doug Bryan, Naghi Prasad, and Daniel Reeves. 2007. "Pennies from eBay: Determinants of Price in Online Auctions." *Journal of Industrial Economics* 55(2): 223–33.

Macrae, C. Neil, Miles Hewstone, and Riana J. Griffiths. 1993. "Processing Load and Memory for Stereotype-Based Information." *European Journal of Social Psychology* 23(1): 77–87.

McAllister, Daniel J. 1995. "Affect- and Cognition-Based Trust as Foundations for Interpersonal Cooperation in Organization." *Academy of Management Journal* 38(1): 24–52.

Mills, Peter K., and Dennis J. Mobert. 1982. "Perspectives on the Technology of Service Operations." *Academy of Management Review* 7(3): 467–78.

Mitroff, Ian I. 1974. "Norms and Counter-Norms in a Select Group of the Apollo Moon Scientists: A Case Study of the Ambivalence of Scientists." *American Sociological Review* 39(4): 579–95.

Molm, Linda D. 2003. "Theoretical Comparisons of Forms of Exchange." *Sociological Theory* 21(1): 1–17.

National White Collar Crime Center and the Federal Bureau of Investigation. 2001. *IFCC 2001 Fraud Report.* Glen Allen, Va.: National White Collar Crime Center. Available at: http://www.nw3c.org.

Oliva, Rogelio, and John Sterman. 2001. "Cutting Corners and Working Overtime: Quality Erosion in the Service Industry." *Management Science* 47(7): 894–914.

Orbell, John M., and Robyn M. Dawes. 1993. "Social Welfare, Cooperators' Advantage and the Option of Not Playing the Game." *American Sociological Review* 58(6): 787–800.

Podolny, Joel M. 1993. "A Status-Based Model of Market Competition." *American Journal of Sociology* 98(4): 829–72.

Resnick, Paul, and Richard Zeckhauser. 2002. "Trust Among Strangers in Internet Transactions: Empirical Analysis of eBay's Reputation System." In *Advances in Applied Microeconomics,* vol. 11, *The Economics of Internet and E-Commerce,* edited by Michael R. Baye. Amsterdam: Elsevier Science.

Resnick, Paul, Richard Zeckhauser, John Swanson, and Kate Lockwood. 2006. "The Value of Reputation on eBay: A Controlled Experiment." *Experimental Economics* 9(2): 79–101.

Ridgeway, Cecilia, and Henry Walker. 1995. "Status Structures." In *Sociological Perspectives on Social Psychology,* edited by Karen Cook, Gary Alan Fine, and James House. Boston: Allyn & Bacon.

Riegelsberger, Jens, M. Angela Sasse, and John D. McCarthy. 2007. "Trust in Mediated Interactions." In *The Oxford Handbook of Internet Psychology,* edited by Adam N. Joinson, Katelyn McKenna, Tom Postmes, and Ulf-Dietrich Reips. Oxford: Oxford University Press.

Rieh, Soo Young, and Daniel R. Danielson. 2007. "Credibility: A Multidisciplinary Framework." In *Annual Review of Information Science and Technology* 41, edited by Blaise Cronin. Medford, N.J.: Information Today.

Rocco, Elena. 1998. "Trust Breaks Down in Electronic Contexts but Can Be Repaired by Some Initial Face-to-Face Contact." In *Proceedings of the SIGCHI Conference on Human Factors in Computing Systems 1998,* edited by Clare-Marie Karat, Arnold Lund, Joëlle Coutaz, and John Karat. New York: ACM Press/ Addison-Wesley.

Rotter, Julian B. 1967. "A New Scale for the Measurement of Interpersonal Trust." *Journal of Personality* 35(1): 1–7.

———. 1980. "Interpersonal Trust, Trustworthiness and Gullibility." *American Psychologist* 35(1): 1–7.

Sabolo, Yves. 1975. *The Service Industries.* Geneva: International Labor Office.

Schneider, Benjamin. 1991. "Service Quality and Profits: Can You Have Your Cake and Eat it, Too?" *Human Resource Planning* 14(2): 151–57.

Schneider, Benjamin, John Parkington, and Virginia Buxton. 1980. "Employee and Customer Perceptions of Services in Banks." *Administrative Science Quarterly* 25(2): 252–67.

Singer, Eleanor. 1981. "Reference Groups and Social Evaluations." In *Social Psychology: Sociological Perspectives*, edited by Morris Rosenberg and Ralph H. Turner. New York: Basic Books.

Snijders, Chris, and Richard Zijdeman. 2004. "Reputation and Internet Auctions: eBay and Beyond." *Analyse & Kritik* 26(1): 158–84.

Spence, Michael. 1973. "Job Market Signaling." *Quarterly Journal of Economics* 87(2): 355–74.

Sproull, Lee, and Sara Kiesler. 1991. *Connections: New Ways of Working in the Networked Organization*. Cambridge, Mass.: MIT Press.

Standifird, Stephen S. 2001. "Reputation and e-Commerce: eBay Auctions and the Asymmetrical Impact of Positive and Negative Ratings." *Journal of Management* 27(3): 279–95.

U.S. Department of Justice. 2002. "Internet and Telemarketing Fraud." Available at: http://www.justice.gov/criminal/fraud/internet (accessed April 9, 2009).

Vance, Anthony, Christophe Elie-Dit-Cosaque, and Detmar W. Straub. 2008. "Examining Trust in Information Technology Artifacts: The Effects of System Quality and Culture." *Journal of Management Information Systems* 24(4): 73–100.

Wang, Ye Diana, and Henry H. Emurian. 2005. "An Overview of Online Trust: Concepts, Elements, and Implications." *Computers in Human Behavior* 21(2005): 105–25.

Wason, Peter C. 1960. "On the Failure to Eliminate Hypotheses in a Conceptual Task." *Quarterly Journal of Experimental Psychology* 12(1): 129–40.

Weber, Elke U., Christopher K. Hsee, and Joanna Sokolowska. 1998. "What Folklore Tells Us about Risk and Risk Taking: Cross-Cultural Comparisons of American, Chinese and German Proverbs." *Organizational Behavior and Human Decision Processes* 75(2): 170–85.

Wilson, Robert. 1985. "Reputation in Games and Markets." In *Game-Theoretical Models of Bargaining*, edited by Alvin E. Roth. Cambridge: Cambridge University Press.

Yamagishi, Toshio. 2001. "Trust as a Form of Social Intelligence." In *Trust in Society*, edited by Karen S. Cook. New York: Russell Sage Foundation.

Yamagishi, Toshio, Masako Kikuchi, and Motoko Kosugi. 1999. "Trust, Gullibility, and Social Intelligence." *Asian Journal of Social Psychology* 2(1): 145–61.

Zeithaml, Valarie, A. Parasuraman, and Leonard L. Berry. 1990. *Delivering Quality Service: Balancing Customer Perceptions and Expectations*. New York: Free Press.

Zheng, Jun, Elizabeth Veinott, Nathan Bos, Judith S. Olson, and Gary M. Olson. 2002. "Trust without Touch: Jumpstarting Long-Distance Trust with Initial Social Activities." In *Proceedings of the SIGCHI Conference on Human Factors in Computing Systems 2002: Changing Our World, Changing Ourselves*, edited by Dennis Wixon. New York: ACM.

Chapter 8

Rebuilding Trust after Negative Feedback: The Role of Communication

Sonja Utz

O NLINE REPUTATION systems, also called feedback systems, are commonly regarded as *the* solution to the trust problem in online markets (see, for example, Ba and Pavlou 2002; Bolton, Katok, and Ockenfels 2004; chapter 1, this volume; Dellarocas 2003; Kollock 1999; Resnick et al. 2000; chapter 3, this volume). However, research has focused mainly on the question of how trust can be built in an online market, but it has neglected the question of how trust can be rebuilt. The chapter provides answers on this understudied question from a social-psychological perspective. The main focus is on the role of communication in rebuilding trust. The central claim is that the effect of a specific communication strategy, such as apology or denial, on perceived trustworthiness depends on the type of trust violation.

Rebuilding trust is important for two reasons. First, negative feedback, such as that in online auctions, decreases trust and in turn probability of sale and price premiums (Eaton 2002; Lucking-Reiley et al. 2007; Melnik and Alm 2002). From the economic perspective of a seller with negative feedback, rebuilding trust is therefore important. Second, rebuilding trust is even more important because online markets are noisy environments. Noise is defined as "discrepancies between actual and desired outcome of an interaction partner due to unintended consequences" (Van Lange, Ouwerkerk, and Tazelaar 2002, 768). An example is a parcel that gets lost in the mail or an e-mail that is never received because the network broke down. Thus people receive negative feedback though they do not deserve it. Social psychological research has shown that noise has detrimental effects on cooperation in social dilemma games in the lab (Van Lange, Ouwerkerk, and Tazelaar 2002). Noise has also been studied in game theory and economics under the term *imperfect monitoring*. Avner Greif argued that there is also a perfect Bayesian equilibrium in markets with imperfect monitoring, but that in this case disputes and conflicts will follow (2006). To overcome these negative effects of noise or imperfect monitoring, rebuilding trust is necessary.

Rebuilding trust in online markets is different from rebuilding trust in face-to-face interactions or online dyadic interactions. First, the target of the trust reparation strategy is different. In online auctions, many interactions are one-shot interactions between strangers (Resnick et al. 2000). Regaining the trust of potential future interaction partners is therefore more important than regaining the trust of the disappointed party. Second, the possibilities for trust repairing attempts are limited. Usually, no extensive communication with all potential future interaction partners takes place; potential future interaction partners use the short comments displayed in the online feedback system to make trustworthiness judgments. This chapter focuses mainly on the role of these short messages in judging the trustworthiness of potential interaction partners.

Trust and Trustworthiness

The chapter builds on the widely accepted trust model that Roger Mayer, James Davis, and David Schoorman developed (1995). These authors define trust as "the willingness of a party to be vulnerable to the actions of another party based on the expectation that the other will perform a particular action important to the trustor, regardless of the ability to monitor or control that other party" (712). Trust has to be distinguished from behavioral trust: "Trust is the willingness to assume risk; behavioral trust is the *assuming* of risk" (724). Trust increases behavioral trust, but behavioral trust can also occur without trust (Cook, Hardin, and Levi 2006; chapter 11, this volume). A buyer might place a bid on a seller with a negative feedback profile simply because the starting price is very low and the chance to make a very good bargain is more tempting than the fear of losing money.

Trust is influenced by two variables: propensity to trust, a dispositional variable, and perceived trustworthiness of the trustee. The latter depends on the respective interaction partner and is therefore less stable than dispositional trust. I therefore focus on perceived trustworthiness. Perceived trustworthiness is comprised by perceived ability, benevolence, and integrity of a trustee. Ability refers to the skills and competencies that enable the trustee to perform the required action. Benevolence is defined as "the extent to which a trustee is believed to want to do good to the trustor, aside from an egocentric profit motive" (Mayer, Davis, and Schoorman 1995, 718). Integrity means that the trustee adheres to a set of acceptable principles.

Mayer and his colleagues argued that all three factors are important for trust, but that each is considered to vary independently from the others (1995). In the context of online markets, benevolence is less important because it assumes that "the trustee has some specific attachment to the trustor" (718). In online markets, most interactions take place between strangers, and the trustee can often not choose the interaction partner (for example, in eBay, the seller does not know which buyers will place a bid), so usually there is no specific attachment. Thus, to find out whom to trust in an online market, one has to find out who is high on integrity and on ability, or—in terms of this chapter—on morality and competence. Adhering to a set of principles can also be seen as motivation to be cooperative and honest. Thus, the factors correspond also to the distinction in motivation and competence used in the previous chapter. Without any prior interactions with a person, as it is often the case in online interactions, judging the morality and competence of a person is difficult. Reputation systems offer a solution to this problem.

Reputation Systems

"A reputation system collects, distributes, and aggregates feedback about participants' past behavior" (Resnick et al. 2000, 46). For example, in eBay, after each transaction, the buyer and the seller can give each other feedback.[1] Feedback can be positive, neutral, or negative. On the member profile, the net amount of positive feedback and the percentage of positive feedback are displayed. Information about the absolute amount of positive, neutral, and negative feedback in general and from unique users is given, and this information is further split up over the past month, the past six months, and the past twelve months. The feedback can also be accompanied by brief additional information, such as "did not send the item," just as the feedback recipient can also respond, such as "item bounced back."

A reputation system has two functions: providing people with information that can be used to judge the trustworthiness of an interaction partner, and eliciting honest behavior of actors (Kollock 1999; chapter 3, this volume). The first function corresponds to the approach of seeing a reputation score as helpful in assessing the character of an actor (Dasgupta 1998). The assumption is that the reputation score clearly indicated how trustworthy and honest the actor is. The second function corresponds to a more strategic, incentive-based view on reputation (Dasgupta 1988). Cheating is tempting in an environment in which most interactions are one-shot interactions between strangers. Reputation systems provide an incentive to behave honestly by introducing a shadow of the future (Axelrod 1984). Cheating does not pay off in the long run if no one wants to interact with a person who has a bad reputation. Providing information about past behavior is thus not enough; the members of the market or group need to sanction sellers with bad reputations (Greif 1989; Kandori 1992; chapter 3, this volume). If such sellers are sanctioned, a reputation system elicits strategically honest behavior even in dishonest persons. This trust building and cooperation enhancing function of reputation systems has been studied extensively (for example, Ba and Pavlou 2002; Bolton, Katok, and Ockenfels 2004; chapter 1, this volume; Resnick and Zeckhauser 2002).

More important for this chapter, the information provided in a feedback profile can be seen as a signal that can be used to judge the trustworthiness of an interaction partner (see also chapter 9, this volume, on relational signals). Depending on the type of market, the information signals mainly the morality or competence of an actor. Reputation systems in online auctions fulfill mainly the function to judge the morality of a potential interaction partner. Packing a parcel and shipping it does not require sophisticated skills, and thus competence is not really an issue. In other environments, such as expert sites or RentACoder.com, reputation systems fulfill mainly the function of judging the competence of a potential interaction partner (see chapter 6, this volume). For example, at Allexperts.com, individuals are judged on the four dimensions of knowledge, clarity of response, timeliness, and politeness on 10-point scales, and a general prestige score is presented. The first two dimensions relate clearly to competence.

Thus, if no additional comments are included, negative feedback should decrease primarily perceived morality in markets where products are traded and perceived competence where knowledge is traded. Depending on the type of market, perceived morality or perceived competence should have a higher impact on the final trustworthiness judgments.

The impact of negative feedback is expected to be stronger when the morality of a trustee is the focus because negative information about morality usually has a stronger impact than negative information about competence. This positive-negative asymmetry of morality and competence information is a robust finding in research on impression formation (for an overview, see Wojciszke 2005). John Skowronski and Donald Carlston argued that the diagnosticity of information is the cause for this asymmetry (1987). In the domain of morality, negative information is more diagnostic. The underlying assumption is that honest people never behave dishonestly. Dishonest people do not behave dishonestly all the time; they behave sometimes honestly as well. Therefore, honest behavior is not diagnostic for the morality of an actor, but dishonest behavior is. In the domain of competence, positive information is more diagnostic. The underlying assumption is that stupid people can never do something intelligently, whereas even very intelligent people sometimes make mistakes. Stupid behavior is therefore not really diagnostic for the competence of an actor, but intelligent behavior is. Consequently, negative feedback has less impact on competence judgments than on morality judgments.

Theoretically, reputation systems are the perfect solution to the trust problem in online markets. Reputation systems face a number of practical problems. They work only in a perfect world—that is, if everyone gives honest feedback after each transaction (see also chapter 1, this volume). Research shows, however, that not every user gives feedback (Jann, Wehrli, and Diekmann 2006; Resnick and Zeckhauser 2002). Submitting feedback is a second-order social dilemma—it takes time and effort, but the one giving the feedback does not profit from it. The key to the value of feedback is that enough users give it that their experiences are representative of the experiences of those who do not give it (Dellarocas 2003). However, it has been observed that some people in eBay avoid giving negative feedback because they are afraid of receiving negative revenge feedback in return (Resnick et al. 2000). This observation has even led to a change in the eBay feedback system: since May 2008, sellers can no longer give negative feedback on buyers.

The present chapter focuses on another hitherto neglected problem on rebuilding trust: noise. Noise can be a parcel lost in the mail, a server breakdown or computer crash, or an accident. Thus, even if all users give feedback that truly corresponds to their experiences, negative feedback is not diagnostic for the immorality or incompetence of the judged person. Noise occurs in all social interactions; however, it occurs more often in online interactions—simply because there are more opportunities for noise to occur. In a traditional shop interaction, buyer and seller are in the same place at the same time, the seller can often inspect the product, and product and money are exchanged immediately. In online transactions, the buyer has to rely on descriptions and pictures of the product. Communication is mediated by technology that can break down (see also chapter 11, this volume). Things can also go wrong with payment and shipping—mixing up numbers of the bank account or letters in an email address, or parcels that get lost. Although all these excuses (my computer crashed, the parcel get lost, I had to go to the hospital) sound like feeble excuses, one has to consider that millions of transactions are conducted on eBay every day. Consider lost parcels. Postal services of most countries report that a very high percentage of all mail is delivered properly (99.8 percent in Holland, for example). Nevertheless, .2 percent of improperly delivered or undelivered parcels means that thousands of transactions go wrong. Consequently, there will be negative feedback in online environments—either caused by fraud or caused by noise. Repairing trust is therefore necessary if these markets are to survive.

Noise has also been studied by economists. Such studies often focus on the role of imperfect monitoring in repeated games (for example, Greif 2006). Imperfect monitoring means that the reputation scores do not always reflect the behavior of the actor; sometimes, the signal indicates that the actor has cheated even if this is not the case. Greif's analysis of community responsibility systems in pre-modern Europe showed that disputes and conflicts are an inevitable consequence of imperfect monitoring systems (2006). Greif focused on the role of institutions; this chapter focuses on the role of communication in rebuilding trust.

The Impact of Negative Feedback

Several field studies on eBay have shown that negative feedback decreases probability of sale and end price (Eaton 2002; Lucking-Reiley et al. 2007; Melnik and Alm 2002). Probability of sale is an indicator for actual risk-taking and thus behavioral trust. These decreases might therefore be caused by other factors than decreased trust. In one experiment, however, trust was measured directly. The results indicate that negative feedback does indeed decrease trust (Ba and Pavlou 2002). In these studies, it has not been examined whether the negative feedback was attributed to fraud or to noise—the implicit underlying assumption was that negative feedback indicates fraud. It is relatively straightforward and also functional to assume that negative feedback caused by fraud lowers trust.

Noise, though, has also detrimental effects. For the most part, what has been studied is the impact of noise on cooperation in social dilemmas, that is, situations in which individual and collective interests are in conflict. On eBay, for example, the individual profit would always be higher if one did not send the product or pay for the product, but if everyone acts according to individual rationality, no transactions take place and the outcome is even worse. Computer simulations have found that noise is detrimental to cooperation rates, especially for reciprocal strategies such as tit-for-tat (Bendor, Kramer, and Stout 1991; Kollock 1993). One incident of noise results in vicious circles of noncooperation. Paul Van Lange, Jaap Ouwerkerk, and Miriam Tazelaar conducted laboratory studies and came to similar conclusions (2002). In all these studies, interaction partners could not be chosen—participants played in dyads (against the computer; Van Lange, Ouwerkerk, and Tazelaar 2002) or strategies were matched randomly or so that each strategy competed against each strategy (tournament matching; Bendor, Kramer, and

Stout 1991; Kollock 1993). The generalizability of these results to online markets is thus somewhat limited.

Paul Pavlou and David Gefen conducted a study in the context of eBay and Amazon (2005). They focused on a psychological variable, psychological contract violation (PCV). This concept stems originally from organizational relationships, but Pavlou and Gefen transferred it to online marketplaces and defined it as "a buyer's beliefs of having been treated wrongly regarding the terms of an exchange agreement with a seller" (373). The focus is on the belief of having been treated wrongly and therefore leaves it open whether the real cause was fraud or an incident of noise. Pavlou and Gefen argued that these subjective beliefs are more important for further trust and risk-taking behavior than objective facts. More important, they show that PCV with an individual seller generalizes to PCV with the whole community of sellers. Moreover, PCV with the community of sellers increases perceived risk and decreases transaction intentions, price premiums, and trust in the community of sellers. This study is interesting for two reasons. First, it looks at psychological processes and subjective constructions of the situation in place of objective facts. Second, it examines how experiences with an individual seller generalize to the whole community of sellers. I take a slightly different perspective and examine how experiences of another seller with a trustee, documented in the feedback profile, influence one's own trust in the same trustee.

Thus, research from various domains shows that negative feedback—even if caused by noise—decreases trust. Repairing trust is therefore necessary. In the next section, I address the solutions that research on noise and rebuilding trust provide.

Dealing with Noise

Computer simulations have shown that noise has detrimental effects on cooperation, especially for reciprocal strategies such as tit-for-tat. However, more generous strategies do pretty well in these environments (for example, Kollock 1993). Paul Van Lange and his colleagues also found that tit-for-tat plus one, a more generous strategy, could overcome the detrimental effects of noise (Van Lange, Ouwerkerk, and Tazelaar 2002). These studies used preprogrammed strategies and looked at which strategies are effective. However, they did not examine which strategies people actually use. Forgiveness in eBay has never been measured explicitly, but many studies on eBay found surprisingly small effects of negative feedback on probability of sale and end price (see Lee, Im, and Lee 2000; Lucking-Reiley et al. 2007; Melnik and Alm 2002; Standifird 2001) and some found no or even positive effects of negative feedback (Eaton 2002; Resnick et al. 2006). This could indicate that people are willing to give the benefit of the doubt to sellers with negative feedback.

People should give the benefit of the doubt especially if they are aware that negative feedback can be caused by noise. To examine whether people are aware of noise in eBay, I conducted a laboratory study. There were three experimental conditions. In the control condition, people received only an explanation of the eBay feedback system. In the noise-underestimates-trustworthiness condition, people were also told that the system works perfectly in theory but less well in real life because things go wrong sometimes—computers crash, parcels get lost, people get sick and so on. The information in the feedback profile could therefore sometimes underestimate the trustworthiness of the seller. In the noise-overestimates-trustworthiness condition, people were told that the system works perfectly in theory but less well in real life because not everyone gives feedback and people are afraid of giving negative feedback. The information in the feedback profile could therefore sometimes overestimate the trustworthiness of the seller.

Perceived awareness of fraud and noise were measured. Participants were presented with seven possible causes for negative feedback on eBay. Some were more related to fraud (such as "does not deliver product" or "sends broken product"), and others were more related to incidents of noise (such as "network broke down" or "misdelivery of parcel"). Factor analysis showed that the items loaded indeed on two factors and the items were combined into a scale on fraud ($\alpha = .85$) and a scale on noise ($\alpha = .71$). People should judge on a 15-point scale how often they thought that this event happened (never—in 30 percent of the cases). It is difficult to judge the exact probabilities of these events; the variable of interest is the relation of fraud to noise.

Analyses of variance showed that the noise awareness manipulation influenced only the fraud ratings, $F(2, 97) = 3.18$, $p < .05$, but not the noise ratings, $F(2, 97) < 1$, ns. In the noise-underestimates-trustworthiness condition, fraud rates were perceived to be lower ($M = 7.64$) than in either the control condition ($M = 8.89$) or the noise-overestimates-trustworthiness condition ($M = 9.13$). The latter two conditions did not differ from each other. Overall, noise was perceived to be somewhat less frequent than fraud ($Ms = 7.38, 7.19, 7.56$ for the noise-underestimates-trustworthiness condition, the control condition, and the noise-overestimates-trustworthiness condition, respectively). These data indicate that people are always aware that negative feedback might be caused by noise. Even in the control condition, in which this fact was not explicitly mentioned, people realized that these things can happen. Interestingly, the manipulation influenced only the fraud-judgments—when people were reminded of noise that underestimates the trustworthiness of sellers, they reported lower levels of fraud, but not higher levels of noise. More important, the fraud rates in the control condition are not significantly different from the ones in the noise-overestimates-trustworthiness; thus the default assumption of eBay users is to assume higher levels of actual fraud than indicated by the reputation score.

For both scales, people varied considerably in their estimations ($SD = 2.61$ for fraud and 2.56 for noise; range 1.5 to 15 for fraud and 2 to 13.33 for noise) indicating that subjective perceptions and attributions play a role. Dispositional trust turned out to influence the ratings. High trusters perceived less fraud ($M = 7.9$) and noise ($M = 6.7$) than low trusters did ($Ms = 9.29$ and 8.14). Another scale was developed to measure general trust in eBay sellers. This scale had six items, ($\alpha = .69$), such as "most sellers on eBay are trustworthy" or "as long as the number of negative feedback is small, I still trust the seller." This scale was related to fraud perceptions, $r(100) = -.34$, $p < .01$, but not to noise perceptions, $r(100) = -.03$, ns. Higher trust in eBay sellers thus lowers fraud perceptions, but is not related to noise perceptions. These results indicate that people are aware that there is noise in eBay transactions, and that these noise perceptions are relatively stable across noise conditions and levels of eBay trust. When people are aware of noise, they should be more willing to give the benefit of the doubt in case of negative feedback. Giving the benefit of the doubt is one strategy buyers can apply to deal with noise. But how can sellers try to regain trust of potential buyers?

eBay recommends that its users communicate if problems arise: "The key to successful transactions on eBay is direct communication between buyers and sellers;"[2] It also offers advice such as "presume good faith from the other side" and reminds visitors that "usually problems are a result of simple miscommunication or mistaken assumptions." These examples indicate that eBay assumes that most unsuccessful transactions are due to noise and that communication is an effective way to resolve these problems. eBay further advises users to focus on the problem rather than the person—that is, to make a situational attribution (something went wrong) in place of a personal attribution (this person is a cheater). Thus, the small effects of negative feedback could also be due to successful trust reparation attempts.

There is also empirical evidence for the beneficial role of communication in noisy environments (Tazelaar, Van Lange, and Ouwerkerk 2004). In this laboratory study, participants played a ten-coin give-some dilemma against an alleged interaction partner, which was in fact a programmed computer strategy. At the beginning of each trial, the participant had ten coins. The alleged interaction partner also had ten coins. Each coin had a value of NFL 0.50 to the person himself or herself, and a value of NFL 1.00 to the interaction partner. Participants have to decide how many of their coins they give to their interaction partner. They then see how much their partner gave. This game was played for fifty-three rounds. There were three conditions: no noise, noise with communication, and noise without communication. Participants were told that one partner would have the option to send a limited number of short messages after several trials and that a lottery would determine who would be allowed to do so. The messages were sent by the alleged partner. The messages explained in different versions the presence of noise—for example, "I wanted to give you six coins, but the computer changed my decision. I think you only received three coins." Some of the messages ended with "I'm sorry." The results showed that cooperation was significantly lower in the noise–no communication condition than in the no noise condition. However, in the noise-communication condition, no drop in cooperation levels occurred, indicating that communication can dilute the detrimental effect of noise. Participants in the noise–no communication condition formed less benign impressions from their interaction partners than participants in the no noise or the noise-communication condition did. Benign impressions partly mediated the effects on cooperation. Trust was not measured in this study, but cooperation can be viewed as trusting behavior.

Does communication also help in eBay? Feedback comments in eBay are restricted to 160 characters. Paul Pavlou and Angelika Dimoka analyzed feedback comments and found that extraordinarily positive comments increase perceived benevolence and credibility and result in a price premium, whereas negative comments decrease perceived benevolence and credibility (2006). Thus there is evidence that the short comments convey additional useful information. Pavlou and Dimoka, however, did not look at the reactions on the negative feedback comments. A first exploratory study examined the effects of these reactions. Participants had to imagine that they wanted to buy a mobile phone for about 175 euro. They were presented with various feedback profiles of sellers. Next to the number on the ID card, they received the comments accompanying the (last) negative feedback. The events were picked from eBay, as well as the reactions. The reactions were samples of reactions found on eBay, and not selected along predefined criteria. However, for each negative event, three conditions were realized: one with no reaction of the seller and two different reactions. In most cases, one of the reactions was friendly and constructive, and the other rather unfriendly. The type of reaction on the negative feedback (none, constructive, destructive) was varied between subjects, and the type of negative feedback was varied within subjects. Type of negative event and feedback profile are therefore confounded variables. Not surprisingly, percentage of positive feedback had the highest impact on trust levels. However, within four of the six scenarios, the type of reaction had a significant effect as well. In most cases, any type of reaction on the negative feedback resulted in higher levels of trustworthiness. For example, when the negative feedback was that the buyer had waited for weeks for delivery and the seller feedback was 97 percent positive, the trust level was $M = 8.88$ on a 15-point-scale in the condition in which the seller did not respond. However, when the seller answered, "had to go to the hospital, sorry for the delay," trust increased to $M = 10.87$. A similar level was obtained for the answer "buyer gave me the wrong zip code, the parcel bounced back," $M = 10.75$. Only in the scenario "fast delivery, but product doesn't work" (seller with 50 percent positive feedback), the reaction "worked at my place, not my fault if he can't install it" resulted in similarly low trust levels ($M = 4.12$) than no reaction did ($M = 4.44$). The reaction of "I offered revocation and refund, but no answer" increased trust levels to $M = 8.41$. Thus the results indicate that communication can enhance trust, but does not necessarily do so. Especially reactions offering an explanation that allowed an attribution to noise (such as hospital or wrong zip code) or described an offer of penance (such as refund) were successful.

The incidents and reactions were sampled from eBay and have therefore a high ecological validity. However, they were not sampled with the goal to vary systematically the type of reaction because the goal of this study was to examine whether the typical reactions found in eBay have any effect. To further determine the effects of communication, the reactions were later given to a different sample and judged on various dimensions such as believability, friendliness, and positivity. People were also asked whether they thought that the seller acted on purpose with malign intent or whether the situation was an accidental incident of noise. All these variables correlated with trustworthiness judgments—the more believable, positive, and friendly a reaction, the more trustworthy the seller was perceived. And the more the negative incident was perceived as accidental and not the fault of the seller, the higher the trustworthiness judgments.

These results indicate that even the short reactions on eBay influence how readers construe the situation. If they attribute it to an incident of noise, trustworthiness judgments increase. Not only the content, but also the style of the reaction plays a role—a friendly and positive reaction results in higher trustworthiness judgments than a unfriendly and destructive reaction, such as the "worked at my place, not my fault if he can't install it" reaction.

Rebuilding Trust after a Trust Violation

Communication has been suggested as a solution not only to overcome the effects of noise (Tazelaar, Van Lange, and Ouwerkerk 2004), but also to rebuild trust after actual trust violations. Rebuilding trust has been neglected in trust research for a quite a long time, but recently the topic has received more attention. William Bottom and his colleagues examined the role of denial versus acknowledgment of intent and the offer of various forms of penance on rebuilding cooperation (2002). Participants played several rounds of a prisoner's dilemma against an alleged interaction partner. The benefits of cooperation were stressed in the beginning to ensure a cooperative interaction. After a certain number of cooperative trials (varying from round 5 to round 15), the interaction partner started to defect. The breach of cooperation was followed by verbal statements providing an explanation that either acknowledged or denied intent. In the denial condition, the experimenter was blamed. A few trials later, the penance manipulation took place, and the partner offered either no penance (mere talk), small or large penance (one or two cooperative moves allowing the partner to get the maximum payoff), or an open-ended offer. Dependent variables were the participant's cooperation in the last five rounds as an indicator of willingness to forgive and return to cooperation (= to trust again). Mere talk was enough to elicit at least one cooperative choice within the last five trials. However, offering penance was more successful. In the case of a short interaction history, acknowledgment of intention was more successful than denial. In the case of a longer interaction history, denial of intention was more successful than acknowledgment because denials are more easily accepted from well-known interaction partners.

The situation in online markets is different, and the results should therefore be generalized only with caution. In online markets, it is more important to repair the trust of potential future interaction partners than of the aggrieved trustee. Some of the strategies are not possible; for example, penance cannot be offered to all potential future interaction partners. However, the basic finding that trust can be rebuilt even by mere talk is important for online markets as well.

Peter Kim and his colleagues developed a model that explains which trust rebuilding strategy is more successful in which situation (2004). They distinguish two types of reactions and two types of trust violations. Reactions can be an apology or denial, and trust violations can be based on either competence or integrity. The latter differentiation corresponds again to the competence-morality dichotomy.

On the basis of the positive-negative asymmetry and the diagnosticity of negative information, Kim and his colleagues came to the proposition that denial should be more effective for morality-based violations of trust and apologies for competence-based violations (2004). The latter is the case because negative competence information is not diagnostic of competence; thus, acknowledging that one made a mistake has no detrimental effects on perceptions of competence and trustworthiness in general. However, because negative morality information is diagnostic, acknowledging a dishonest intention would be decidedly bad for any perception of morality and trustworthiness in general. Note that this model makes predictions only about the success of different strategies in repairing trust. It says nothing about the motives for using these strategies. Thus, if reputation is seen as a signal of the character of an actor, an honest actor who received a negative rating because of noise might want to use the most successful strategy to repair his or her reputation. However, an actor who cooperates only for strategic reasons (the incentive-based view of reputation) might try to find the right balance between occasional cheating and using the appropriate repair strategy.

Kim and his colleagues tested these assumptions in an experiment in which participants saw videos of an alleged job applicant (2004). The candidate applied for a job as a tax accountant and was accused of having filed an incorrect tax return. In the competence-based trust violation condition, this was framed as lack of knowledge of the appropriate tax codes. In the morality-based trust violation condition, it was framed as intentional action with the goal to increase the client's tax return. The dependent measures were indicators of behavioral trust—willingness to risk, hiring, and giving job responsibilities to the applicant. Indeed, denial was more successful for a morality-based violation of trust, and apology for a competence-based violation. In general, the effects of type of communication were stronger for the morality-based violation of trust. The effects were mediated by trusting beliefs—more specifically, perceived morality and perceived competence. In this experiment, participants received video segments of a job interview. Videos, of course, include both verbal and nonverbal information. In eBay, only short text-based comments and reactions are possible; nonverbal cues are missing. Thus the question remains on how far the predictions hold true for short text-based comments. More important, the model captures neither all possible causes nor all possible responses to trust violations. Kim and his colleagues distinguished a difference between competence-based and morality-based trust violations, but did not address the role of noise. With regard to the responses, denial was defined as denial of the entire incident. However, at eBay, reactions are also found in which people acknowledge the incident but deny responsibility. An integrative model that captures also the role of noise is therefore proposed.

Toward an Integrative Model: Rebuilding Trust in Noisy Environments

The main lesson from research on noise was that the detrimental effects of noise can be overcome when the existence of noise is brought into awareness by communication. The main lesson from literature on rebuilding trust was that apologies should do better in cases of competence-based violations of trust, and denial in cases of morality-based violations of trust. These lines of research are combined into the model presented in figure 8.1.

Figure 8.1   The Trust Reparation Model

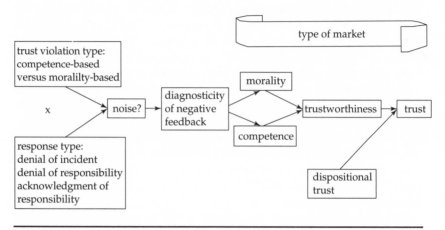

Source: Author's compilation.

The right part of the model—that is, how perceived morality and competence influence trustworthiness, and how trustworthiness and dispositional trust together influence trust—has been confirmed by many studies (for example, Mayer, Davis, and Schoorman 1995; McKnight, Choudhury, and Kacmar 2002). However, the model extends previous research in several ways. First, it places trust violations in a larger context and makes assumptions about the relative importance of perceived morality and perceived competence on final trustworthiness judgments in different online markets. If nothing is known about the type of trust violation, such as negative feedback in eBay without an accompanying comment, the type of market determines the impact of perceived morality and perceived competence on final trustworthiness judgments. Despite the general dominance of morality in impression formation, morality judgments are expected to have a higher impact on final trustworthiness judgments and trust in morality markets than in competence markets (Wojciszke, Bazinska, and Jaworski 1998). Competence judgments are expected to have a higher impact on final trustworthiness judgments and trust in competence markets than in morality markets. Chapter 6 in this volume provides indirect support for this assumption. The authors examined a market in which coders could be hired for programming projects and found that positive feedback had a much higher impact on probability of being chosen for a project than it usually has on probability of sale in online auctions. In this type of market, mainly the competence of a coder is judged, and positive competence information is highly diagnostic. Thus the results might indicate that perceived competence is more important in judging the trustworthiness of a coder than of a seller.

The type of trust violation should influence the relative importance of morality and competence judgments in a similar way. Morality judgments are more important in instances of morality-based trust violations, and competence judgments in instances of competence-based trust violations because the type of violation turns the attention to the corresponding quality of the trustee. Sonja Utz, Uwe Matzat, and Chris Snijders found in two scenario-studies with actual eBay users that competence-based trust violations are perceived as less severe than morality-based trust violations (2009). Respondents judged the trustworthiness of eBay sellers with identical reputation scores; only the accompanying comment framed the trust violation as being morality-based or competence-based.

The basic assumption of the model is still that the effectiveness of a response depends on the type of violation. However, the typology of responses is extended. Kim and his colleagues defined apology as acknowledgement of responsibility and regret, and denial as denial of the incident and therefore also responsibility (2004). This definition is commonly used in the trust-rebuilding literature as well as in the *Oxford English Dictionary* but confounds the acknowledgement of responsibility and regret. Moreover, if noise is considered, it can happen that people acknowledge the negative incident, but deny responsibility. The definition of denial does not cover these situations. In the proposed model, a different typology is used. First, a trust reparation attempt can deny or acknowledge the incident. If the incident is acknowledged, a further distinction in denial or acknowledgment of responsibility is made, resulting in three different responses: denying the incident, denying responsibility, and acknowledging responsibility. Denying the incident and acknowledging responsibility correspond to the typology of Kim and his colleagues, with the difference that acknowledging responsibility and regret are no longer confounded (2004). Denying responsibility while acknowledging the incident corresponds to communication about noise.

In a morality-based violation, denying responsibility is predicted to be more successful in repairing trust than denying the incident, which is in turn more successful than acknowledging responsibility. Acknowledging responsibility is the worst response because it is a clear and highly diagnostic indicator of low morality and is thus even worse than denying the incident. In the case of a competence-based violation of trust, acknowledging responsibility is predicted to be more successful in repairing trust than denying responsibility, which is in turn more successful in repairing trust than denying the incident. The latter is considered as worst because people are so afraid of negative revenge feedback that negative feedback is usually not given groundlessly (Resnick and Zeckhauser 2002). Denying the situation might therefore be not credible.

The model assumes that communication influences the responsibility attributions, which influence impression formation. If a negative incident is attributed to noise, the negative feedback is not perceived as diagnostic and perceived morality and competence of the potential interaction partner should not or only slightly decrease. The trust repair strategy is successful. However, if a negative incident is still attributed to the responsibility of the trustee, the negative feedback is perceived as diagnostic, and perceived morality and competence of the potential interaction partner should decrease. Whether mainly perceived morality or mainly perceived competence is decreased depends on the type of trust violation—in case of a competence-based trust violation, perceived competence of the trustee is more affected; in case of a morality-based trust violation, perceived morality of the trustee is more affected.

Empirical Studies on the Reparation of Trust in eBay

To test whether the original predictions also hold in eBay, an experiment with a 2 (type of trust violation) × 3 (response: apology, denial, none) experiment was conducted (Utz 2005). The condition without a response was added to examine whether the two responses differed only in their success in repairing trust or whether the wrong response decreased trust. Participants were to imagine that they wanted to buy a mobile phone. The offers were comparable; only the sellers differed. Participants were then presented with a list of sellers and to indicate the trustworthiness of each. The competence-based violation of integrity was "used wrong zip code, took therefore quite a long time." The apology was "sorry, my mistake, I mixed up two numbers." The denial was "not true, buyer gave me the wrong zip code." The morality-based violation of trust was "sends broken product, soundcard did not work!" The apology was "sorry, I offered refund." The denial was "did work at my place, not my fault if he can't install it." In the no-response condition, no reaction was presented.

Dependent measures were: trustworthiness of the seller, responsibility attributions (seller is responsible; somebody else or noise is responsible), and believability. The analysis of trust did not reveal the expected interaction between type of trust violation and type of response. Instead, two main effects emerged.

As presented in figure 8.2, the seller with the competence-based violation was always perceived as more trustworthy than the seller with the morality-based violation. The no-response condition can be seen as a

Figure 8.2   Trustworthiness Judgments

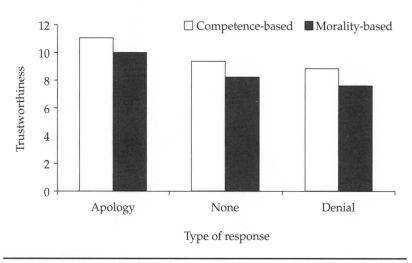

Type of response

Source: Author's compilation.

sort of baseline—even without a response, the type of negative feedback influenced perceived trustworthiness. This shows that the information given in the comments is indeed used to construe the situation in terms of competence-based or morality-based trust violations. Moreover, it confirms the prediction that competence-based violations are perceived as less severe than morality-based violations in morality markets. The main effect of type of response indicated that an apology was more successful than no reaction, which was in turn more successful than denial. Thus, in competence-based violations of trust, the hypotheses of Kim and his colleagues were supported, but in morality-based violations they were not (2004).

The analyses of the responsibility attributions showed clearly that the type of response altered the attributions. For the attribution that the seller acted on purpose, again, two main effects emerged. The morality-based violation of trust was attributed more to the seller than the competence-based violation of trust. This is in line with the positive-negative asymmetry; negative information in the competence domain is less diagnostic and less interpreted as a purposeful attempt at fraud by the seller. When an apology was rendered, the trust-violation was significantly less attributed to the seller than when no response was given or the incident was denied. The nonresponse and the denial condition did not differ significantly; this might indicate that an attribution to a malign seller is the default attribution in morality markets such as eBay. An

Figure 8.3   Responsibility Attributions (Somebody Else's Fault)

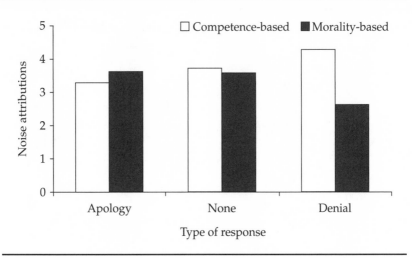

Source: Author's compilation.

apology can alter this default attribution. For the noise attribution (someone else's fault), a different pattern emerged (see figure 8.3).

The main effect of type of response was not significant, and the main effect of type of trust violation was only marginally significant. The competence-based violation was more easily attributed to noise than the morality-based violation. However, there was a significant interaction between type of violation and type of response. A significant effect emerged only in the denial condition, indicating that people believed the denial in the competence-based scenario ("buyer gave me the wrong zip code"), but not in the morality-based scenario ("did work at my place"). When the responsibility attributions were included as a covariate in the analysis of variance with trustworthiness as dependent variable, the main effect of type of response was no longer significant. Thus, the effect of communication (type of response) on trustworthiness judgments is mediated by attributions. This result supports the assumption of the model that people use the information given in the text comments to judge whether the negative incident might be caused by noise. If an incident is attributed to noise, trust is not violated and there is less need to repair trust; it therefore does not matter whether the accused person reacts with denial or an apology.

Further analysis of the judgments of the reactions in the apology and denial conditions revealed that the denial in the morality-based scenario was perceived as less believable than the denial in the competence-

Figure 8.4   Trustworthiness Judgments as a Function of Type of Trust
            Violation and Type of Response, with Believability of
            Response as Covariate

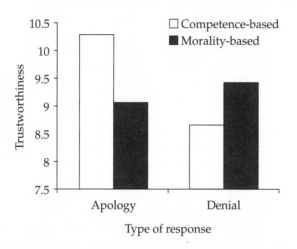

Source: Author's compilation.

based scenario. If believability was included as a covariate, a marginally
significant interaction between type of response and type of trust violation occurred. As can be seen in figure 8.4, the pattern was as predicted
according to the Kim et al. model (2004). In the case of a competence-
based violation, an apology is more successful in repairing trust than denial. In the case of a morality-based violation, denial is more successful
than an apology.

This study revealed several interesting results. First, it showed that communication, a factor neglected in most previous studies on the eBay reputation system (for an exception, see Pavlou and Dimoka 2006), influences
trustworthiness judgments. Even in the no-response condition, the difference between the competence-based and the morality-based scenarios was
significant. The type of negative feedback influences the perception of the
situation and the construction in terms of a morality-based or competence-
based violation. As can be predicted from the work on the positive-negative asymmetry, trustworthiness judgments are higher in the competence-
based scenario than in the morality-based scenario. Negative information
in the competence domain is not really diagnostic and has therefore less
impact on trustworthiness judgments. Second, and in contrast with the
predictions of Kim and his colleagues, an apology always proved more
successful in repairing trust than denial, not only in a competence-based
trust violation (2004). Denial was worse than no response.

Why did the expected trust-repairing effect of denial in the morality-based trust violation not occur? The differences in setting between the studies might be one reason. Kim and his colleagues used videotapes, and therefore both verbal and nonverbal communication, whereas the present study provided people with only short text-based comments (2004). Longer messages with more channels are less ambiguous than short text-messages (see also chapter 11, this volume). More important, people differed in how much they believed the explanations. When believability was used as a covariate, the predicted pattern occurred. Thus, it might be that the denial in the Kim et al. study was more believable (2004). Guda Van Noort, Peter Kerkhof, and Bob Fennis found that people who shop online are in a prevention focus and perceive higher risks than those who shop in a brick-and-mortar shop (2005). In a similar vein, the setting of an online auction might have triggered a prevention focus that led to skepticism and discounting the denial. Two recent studies by Utz and her colleagues also stress the important role of believability (Utz, Matzat, and Snijders 2009). Believability of reactions turned out to mediate the effects of the reactions on trustworthiness. In these experiments, respondents did not believe the denials and behaved as if guilt had been proven by showing low levels of trustworthiness after the denial of a morality-based trust violation (Kim et al. 2004, exp. 2).

It is also possible that apologies were more successful because of the regret component. The apologies in the present experiment were always perceived as friendlier and as more polite than denials, but this could be mainly due to the word *sorry*. Thus the results show that it makes sense to separate the regret component from the apology. Instead, it is more important to distinguish between acknowledging the incident and acknowledging responsibility. Plain apologies, that is, pure regrets, have been more successful in repairing trust than apologies that offer an explanation (Utz, Matzat, and Snijders 2009). Pure regrets are an unambiguous signal of regret. Explanations are more ambiguous; believability of the specific apology and the dispositional propensity to trust and believe apologies play a significant role.

Conclusion

The main goal of this chapter was to turn the attention to two topics that have so far been neglected in social psychological research on reputation systems in online markets: the role of noise and the rebuilding of trust. Noise posits a threat to the function of reputation systems because it lowers the diagnosticity of negative feedback. This can have detrimental consequences for the entire marketplace because negative experiences with individual sellers generalize easily to the community and decrease trust in the community of sellers, transaction intentions, and price premiums (Pavlou and Gefen 2005). Given these findings, the success of online marketplaces such as eBay or Amazon is surprising and can partly be explained by successful trust-repairing strategies. Research should therefore turn to trust-rebuilding strategies in online interactions. The chapter takes a first step toward this goal by deducting a model from two lines of research. Not all predictions of the model have yet been tested empirically, but it provides a useful framework for a research agenda. First, it is important to examine the effects of the three response types on perceived competence and morality and final trustworthiness judgments. Attributions to noise and perceived diagnosticity of feedback should be measured as well—these variables have not been considered in prior research. Research should also be extended by comparing types of markets. Most studies on reputation systems focus on eBay, but rebuilding trust is expected to be easier in competence markets.

The trust-building function of reputation systems in online markets has been studied extensively, and the primary focus has been the deleterious effect of negative feedback. It is also and equally important to focus on positive outcomes and to study how trust can be rebuilt in noisy environments.

Notes

1. In May 2008, eBay changed the system. Sellers can no longer give negative feedback on buyers because eBay management assumed that many buyers would not give well-deserved negative feedback in fear of negative revenge-feedback.
2. Available at: http://pages.ebay.com/help/buy/communicate.html.

References

Axelrod, Robert M. 1984. *The Evolution of Cooperation*. New York: Basic Books.

Ba, Sulin, and Paul A. Pavlou. 2002. "Evidence of the Effect of Trust Building Technology in Electronic Markets: Price Premiums and Buyer Behavior." *MIS Quarterly* 26(3): 243–68.

Bendor, Jonathan, Roderick M. Kramer, and Suzanne Stout. 1991. "When in Doubt: Cooperation in a Noisy Prisoner's Dilemma." *Journal of Conflict Resolution* 35(4): 691–719.

Bolton, Gary E., Elena Katok, and Axel Ockenfels. 2004. "How Effective Are Electronic Reputation Mechanisms? An Experimental Investigation." *Management Science* 50(11): 1587–602.

Bottom, William P., Kevin Gibson, Steven E. Daniels, and J. Keith Murnighan. 2002. "When Talk Is Not Cheap: Substantive Penance and Expressions of Intent in Rebuilding Cooperation." *Organization Science* 13(5): 497–513.

Cook, Karen S., Russell Hardin, and Margaret Levi. 2006. *Cooperation without Trust*. New York: Russell Sage Foundation.

Dasgupta, Partha. 1988. "Trust as a Commodity." In *Trust: The Making and Breaking of Cooperative Relations*, edited by Diego Gambetta. Oxford: Blackwell Publishers.

Dellarocas, Chrysanthos. 2003. "The Digitization of Word-of-Mouth: Promise and Challenges of Online Reputation Mechanisms." *Management Science* 40(10): 1407–24.

Eaton, David H. 2002. "Valuing Information: Evidence from Guitar Auctions on eBay." Department of Economics and Finance working paper 0201. Murray, Ky.: Murray State University. Available at: http://databases.si.umich.edu/reputations/bib/papers/eatonpaper.pdf (accessed April 5, 2009).

Greif, Avner. 1989. "Reputation and Coalitions in Medieval Trade: Evidence on the Maghribi Traders." *Journal of Economic History* 49(4): 857–82.

———. 2006. *Institutions and the Path to Modern Economy: Lessons from Medieval Trade*. Cambridge: Cambridge University Press.

Jann, Ben, Stefan Wehrli, and Andreas Diekmann. 2006. "Reciprocity of Feedback in Internet Auctions." Paper presented at the Eighth General Online Research Conference. Bielefeld, Germany (March 21–22).

Kandori, Michihiro. 1992. "Social Norms and Community Enforcement." *Review of Economic Studies* 59(1): 63–80.

Kim, Peter H., Donald L. Ferrin, Cecily D. Cooper, and Kurt T. Dirks. 2004. "Removing the Shadow of Suspicion: The Effects of Apology Versus Denial for Repairing Competence—Versus Integrity-Based Trust Violations." *Journal of Applied Psychology* 89(1): 104–18.

Kollock, Peter. 1993. "'An Eye for an Eye Leaves Everyone Blind': Cooperation and Accounting Systems." *American Sociological Review* 58(6): 768–86.

———. 1999. "The Production of Trust in Online Markets." In *Advances in Group Processes*, vol. 16, edited by Edward J. Lawler, Shane R. Thye, Michael W. Macy, and Henry A. Walker. Greenwich, Conn.: JAI Press.

Lee, Zoonky, Il Im, and San Jun Lee. 2000. "The Effect of Negative Buyer Feedback on Prices in Internet Auction Markets." In *Proceedings of the 21st International Conference on Information Systems*, edited by Wanda Orlikowski, Peter Weill, Soon Ang, and Helmut Krcmar. Atlanta: Association for Information Systems.

Lucking-Reiley, David, Doug Bryan, Naghi Prasad, and Danie Reeves. 2007. "Pennies from eBay: The Determinants of Price in Online Auctions." *Journal of Industrial Economics* 55(2): 223–33.

Mayer, Roger C., James H. Davis, and F. David Schoorman. 1995. "An Integrative Model of Organizational Trust." *Academy of Management Review* 20(3): 709–34.

McKnight, Harrison D., Vivek Choudhury, and Charles Kacmar. 2002. "Developing and Validating Trust Measures for e-Commerce." *Information Systems Research* 13(3): 334–59.

Melnik, Mikhail I., and James Alm. 2002. "Does a Seller's Ecommerce Reputation Matter? Evidence from eBay Auctions." *Journal of Industrial Economics* 50(3): 337–49.

Pavlou, Paul A., and Angelika Dimoka. 2006. "The Nature and Role of Feedback Text Comments in Online Marketplaces." *Information Systems Research* 17(4): 392–414.

Pavlou, Paul A., and David Gefen. 2005. "Psychological Contract Violation in Online Marketplaces: Antecedents, Consequences, and Moderating Role." *Information Systems Research* 16(4): 372–99.

Resnick, Paul, and Richard Zeckhauser. 2002. "Trust Among Strangers in Internet Transactions: Empirical Analysis of eBay's Reputation System." In *Advances in Applied Microeconomics*, vol. 11, *The Economics of the Internet and E-Commerce*, edited by Michael R. Baye. Amsterdam: Elsevier Science.

Resnick, Paul, Richard Zeckhauser, Eric Friedman, and Ko Kuwabara. 2000. "Reputation Systems." *Communications of the ACM* 43(12): 45–48.

Resnick, Paul, Richard Zeckhauser, John Swanson, and Kate Lockwood. 2006. "The Value of Reputation on eBay: A Controlled Experiment." *Experimental Economics* 9(2): 79–101.

Skowronski, John J., and Donald E. Carlston. 1987. "Social Judgment and Social Memory: The Role of Cue Diagnosticity in Negativity, Positivity, and Extremity Biases." *Journal of Personality and Social Psychology* 52(4): 689–99.

Standifird, Stephen S. 2001. "Reputation and e-Commerce: eBay Auctions and the Asymmetrical Impact of Positive and Negative Ratings." *Journal of Management* 27(3): 279–95.

Tazelaar, Miriam J. A., Paul A. M. Van Lange, and Jaap W. Ouwerkerk. 2004. "How to Cope with 'Noise' in Social Dilemmas: The Benefits of Communication." *Journal of Personality and Social Psychology* 87(4): 845–59.

Utz, Sonja. 2005. "Rebuilding Trust after Negative Feedback: The Role of Communication." Paper presented at the KNAW Academy Colloquium, "Trust and Cooperation in Online Interaction." Amsterdam (May 2–4).

Utz, Sonja, Uwe Matzat, and Chris Snijders. 2009. "Online Reputation Systems: The Effects of Feedback Comments and Reactions on Building and Rebuilding Trust in Online Auctions." *International Journal of Electronic Commerce* 13(3): 95–118.

Van Lange, Paul A. M., Jaap W. Ouwerkerk, and Miriam J. A. Tazelaar. 2002. "How to Overcome the Detrimental Effects of Noise in Social Interaction: The Benefits of Generosity." *Journal of Personality and Social Psychology* 82(5): 768–80.

Van Noort, Guda, Peter Kerkhof, and Bob Fennis. 2005. "Online winkelen en regulatieve focus" In *Jaarboek Sociale Psychologie 2004*, edited by Ernestine H. Gordijn, Rob Holland, Anneloes Meijnders, and Jaap W. Ouwerkerk. Groningen, The Netherlands: Aspo Pers.

Wojciszke, Bogdan. 2005. "Affective Concomitants of Information on Morality and Competence." *European Psychologist* 10(1): 60–70.

Wojciszke, Bogdan, Roza Bazinska, and Marcin Jaworski. 1998. "On the Dominance of Moral Categories in Impression Formation." *Personality and Social Psychology Bulletin* 24(12): 1251–263.

Chapter 9

The Acceptance and Effectiveness of Social Control on the Internet

Uwe Matzat

S OCIAL CONTROL is applied on the Internet in many forms. In leisure time communities, administrators may resort to drastic measures and banish misbehaving members (Suler and Phillips 1998), whereas scientific email list administrators influence member behavior successfully by simply appealing to norms (Matzat 2004). Between the two extremes is a continuum of forms that spans the entire range between direct and indirect control, which can be very effective (see Peterson 1997). Online auctions such as eBay apply a direct form of social control by allowing members to evaluate each other's behavior during financial transactions. The resulting reputation score directly affects the benefits to an eBay user by influencing the auction price of his offered goods (Diekmann and Wyder 2002; Snijders and Zijdemann 2004; chapters 5 and 6, this volume). In open source communities, some members are subject to almost invisible social control in that potential employers can observe their achievement by looking at their software output (Osterloh and Rota 2004).

Within online communities, the administrators have special power based on opportunities to use technical tools to administer control (Reid 1999). Nevertheless, social control is more than simply applying ICT (information and communication technology) tools. The deliberate use of group rituals, for example, plays an important role as well (Reid 1999). Various forms of social control are often applied but can at times have unintended effects. One such example is the manager of a multimedia chat community called "The Palace." He removed several misbehaving members and was then confronted by several other disgruntled members (Suler 2000). Very little is known about which types of social control are adequate for specific online groups.

Establishing communities on the Web rests to a large extent on the thoughtful preparation and application of social control. Literature based on the advice of consultants has emerged that offers how-to recommendations, such as Amy Kim's best practices of successful online community managers (2000). One of her recommendations includes using data automatically collected on posting behaviors of community members to construct members' rankings. This practice would provide an incentive for members to increase activity to gain a higher position in the public rankings. Additional recommendations are provided in a number of books, suggesting that the popularity of such literature may influence many online community administrators (see Figallo 1998).

Herein lies the problem—that we cannot prove the validity of such recommendations from consultants because it is difficult to generalize from a few best practice examples. Additional knowledge is needed on the effects of different forms of social control under different conditions and within different types of online groups. This chapter contributes to the existing knowledge base with a systematic comparison of the acceptance and effectiveness of different forms of social control by members of two types of online groups.

In this study, members of knowledge-sharing online groups and members of eBay are confronted with examples of direct and indirect social control applied to their groups. These examples are presented in a number of scenarios, and members are asked to evaluate both the acceptance and effectiveness of the controls through indirect questioning (Fisher 1993).

Management at eBay claims that members constitute a community with special values and willingness to follow community norms (eBay Inc. 2006b). Consequently, we should expect that appeals to such norms and rules by the management are strongly accepted and efficient, given that they are in tight, knowledge-based communities (for example, Matzat 2004).

The eBay management point of view is contrasted with another approach. The theory of relational signals in online groups distinguishes different types of social control by predicting which conditions affect the outcomes when social controls are applied. Arguments derived from the theory are used as a framework to examine empirically which types of social control are regarded as more acceptable and efficient by members of eBay and of knowledge-sharing groups. This contributes to assessing whether online auctions differ from other communities on the Internet in the sense that they accept and need stronger forms of social control.

Online auctions, it is argued, face problems of trust in such a way that they need direct forms of social control much more than knowledge-sharing groups.

A Relational Signaling Approach to Social Control

My theory of relational signals in online groups (Matzat 2009) stems from ideas of David Kreps and his colleagues and Eric Rasmusen, which portray how the lack of information affects outcomes in strategic decision situations (Kreps et al. 1982; Rasmusen 1989). Robert Frank applied these ideas to a number of social phenomena outside the economic sphere (1988).

I develop an informal version that is only loosely related to economic signaling theory. Rather, it stresses the importance of how individuals perceive the relations they have with each other, and includes the idea that these perceptions are affected by framing effects (Lindenberg 1997). The extent to which individuals take into account or neglect a common group frame sends information (signals) about their behavior that others can expect from them in the future.

The theory presented in the next section cannot immediately be used to derive predictions about differences between knowledge-sharing groups and online auctions. Additional related arguments about group differences are therefore developed and tested in a later section.

The Theory of Relational Signals in Online Groups

Members of online groups can exhibit two types of interest in online interaction with other members. In some groups, members are strongly motivated by their material interests, which do not necessarily require social interaction for fulfillment, for example, the attainment of a product or information. In other groups, relational interests play an important role. These require social interaction for fulfillment (De Vos 2004). One example is acquiring new contacts or maintaining existing contacts.

Online groups are established to fulfill either the material or relational interests of their members, or will address both types of interests. That is, when members interact on the Internet, they have some common interests as a group. Members also have, of course, their own unique, individual interests. Active participation in online groups may help them realize their common group interests, but will compete for the time they need to fulfill their individual interests. Under other conditions, active participation in the group allows a member to fulfill common group interests and individual interests simultaneously (Lindenberg 1997). For example, in a knowledge-sharing online group for teachers answering questions during group discussion, the discussion may fulfill the group's interest in composing a knowledge resource that is available to all teachers. At the same time, it may help individual teachers build new professional contacts or maintain friendly relations.

If a member's individual and group interests are mutually competitive, the question lies in which goal dominates. A member may evaluate the adequacy of his behavior, for example, by responding to a question on basis of the criterion whether it fits with the common group goal or with his competing individual goals. The goal that dominates this decisive situation is called the frame of the decision (Lindenberg 1997). Some forms of social control may attempt to manipulate the member's decision frame.

Interaction in online groups gives members important information about how any individual regards his relationship with others and the group. Three kinds of relational signals are found to be sent during online interaction (Matzat 2009). First, in bilateral interaction, the behavior of Ego can give Alter, the interaction partner, information about how Ego regards the relationship. This is especially true if Ego's behavior can indicate whether he regards the relationship as purely instrumental for maximizing his own short-term benefits, or whether he takes into account the interests of Alter as well. Second, the participation or lack of participation during group interaction indicates the extent to which Ego takes the norms, rules, and common interests of the whole group into account. Third, and very important, the group administrator's behavior sends signals that indicate what behavioral standards he expects from the members. For example, an administrator who appeals to norms of fairness clearly expresses that these norms should be a point of concern for all members. At the same time, an administrator who removes members without warning after an initial small deviation from a norm indicates that the group does not appreciate members as individuals.

Three Types of Social Control   The theory distinguishes between three types of social control that can be applied by members or the group administrator, which vary from weak to strong. The first kind of (weak) social control is applied through what are called frame stabilizing tools. These tools work through increasing the cognitive salience of the common group goal, thus pushing the potential costs of neglecting competing individual goals to the background (Lindenberg 1997). Frame stabilizing tools are those that increase the salience of the group, its boundaries, and its common rules and norms. Examples include the definition of the group in contrast to other groups, the use of group-specific symbols, or the appeal to group norms that help to reach the common group goal.

The second type of social control is applied with indirect monitoring tools. These give members the opportunity, as a by-product of their group participation, to send signals to the group that indicate their approval of the group's goals, norms, and rules. These tools cause a member to restrict the fulfillment of his competing individual interests, because the unlimited fulfillment would send signals to other members that lead to disapproval. An indirect monitoring tool was applied by an administrator in the famous "WELL" community by kicking off a discussion and affecting its outcome (Hafner 1997). Serious problems with deviating members made the administrator initiate a public discussion about group goals and related norms and rules. During the discussion, it was concluded that future deviating members should not be excluded, but other members should impose informal sanctions on them. This gave other members the opportunity to express their disapproval of the deviating members in public, thereby signaling their own compliance with group norms and rules.

The third and strongest form of social control is direct control. These tools directly change the costs and benefits of the decision alternatives of the members, in contrast to frame stabilizing tools, which change only perceived measures (Lindenberg 1997). An example of direct control is the use of automatically collected data about the posting behavior of members for the publication of public rankings. In this case, the decision alternative to post is made more attractive because achieving high status in the group is an added benefit to posting behavior. eBay's reputation system and that of the online programmers' market discussed in chapter 6 of this volume are also examples of using a direct social control tool.

The question posed is, therefore, "under which conditions are particular types of social control more adequate for stimulating active participation?" That management applies a tool sends certain signals to members that can be evaluated either positively or negatively, depending on the type of group. The three types of tools we have identified constitute a hierarchy of social control that, when applied, indicate relational disinterest on the part of the administration in an ascending order (Lindenberg 1997). This insight is used to predict the effects of these different forms of control in online groups, which vary in degree of relational interest to the members.

If the group administrator applies direct forms of social control that change the direct benefits for the member, a clear signal is sent. This type of signal indicates that, according to the administrator, the best way to influence the member's behavior is not to appeal to his concern for his colleagues' interests, but to transform his opportunities for the short-term maximization of his own benefits. That is, members receive the signal that they are not expected to have a high degree of relational interest. This may lead to desired changes in member behavior in groups with only a limited degree of relational interest. However, it will be less accepted in online groups with strong relational interest. The results are different for indirect monitoring and the application of frame stabilizing tools.

If the group administrator applies indirect monitoring, he or she is offering members an opportunity to signal accordance with group norms. Members will not make use of this opportunity unless they have an interest in avoiding (or obtaining) other members' disapproval (or approval). If they do not have any interest in maintaining a satisfying relation with the other members, either for instrumental or intrinsic reasons, then indirect monitoring does not provide any incentive for behavioral change. Frame stabilizing tools also exhibit limited impact when the degree of relational interest is low. If members are interested only in maximizing their own interests, then a common group goal will hardly be salient. This is explained primarily by the fact that contributing to the public good implies higher costs than benefits in terms of the realization of one's narrow self-interests. Thus indirect monitoring and weak forms of social control will be more effective in online groups with strong relational interests than in those with weaker relational interests.

Group Characteristics and Relational Interests   The next question is about the conditions under which online groups are characterized by stronger relational interest. Only one is mentioned here (see Matzat 2009). Some online group members interact only through the group, whereas other groups' online interaction is embedded in networks of relations that exist offline. This is referred to as a high degree of social embeddedness of the online interaction in offline networks. For example, in a knowledge-sharing group for teachers, some members may know each other from collaboration in school-encompassing projects or from being members of the same professional association.

A high degree of social embeddedness dramatically changes the character of the group. Members know that it is likely they will meet each other again, and depend on one another for successful interaction outside the group. Even if some members do not have close contact with other members, they will realize the interactions between others, and this informal network among members has a high density. High network density increases the likelihood that information about misbehavior spreads quickly, and strong forms of misbehavior may be sanctioned by collective action (Coleman 1990). Consequently, under the condition of a high degree of social embeddedness of the group, members depend more on each other. If Ego is more dependent on Alter, then it is likely that Ego will develop an interest in maintaining a satisfying relation with Alter. Thus a high degree of embeddedness leads to a higher degree of relational interest in the group, which in turn affects the outcomes of the three forms of social control. Moreover, a high degree of embeddedness directly diminishes problems of trust. These problems are reduced because a high degree of embeddedness typically means that members are likely to meet each other in the future. Members will also be more willing to place trust in one another because they realize their ability to sanction the abuse of trust by other members of the network.

Common Interest and Transaction Online Groups

The arguments contained in the theory of relational signals can be used to predict the conditions under which a specific form of social control has desirable or undesirable effects. It does not, however, directly lead to predictions on whether strong or weak forms of social control are more effective or accepted in either online auctions or knowledge-sharing groups. One must first distinguish between the main functions of different types of online groups. In so-called transaction online groups, the main purpose of the interaction is to conduct business, such as in eBay. Online groups of interest allow fulfillment of at least one common goal that unites the members (see Matzat 2009; Armstrong and Hagel 1996). Knowledge-sharing groups for teachers are one such example. Their members have the common goal to increase a common knowledge resource all members can use.

Both groups face problems of trust that create a barrier to their reaching their full potential. In eBay transactions, the buyer first must send payment to the seller. Risks include that the seller may fail to send the product, sending with a serious delay, or sending a product with lower quality than promised. In knowledge-sharing groups of teachers, several problems of trust emerge. For example, a teacher might hesitate to send teaching material to the group. When sending material, a teacher runs the risk of not receiving anything in return, in addition to being criticized for inadequate quality of the material, witnessed by hundreds of colleagues. Although such forms of abuse of trust cannot be called cheating, their consequences nevertheless may be more fundamental than the loss of money on eBay.

Consequently, application of social control by the administration is one useful way to reduce the risk that placed trust is misused. If the social control shows its intended effect, members will be more willing to place trust, and thus the entire group profits. In online transaction groups, one form of direct social control uses a reputation system, such as that at eBay. Additionally, eBay claims to constitute a community and appeals to community norms (2006a, 2006b). In common-interest online groups for teachers, the administrators also appeal to group norms.

However, more direct forms of social control are also viable options (see Verhulp 2005). It is thus useful to determine what effects are to be expected when strong and weak forms of social control are applied to each type of online group.

Although both groups face problems of trust, the details of the problems differ remarkably. Teachers run the risk of ruining their reputation, whereas eBay members run the risk of losing their money. It is unclear which problem is more threatening to the groups in the sense that it prevents a larger number of members from becoming active and placing trust. Thus the first research question is about the extent to which members of common-interest groups and of transaction groups face problems of trust. The two groups are different not only with respect to the type of resources their members run the risk of losing (money or reputation). Members of transaction groups interact with each other only to conduct business. The main function of a transaction group dominates the social interaction, making all other measures largely irrelevant. This is different for most knowledge-sharing groups, many members of which take into account that meeting another member in another social context is possible, whereas most members of transaction groups meet only as online transaction partners. The degree of relational interest in transaction groups is thus much more limited than in knowledge-sharing groups.

Accordingly, members of transaction groups tolerate appeals to norms and rules of conduct, but they realize that the overlap of common interests is minute given the conflict built into their interaction. To some extent, what the seller has won, the buyer has lost. The high degree of conflicting interests and low degree of social embeddedness prevents strong relational interests from developing. From the point of view of the member, problems of trust therefore cannot effectively be solved through weak forms of social control; stronger forms are needed. Members of common interests groups, on the other hand, have stronger relational interests they do not want destroyed through the use of harsh instruments. They believe that milder forms of social control have a measurable effect. These observations lead to the following two predictions:

Hypothesis 1. Direct control is more accepted in online transaction groups than in online common-interest groups.

Hypothesis 2. Indirect control is (evaluated as) more efficient in online common-interest groups than in online transaction groups.

Differences between these two types of groups are expected for reasons other than one concerning money and the other not. Rather, the differences are expected because of conflicting interests dominant in the interaction that are not dampened by interaction in other social contexts.

This limits the degree of relational interest in transactional groups. If the same transaction were to take place under the condition of a high degree of social embeddedness, the problem of trust would be less severe and members more willing to place trust. This observation leads to the following predictions:

> *Hypothesis 3.* Members of online transaction groups possess less relational interest than members of online common-interest groups.
>
> *Hypothesis 4.* Members of online transaction groups face fewer problems of trust in their transactions when they are socially embedded versus when they are not. That is, under a high degree of embeddedness, members of online transaction groups are more willing to place trust than when embeddedness is low.

Finally, it is interesting to note how members of the same group evaluate these types of social control in comparison to one another. This leads to research question 2: Which forms of social control (weak or strong) are more accepted among members of transaction groups and members of knowledge-sharing groups?

Design of the Study

This study uses data on social control in two types of online communities (OLCs). Data on Dutch members of eBay is used as an example of a transaction OLC. The behavior of Dutch teachers sharing knowledge in a number of online groups of the same virtual organization is used as an example of common-interest OLCs.

The data on knowledge-sharing communities was collected between November 2005 and February 2006 in thirty-three OLCs in a large virtual organization. This study focuses on teachers who use the OLCs for secondary education, and these communities offer multiple comparable measures. They each have a goal to stimulate the exchange of knowledge among teachers to encourage learning from each other and facilitating their professional development. Teachers must register to become a member of the OLC, which has one manager responsible for informing members and resolving problems. All OLCs provide their members an opportunity to share teaching materials, and each has a discussion forum in which members can exchange questions and answers with their colleagues. The managers regularly send an electronic newsletter to all subscribed members, who also have the opportunity to contribute by writing short pieces. In some OLCs, an email list allows interested teachers to hold more intensive discussions with each other. To collect the data, we sent every member an email invitation to participate in an online survey. Answering questions required approximately ten to twenty minutes, which led to a response rate of 38 percent. After removal of some outliers, 2,547 usable answers remained.

The data on Dutch eBay users was collected in July and August 2006. Because it was not feasible to obtain a random sample of all eBay users, a different approach was used. An invitation to participate in our survey was sent by email to a random sample of members of a large Dutch commercial opt-in access panel. Among these, 1,141 members (response rate 44.3 percent) who were also subscribers of eBay and bought or sold at least one item on the site during the last twelve months completed the survey, which required approximately twenty minutes. The sample was stratified so that different age groups and groups with different lengths of membership were selected.

Because only active eBay members were included, the sample of teaching community members was divided into 854 active and 1,693 passive members for more adequate comparisons. An active member was a respondent who had ever sent a contribution to the community newsletter, had sent teaching material to the community, had sent at least one email per month to the community email list, had posted at least one message per month to the community forum, or had answered yes to the question of whether he or she had ever been active in some another way. The most interesting comparisons are conducted between 1,141 active eBay members and 854 active members of the online teacher communities.

To reduce the questionnaire length, some questions were asked only of a random selection of all respondents. Moreover, to ensure that the teachers were able to answer the questions about social control, we presented them only to those who subscribed for at least six months. The number of cases in the different analyses varies and is reported separately for each analysis.

Measurement

The *acceptance and effectiveness of social control* was analyzed using a scenario approach combined with the method of indirect questioning (Fisher 1993). Members were confronted with a hypothetical but realistic scenario that presented the application of social control as a remedy for a problem of cooperation in their own online group. The scenario was preceded by a short description of a problem of cooperation, such as this: "On eBay [in every community on the Internet], there are some rules. For example, it is expected that buyers pay in time and that sellers deliver in time. [For example, it is expected that members are polite and do not offend others.] What do you think of the following way that the eBay management [that the management of your community] might use to deal with problematic behavior?" A tool of social control was presented in the second step (see the following). Finally, the member was asked to evaluate the acceptance and effectiveness of the tool to solve the presented problem—in this case, to increase rule compliance among members.

Of course, it is not unproblematic to ask whether the respondent would accept such a tool and change his or her behavior, because rule compliance might be socially desirable. Thus two measures were taken to reduce this effect. First, we control for the general tendency to give socially desirable answers by including the scores on the shortened version of the BIDR-6 scale (see Paulhus 1991). Second, we reduce this tendency by using indirect questioning. This projective technique is often used. It entails asking respondents to answer questions from the perspective of another typical person or group (see, for example, Miller and Thomas 2005; Steenhaut and Van Kenhove 2005) and reduces social desirability bias by giving respondents the opportunity to attribute undesirable behavior to a typical other (Fisher 1993; Vargas, von Hippel, and Petty 2004; Neeley and Cronley 2004).

After the presentation of the scenario that described the application of some form of social control within the respondent's group, the respondent was asked two questions: "How acceptable do you think such an approach would be for a typical member of eBay [your community]?" and "What do you think about how such an approach would change the behavior of a typical member of eBay [your community]? Would he or she show more, less, or just as much rule compliance as before?" Each question was answered on a 7-point Likert scale ranging from "completely unacceptable" to "completely acceptable", and from "less" or "unchanged" to "more." The scenarios used in the second step, after the description of the problem (see appendix) were as follows:

[eBay] The management of eBay publishes some rules on the Web. Every member of eBay receives an email informing him or her about their meaning for the whole community. Occasionally, and at appropriate times, the management again draws attention to the rules, explaining why they were set up in this way and emphasizes the importance of compliance to the rules for the whole community.

[Knowledge-sharing group] The community manager publishes some rules on the Web, such as "Be polite and friendly. You are not allowed to offend others during discussion or when you have diverging opinions." Every member receives an email informing him or her about their meaning for the whole community. Occasionally, and at appropriate times, the management again draws attention to the rules, explaining why they were set up in this way and emphasizes the importance of compliance to the rules for the whole community.

Other scenarios used in the surveys are included in the appendix.

Relational interests were measured by perceived importance of fulfilling numerous interests through the group. These relational interests need social interaction for their fulfillment, such as making contacts, attaining status in the group, and the like. Respondents were asked to assess the following statements on a 7-point Likert scale ranging from "completely disagree" to "completely agree":

> It is important to me to make new contacts with other members of eBay [with other colleagues within my community]. . . . There is a group of members whose sympathy is important to me. . . . I like having the attention of other members of eBay [of my community]. . . . I would dislike having nothing to contribute to eBay [of my community]. . . . I like being popular at eBay [in my community].

Cronbach's alpha for a scale consisting of the five items is 0.91 within eBay and 0.79 within the teachers' OLCs.

Whether problems of trust within eBay differ in online *transactions in embedded versus nonembedded settings* was tested by means of two 1-factorial experiments (two steps) with a within-person design. We presented the respondent with the following baseline condition: "Imagine that you intend to buy a modern and highly valuable mobile phone with many extra functions. You are willing to pay up to about 300 € for the product and you expect that it is a realistic option to get the mobile for this price at eBay." Additionally, the respondent saw a (hypothetical) profile of an eBay seller with a feedback score of 0 (no transaction during the last six months), as presented in figure 9.1:

We asked the respondent, "Would you take part in the online auction of this seller and finally buy the product?" On a 5-point Likert scale, answer options included "definitely not," "probably not," "maybe yes/maybe no," "probably," and "sure." On the next screen, the respondent was confronted with the same scenario and profile, with the addition of one of two treatment descriptions: The first was, "With the help of the information in the member's profile, you discover that he or she is a baker in your neighborhood. You do not know the baker personally, but you do your shopping at his or her bakery." The second was, "With the help of the information in the member's profile, you discover that he or she is a helpdesk employee of your online provider. You have never seen this person in a face to face meeting, but every now and then you exchange emails with the employee about computer related topics." This treatment increased the degree of embeddedness, which is low in the baseline condition and high in the two treatment conditions. At the end of the scenario, we once more

Figure 9.1   Profile of the Seller

Gebruikersprofiel: Verkoper XY (0)				
Feedbackscore: 0	recente feedback			
Positieve feedback:		afgelopen	afgelopen	afgelopen
0 positieve feedback		maand	6 maanden	12 maanden
0 neutrale feedback	Positief	0	0	0
0 negatieve feedback	Neutraal	0	0	0
	Negatief	0	0	0

Source: Author's compilation.

asked the respondent, "Would you take part in the online auction of this seller and finally buy the product?"

To measure the *problems of trust*, we included indicators of the respondents' *actual placement of trust*, their *willingness to place trust* under different conditions, and the extent to which they *subjectively perceived problems of trust* in the group. The extent was assessed by members' reactions to the statement, "Members do not trust each other" on a 7-point Likert rating scale with the labels "not," "hardly," "to a limited extent," "to some extent," "to a reasonable extent," "to a large extent," and "to a very large extent." *Actual placement of trust* was indicated by asking, "During the last twelve months, how often did you participate in an online auction with a bid of 100 € or more under the condition that you had no information about the past transactions of the seller, that is, you had no information about his reputation score?" The teachers were asked, "Did you ever send teaching material to your community?"

Willingness to place trust included two questions for eBay members. The first question was, "Assume that you would like to buy a modern mobile phone with many additional functions. You expect to get such a phone for about 300 €. Moreover, assume that such a product would be offered by a seller about whom no information about his past transactions is known. Would you take part in the online auction of this seller and finally buy the product?" The second question was, "Assume that you had bought a product on eBay for about 300 €. The product was delivered ten days later than promised. Would you, under such circumstances, provide feedback before your seller did so?"

Members of the teachers' community were also asked two questions. The first question was, "Assume that in your community there is a discussion forum where members have the opportunity to exchange information about the problems they have with their pupils. Would you discuss your own problems in such a community when your name is attached to the postings?" The second question was, "Would you be willing to send teaching material with your name on it to the community under the precondition that disposal of the material would be easy?" All questions could be answered on a 5-point Likert scale with the labels "definitely not," "probably not," "maybe yes/maybe no," "probably," and "sure."

In the analyses, we include a number of control variables. *General trusting disposition* consists of one factor from four items on the scale proposed by Sirkka Jarvenpaa, Kathleen Knoll, and Dorothy Leidner (1998). *Pro-social orientation* is indicated by a score that stems from a shortened version of the "decomposed games method" (see Snijders and Weesie 1999), and *digital literacy* was measured by an extended version of a scale proposed by Eszter Hargittai (2005).

Results

In both samples, the proportion of women was 54.8 percent. Both groups consist of members with a comparable number of years of Internet use (more than seven years constitutes 54 percent in both groups), a comparable length of membership in the community (on average between one and two years), and the eBay members score only slightly higher on the scale of social desirability ($t = 1.68$, $p = .09$). The eBay members are significantly younger ($\bar{X}_1 = 40$ versus $\bar{X}_2 = 45$ years, $t = -9.9$, $p < .01$). They score significantly higher on the digital literacy scale ($t = 6.4$, $p < .01$), and significantly lower on the scales of prosocial attitudes ($t = -19.3$, $p < .01$) and general trusting disposition ($t = -7.4$, $p < .01$).

With respect to the first question, about the intensity of problems of trust, we find that eBay members score significantly higher in their answer to the question, "To what extent do members not trust each other?" ($\bar{X}_1 = 3.1$, $\bar{X}_2 = 2.1$, $n_1 = 1141$, $n_2 = 344$), $t = 13.3$, $p < .01$). Significantly fewer eBay members dared participate during the previous year in an auction of a seller with an unknown reputation score than teachers ever dared send teaching material to their community (19 percent versus 44 percent, $X^2 = 146.2$, $p < .01$). Although the differences can partly be explained by the difference in the time frame of the questions ("one year" versus "ever"), they do not disappear when we restrict the analysis to those who subscribed as members no longer than one year (14.5 percent versus 32.9 percent, $X^2 = 28.5$, $p < .01$).

In regard to the willingness to place trust in typical situations that demand trust, we also see differences between the groups. On the 5-point scale measuring the willingness to place trust in a seller with unknown reputation, the eBay members score a 2.4. Teachers have a score of 2.7 on a comparable scale measuring the willingness to post messages about problems with their pupils ($t = -3.7$, $p < .01$, $n_1 = 229$, $n_2 = 373$). In turn, eBay members are significantly more willing to give negative feedback though the partner did not yet do so ($\bar{X} = 3.3$, $t(3.3, 2.7) = 7.6$, $p < .01$, $n_1 = 329$, $n_2 = 373$). It is even more likely that teachers will send teaching material bearing their name ($\bar{X} = 4.0$, $t(4.0, 3.3) = -9.5$, $p < .01$, $n_1 = 329$, $n_2 = 373$).

The numbers show that, for the teachers, discussing with colleagues the problems they have with pupils is a more serious problem of trust than sending teaching material to colleagues. eBay members consider it more serious to trust an unknown seller than to give negative feedback as the first of the two transaction partners.[1] If we compare the two more serious problems, that is, the collegial discussion of teachers' problems with pupils and sending a bid in an online auction of an unknown and new seller, eBay members are less willing to place trust than teachers are. With respect to the first question, this finding, combined with the fact that eBay members, much more than teachers, agree with the statement "members do not trust each other," suggests that problems of trust tend to be more serious for members of eBay than for teachers.

The acceptance of weak and strong forms of social control in both types of groups is analyzed for two types of problems in these communities—namely, compliance with basic rules that govern conflicts, and the stimulation of members' active contributions to community activities (see appendix). We presented eBay members three scenarios with solutions to the problem of rule compliance. One scenario proposed using weak social control for rule compliance—specifically, appealing to norms (see appendix, scenario eBay-1). Two others proposed forms of strong control—namely, the exclusion of members (see appendix, scenario eBay-2) and an automated ranking of members (see appendix, scenario eBay-3). On a 7-point scale ranging from "completely unacceptable" to "completely acceptable," there are no significant differences in the acceptance of the three tools (all three p-values $>.1$, $n = 1141$). All three forms of social control are judged as acceptable by the eBay members ($\bar{X} = 5.4$ for norm appeals, $\bar{X} = 5.4$ for member exclusion, $\bar{X} = 5.3$ for automated ranking). This comes as no surprise given that all three tools are common practice within eBay.

In addition, we presented two forms of control designed to stimulate eBay member activity in providing feedback on transaction partners. Scenario eBay-4 proposed appealing to norms (weak control), and scenario eBay-5 proposed member exclusion (strong control). Norm appeal is judged moderately acceptable ($\bar{X} = 5.2$), the exclusion of members acceptable, but to a somewhat lesser degree ($\bar{X} = 5.0$). The acceptance of weak social control is significantly higher than the acceptance of strong social control (paired samples test: $t = 3.8$, $p < .01$, n = 1141) for the stimulation of feedback.

We presented two similar scenarios to members of the teachers' OLCs, in this case, for solving rule compliance problems. The first scenario, as with the eBay scenario, proposed norm appeal as an example of weak social control (see appendix, scenario teacher-1). The second, also as with the eBay scenario, proposed excluding members (see appendix, scenario teacher-2) as strong social control. Because the two scenarios were part of a larger set, we were not able to present every scenario to all respondents. One group of respondents received both scenarios, one group received only the first, and a third group received only the second. The respondents who judged both scenarios determined direct control to be being only marginally more acceptable than weak control ($\bar{X} = 5.7$ versus $\bar{X} = 5.5$, paired samples test: $t = 1.8$, $p = .07$, n = 96). There are no differences between the judgments in the groups who were presented with only one of the two forms of social control (both $\bar{X} = 5.7$, independent samples test: $t = .08$, $p > .10$, $n_1 = 94$, $n_2 = 66$). Combining both analyses into one generalized least square regression shows no significant differences between the two scenarios ($z = -1.62$, $p > .10$). Thus we can conclude that for the teachers, strong and weak forms of social control are equally acceptable in addressing rule compliance, and this degree of acceptance is strong.

Three scenarios were presented to members of the teachers' OLCs, this time for the problem of membership stimulation. One proposed direct control in the form of book and CD vouchers for the most active posters (see appendix, scenario teacher-3), and another proposed it in the form of an automated public member ranking (see appendix, scenario teacher-4). The third proposed weak social control, in the form of appeals to norms (see appendix, scenario teacher-5). Among respondents who received all three scenarios, direct control in the form of vouchers was neither clearly acceptable nor unacceptable ($\bar{X} = 4.3$), direct control in the form of a member ranking was generally unacceptable ($\bar{X} = 3.2$), and weak control in the form of norm appeals was acceptable ($\bar{X} = 5.3$). The differences between the acceptance of the weak and strong forms of social control are significant (paired samples test: $t = 4.4$, $p < .01$ for the difference between vouchers and norm appeals, and $t = 10.1$, $p < .01$ for the difference between automated ranking and norm appeals, n = 96).

When we compare the answers of the group that received only the direct control scenarios with the answers of the group that received only the weak control scenario, we find similar differences. Social control with the help of vouchers is neither acceptable nor unacceptable ($\bar{X} = 4.3$, n = 94), social control with the help of an automated ranking is generally unacceptable ($\bar{X} = 3.4$, n = 94), and social control by an appeal to norms is clearly acceptable ($\bar{X} = 5.6$, n = 66). Differences in the acceptability of the weak and strong forms of social control are significant ($t = 5.5$, $p < .01$ for the difference between vouchers and norm appeals, $t = 9.3$, $p < .01$ for the difference between automated ranking and norm appeals). Combining the two analyses into one generalized least square regression shows that weak social control is significantly more accepted than the two forms of strong control ($z_1 = -7.1$, $z_2 = -13.7$, both $p < .01$).

We can summarize the findings on the second question for both groups as follows. In regard to rule compliance in both groups, eBay and teachers' communities, strong and weak forms of social control are equally acceptable and the level of acceptance is moderately high. When considering the problem of membership stimulation, weak forms are significantly more accepted. In teachers' communities, strong social control in the form of an automated ranking of members is unacceptable, whereas eBay members find it acceptable, though less so than weak social control.

Next, we test hypothesis 1, which claims that direct control is more accepted in transaction OLCs than in common-interest OLCs. First, we analyze the acceptance of direct control for problems of rule compliance by comparing the acceptance of the exclusion of members (scenario eBay-2) and the automated ranking system among eBay members (scenario eBay-1) with the proposal to exclude members of the teaching communities when they regularly do not comply with rules (scenario teacher-2). Contrary to the hypothesis, we see that strong control is accepted more among members of the teachers' community than among members of eBay ($\bar{X} = 5.4$ for exclusion of eBay members, $\bar{X} = 5.4$ for the ranking of eBay members, $\bar{X} = 5.7$ for the exclusion of teachers, $t_1 = 3.1$, $p < .01$, $t_2 = 3.3$, $p < .01$). The difference can be explained largely by the higher degree of trusting dispositions among the teachers that is positively associated with the acceptance of direct control, as the following results of multiple regression analyses presented in table 9.1 show.

The acceptance of direct control increases with higher levels of a general trusting disposition. When we control for these other differences between the samples, the differing acceptance between the groups is no longer significant. Nevertheless, there is no evidence for the hypothesis that the members of eBay are more willing than the teachers to accept strong forms of social control to solve the problem of rule compliance.

The acceptance of direct control for membership stimulation of activity is analyzed by comparing the acceptance of members' exclusion for the stimulation of feedback (scenario eBay-5, $\bar{X} = 5.0$) with the acceptance of an automated ranking (scenario teacher-4, $\bar{X} = 3.3$), and a voucher (scenario teacher-3, $\bar{X} = 4.3$) for the stimulation of active postings in the teachers' communities. Both differences are significant and measured in the expected directions ($t_1 = -5.3$, $p < .01$, $t_2 = -13.2$, $p < .01$).

Table 9.1   Multiple Regression of the Acceptance of Direct Control for Rule Compliance

	1: Exclusion of eBay Members and Exclusion of Teachers	2: Ranking of eBay Members and Exclusion of Teachers
Group membership (teachers' communities = 1)	0.031 (.313)	0.052 (.091)
Prosocial attitudes	0.068 (.029)*	0.048 (.125)
Social desirability	0.092 (.003)**	0.091 (.003)**
Trusting disposition	0.150 (.000)**	0.173 (.000)**
Years of Internet use	0.015 (.641)	0.011 (.740)
Gender (female = 1)	0.096 (.002)**	0.077 (.013)*
Age	0.043 (.182)	0.004 (.890)
Digital literacy	0.047 (.161)	0.110 (.001)**
	n = 1088	n = 1088

Source: Author's compilation.
Note: Standardized regression coefficients, two-sided p-values in parentheses.
* $p < .05$, ** $p < .01$

Multiple regression analyses presented in table 9.2 show that the differences cannot be explained with respect to prosocial attitudes, general trusting dispositions, digital literacy, or other factors within the groups.

Members of the teachers' communities accept forms of strong social control much less than their eBay counterparts to stimulate membership

Table 9.2   Multiple Regression of the Acceptance of Direct Control for Membership Stimulation

	1: Exclusion of eBay Members and Voucher for Teachers	2: Exclusion of eBay Members and Ranking of Teachers
Group membership (teachers' communities = 1)	−0.182 (.000)**	−0.363 (.000)**
Prosocial attitudes	0.075 (.017)*	0.071 (.018)*
Social desirability	0.130 (.000)**	0.125 (.000)**
Trusting disposition	0.049 (.099)	0.047 (.101)
Years of Internet use	−0.024 (.460)	−0.031 (.324)
Gender (female = 1)	0.034 (.275)	0.008 (.789)
Age	−0.014 (.660)	−0.029 (.344)
Digital literacy	−0.013 (.699)	−0.004 (.891)
	n = 1088	n = 1088

Source: Author's compilation.
Note: Standardized regression coefficients, two-sided p-values in parentheses.
* $p < .05$, ** $p < .01$

Table 9.3   Multiple Regression of the Effectiveness of Weak Control for Membership

Group membership (teachers' communities = 1)	–0.109 (.001)**
Prosocial attitudes	0.046 (.153)
Social desirability	0.103 (.001)**
Trusting disposition	0.102 (.001)**
Years of Internet use	–0.022 (.526)
Gender (female = 1)	0.037 (.238)
Age	0.019 (.565)
Digital literacy	0.047 (.177)
	n = 1066

Source: Author's compilation.
Note: Standardized regression coefficients, two-sided p values in parentheses.
* $p < .05$, ** $p < .01$

activities, even after controlling for other factors of influence. Thus we find evidence for hypothesis 1, claiming that members of common-interest communities are less willing to accept direct control than members of online transaction communities. However, this is only true for the problem of membership stimulation, and not for that of rule compliance.

The next results show differences in the perceived effectiveness of weak forms of social control. We test this effect for the problem of rule compliance (scenarios eBay-1 versus teacher-1) and for the problem of membership stimulation (scenarios eBay-4 versus teacher-4). There are no differences between the two types of online communities with respect to the perceived effectiveness of weak social control for the problem of rule compliance ($\bar{X}_1 = 4.8$ $\bar{X}_2 = 4.9$, $t = 1.5$, $p > .10$, $n_1 = 161$, $n_2 = 1141$). Differences with respect to the perceived effectiveness of weak social control for the problem of membership stimulation, however, are significant ($\bar{X}_1 = 4.8$, $\bar{X}_2 = 5.1$, $t = 3.2$, $p < .01$, $n_1 = 161$, $n_2 = 1141$). That is, members of eBay tend to perceive weak social control as more effective than members of the teachers' community do. This difference does not disappear when we control for variances in other characteristics of the two groups, as the results of a multiple linear regression analysis presented in table 9.3 show.

The results do not support hypothesis 2; thus it must be rejected. When considering the problem of rule compliance, both groups perceive weak social control as effective. However, members of eBay see it as more effective for stimulating membership activity than members of the teachers' community do.

A test of hypothesis 3 shows that the degree of relational interests is significantly larger among the members of the teachers' community than among the members of eBay ($\bar{X}_1 = 15.5$ $\bar{X}_2 = 14.5$, $t = 3.4$, $p < .01$, $n_1 = 804$, $n_2 = 1141$).

Table 9.4   Relational Interests

Group membership (teachers' communities = 1)	0.074 (.008)**
Prosocial attitudes	0.013 (.650)
Social desirability	0.044 (.084)**
Trusting disposition	0.080 (.002)**
Years of Internet use	−0.083 (.002)**
Gender (female = 1)	−0.100 (.000)**
Age	0.059 (.030)*
Digital literacy	0.082 (.004)**
	n = 1555

Source: Author's compilation.
Note: Standardized regression coefficients, two-sided *p*-values in parentheses.
* *p* < .05, ** *p* < .01

The multiple regression analysis in table 9.4 shows that relational interests depend on factors such as age, digital literacy, trusting disposition, gender, and years of Internet use, some measures of which vary between the groups. Nevertheless, after controlling for the factors of influence, members have significantly more relational interests in the teachers' communities than in eBay. This finding supports hypothesis 3.

Finally, we test whether the problem of trust in eBay is diminished under the condition of a high degree of social embeddedness. We compare the willingness to place trust in a seller without a reputation score under the condition of not knowing each other (baseline condition), which is the usual condition in eBay. Also included were two treatment conditions in which the seller and buyer by chance are likely to interact in another context. Because the questions about the baseline and the treatment conditions were independently shown only to random selections of the eBay respondents, the number of respondents in the baseline and one of the treatment conditions is very small. Whereas in one comparison, the willingness to place trust increases from $\bar{X} = 2.3$ to $\bar{X} = 3.0$, it increases from $\bar{X} = 1.7$ to $\bar{X} = 2.2$ in the other. These increases are both significant (Wilcoxon signed ranks exact tests: $z_1 = -2.2$, $p < .03$, $n_1 = 22$, $z_2 = -3.0$, $p < .01$, $n_2 = 18$), and the findings are in line with hypothesis 4.

Overall, the findings can be summarized as follows:

First, eBay members agree significantly more than members of the teachers' communities to the statement that members do not trust each other. Moreover, among teachers, the opportunity to discuss the difficulties they have with their pupils is less often used than the opportunity to send their teaching materials to the community. Among eBay members, the opportunity to trade with sellers without a reputation score is less often used than the opportunity to provide unpleasant feedback first if the seller had not yet provided feedback. When we compare the two more challenging problems of trust, we find that eBay members are significantly less willing than teachers to place trust in their problematic interaction situations that demand trust. Thus, problems of trust are more severe in eBay than they are in the online teachers' communities.

Second, the analysis of the acceptance and effectiveness of social control focuses on two problems—namely, the problem of rule compliance and that of membership stimulation.

Several similar characteristics were found in both groups. As a remedy for the problem of rule compliance, both determined that weak and strong forms of social control are equally acceptable. When considering the problem of membership stimulation, strong forms of social control in both groups are less acceptable than weak forms of social control. In accepting strong forms of social control as a solution to the problem of rule compliance, no significant differences between the two types of groups were found. Overall, strong forms of social control tend to be accepted as a remedy for rule compliance.

However, there are some differences between the groups. In accordance with hypothesis 1, the strong forms of social control as a solution to the problem of membership stimulation were significantly less accepted in the teachers' communities than among eBay members. Weak social control as a solution to the problem of rule compliance was perceived as similarly effective in both groups. Contrary to hypothesis 2, weak social control as a solution to the problem of membership stimulation was regarded as being significantly less effective in the teachers' communities than within eBay.

Third, it was also found that the degree of relational interests was significantly lower among eBay members than in the teachers' communities. Finally, the willingness to place trust is stimulated among the members of eBay if the buyer also interacts with the seller in social contexts outside eBay.

Discussion and Conclusions

In communities on the Internet, various forms of social control are often applied. It is unclear, however, whether all types are equally acceptable among community members. Also uncertain is whether any differences between types of online groups in the acceptance and perceived effectiveness of social control are characteristic.

This study compared the intensity of problems of trust and the acceptance and effectiveness of weak and strong forms of social control in two common types of online groups. Online communities for teachers were used as an example of common-interest communities, and eBay as an example of an online transaction community. Both types are common.

eBay management claims that eBay has community values and habits that make it similar to other Internet communities. This study used a relational signaling perspective to examine possible differences between the two types of groups.

Common interest and transaction groups have several similar characteristics. In regard to compliance with rules, weak and strong forms of social control are equally acceptable. Membership stimulation in both types of groups using weak forms of social control are much more acceptable than strong forms. A number of striking differences also emerged, however. Problems of trust between the members are perceived as more severe within eBay than within the online teachers' communities. Members of eBay hesitate much more than teachers in placing trust in situations where it is needed. Moreover, in accordance with the third and fourth hypotheses, we found that interaction within eBay is far less characterized by interests to build and maintain relations with other members than in teachers' communities. That interaction in eBay about financial transactions per se is not a barrier for the development of trust. The experimental findings show that trust would be placed more often when such transactions are embedded within interactions in other contexts outside of the transaction online group. Because transaction online groups usually do not have such social embeddedness, I conclude that this type of interaction is characterized by a narrowness which limits the development of trust.

Other group dissimilarities have important implications for the management of online communities. In partial accordance with the first hypothesis, acceptance of strong social control as a solution to the problem of membership stimulation is much lower in the teachers' communities than at eBay. Although strong forms of social control were acceptable within eBay, they tend to not be so in teacher communities.

Contrary to the second hypothesis, eBay members consider weak social control to be more effective in stimulating membership activity than teacher community members. This unexpected finding may be explained by the fact that the problem of membership stimulation within eBay is related to feedback. Although it may be somewhat unpleasant to provide negative feedback, the numbers show that many members do not hesitate in doing so, even when the partner has not yet provided his or her feedback and may be provoked to return negative comments. These numbers suggest that eBay members are highly motivated to provide feedback so that appeals to norms can work as an efficient reminder to fulfill a member's duty. Stimulation of members' postings in teacher community discussion groups, however, is a much more serious problem. Research regularly finds that few members in knowledge-sharing groups are motivated to actively post responses during discussions (see Rojo and Ragsdale 1997; Stegbauer and Rausch 2001; Ardichvili, Page, and Wentling 2003;

Matzat 2004; Preece, Nonnecke, and Andrews 2004). Therefore, simply appealing to norms might be evaluated as ineffective. If this is true, the found group difference would be a result of the large variance in the severity of the two selected problems, rather than a general or typical difference between transaction and common-interest communities. Stated differently, the two selected problems were incomparable and testing the hypothesis by selecting comparable problems might lead to a different result. Further research is needed to test this explanation.

These findings have important implications for managing online communities. They point to large simplifications in the literature on recommendations about the hosting of Web communities (Kim 2000; Figallo 1998). The best-practice examples in the literature of consultants may provide acceptable starting points for an online community manager. Nevertheless, community management would profit from the insights of research that compares the recommendations for different types of online groups. First, the findings show that the different tools of social control are not of equal value. Strong forms of social control are less acceptable than weak for encouraging membership stimulation. Second, they show that the adequacy of the same tool depends on the social context. Strong forms of social control are much more accepted in online transaction communities than in communities of common interest. The findings support the hypothesis that common-interest communities need a different management policy than transaction communities. Whatever community values eBay may have, its members accept a kind of community policy that rests on strong social control. Additionally, members of eBay face larger problems of trust and have fewer relational interests. In that sense, eBay, as a transaction group, is clearly different from the teachers' communities investigated.

Although the findings show important differences between the examples of two prominent types of online communities, further research should examine to what extent they describe general differences. Additionally, other types of online groups should be studied. For instance, health communities that often provide social support to their members may have even more relational interests than the teachers' communities (Eysenbach et al. 2004). Accordingly, acceptance of strong forms of social control should be rather low. A study's typology of online groups related to differences in members' relational interests may guide further research (Matzat 2009). The presented results, however, support the proposal that recommendations about hosting Web communities should be based on a theory of online community interaction and community management. In such a theory, hypotheses about the acceptance and effectiveness of social control on the Internet should be a cornerstone. Relational signaling theory provides a framework and hypotheses for a needed topography of the adequacy of social control in different locations on the Internet. Insight into the consequences of social control on the Internet is an important ingredient when designing communities.

Appendix: Measurements of Acceptance and Effectiveness

Rule Compliance Scenario Introduction

On eBay [every community on the Internet] there are some rules. For example, it is expected that buyers pay in time and that sellers deliver in time. [For example, it is expected that members are polite and do not offend others.] What do you think of the following way that the eBay management [that the management of your community] might use to deal with problematic behavior?

- Scenario eBay-1. The management of eBay publishes some rules on the Web. Every member of eBay receives an email informing him or her about their meaning for the whole community. Occasionally, and at appropriate times, the management draws attention to the rules, explaining why they were set up the way they were, and emphasizing the importance of compliance to the rules for the whole community.

- Scenario eBay-2. Every member who violates an important rule will be excluded from future use of eBay. However, members are informed about this policy beforehand.

- Scenario eBay-3. A database with the ranking of every member is set up. The more positive evaluations a member receives from others, the higher the member's position. These rankings are made available to every member, and every member has the opportunity to look up the position of every other member in this ranking.

- Scenario teacher-1. The community manager publishes some rules on the Web, such as, "Be polite and friendly. You are not allowed to offend others during discussion or when you have diverging opinions." Every member receives an email informing him or her about their meaning for the whole community. Occasionally, and at appropriate times, the management draws attention to the rules, explaining why they were set up this way, emphasizing the importance of compliance to the rules for the whole community.

- Scenario teacher-2. The community manager publishes a number of rules on the community website, such as, "You are not allowed to offend other members." Every member is informed about the rules. Moreover, the management announces that every member who violates an important rule twice (or more often) will be excluded. Rule violation will be controlled regularly. If a member does not comply with a rule, then he will first receive a warning. If a second violation takes place within a period of 12 months, he or she will be excluded. It is the aim of this policy to prevent members from failing to comply with the rules in the future.

Membership Stimulation Scenario Introduction

eBay: For eBay, it is crucial that members are willing to provide feedback on the behavior of a transaction partner after the completion of a transaction. Giving feedback takes time, however, and not everyone provides feedback. What do you think of the following proposals to facilitate the provision of feedback among members of eBay?

Teachers: The teachers' community needs member contributions. It is crucial that members not only take information, but also share their knowledge with others. What do you think of the following proposals to facilitate the contributions of members?

- Scenario eBay-4. The management emphasizes on eBay and in email communication that the community has the common goal to buy and sell products in a safe online environment. The management also emphasizes that the whole community profits from the provision of feedback. It is in the interest of everyone that feedback is provided about every transaction partner. Management repeats this message in emails and on eBay, when appropriate, or when it becomes clear that the enthusiasm for providing feedback is decreasing.

- Scenario eBay-5. EBay management makes it clear that providing feedback is critical for the security of the auction system. All members are sent an email that informs them of the importance of feedback provision. Moreover, every member is informed that access to eBay can be denied to anyone who did not provide feedback in more than 50 percent of his transactions. There will be regular control on the issue of feedback provision. If a member violates the rule once, he will receive a warning. If he violates the rule a second time within the following twelve months, then he will be excluded for a period of three months. It is the aim of this policy to prevent other members from failing to provide enough feedback in the future.

- Scenario teacher-3. To increase the number of postings in a discussion forum, every three months each member's nonanonymous postings are counted. The five members with the highest number of postings receive a book or CD voucher as a reward. This rule will be announced to the community at the beginning of the three-month period.

- Scenario teacher-4. To increase the number of postings in a discussion forum, every three months each member's non-anonymous postings are counted. Every member is ranked according to the number of posts. The higher the number of postings, the higher the position in the ranking. The ranking is made public within the community, and brought to the attention of every community member.

- Scenario teacher-5. On the websites of the community, the community manager makes clear that it is the common intention of the whole community to exchange knowledge. He emphasizes that the entire community of teachers profits from the members' contributions and that active members are of special value to all other members and the community. He draws attention to the opportunity to actively contribute to this goal by posting messages in a discussion forum and by answering the questions of other members. At appropriate times, this message is repeated in the newsletter and on the webpages of the community if the members' activities are decreasing.

Note

1. This finding casts doubt on the adequacy of the comparison between the problem of sending teaching material, which turns out to be the less serious problem of trust in the teachers' communities, and the problem of trusting an unknown seller, which turns out to be the more serious problem within eBay.

References

Ardichvili, Alexander, Vaugh Page, and Tim Wentling. 2003. "Motivation and Barriers to Participation in Virtual Knowledge-Sharing Communities of Practice." *Journal of Knowledge Management* 7(1): 64–77.

Armstrong, Arthur, and John Hagel III. 1996. "The Real Value of On-Line Communities." *Harvard Business Review* 74(May-June): 134–41.

Coleman, James S. 1990. *Foundations of Social Theory*. Cambridge, Mass.: Harvard University Press.

De Vos, Henk. 2004. "Community and Human Social Nature in Contemporary Society." *Analyse & Kritik* 26(1): 7–29.

Diekmann, Andreas, and David Wyder. 2002. "Vertrauen und Reputationseffekte bei Internet-Auktionen." *Kölner Zeitschrift für Soziologie und Sozialpsychologie* 54(4): 674–93.

eBay Inc. 2006a. "About the eBay Community." Available at: http://pages .ebay.com/aboutebay/community.html (accessed April 6, 2009).

———. 2006b. "Ebay Community Values." Available at: http://pages.ebay .com/community/people/values.html (accessed July 5, 2006).

Eysenbach, Gunther, John Powell, Marina Englesakis, Carlos Rizo, and Anita

Stern. 2004. "Health Related Virtual Communities and Electronic Support Groups: Systematic Review of the Effects of Online Peer to Peer Interactions." *British Medical Journal* 328(May 15): 1166–170.

Figallo, Cliff. 1998. *Hosting Web Communities.* New York: John Wiley & Sons.

Fisher, Robert J. 1993. "Social Desirability Bias and the Validity of Indirect Questioning." *Journal of Consumer Research* 20(2): 303–15.

Frank, Robert H. 1988. *Passions within Reason: The Strategic Role of the Emotions.* New York: W. W. Norton.

Hafner, Katie. 1997. "The Epic Saga of the Well." *Wired.* Available at: http://www.wired.com/wired/archive/5.05/ff_well_pr.html (accessed February 17, 2007).

Hargittai, Eszter. 2005. "Survey Measures of Web-Oriented Digital Literacy." *Social Science Computer Review* 23(2): 371–79.

Jarvenpaa, Sirkka L., Kathleen Knoll, and Dorothy E. Leidner. 1998. "Is Anybody Out There? Antecedents of Trust in Global Virtual Teams." *Journal of Management Information Systems* 14(4): 20–64.

Kim, Amy Jo. 2000. *Community Building on the Web.* Berkeley, Calif.: Peachpit Press.

Kreps, David M., Paul Milgram, John Roberts, and Robert Wilson. 1982. "Rational Cooperation in the Finitely Repeated Prisoner's Dilemma." *Journal of Economic Theory* 27(2): 245–52.

Lindenberg, Siegwart. 1997. "Grounding Groups in Theory: Functional, Cognitive, and Structural Interdependencies." In *Advances in Group Processes*, vol. 14, edited by Shane R. Thye and Edward J. Lawler. Greenwich, Conn.: JAI Press.

Matzat, Uwe. 2004. "The Social Embeddedness of Academic Online Groups as a Norm Generating Structure: A Test of the Coleman Model on Norm Emergence." *Computational and Mathematical Organization Theory* 10(3): 205–26.

———. 2009. "A Theory of Relational Signals in Online Groups." New Media and Society 11(3): 375–94.

Miller, Diane L., and Stuart Thomas. 2005. "The Impact of Relative Position and Relational Closeness on the Reporting of Unethical Acts." *Journal of Business Ethics* 61(4): 315–28.

Neeley, Sabrina M., and Maria L. Cronley. 2004. "When Research Participants Don't Tell It Like It Is: Pinpointing the Effects of Social Desirability Bias Using Self vs. Indirect-Questioning." In *Advances in Consumer Research*, vol. 31, edited by Barbare E. Kahn and M. F. Luce. Duluth, Minn.: Association for Consumer Research.

Osterloh, Margit, and Sandra Rota. 2004. "Trust and Community in Open Source Software Production." *Analyse & Kritik* 26(2): 279–301.

Paulhus, Delroy L. 1991. "Measurement and Control of Response Bias." In *Measures of Personality and Social Psychological Attitudes*, edited by John P. Robinson and L. S. Wrightsman. New York: Academic Press.

Peterson, Patricia J. 1997. "'They've Got the Whole World in Their Hands': A Case Study of Social Control on the Internet." In *Mapping Cyberspace: Social Research on the Electronic Frontier*, edited by Joseph E. Behar. Binghamton, N.Y.: Dowling College Press.

Preece, Jenny, Blair Nonnecke, and Dorine Andrews. 2004. "The Top Five Reasons for Lurking: Improving Community Experiences for Everyone." *Computers in Human Behavior* 20(2): 201–23.

Rasmusen, Eric. 1989. *Games and Information*. Malden, Mass.: Blackwell Publishers.

Reid, Elizabeth. 1999. "Hierarchy and Power: Social Control in Cyberspace." In *Communities in Cyberspace*, edited by Marc A. Smith and Peter Kollock. London: Routledge.

Rojo, Alejandra, and Ronald G. Ragsdale. 1997. "Participation in Electronic Forums: Implications for the Design and Implementation of Collaborative Distributed Multimedia." *Telematics and Informatics* 14(1): 83–96.

Snijders, Chris, and Jeroen Weesie. 1999. "Sociale oriëntaties, tijdspreferenties en de stabiliteit van relaties." In *Huwelijks- en samenwoonrelaties in Nederland: De organisatie van afhankelijkheid*, edited by Kalmijn Matthijs, Wim Bernasco, and Jeroen Weesie. Assen, The Netherlands: van Gorcum.

Snijders, Chris, and Richard Zijdemann. 2004. "Reputation and Internet Auctions: EBay and Beyond." *Analyse & Kritik* 26(1): 158–84.

Steenhaut, Sarah, and Peter Van Kenhove. 2005. "Relationship Commitment and Ethical Consumer Behavior in a Retail Setting: The Case of Receiving Too Much Change at the Checkout." *Journal of Business Ethics* 56(4): 335–53.

Stegbauer, Christian, and Alexander Rausch. 2001. "Die schweigende Mehrheit-"Lurker" in Internetbasierten Diskussionsforen." *Zeitschrift für Soziologie* 30(1): 48–64.

Suler, John R. 2000. "From Conception to Toddlerhood: A History of the First Year (or So) of the Palace." Available at: http://www.rider.edu/users/suler/psycyber/palhistory.html (accessed July 4, 2006).

Suler, John R., and W. L. Phillips. 1998. "The Bad Boys of Cyberspace: Deviant Behavior in Multimedia Chat Communities." *Cyberpsychology and Behavior* 1: 275–94.

Verhulp, Eric. 2005. "Eigen inbreng van docenten stimuleren." *Kennisnet in Druk* (2): 3.

Vargas, Patrick T., William von Hippel, and Richard E. Petty. 2004. "Using Partially Structured Attitude Measures to Enhance the Attitude-Behavior Relationship." *Personality and Social Psychology Bulletin* 30(2): 197–211.

Chapter 10

Order, Coordination, and Uncertainty

Coye Cheshire and Judd Antin

O NLINE EXCHANGE systems that allow individuals to view, share, and edit text, images, audio, and video are now a key element of the Internet landscape. Millions of people who were once passive consumers of information provided by privileged gatekeepers can produce and share content at very low cost. The continued evolution of large-scale online systems has also helped facilitate large-scale collective action in which information is the object of value and exchange.

According to one estimate, the Internet contained more than 500,000 terabytes of information in 2002 and was growing at an exponential rate (Lyman and Varian 2003). It would be misleading, however, to view the volume of information now produced and exchanged on the Internet as a by-product of the mere availability of new technologies. Rather, we must examine the patterns of use that link these technologies to the flood of new content. What factors encourage us to contribute information on the Internet? How do we develop trust, credibility, or reliability in the information systems with which we interact? As we increasingly rely on the Internet to exchange private and public information, these and many other questions deserve close scrutiny.

We begin this chapter by classifying types of Internet information exchange systems according to a simple and versatile scheme. Despite the increasing growth of large-scale participatory online exchange systems, there have been few efforts to systematically organize them using a coherent taxonomy. To date, much of the public discourse about online information exchange systems has occurred in the popular press, which often lumps diverse systems into broad categories such as user-generated content systems or simply Web 2.0.[1] Here we aim to produce a typology of Internet systems that produce large public goods through smaller, individual contributions of information. To accomplish this, we categorize systems along two key dimensions: order and coordination.

Information Pools: Group-Generalized and Productive Exchange

When information from many sources is collectively transmitted over a computer network so that it can be accessed for public, club, or private consumption, it creates what we call an information pool (Cheshire and Antin 2008). The digital information goods in these systems may include, but are not limited to, text, software, photographs, audio, and video (Kollock 1999; Shapiro and Varian 1998). Examples of information pools include peer-to-peer file-sharing systems in which individuals exchange music, movies, and software (BitTorrent, Gnutella, Napster); collaborative content systems in which individuals contribute and collectively edit, organize, and manage content (Wikipedia, Flickr, YouTube); social voting and filtering systems (Digg, del.icio.us); and distributed work systems in which individuals contribute small quantities of information to help complete large tasks (Amazon Mechanical Turk, NASA ClickWorkers, Mycroft).

Two noteworthy characteristics of information help reduce the costs of contributing to information pools. First, information can be consumed by many individuals without affecting the consumption of anyone else. This means that information goods have high jointness of supply (Kollock 1999; Cheshire 2007) or are nonrival goods (Shapiro and Varian 1998). Second, information can be replicable, a property of information by which perfect copies can be made at a near zero cost and an important means by which digital information achieves high jointness of supply (Cheshire 2007).[2] These two qualities are important for understanding the creation of information pools because they make it possible for an individual to keep the full value of the public good without impeding others' ability to consume it. Or, as Carl Shapiro and Hal Varian pointed out, information often has high fixed costs of production but low marginal costs of reproduction (1998). Digital information goods are also distinct from other goods and services because the costs associated with sharing them are typically quite small (Kollock 1999; Shapiro and Varian 1998). There are certainly some costs, such as the time required to copy and transmit information or the cost of an Internet connection. However, these are arguably much smaller than the actual content value of the information.

The design, information architecture, and user interface of any information pool influence how contributions are made and outcomes are produced. As Judith Donath pointed out, online spaces are limited in the same way that our physical environment is limited by the constraints of buildings, land, and architecture (1999). The users of an online information system must work within the constraints of the technical framework established by the designers, such as the MediaWiki software that runs Wikipedia or the BitTorrent file-sharing protocol. These constraints define and constrain the way that interaction takes place on Wikipedia and peer-to-peer file sharing systems. Finally, individuals are limited by the interaction mechanism strictly defined by the keyboard, mouse, and computer screen. Each of these constraints bound the environment in which potential participants weigh the costs and benefits of social interaction, make decisions about contributing to an online system, and consume information.

Order and Group-Generalized Exchange

Individuals contributing information to create an information pool from which many can benefit can establish a type of group-generalized exchange system. Following Peter Ekeh's description of generalized exchange (1974), Toshio Yamagishi and Karen Cook defined a group-generalized exchange system as one in which individuals contribute to a public good yet receive benefits only from the contributions of others (1993).[3] This creates a collective action problem—the public good can be created only if many individuals contribute, yet each individual is better off not contributing and instead taking advantage of the efforts of others.

In many situations, contributions are evenly redistributed to all recipients of the public good. For example, individuals who work to reduce air pollution will enjoy cleaner air both as a result of their own contributions and those of others. On the other hand, consider the example of those who contribute recipes to a cookbook. All contributors receive benefits from the collection but a given individual's contributions do not carry the same value as that of others because the individual already has the recipe. This distinction is important because it highlights the fact that an individual must bear the cost associated with contributing to the public good but must also rely entirely on the contributions of others to receive many types of rewards. Of course, in some information pools the rewards are distributed back to everyone—including the original contributor. For example, programmers who contribute to open source software projects (that is, Linux) receive the benefits of their contributions just as much as they receive the benefits of others' efforts. In such cases, the information pool is more analogous to classic public goods problems such as sharing a common area, constructing a town bridge, and so on.

The relative costs and benefits associated with contributing to an information pool and the source of one's rewards highlight the importance of incentives. For example, if an individual does not fully understand how the pool is produced, what the product will ultimately look like, or how it will prove beneficial, the incentive to contribute may be quite low. Furthermore, if individual contributions are not organized, individuals may feel that their contributions are being wasted. For example, a community-created cookbook with no theme, table of contents, or index introduces barriers to assessing the utility of one's contribution or the collective outcome, especially when the cookbook is large.

We refer to the organization of contributions through specific means and toward a focused outcome as the problem of order. The order in a given information pool is the organization of individual contributions and the clarity of the intended collective outcome. In ordered systems, the process of production and exchange is well defined and the products are clearly specified. A scaffold is in place which determines when, how, and in what form exchanges and contributions to the public good are made. Individuals know what they should do to contribute, know what their contribution will ultimately create, and have a reasonable concept of how the outcome will benefit them. On the other hand, in less ordered systems there are few restrictions on the process of contribution and the final product may be entirely emergent or simply undefined. We do not propose that a more ordered system is qualitatively better or worse than a less ordered one. Rather, we argue that the property of order influences how participants interpret and understand the outcome in a given information pool.

Coordination and Productive Exchange

Information pools can also be examples of productive exchange, that is, situations in which mutual interdependencies between actors are strong enough to make collaboration the most rewarding option (Emerson 1972; Lawler, Thye, and Yoon 2000). Individual contributions to an information pool are often interdependent because they combine to create a good that is greater than the sum of its parts. For example, individual contributions to Wikipedia are valuable as stand-alone bits of information, but the value generated by the synthesis of many such bits, which no individual user could create alone, arguably exceeds their additive value. User-generated content systems, in which individuals contribute images, digital audio, and digital video files, gain value from the eclectic nature of the material as well as the overall size of the collection (thereby increasing the likelihood of finding desired content).

An important component of productive exchange systems is the coordination of contributions. Specifically, "in productive exchange, there are strong incentives for exchange, and the main question is whether the actors can coordinate their actions to forge agreements" (Lawler, Thye, and Yoon 2000, 617). For example, if one individual has rice and the other fish, there will be no sushi unless each is aware of the other and a structure is in place to allow them to exchange (see Yamagishi 1995). Peter Kollock argued that when individuals contribute digital information to produce public goods in online environments, the coordination and communication costs are often much lower than in other types of interaction situations, such as face-to-face communication (1999). But even among online systems, structural designs that constrain or allow interactions among individuals are likely to affect the overall coordination costs.

We refer to the organization of contributors into roles with well-defined duties and responsibilities as the problem of coordination. Participants in coordinated systems undertake specific types of work and responsibilities and interact according to guidelines determined by the roles they have chosen or to which they have been assigned. As a result, higher levels of coordination may imply less discretion for individual contributors. On the other hand, less coordinated systems leave roles and responsibilities underspecified and allow participants to decide for themselves which roles to fill and how to fill them.

Classifying Information Pools by Order and Coordination

The two key characteristics of order and coordination intersect to create a simple typology of information pools (see figure 10.1). Order and coordination are not orthogonal concepts but instead distinct yet related features. For example, higher levels of order can lead to higher levels of coordination, and vice versa. Highly bounded processes and products tend to coincide with highly bounded roles and actions within them. Furthermore, order and coordination should be viewed as continuous characteristics rather than discrete categories—a given system is not simply ordered or unordered, coordinated or uncoordinated. Rather, systems have sociotechnical properties that make them more or less ordered or coordinated, and enable the evolution of order and coordination over time. Thus it is instructive to examine the relationship between the two concepts because the degree to which a system is ordered and coordinated relates to very different types of information pools.

Low order and low coordination systems   provide very few (if any) well-defined structures for exchanging and sharing information. The technical constraints of a system's software provide a lower boundary for order and coordination, in that users are free to choose only those activities and roles allowed by design. Beyond these minimal constraints,

Figure 10.1   Categorization of Information Pools

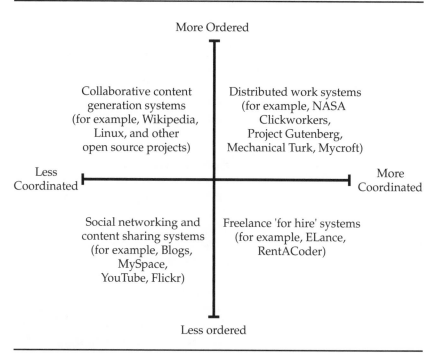

More Ordered

Collaborative content
generation systems
(for example, Wikipedia,
Linux, and other
open source projects)

Distributed work systems
(for example, NASA
Clickworkers,
Project Gutenberg,
Mechanical Turk, Mycroft)

Less
Coordinated

More
Coordinated

Social networking and
content sharing systems
(for example, Blogs,
MySpace,
YouTube, Flickr)

Freelance 'for hire' systems
(for example, ELance,
RentACoder)

Less ordered

Source: Authors' compilation.
Note: Order refers to the organization of individual contributions and the clarity of the intended collective outcomes. *Coordination* refers to the organization of contributors into roles with well-defined duties and responsibilities.

however, low order and low coordination systems leave their processes and products ambiguously defined, and leave users to decide for themselves which tasks to do and how to do them.

Blogs are one of the most common examples of unordered and uncoordinated systems. The software that supports blogging—Wordpress, TypePad, and Blogger, for example—provides a basic limiting framework for the processes and products that users can undertake and the roles they can fulfill. Beyond this loose framework, however, there is little agreement about what constitutes a blog or the practice of blogging. The *Oxford English Dictionary* has defined a blog in this way: "A frequently updated web site consisting of personal observations, excerpts from other sources, etc., typically run by a single person, and usually with hyperlinks to other sites; an online journal or diary" (OED Online 2008). However, recent research has outlined great diversity in the definition of blogging between blog software producers, researchers, and bloggers themselves (Boyd 2006). Similarly, Bonnie Nardi, Diane Schiano, and Michelle Gumbrecht found "tremendous diversity in blog content" and noted that though some individuals blog frequently, as the *OED* definition implies, the frequency or regularity of posts varied widely and was not a key element of bloggers own conception of blogging (2004, 42). Although the confessional style of many blogs has been highlighted in the popular press (Nardi et al. 2004), many blogs also take the form of filters for highlighting interesting content on the Web and knowledge logs in which bloggers share their expertise (Herring et al. 2004). Finally, Jan Schmidt has drawn from social structuration theory to note that the open-ended nature of blogging roles—reader, writer, commenter, and so on—are related to distinct classes of procedural rules for interaction (2007).

Blogs illustrate the intersection of technical systems that provide low order and low coordination with social practices to create diverse definitions and usages. In part because of the open-ended nature of blogs as a platform for communication, expression, and social interaction, this research illustrates that they come to constitute many types of content and fill many distinct roles. Anyone can create a blog and decide what it will or will not contain, regardless of what anyone else does with their own blogs. Nevertheless, the content that is created produces public goods of varying quality and use value. Individual blogs and collections of blogs present news, gossip, firsthand accounts of events, and links to related content, among other things. Anyone can benefit from this material, regardless of whether one is a blogger.

High order and low coordination systems   are those in which a structure for the process of exchange is in place, but in which individual actors are left to choose their role and how they carry it out. A high degree of order is usually created through a combination of technical mechanisms and social norms. Many open source software projects, for example, use Web-based systems to track software bugs. When individuals report a bug, they contribute content about the bug through a highly ordered system that requires them to provide a prescribed set of details about the problem. Social norms about the proper way to describe bugs, however, also add to the degree of order in the system. For example, providing exact, numbered steps to reproduce a bug rather than simply a general description of the problem is encouraged.

A low degree of coordination, on the other hand, can have several contributing factors. Most systems have at least a few roles. For example, a small group of individuals who design or maintain the system may occupy administrator roles. Most individuals, however, will not have the duties or privileges associated with administrator status. In other systems, technical and social constraints may define broad roles such as author or editor, but provide no guidance on how the roles should be carried out. Finally, low coordination systems may face what we call the pot-luck problem: without a structure in place to distribute individuals' to each of the necessary roles, some roles may be overfilled and others underfilled.

Wikipedia is a good example of a high order and low coordination system. A great deal of Wikipedia's order is prescribed by the system's narrow focus on the production of encyclopedic content. In addition to the constraints on users' actions provided by the MediaWiki software that runs Wikipedia, the system has developed a rigorous set of norms around issues such as appropriate article topics and tone. Fernanda Viégas, Martin Wattenberg, and Matthew McKeon detailed the hundreds, if not thousands, of detailed rules and procedures that Wikipedia's contributors in the course of creating content, and illustrate the high degree of order through the case study of the featured article nomination process (2007). Brian Butler, Elisabeth Joyce, and Jacqueline Pike noted that, as of September 2007, Wikipedia's official policies comprised forty-four pages on the site, and 248 pages were dedicated to Wikipedia guidelines (2008). Research has also suggested that an important part of participating on Wikipedia is the gradual learning, acceptance, and adoption of rules and processes that constitute Wikipedia's ordered system (Bryant, Forte, and Bruckman 2005).

Certainly this high degree of order constrains the diversity of roles within the system. Wikipedia, however, is subject to many of the challenges of low coordination that we described earlier. Although individuals can choose to write, edit, or discuss content, and are bound to a degree by the system's guidelines, how those roles are carried out is open to a great deal of interpretation. One individual who edits may go word by word, attempting to maintain as much of the original author's material as possible, whereas another may delete the content wholesale and replace it with comparable text. Similarly, though administrators are bound by certain guidelines when arbitrating disputes, one may take a compassionate, conciliatory route towards compromise and another may choose a side simply to bring the argument to a swift conclusion. In addition, the pot-luck problem is evident in Wikipedia. The development of an article requires that individuals both contribute new content and edit existing content. However, many more users choose to edit than to add (Swartz 2006). Even fewer individuals contribute their effort toward the higher-level administrative and bureaucratic needs of the system, despite the increasing importance of those roles. Viégas and her colleagues, for example, found that Wikipedia Talk pages, which are primarily used for coordinating editing activities, resolving disputes, and enforcing guidelines, are growing at a faster rate than the Wikipedia encyclopedia pages themselves (Viegas et al. 2007).

Low order and high coordination systems are perhaps more rare because defined roles often engender structured processes. A useful way to think of these systems is populations of uncommitted freelancers: actors who have well-defined roles but no applications for them. In this respect they function much like simple for-hire classified advertisements. ELance and RentACoder, both online markets for skilled service providers, are good examples of such systems. They are highly coordinated because individual roles, such as service requestors and service providers, are clearly defined in the design of the system (Kim and Altinkemer 2005). In this respect, they closely follow the description of productive exchange provided earlier. The value of an information pool such as ELance, for example, is provided by allowing individuals to clearly specify their skills, experience, and desired responsibilities, and at the same time allowing employers to describe roles that need to be filled. The key value exchange is in coordinating, matching, and managing individuals who need each other.

At the same time, for-hire systems illustrate the potentially multifaceted nature of order. ELance is a low order system because the process by which employers and employees seek and find each other is completely unspecified, and the product is only loosely defined as a body of classified advertisements that allow employers and employees to find each other. At the same time, ELance provides a higher degree of order to specify the details of work assignments and worker skills that individuals must provide. This example, then, shows that an information pool's degree of order and coordination depends in part on the resolution of the analysis. Examining ELance as a whole, we may classify it as a distinctly low order system, but at the same time elements within it exhibit higher degrees of order.

High order and high coordination systems are those that use a rigorously structured approach, imposing narrow boundaries on the process of exchange and limiting participants to only a few well-defined roles. Such systems are usually focused on extremely specific tasks and products. NASA's ClickWorkers project, which has engaged thousands of amateur volunteers to undertake the tedious task of labeling craters on various moons and planets, is an early example of a high order and high coordination system. In the interest of furthering the public good of scientific knowledge, NASA engaged volunteers to do one and only one thing, and provided a highly restricted user interface for accomplishing this task.

A second example is Project Gutenberg, which has undertaken the immense task of digitizing public domain books so that they can be available to anyone through the Internet. Like ClickWorkers, Project Gutenberg has a specific work task that must be repeated on such a massive scale that using the Internet to engage volunteers became an opportune solution. Although Project Gutenberg engages volunteers in several additional roles that are more loosely defined, the majority of the work consists of the highly organized and focused task of transcribing text depicted in scanned images.

Uncertainty and Contributions to Information Pools

The notion of uncertainty is essential to understanding whether individuals will choose to interact with an information pool. We define uncertainty as an individual's degree of confidence about a particular outcome. There are several possible sources of uncertainty in interpersonal exchange, such as the quality of the goods at stake (Kollock 1994) and the likelihood of finding an exchange partner (Gerbasi 2005). When individuals can identify and interact with specific others over time, increased uncertainty often leads to commitment (Cook and Emerson 1978; Kollock 1999).

Uncertainty directly relates to how individuals assess the reliability, security, or trustworthiness of others who use an online information exchange system. In a system such as the online auction service eBay, experiential and third-party reputations allow individuals to make informed decisions about potential exchange partners. In such cases, reputations are tools for reducing uncertainty and inferring trustworthiness (Cook and Hardin 2001). However, reputation information is not always available. When individuals cannot be persistently and uniquely identified and no reputation information is available, it may lead to increased uncertainty and collectively deficient outcomes (see chapter 3, this volume).

When individuals cannot develop experiential or third-party information about other people over time, what matters most is institutional backing for failed trust or reliance (Cheshire and Cook 2004). In many information pools, however, the only institutional backing is the system itself rather than a third party. Thus the key to understanding when and why individuals contribute to information pools, often with anonymous contributions and no reputation systems, is tied to the extent to which individuals believe the system is reliable and secure.

Some online systems convey a sense of consistency, dependability, and security. Others may not or do not. We refer to these expectations as a sense of reliability. Reliability is similar but distinct from the concept of trustworthiness, which is a property we infer about others in whom we trust to do a specific task (Hardin 2002). A crucial component of interpersonal trust and trustworthiness is the ability to be betrayed (Baier 1986). An online system cannot really betray us through choice because it does not have agency or the ability to consider our interests, desires, or needs. Yet, as users, we expect that an online system will do what it claims to do, such as transferring our information securely and consistently or being available and responsive when we choose to use it. Issues of uncertainty and reliability have become important to research on Internet exchange, especially among e-commerce systems where the measurable financial risks are potentially very high.[4] Indeed, lack of trust is often cited as a reason consumers shy away from making online exchanges and transactions in some systems (Ang and Lee 2000).

Assessments about the reliability of an online system are largely influenced by the way the system collects, uses, and redistributes personal information. When individuals attempt to assess the reliability and credibility of websites, for example, some factors they may consider are the structure or focus of the information displayed, and overall website design (Fogg 2003). Many different specific design features of a system or website (that is, use of photographs, layout of text, professionalism of graphics, and the like) affect an individual's perceptions about its reliability (Fogg et al. 2001; Fogg 2003). Thus, in the absence of ongoing, firsthand experiential information, individuals infer reliability based on presentation and design—even if this information is tangentially or dubiously related to any real measure of reliability or online security.

System Uncertainty and Environmental Uncertainty

We have described order and coordination as characteristics tied to design decisions to allow, constrain, and define the conditions of exchange between participants in a given online system. We refer to system uncertainty as the ambiguity, created by design and patterns of use, about how interactions and contributions will be managed in an information pool. Systems with high order and coordination have clear outcomes and are more transparent to users, whereas those with low order and coordination have more ambiguous interaction processes, imprecise products, and undefined roles for participants. Thus, information pools with higher degrees of order and coordination have lower levels of system uncertainty, and vice versa.[5]

The differences in system uncertainty between information pools with more or less order and coordination are apparent in our earlier examples. An individual who interacts with Project Gutenberg knows exactly what the purpose of the system is and how contributions are made because all this information is expressly presented to users before they can make a contribution. Although there are certainly no guarantees that the system will never experience a problem, the key is that Project

Gutenberg presents a clear order and method of coordinating potential contributions. In contrast, blogs create many types of content with numerous roles such as content creator, commenter, reader, etc. This is not to say that blogs and systems of interrelated blogs do not have a purpose or methods of contribution and interaction. Rather, the crucial issue is that the overall amount of system uncertainty is relatively higher for the low order and low coordination blogosphere than for rigorously structured and controlled systems such as Project Gutenberg.

The structural affordances of an information pool, however, are not the sole influence on user attitudes and behaviors. Many other factors can shape a user's perception of the system and propensity to interact with it. We refer to the ambiguity of the context of interaction in an information pool as environmental uncertainty. Interpersonal relationships are embedded in more or less certain environments that foster or inhibit trust and commitment (Kollock 1994). The large and diverse environments of the Internet are rife with uncertainty and risk, creating a clear analog to the environmental uncertainties that occupy the offline world.

The sources of online environmental uncertainty are numerous, including familiarity with domain names that host a site, the lack or presence of commercial interests, and the surrounding website or websites in which a given information pool is embedded. For example, if an information pool collects contributions through an interface on one or more Web pages, then the host websites themselves may influence the perceptions that potential contributors have about the information pool. Thus, independent of the order and coordination of an information pool, the surrounding Internet environment must be considered as an underlying influence on contribution or noncontribution behavior.

Uncertainty and User Contributions

To illustrate and explore contribution behavior in online information exchange in the presence of system and environmental uncertainty, we examine a real-world information pool called Mycroft.[6] This system creates information goods by synthesizing the efforts of many people who each contribute one small piece of information at a time. Mycroft accepts large jobs that cannot technically or efficiently be completed by computers and breaks them down into many constituent parts called puzzles. The puzzles are distributed through banner ads on existing websites in place of traditional advertising materials (see figure 10.2). As each puzzle is answered, the results are combined with others at successively larger levels until the top-level job is complete. Mycroft produces public goods that are the synthesis of many small contributions; participants must rely on the contributions of others to produce the collective outcome.

Figure 10.2   Mycroft Banner Interface

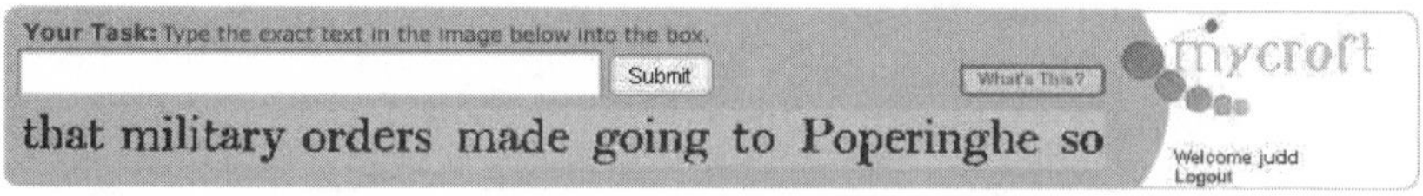

Source: Authors' compilation.

Mycroft banners exist on many diverse websites and are designed to facilitate entirely self-contained interactions within the banner. Users who visit a blog, shopping, or news site and find a Mycroft banner there can contribute to the information pool without leaving that page. Individuals can contribute anonymously or create persistent user accounts on the system.[7] This architecture takes advantage of casual contributions, turning collective action into something that individuals might do while surfing from one website to the next. Individuals can also contribute through banners they find on the Mycroft project's home site.

In the two field studies that follow we use the Mycroft system to examine user contributions in conditions of varying uncertainty. Mycroft is a particularly advantageous platform for this examination. First, as an example of a highly ordered and coordinated system, it is relatively low in system uncertainty because the processes, products, and roles are both narrowly defined and made explicit to potential contributors. This makes Mycroft a good baseline from which to modify conditions of uncertainty and investigate contribution behavior. Second, Mycroft's architecture requires that it exists out in the wild on a variety of real websites—a primary home website, personal home pages, blogs, commercial sites, and so on. Mycroft provides an online test bed that is subject to the intangible, difficult to reproduce, contextual influences of real-world online behavior.

Data and Measurement

We collected data on the contributions of more than 5,000 people who viewed Mycroft banners more than 100,000 times between March 2006 and October 2006. During this period, Mycroft banners were hosted on more than twenty diverse sites as well as on an internal home website. Internet traffic was approximately evenly divided between the internal and the external sites. Those who visited and contributed through the internal site were recruited through messages distributed by e-mail, word-of-mouth, and other electronic notices. Thus the sample of con-

Table 10.1   Tasks in Mycroft Banners

Task	Task Description	Answer Format
Tagging descriptions	Assign keywords to an item of user-generated content which includes a text description and an optional image	Keywords/"tags"
Interpreting scanned text	Enter the text displayed in a small image which represents a section of a scanned page of text (see figure 10.2)	Sentence fragments/ text strings
Tagging images	Assign keywords to an image	Keywords/"tags"

Source: Authors' compilation.

tributors to the internal site included members of the researchers' social networks, members of the local academic community where the study was conducted, and others who heard about the project through these announcements. Individuals who contributed through external websites were simply those who happened to discover the Mycroft banner in the course of their normal Web browsing experiences. We take each of these samples into consideration in interpreting all findings.

During the data collection period, Mycroft distributed three types of puzzles (see table 10.1). One type asked individuals to label images drawn from a publicly available set of images on the Internet. The second type asked individuals to type in small portions of text that appeared in a scanned image of text. The third asked individuals to read a description of an item and then apply keywords to it. All of the puzzles exist within the same banner interface and require a very small input from the user in the form of a few words of text.

In the following section, we use two ways to measure contributions to the Mycroft system. The first is the contribution-by-view ratio (C/V ratio), which is calculated by dividing the number of people who contribute to Mycroft on a specific page by the total number of people who viewed that same page. For example, if a Mycroft banner is viewed 100 times on website X and only five contributions are made, the C/V ratio is 5 percent. The C/V ratio is a rough measure of capture—that is, how many users are motivated to interact with a Mycroft banner given the amount of traffic to the site that hosts the banner. This measure is appropriate when the unit of analysis is the host site that displays Mycroft banners.

The second metric we use in our analysis is the total number of contributions to Mycroft that a single individual makes during a specified research period. When we use the total number of contributions, however, we control for the number of banners that an individual viewed. It is important to note that banner views are not necessarily greater than or equal to the number of contributions.[8]

Two limitations add important caveats to all of our analyses. First, we acknowledge the general problems of sampling inherent in much online research, such as anonymous online survey responses (see Bainbridge 2002). We did not apply any constraints to who viewed or interacted with Mycroft through the variety of websites on which it is displayed. However, though we made every attempt to make the Mycroft system available for anyone to use, we have no way to determine the demographic composition of our internal home site or external website samples. Second, although Mycroft incorporates a robust mechanism for tracking both anonymous and known-identity users across many interactions on many sites, no mechanism is completely free of potential error.[9] We have taken every possible precaution when analyzing the data to account for and eliminate redundant and erroneous contributions to the system.

Study 1: System Uncertainty and Contribution Behavior

Even when the role of a potential contributor in an information pool is clear and the purpose is well-defined, additional information can enhance one's knowledge of the intended recipient and goal of the collective effort. When the goal and recipient is highlighted, potential contributors know exactly why they are contributing and how their efforts will produce a collective outcome. The presence of this type of information should reduce overall system uncertainty, and therefore increase the likelihood that individuals will make one or more contributions.

To examine the effect of highlighting the recipient of participants' efforts on contribution behavior, we designed a simple field experiment using the Mycroft system. The first time any user viewed a Mycroft banner between September and November of 2006, he or she was randomly and persistently assigned to one of two conditions: a control condition in which the banner contained only the Mycroft logo, or the experimental condition in which the Mycroft logo was displayed alongside the logo of the host company for whom Mycroft was collecting information.

We conducted this experiment on the website of the organization whose logo was integrated into Mycroft's user interface. Because we were not able to use the host company's logo on other external websites, we also conducted the same experiment on our own internal project site. We did this so that we could compare the effect of the logo on Mycroft banners placed on the organization's website to those placed on a website not affiliated with the host company. Furthermore, we used only tagging puzzles for this field experiment. This was done to ensure that the tasks were exactly the same and the only difference between the Mycroft banner puzzles in the two conditions was the presence (or lack) of the visual logo from the host organization.

Results and Interpretation   We conducted an analysis of covariance (ANCOVA) with the number of total contributions that an individual made as the dependent variable, the presence of the visual logo and whether the participant used an internal or external website as the independent variables, and the number of banner views (per individual) as the covariate. Controlling for all other factors, the number of times that individuals viewed a Mycroft banner had a strong and significant effect on the number of contributions he or she made, $F(1, 1470) = 45.5$, $p < .001$. Thus the more an individual was exposed to Mycroft banners, the more he or she contributed overall. Controlling for the number of banner views, individuals who came to Mycroft's internal website also contributed significantly more ($M = 1.7$, $SE = .25$) than those who came across the Mycroft banners on the external site ($M = .03$, $SE = .16$), $F(1, 1470) = 32.4$, $p < .001$.

Controlling for both the number of banner views and the internal-external site distinction, the presence of the visual logo had a significant and positive effect on the number of contributions, $F(1, 1470) = 3.99$, $p < .05$. The interaction between the presence of the logo and the internal-external sites was also significant, $F(1, 1470) = 3.7$, $p = .05$. As figure 10.3 shows, this interaction effect explains where the real differences exist. Among those who visited the external site (that is, the website of the company whose logo was used), there was essentially no difference in the number of contributions for those who viewed the additional logo and those who did not. However, among those who visited the internal site, the presence of the visual logo had a clear, positive effect on the number of contributions to Mycroft.

These results support our prediction that the presence of the affiliate logo can decrease system uncertainty by clarifying the simple question, "Who will be the recipient of my effort?" For individuals who visited the internal site, the presence of the affiliate logo may establish more order, and therefore less system uncertainty, by clearly answering this question. For those who visited the external site, the visual logo may only establish an explicit link between the Mycroft banners and the host site. Because the visual logo belonged to the external host site, it may simply have been redundant information.

Figure 10.3   Number of Contributions

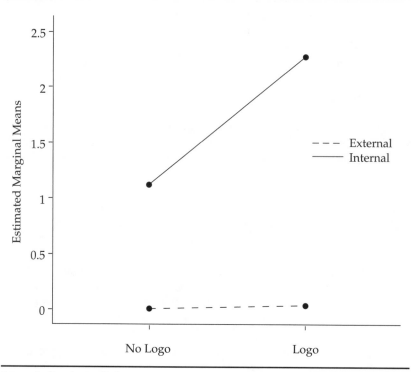

Source: Authors' compilation.

Study 2: Environmental Uncertainty and Guilt by Association

Potential contributors interact through Mycroft banners that look like standard banner advertisements and exist in locations where advertisements normally are located on the Web. Research has consistently shown that perceptions of Web advertisements are extremely negative and can negatively impact online interaction in some contexts (Fox 2000; Metzger 2004). Furthermore, the existence of commercial advertising on a website can also lead to an overall lack of perceived credibility in the website content as a whole (Fogg et al. 2001). Thus, the co-presence of commercial advertising may function as a source of environmental uncertainty for the Mycroft system. We suggest that the presence of advertising on websites that host Mycroft banners should lead to lower contribution rates by increasing environmental uncertainty.

Methodology

Using data collected between March and August of 2006, including more than 137,000 views and about 3,300 contributions, we examined the difference in contributions between websites that displayed commercial banner advertising alongside Mycroft banners and those that did not. During the data collection period, we examined twenty external volunteer sites that hosted Mycroft banners. The external sites were classified according to whether the pages contained Mycroft banners only (N = 16 host sites), or Mycroft banners and commercial advertisements (N = 4 host sites).

Results and Interpretation

As figure 10.4 shows, the average contribution-by-view rate for sites that also featured banner advertisements was nearly three times lower (M = .84) than the mean for those sites that did not (M = 2.43). A simple *t*-test comparison yields a borderline significant effect ($p < .10$). In addition, a Mann-Whitney U (nonparametric) comparison of the means also

Figure 10.4   Average Contribution-to-View Rate

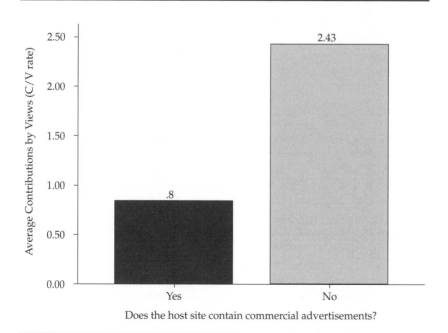

Does the host site contain commercial advertisements?

Source: Authors' compilation.

showed borderline significance ($p = .08$). This result lends modest support to the assertion that the co-presence of commercial advertising may increase environmental uncertainty, leading to lower overall contribution-to-view rates.

Although the results of this second study are not highly statistically significant, we are severely limited by the small number of sites in this analysis ($N = 20$). The number of sites in our study was limited by practical issues associated with acquiring the necessary cooperation and support from the host website administrators. The overall effect size for the mean difference was .30, indicating that the effect is noteworthy even if the difference is borderline significant. Despite the limitations, the findings are consistent with our general predictions.

Conclusion

We began this chapter by describing how order and coordination define the ways that contributions are organized and roles are presented in information pools. We argued that the levels of order and coordination in a given system are influenced by the design decisions of its creators, whether intentional or not. We introduced a typology of information pools by order and coordination and explored representative online systems for each quadrant in our classification.

Order and coordination help define the base levels of system uncertainty in information pools. System uncertainty is important to understanding how the design and use of a system can affect the way that interactions and contributions are managed. In addition, the surrounding Internet environment can influence behavior independent of existing levels of system uncertainty. Both types of uncertainty are essential to understanding contribution and noncontribution behaviors in information pools.

In our exploratory field experiments, we examined specific factors that can influence system and environmental uncertainty. Using a highly ordered and coordinated information pool, we investigated the effect of highlighting the intended recipient of participants' contribution behavior and the effect of co-location with commercial advertisements. Our first study showed that using a visual logo to clarify and highlight the intended recipient of user contributions led to significantly more contributions in the internal sample but had no effect in the external sample. For individuals who visited the internal site, the presence of the affiliate logo may have established an additional degree of order but had no effect for those who visited the external site. The second study provided modest evidence that the co-presence of commercial advertisements can negatively affect contributions to an information pool. In our examination of external websites that hosted Mycroft banners, sites that included other commercial advertisements had nearly three times fewer contributions-per-view than those that did not. Negative associations with commercial advertising may thus increase environmental uncertainty, leading to a reduction in the number of contributions relative to banner views.

We limited our examination to a highly ordered and coordinated system so that the relative effect of system uncertainty would be minimized. That is, we wanted participants to have a clear role and a stated purpose for contributing so that we could focus on specific factors that might influence perceptions of reliability and rates of contribution. Although these exploratory field experiments were never intended to be conclusive tests, they highlight the importance of both structural and environmental uncertainty in information pools and at the same time provide numerous possibilities for future field and lab studies.

The Future of Information Pools

Information pools are likely to evolve over time through social uses of technologies and ongoing design modifications. We suggest that some systems tend toward more order and coordination as they grow over time, just as social communities and systems often do in the offline world. However, whether such a shift occurs, and in which direction, may largely depend on the nature of the public good produced. Well-defined public goods may tend toward more order and coordination over time, and an amorphous public good may persist precisely because it is unordered and uncoordinated.

Wikipedia is an example of an information pool that began as a more ordered and less coordinated system with the stated goal of producing encyclopedic content through a specific series of open editing processes. As the system grew in size and popularity, however, the natural consequence of those goals appeared to push Wikipedia to establish more coordination—despite the existence of an ideology of openness that might have discouraged the shift. Current empirical work on Wikipedia is already beginning to show evidence of this kind of shift (Zhang and Zhu 2006; Viégas et al. 2007). In Wikipedia's early development, small groups of individuals emerged to become editors, arbitrators, and proctors for the system. These informal, self-assigned roles satisfied the quality standards of the community for a time, but, as Wikipedia grew, the scope of the problems apparently overcame the abilities of the informally coordinated contributors to insure all of the information in the online encyclopedia (Katie Hafner, "Growing Wikipedia Revises Its 'Anyone Can Edit' Policy," New York Times, June 17, 2006).

Vandalism and other forms of abuse became so problematic that they threatened the production of an ordered public good. Faced with these new problems, Wikipedia co-opted the informal coordination mechanisms into more formal ones, instituting new system-level limitations on some topics, and increasing the need for more powerful, well-defined roles (such as administrators who can lock or unlock topics). Furthermore, additional features such as Talk Pages were added by designers to facilitate discussion and to discourage editing wars on the public content pages (Viégas et al. 2007). Thus, many responsibilities of coordination have increasingly shifted from the users to the system itself.

Unlike ordered systems like Wikipedia, social networking and content sharing systems present us with examples of systems that may exist precisely because of their relatively low levels of order or coordination. These systems rely on the free expression and personal creativity of individual contributors. The public goods in these cases are amorphous and emergent, along with the base of contributors who help create them. For example, content sharing systems such as YouTube.com rose in popularity when relatively small amounts of original user-created content were widely disseminated (Hardy 2006). Indeed, the purpose of many user-created content sharing sites is to avoid too much structure so that unpredictable, unique, and interesting new content can emerge. Thus, too much imposed order and coordination could be stifling or even lead to the collapse of the system.

Of course, these final points are based on a few select examples. We believe they raise exciting questions about the relationships between the structure of online exchange systems and the public goods that they produce. At the time of this writing, many of these collaborative content and content-sharing sites are just beginning to gain widespread attention. Future theory and research should examine the locus of order and coordination within information pools, with attention to both technical designs and emergent social structures. The longitudinal evolution of order and coordination within different information pools is another exciting research area. It will be interesting to observe changes in the order and coordination of these systems as they grow and expand, as well as how this affects both the social uses of the systems and the nature of the content that is created and distributed.

Future research might expand our understanding of how and why individuals contribute to information pools under various conditions and contexts of interaction. Although we did find an effect from the mere presence of an affiliation logo, this generally suggestive finding would benefit from more targeted follow-up studies. Understanding what types of other visual cues are more or less effective at reducing different types of uncertainty as well as providing different avenues for contributing information are just two intriguing areas of future research. Regarding the negative effect of commercial advertising, future studies might also control for the type of advertisement or the position of the advertisements (that is, in relation to a Mycroft banner). Of course, many other factors may influence environmental uncertainty, and the changing landscape of the Internet makes the sources of environmental uncertainty a perpetually moving target.

This is an exciting time for the social scientific study of collective action in online environments. New systems are constantly emerging, just as others are evolving technically and through the capricious actions of users. The information pools we have classified in this chapter are undeniably complex systems that require an understanding of both technical designs and the social relations and interactions enabled by these arrangements. As we have demonstrated through exploratory field experiments, the context in which users interact with an information pool may influence perceptions of reliability, thereby affecting overall contributions of information to the system. The issues of uncertainty and reliability, though of principal importance, are just the tip of the proverbial iceberg when it comes to our understanding of antecedents and consequences of information pools and other types of online collective action. The opportunities for continuing research in this area are evident, and we believe that the classification framework and analyses presented here will prove a useful tool in future investigations.

Notes

1. The general phenomenon of using large numbers of individuals on the Internet to produce information is sometimes dubbed Web 2.0. In the early 2000s, the term quickly became more of a marketing buzzword and less of a descriptive term for a defined set of technologies or systems (Madden and Fox 2006). Still, the types of Internet information contribution systems that we describe in this chapter are often aligned with the Web 2.0 concept of participatory Internet applications (see O'Reilly 2005).

2. It is important to note that information can have the qualities of high jointness of supply and replication, but these are not necessary features of all information goods. Indeed, many types of information have very low jointness of supply because each person's use of it reduces its availability to others. For example, a book can be checked out from a library by only one person at a time. Yet the same material in the book could be made available as an electronic file. In both cases, the physical book and the electronic book, the information could theoretically be replicated through photocopies or downloads, yet the electronic download has higher jointness of supply than the physical manifestation of the book, because many can download and use the information at the same time without affecting another's use of it.

3. Peter Ekeh made several other distinctions between types of group-generalized exchange systems (1974). For example, some systems involve individuals receiving benefits from others (A ← B, C, D; B ← A, C, D) and other systems involve individuals who take turns giving to all others (A → B, C, D; B → A, C, D)

4. Whereas uncertainty (structural or perceived) deals with how confident an individual may feel about a particular outcome based on various factors, risk deals with what is actually at stake in a situation. In the online information pools we present, one essential shared feature is that they are low-risk systems (see figure 10.1). Of course, this could just be an unintended consequence of our own example selection. Another possibility is that these example systems survive on the Internet precisely because of their low risks for contributors. In this view, examples of high-risk information pools may be hard to find because it is difficult to encourage information contributions among potentially anonymous partners if the risks (and potential costs) are fairly high.

5. Of course, there are other types of uncertainty in different online systems, such as the quality of the information provided by contributors or the likelihood of finding a partner in dyadic exchanges. Here we are only dealing with the system uncertainty associated with direct interaction with a given system.

6. Alluding to knowledge-building through deduction, Mycroft is appropriately named after Sherlock Holmes' older and wiser brother.

7. Although users can register with Mycroft, we do not use any of the information about registered users in any of the exploratory research reported here. In addition, the actual number of registered users is extremely small (less than 1 percent).

8. A view is counted only when an individual loads the Web page that hosts a Mycroft banner, but that individual can contribute repeatedly through the banner without reloading the page and registering another view.

9. Mycroft uses a system for assigning persistent unique IDs to anonymous users so that they always receive the same experimental condition, as long as they use the same physical computer on subsequent visits.

References

Ang, Lawrence, and Boon-Chye Lee. 2000. "Engendering Trust in Internet Commerce: A Qualitative Investigation." In *Proceedings of the ANZAM 2000 Conference*. Sydney: Macquarie University.

Baier, Annette. 1986. "Trust and Antitrust." *Ethics* 96(2): 231–60.

Bainbridge, William S. 2002. "Validity of Web-Based Surveys." In *Computing in the Social Sciences and Humanities*, edited by Orville Vernon Burton. Urbana: University of Illinois Press.

Boyd, Danah. 2006. "A Blogger's Blog: Exploring the Definition of a Medium." *Reconstruction* 6(4); online only. Available at: http://danah.org/papers/ABloggersBlog.pdf (accessed April 9, 2009).

Bryant, Susan L., Andrea Forte, and Amy Bruckman. 2005. "Becoming Wikipedian: Transformation of Participation in a Collaborative Online Encyclopedia." In *GROUP 2005: Proceedings of the 2005 International ACM SIG-GROUP Conference on Supporting Group Work*. New York: ACM. Available at: http://www.cc.gatech.edu/~asb/papers/bryant-forte-bruckman-group05.pdf (accessed April 9, 2009).

Butler, Brian, Elisabeth Joyce, and Jacqueline Pike. 2008. "Don't Look Now, but We've Created a Bureaucracy: The Nature and Roles of Policies and Rules in Wikipedia." In *Proceedings of the 26th Annual SIGCHI Conference on Human Factors in Computing Systems*, edited by Mary Czerwinski and Arnie Lund. New York: ACM.

Cheshire, Coye. 2007. "Selective Incentives and Generalized Information Exchange." *Social Psychology Quarterly* 70(1): 82–100.

Cheshire, Coye, and Judd Antin. 2008. "The Social Psychological Effects of Feedback on the Production of Internet Information Pools." *Journal of Computer Mediated Communication* 13(3): 705–27.

Cheshire, Coye, and Karen S. Cook. 2004. "The Emergence of Trust Networks: Implications for Online Interaction." *Analyse & Kritik* 26(1): 220–40.

Cook, Karen S., and Richard M. Emerson. 1978. "Power, Equity and Commitment in Exchange Networks." *American Sociological Review* 43(5): 721–39.

Cook, Karen S., and Russell Hardin. 2001. "Norms of Cooperativeness and Networks of Trust." In *Social Norms*, edited by Michael Hechter and Karl-Dieter Opp. New York: Russell Sage Foundation.

Donath, Judith. 1999. "Identity and Deception in the Virtual Community." In *Communities in Cyberspace*, edited by Peter Kollock and Marc Smith. London: Routledge.

Ekeh, Peter Palmer. 1974. *Social Exchange Theory: The Two Traditions*. London: Heinemann Educational.

Emerson, Richard M. 1972. "Exchange Theory Part I: A Psychological Basis for Social Exchange." In *Sociological Theories in Progress*, vol. 2., edited by Joseph Berger, Morris Zelditch Jr., and Bo Anderson. Boston: Houghton-Mifflin.

Fogg, B. J. 2003. "Prominence-Interpretation Theory: Explaining How People Assess Credibility Online." In *CHI '03 Extended Abstracts on Human Factors in Computing Systems*, edited by Gilbert Cockton and Panu Korhonen. New York: ACM.

Fogg, B. J., Marshall Jonathan, Kameda Tami, Solomon Joshua, Rangnekar Akshay, Boyd John, and Brown Bonny. 2001. "Web Credibility Research: A Method for Online Experiments and Early Study Results." In *CHI '01 Extended Abstracts on Human Factors in Computing Systems*, edited by Marilyn Mantei Tremaine. New York: ACM. Available at: http://captology.stanford.edu/pdf/WebCred%20Fogg%20CHI%202001%20short%20paper.PDF.

Fox, Susannah. 2000. "Trust and Privacy Online: Why Americans Want to Rewrite the Rules." Washington, D.C.: Pew Internet & American Life Project.

Gerbasi, Alexandra. 2005. "Attribution and Commitment in Different Types of Exchange." Presented at the annual meetings of the American Sociological Association. Philadelphia, Pa. (August 12). Available at: http://www.allacademic.com/meta/p19488_index.html (accessed April 7, 2009).

Hardin, Russell. 2002. *Trust and Trustworthiness*. New York: Russell Sage Foundation.

Hardy, Ian. 2006. "The Viral Video Online Revolution." BBC News. Available at: http://news.bbc.co.uk/1/hi/programmes/click_online/5020364.stm (accessed November 7, 2006).

Herring, Susan C., Lois Ann Scheidt, Sabrina Bonus, and Elijah Wright. 2004. "Bridging the Gap: A Genre Analysis of Weblogs." In *Proceedings of the 37th*

Annual Hawaii International Conference on System Sciences, vol. 4. Washington, D.C.: IEEE Computer Society.

Kim, Joung Yeon, and Kernal Altinkemer. 2005. "E-lancing: A Tool for Yield Management in the IT Service Industry." Working paper. Krannert School of Management, Purdue University.

Kollock, Peter. 1994. "The Emergence of Exchange Structures: An Experimental-Study of Uncertainty, Commitment, and Trust." *American Journal of Sociology* 100(2): 313–45.

———. 1999. "The Economies of Online Cooperation: Gifts and Public Goods in Cyberspace." In *Communities in Cyberspace*, edited by Peter Kollock and Marc Smith. London: Routledge.

Lawler, Edward J., Shane R. Thye, and Jeongkoo Yoon. 2000. "Emotion and Group Cohesion in Productive Exchange." *American Journal of Sociology* 106(3): 616–57.

Lyman, Peter, and Hal R. Varian. 2003. "How Much Information?" *How Much Information 2000*. University of California–Berkeley. Available at: http://www.sims.berkeley.edu/how-much-info (accessed November 7, 2006).

Madden, Mary, and Susannah Fox. 2006. "Finding Answers Online in Sickness and in Health." Washington, D.C.: Pew Internet & American Life Project. Available at: http://www.pewinternet.org/Reports/2006/Finding-Answers-Online-in-Sickness-and-in-Health.aspx (accessed April 9, 2009).

Metzger, Miriam J. 2004. "Privacy, Trust, and Disclosure: Exploring Barriers to Electronic Commerce." *Journal of Computer Mediated Communication* 9(4): 2158–171.

Nardi, Bonnie, Diane J. Schiano, and Michelle Gumbrecht. 2004. "Blogging as Social Activity, or, Would You Let 900 Million People Read Your Diary?" In *Proceedings of the 2004 ACM Conference on Computer Supported Cooperative Work*, edited by Jim Herbsleb and Gary Olson. New York: ACM.

Nardi, Bonnie, Diane J. Schiano, Michelle Gumbrecht, and Luke Swartz. 2004. "Why We Blog." *Communications of the ACM* 47(1): 41–46.

O'Reilly, Tim. 2005. "What is Web 2.0?" *O'Reilly Media*. Available at: http://www.oreillynet.com/pub/a/oreilly/tim/news/2005/09/30/what-is-web-20.html (accessed November 22, 2006).

OED Online. 2008. *Oxford English Dictionary*. "blog, n." Available at: http://dictionary.oed.com/cgi/entry/00319399 (accessed December 2008).

Shapiro, Carl, and Hal R. Varian. 1998. *Information Rules: A Strategic Guide to the Network Economy*. Boston: Harvard Business School Press.

Schmidt, Jan. 2007. "Blogging Practices: An Analytical Framework." *Journal of Computer-Mediated Communication* 12(4): 1409–427.

Swartz, Aaron. 2006. "Who Writes Wikipedia?" *Raw Thought*. Available at: http://www.aaronsw.com/weblog/whowriteswikipedia (accessed December 31, 2008).

Viégas, Fernanda, Martin Wattenberg, Jesse Kriss, and Frank van Ham. 2007. "Talk Before You Type: Coordination in Wikipedia." Presented at the 40th Annual Hawaii International Conference on System Sciences (HICSS). Oahu, Hawaii (January 3–6). Available at: http://www.research.ibm.com/visual/papers/wikipedia_coordination_final.pdf.

Viégas, Fernanda, Martin Wattenberg, and Matthew McKeon. 2007. "The Hidden Order of Wikipedia." In *Online Communities and Social Computing*, edited by Douglas Shuler. New York: Springer-Verlag.

Yamagishi, Toshio. 1995. "Social Dilemmas." In *Sociological Perspectives on Social Psychology*, edited by Karen S. Cook, Gary A. Fine, and James S. House. Boston: Allyn & Bacon.

Yamagishi, Toshio, and Karen S. Cook. 1993. "Generalized Exchange and Social Dilemmas." *Social Psychology Quarterly* 56(1): 235–48.

Zhang, Michael, and Feng Zhu. 2006. "Intrinsic Motivation of Open Content Contributors: The Case of Wikipedia." Working paper. Cambridge, Mass.: Massachusetts Institute of Technology. Available at: http://digital.mit.edu/wise2006/papers/3A-1_wise2006.pdf (accessed April 8, 2009).

Chapter 11

Cooperation with and without Trust Online

Azi Lev-On

THE SWEEPING and extensive penetration of the Internet generates endless possibilities for emergent associations and exchange. Engendering trust may be critical to enabling agents to gain from such exchange; for example, trust can assist in overcoming dilemmas related to multinational organizations, global virtual teams, auction and barter sites, house exchange sites, peer-to-peer file swapping sites, and on and on (Iacono and Weisband 1997; Jarvenpaa and Leidner 1999; Kirkman et al. 2002).

The formation and continuance of trust online, however, runs into obstacles that jeopardize the fulfillment of the great potentials of the Internet for mutually beneficial exchange (see Nissenbaum 2004; Dutton and Shepherd 2003; Ben-Ner and Putterman 2003.) The logic of repetition and expectation of future exchange is a primary generator of trust in everyday life (Hardin 2002). But online exchanges are often singular, and may not be supported by thick relationships, geographic proximity, or FtF (face-to-face) interaction between agents. The formation of local norms can engender cooperation as well (Cook and Hardin 2001), but online spaces are often normatively thin. Without trust the great potential of the Internet for exchange may be jeopardized, crowding out entrepreneurs and traders.

This chapter explores the possibilities of generating trust and cooperation online, and looks at mechanisms that emerge to overcome risk and facilitate cooperation. Following Harvey James (2002), I distinguish between two methods of managing trust problems. One is generating trust by altering agents' expectations about the future behavior of others, without institutional intervention and leaving agents' vulnerability intact. A second approach involves establishing institutions that alter the strategic setting, transforming the problem of trust into one about the competence of third parties. The distinction between trust-based cooperation and cooperation without trust frames the rest of this chapter.

Lack of Identity and Contextual Cues

In spite of the recent explosion of the academic literature on trust, the concept of trust is often left undefined or ambiguous (McKnight and Chervany 1996). In particular, in the literature on trust in the Internet, trust is often confounded with security (Nissenbaum 2004).[1] Its focus thus ranges from technological infrastructure to computers and network equipment, from system administrators and users to corporations and governments, and so on.

In this chapter, I use Russell Hardin's cognitive account of trust as encapsulated interest, which conceptualizes trust in terms of expectations about the future behaviors of interdependent agents (2002). In a choice situation involving two agents (without loss of generality), agent X trusts agent Y in a particular context when X is willing to become vulnerable to future actions by Y, who acts only after X's action is known. Such willingness is based on the expectation that agent Y will perform in the future some action that would bring about a state of the world that is desirable to X.[2]

Trust judgments do not immediately or necessarily have behavioral outcomes, but they inform decisions to act, and so "inspire courses of action" (Levi and Stoker 2000, 476). These judgments are based on the would-be trustor's assessment of the interests, commitments and character of the trustee, given institutional, social, or other constraints (Hardin 2002). To be able to make informed assessments of the trustworthiness of Y, X must acquire information about Y's interests, commitment, and character. Such assessments of trustworthiness can be based on *visual cues* that can involve bodily discipline and gestures, eye contact, facial expressions, and manner of dressing, among others. Assessments of trustworthiness can also be inferred from verbal cues (tone of voice, fluency, and so on) and social cues (gender, age, status, group membership, and the like). Identity can signal trustworthiness when it consists of specific properties associated with trustworthiness for specific agents. Trustworthiness assessments can also be based on an extended observation of performance (Sztompka 1999). Cues provide information about qualities that the trustor correlates with trustworthiness, and can focus attention on the presence or absence of such qualities in the would-be trustee (Bacharach and Gambetta 2001).

In this section, I analyze the main barriers to the formation of online trust, that is, the obstacles individuals encounter in assessing interests, commitments, and character online, which may be necessary to reach informed and sound judgments about the trustworthiness of other agents. I focus on two such obstacles: the absence of identity cues (anonymity) and the lack of contextual cues.

As Helen Nissenbaum has showed, anonymity is often singled out as the major obstacle for creating trust online (1999, 2004). Anonymity denotes the absence of identifying information about an agent in a particular context, such as a transaction, negotiations, and the like.[3] In an anonymous transaction, for example, the identity of one or more of the transacting parties cannot be extracted from the data, or established by combining the transaction data with other data. Many online activities—from sending e-mail, to participating in discussion forums, to engaging in electronic commerce, to participating in online systems that support teamwork, decision-making, or negotiations—involve different degrees of anonymity (Nissenbaum 1999).

Online exchange enables various forms of anonymity. One of the more robust involves the use of remailers, that is, servers that strip all identifying information from a message and then forward it to its destination. Sometimes a chain of remailers is used to even better conceal the identity of the sender. When combined with encryption, not only the identity of the sender is concealed, but all the identifying information included in the message itself is also scrambled and thus unrecognizable except to authorized readers. A robust form of anonymity can also be achieved by using anonymous browsers that encrypt all information that passes through the browser and allow users to send e-mails and browse the web anonymously. Anonymity can also be obtained by connecting to the Internet through public hot-spots or Internet cafés, where it may be impossible to keep track of users' identities. Agents often use less robust forms, where real-world identities can be verified by service providers or router operators. Sometimes agents can be identified by a pseudonym, which does not correspond to and cannot be associated with their real-world identity (pseudonymity). A pseudonym can serve as a model for the public online identity of an agent, even if it is different from her offline identity (Clarke 1999). But even without the use of robust techniques such as remailing or anonymous browsing, users can still be effectively anonymous to others. This is possible because the vast majority of users do not have the time, resources, technical abilities, or legal authority required to expose the identity of an agent who provides no identifying information, or to disclose the identity behind a pseudonym (Clarke 1999).

Anonymity sets obstacles to the formation of trust because it enables agents to minimize or even eliminate the consequences of being detected, monitored, and punished.[4] Anonymity allows agents to circumvent accountability for their actions, and can mask fraud, blackmail, harassment, and forms of speech that can lead to physical or psychological harm to others at low risk (Froomkin 1995; Levine 1996; Nissenbaum 2004). When an anonymous agent acts in such ways, it is impossible to authenticate her identity, monitor her actions, or hold her accountable and responsible.

Anonymity can be detrimental to trust in other ways as well. Anonymity prevents agents from building up and utilizing a reputation. The inability to inquire about the reputation of agents, in the absence of other trust-generating cues, can prevent positive judgments about trustworthiness, even when such judgments are appropriate. The use of anonymity also effectively disables expert authority in situations when it could be valuable. Moreover, in some cases, the very use of anonymity, even without malicious intent, can raise suspicion and distrust and prevent exchange. Agents may suspect that if someone is willing to take on the technical difficulties required to conceal one's identity, that person may have something to hide.

When no structural solutions to such problems are available, agents may fail to enjoy the benefits of a mutually beneficial online exchange. Over time, agents can develop risk-averse dispositions, and even generalize an unpleasant experience of an online breach of trust to the Internet user population at large. The use of effective anonymity online can thus jeopardize the establishment and persistence of trust.

Another obstacle to the development of online trust has to do with contextual cues. Even when agents expose their identity, a variety of cues that would allow inferences about them are unavailable online (Nissenbaum 2004). Visual, verbal, and social cues can be restricted or absent and thus a range of indications about the intentions of agents is unavailable. In the absence of such cues, others may not be able to confirm an agent's self-presentation.

The remaining cues may not support the cognitive groundwork necessary to reach an informed decision about trusting a particular agent in a particular context. Visual, verbal, and social cues that agents learn to anticipate and recognize in repeated settings are often replaced by textual signs. An agent's e-mail address can in some cases be the only identity cue available.[5] The content and design of websites or blogs do provide cues about character, commitment, and interests. These, however, seem pale in comparison with the variety and richness of cues available through other media.

The poverty of cues in Internet communication is primarily a consequence of the limitations of the medium. Bandwidth restrictions may confine users to text-based communication and allow them to recreate only vague approximations of the audio and visual qualities of FtF communication, even for those with high-speed Internet connections. Video and audio capabilities in CMC (computer-mediated communication) can indeed generate additional cues and frame social settings in more recognizable and familiar ways. However, such capabilities require a broad bandwidth that may be costly or even unavailable.

The poverty of cues will persist even if technical improvements, such as innovative communication protocols and especially wider bandwidth, enable the enrichment of communication channels. First, bandwidth enhancements will not necessarily be available to all users equally, and thus even if user X enriches her communicative capabilities, such capabilities may not be available to her partner Y, in which case the communication has to correspond to the abilities of Y. Second, different pricing schemes may encourage users to prefer less costly text-based communication to audio- and video-enabled communication, even when they are available. Third, when available software and hardware are incompatible, text-based communication will be an alternative to richer CMC environments even when enhanced communicative capabilities exist for both communicators.

Experimental Evidence: Social Dilemma and Trust Games

Laboratory experiments lend further support to claims regarding the adverse consequences of the lack of identity and context cues for cooperation.

The experimental laboratory is a first-rate environment in which to study trust, reciprocity, and cooperation because it permits manipulating and controlling for multiple variables, desegregating their effects, and conducting multiple treatments to rule out competing hypotheses. Laboratory experiments involving communication face an external validity problem, in that the arenas for communication are provided by the experimenters and (in most cases) cost the experimental subjects nothing. By contrast, in real-world social dilemmas, the transaction and opportunity costs of communication (especially discussion) can be quite high. Public spaces for communication are public goods in themselves. David Messick and Marilyn Brewer asserted that outside the laboratory, "the implications of [the effect of communication on cooperation] are limited . . . in that for many real-world dilemmas, such direct communication among group members is not an available solution to the problem. Most social dilemmas involve large collectives that are extended in time and space, offering little or no opportunity for group members to communicate or negotiate a solution to the choice problem" (1983, 23).

Nevertheless, the large-scale coordination on Internet communication infrastructure enables inexpensive and accessible communication channels in many dilemma situations, and therefore relaxes the provision problem and, with it, the external validity problem.

I review results from three relevant avenues of experimental research regarding computer-mediated communication and cooperation: social dilemma experiments that involve simultaneous choice games; trust games that involve sequential choices (including some experimental findings from our recent research conducted at the University of Pennsylvania); and experiments on efficiency, productivity, and collaborative decision making in workgroups (for a review of various experimental designs, see Cook and Cooper 2003). Let me start with social dilemma games.

Social dilemmas are choice situations involving interdependent agents, where the choices of each influence the welfare of all. These choice situations are dilemmas because the strategic setting is such that short-term rational decisions of narrowly self-interested agents lead to socially suboptimal outcomes—that is, the Nash equilibrium is also Pareto suboptimal. In typical social dilemma experiments, subjects are divided into groups greater than two. All subjects receive an endowment and then decide to send some, all, or none of this amount to a group account. The amount the subjects do not send is theirs to keep. The amount accumulated in the group account is then multiplied by the experimenters and equally divided among group members. These games use the mixed-motive structure of a social dilemma, where it is individually best for subjects to keep their money in their personal account, but all are better off if everyone makes a cooperative decision and contributes their endowments to the group account.

A robust experimental finding in the study of social dilemmas is the positive effect of (interactive and unrestricted) communication on cooperation, which elsewhere we denote as a communication effect (Bicchieri and Lev-On 2007). John Ledyard, in an extensive survey of the experimental literature on public goods, singled out communication and the marginal per capita return as the two variables most conducive to cooperation (1995). David Sally, in a meta-analysis of thirty-five years of social dilemma experiments, showed that the ability to communicate increases cooperation over base rates by 40 percent (1995).

The communication effect has mostly been studied in face-to-face settings, but it is present in computer-mediated environments as well; that is, CMC produces higher cooperation rates than equivalent environments in which communication is not allowed. Here are some additional features of the computer-mediated communication effect, as shown in social dilemma games: [6]

1.   The communication effect varies in degree according to the richness of the communication channel. Videoconferencing produces cooper-

ation rates very close to FtF communication, whereas text-based communication produces substantially less. Generally, the CMC effect approximates the FtF communication effect the closer the communication channel comes to reproduce the features of face-to-face communication.

2.   When using CMC to communicate in social dilemmas, communication is normatively charged—even more charged than FtF communication. This could be explained by the need to compensate for the lack of contextual cues in computer-mediated environments (see Frohlich and Oppenheimer 1998, 401; Rocco 1998; Brosig, Ockenfels, and Weimann 2003).

3.   Compared to FtF communication, it takes more time to establish cooperation, especially when using "poorer" CMC channels. In the absence of continuing communication, cooperation deteriorates over time. But after communication resumes, cooperation rates improve again.

4.   Especially with asynchronous communication, it is more difficult to establish social contracts in CMC, and even when such agreements are reached, they are violated more frequently than agreements reached using FtF communication.

An experiment by Jeannette Brosig, Axel Ockenfels, and Joachim Weimann nicely captured some of the points we make, and is worth reviewing in some detail (2003). The experiment is about a repeated public-good game with seven conditions, most of which involved preplay communication. The only difference between the communication conditions was the medium. The seven conditions included a control no-communication condition, and an identification condition in which players saw one another for ten seconds but could not talk. Two of the other conditions involved unidirectional communication, in which players were exposed to communication from others but could not actively participate. These were, respectively, a lecture condition and a talk-show condition.[7] In the fifth condition, the group communicated through an audio-conference system. In the last two conditions, groups communicated using either a videoconference system or a table conference, at which subjects sat around the same table and could talk to each other for up to ten minutes.

The authors found that different media produced distinct communication effects, and that contributions in the videoconferencing and table-conference conditions were significantly higher than in other conditions. The seven communication conditions were divided into three subgroups according to the extent and stability of cooperation. Each subgroup includes similar conditions, but such conditions differ significantly from those of other subgroups:

- Control and identification conditions were characterized by relatively low initial contribution rates (less than 50 percent), but relatively stable cooperation (decline of less than 20 percent).

- The audio-conference condition, as well as the two conditions of unidirectional communication, lecture and talk show, were characterized by intermediate initial contribution rates (between 50 and 60 percent), but relatively unstable cooperation (decline of more than 30 percent).

- The videoconference and table conference conditions were characterized by high initial contribution rates (more than 90 percent) and relatively stable cooperation (decline of less than 20 percent).

The communication effect was present in all communication conditions, but different CMC channels produced different levels of contributions to the production of the public good. In the absence of continuous communication, there was a decline in cooperation rates in all conditions, though the extent of the decline varied across conditions (see also Frohlich and Oppenheimer 1998; Bos et al. 2001; Rocco 1998; Zheng et al. 2001).

Elsewhere we have argued that communication affects cooperation in social dilemmas because it focuses agents on prosocial norms, notably promise-keeping (Bicchieri and Lev-On 2007). Consequently, the dilemma situation is perceived as representative of other situations in which agents make and keep their promises. This scripted interaction allows agents to form expectations about the behavior of other parties and beliefs that others expect them to honor their promises as well.

Computer-mediated communication hinders cooperation because of the relative absence of individual and social cues, which impedes the generation of normative settings where promises to cooperate are perceived as credible. Cues about the norms that govern the interaction allow agents to infer whether the situation is similar to and representative of familiar settings. Cues about the intentions of players enable "mindreading" (McCabe, Smith, and LePore 2000). Media that are richer with cues, especially videoconferencing systems, allow agents to gain public knowledge of their respective promises, as well as to perceive promises as credible and thus feel it is safe to cooperate. Thinner communication channels instead may fail to convey enough cues to generate the right kind of expectations that support norm-abiding behavior (Bicchieri and Lev-On 2007).

Close cousins of social dilemma games are trust games, which are in essence sequential dilemma games. In a typical trust experiment, subjects are assigned to one of two roles, first movers or second movers. Experiments contain two decision periods.[8] In the first decision period, each first mover receives an endowment and then decides to send some, all, or none of it to the second mover. The amount the first mover does not send is hers to keep. In the second decision period, the amount first movers sent to second movers is multiplied by the experimenters. The second mover can send some, all, or none of this amount to the first mover. The amount the second mover does not send is hers to keep. Unlike in social dilemma games with communication, in trust games with communication the trustee (second mover) knows both the trustor's promise and action, before playing. A big discrepancy between promise and performance can result in sanctioning, which is impossible in simultaneous-move social dilemma games. As a result, communication in trust games can be even more conducive to cooperation than in social dilemma games. This hypothesis remains to be explored, however (see McCabe, Smith, and LePore 2000).

In recent years there has been an upsurge in both the theoretical and the empirical study of trust and reciprocity. Unfortunately, experimental literature that directly tests the effects of interactive communication on behavior in trust games is only just emerging.

A few studies demonstrate that the communication effect exists in trust games as well. Avner Ben-Ner and Louis Putterman introduced four relevant communication conditions before trust games: no-communication, a one-stage computerized negotiation between first and second mover during which subjects could make choices out of a table of possible distributions and possibly enter a contract; a three-stage computerized negotiation along similar lines; and a computerized preplay chat (2006). The authors found significant differences in terms of both trust and trustworthiness between all communication conditions and the no-communication condition. They also found significant differences between the no-binding chat and negotiations conditions.

Gary Charness and Martin Dufwenberg allowed unrestricted written messages from second movers to first movers before trust games (2006). They also found significant differences between the communication and the no-communication conditions in terms of both trusting and reciprocal behaviors. Tore Ellingsen and Magnus Johannseeon obtained similar results (2004). Cristina Bicchieri, Azi Lev-On, and Alex Chavez allowed subjects to communicate before playing trust games; the richness of the communication media and the topics of conversation were manipulated (2009). The authors found that first movers' expectations of second movers' reciprocation were influenced by communication and strongly predicted their levels of investment.

Last, in a quasi-experiment, Iris Bohnet and Yael Baytelman conducted surveys in which senior executives were asked to make choices in emulated trust games (2007). Treatments included an anonymous one-shot trust game scenario without communication, and a one-shot scenario with preplay face-to-face communication. The authors found, again, significant differences between the communication and the no-communication conditions in terms of amounts sent and received, and the expectations of both first and second movers. They also found that following FtF communication, second movers returned greater portions of the amounts sent to them by first movers. The quasi-experiment, however, did not include CMC treatments, and did not involve monetary incentives.

Experimental Evidence from Workgroups

A third and last relevant avenue of research includes findings from the study of efficiency, productivity, and decision-making in virtual collaborations and workgroups.

In line with the findings surveyed on cooperation patterns in one-shot social dilemma experiments, early research found that CMC could not sustain elaborate forms of relational development and support as FtF communication. Reduced cues (or cues-filtered-out) theory suggests that communication mediums have sets of objective characteristics that correspond to distinct levels of richness. Richer communication media support more cues and help bring about higher levels of social presence. Arguably, higher levels of social presence result in greater attention to the presence of others and greater awareness of, and conformity to, social norms (see Kiesler, Siegel, and McGuire 1984; Sproull and Kiesler 1986; Kiesler and Sproull 1992). The lack of cues in CMC leads to reduced awareness of the social environment, and consequently to reduced concerns for social approbation, decreased awareness of and adherence to social norms, and reduced opportunities for social control and regulation. According to the reduced cues theory, CMC encourages antinormative and uninhibited behaviors such as flaming—that is, inappropriate and hostile assaults on others.

The reduced cues theory has been criticized for failing to provide a comprehensive explanation of behavior online. Scholars argue that the theory is based on research designs that involve one-shot interactions, where participants have no previous knowledge of each other and expect no future interactions (Walther 1996). The theory is also grounded on text-based interactions and ignores richer CMC environments, which may be more conducive to cooperation (Soukup 2000).

Further empirical work challenges the claim that CMC is inherently antinormative and inhospitable. Instead, scholars argue that over time individual CMC users create and modify impressions based on information and cues they receive, establish socioemotional contexts (Rice and Love 1987), and develop social and even warm relationships just as users of other communication media do (Parks and Floyd 1996; Walther 1996). The inhospitable character of CMC seems limited to initial interactions among previously unacquainted partners who do not expect future relationships (Walther, Anderson, and Park 1994). Despite its limited scope, reduced cues theory may still be applicable to time-limited and socially impoverished settings. Its findings, however, should be integrated into a wider framework that involves longitudinal research and considers the social context of communication as well (Walther 1996).

Such a framework is provided by the social information processing (SIP) theory, which recognizes that continuing communication enables the normative conditions for cooperation in CMC to develop, even if cooperation is established more slowly than in FtF environments (Walther, Anderson, and Park 1994; Walther 1996). Repeated interaction involves continuous and mutual reception and verification of cues. Agents find ways to adapt to the limitations of the medium and to reduce uncertainty (Chidambaram 1996; Walther 1996). Specifically, when future relationships are anticipated, communication itself fails to account for relational development; users disclose more information about themselves as they seek and acquire information about their partners. Based on this information, they develop interpersonal knowledge and stable relations with partners. When the amount of trustworthiness-relevant information crosses some subjective thresholds, agents feel comfortable in making projections about the future behaviors of other agents. Consequently, cooperation increases over time and converges to rates observed in FtF communication (Walther 1996; Wilson, Straus, and McEvily 2006).

A third theory, which I only briefly present, is the SIDE theory (social identity model of depersonalization effects), which is supported by a growing body of research (for reviews, see Postmes, Spears, and Lea 1998; Spears and Lea 1994; Watt, Lea, and Spears 2002), and specifically research in CMC environments (Postmes et al. 2001). Both SIP theory and SIDE theory emphasize the social context of CMC. SIDE theory shows, however, perhaps counterintuitively, that the social context of communication may be especially salient and the influence of social norms particularly effective, at the relative absence of information about agents. Social influence and social norms can be most prominent without the immediate presence of other agents.

According to SIDE theory, when a CMC environment is characterized by a salient sense of group membership, the lack of other cues leads to a stronger influence of social norms on behavior and to compliance with situational norms. Although CMC indeed blocks a range of interpersonal cues, it often leaves some group-level social cues intact. These may be the only cues available for agents. Such cues can be inferred from the group goal or documentation, and are similarly available and comprehensible to all agents simply by virtue of their belonging to the same group. Research demonstrates that in such circumstances group membership becomes situationally relevant and agents are more likely to adapt to the situational norms, even in groups with no history. Russell Spears and Martin Lea argued that in CMC, the overreliance on minimal cues to "cognitively compensate" for the absence of other cues can lead to in-group favoritism, stereotyping, and disapproval of out-groups. In such conditions, they claimed, CMC generates a "panoptic power" (1994, 427).

In conclusion, research from various disciplines converges on similar conclusions. Computer-mediated communication should be understood within its social context as an "amplifier or magnifier of social psychological and communication phenomena" (Walther 1997, 360; see also DeSanctis and Poole 1994). The possibilities of relational development, trust and cooperation should be explored using a "contextually sensitive approach" (Spears and Lea 1994, 452). Trust can be established in repeated interactions where future exchange is expected, even if slower than offline. When the group context of communication is salient (as in various support groups), the lack of cues can actually be conducive to trust. Still, in dilemma situations where agents neither share a common background nor expect future interactions, the absence of cues may impede the cognitive processes that ordinarily result in informed judgments of others' trustworthiness.

Emergent Internet-Based Institutions

In the first part of this chapter I argued that poor Internet communication channels impede the cognitive groundwork necessary for creating the right kinds of expectations in mixed-motive scenarios. In the absence of information and cues about others' motivations, character, and commitments, agents may choose to exchange only with those with whom they have established long-term relations, and thus fail to gain from large-scale online trade.

I now look at the unique contribution of the Internet to facilitating the institutional scaffolding needed for overcoming the problem of trust-based cooperation. I introduce several solutions that have evolved in response to the problems of online trust, and focus on reputation systems, which are based on pooling a large number of small reputational contributions from many relevant agents. Lack of identity and context cues can be inhospitable to trust and cooperation online. Such disadvantages are minimized by use of the Internet to reduce the costs of emergent organization needed to overcome trust problems (Lev-On and Hardin 2007).

Before moving to reputation systems, let me briefly review a few other avenues to addressing the problems of trust-based cooperation. One option involves enriching the channels used for communication, leaving agents' vulnerability to deception intact. In the absence of FtF contact, interface design can provide signals that influence trust judgments. Unlike in the offline world, where body language can send cues that conflict with verbal substance, Web designers have decisive control over the appearance of websites. They can determine the information that becomes publicly available and how it is framed, how agents are presented, and what tools are available to make searches, queries, or comments.

Generally, designers should be attentive to factors that influence the perceptions of Internet users about trustworthiness (Shneiderman 2000). For example, B. J. Fogg and his colleagues used an online survey to determine which factors influence users' perceptions of the credibility of websites (2002). The variables found to have the most substantial influence included a site's usefulness in previous visits (that is, impressions from previous exchange); the presence of identifying details such as a street address, telephone number, and e-mail address; the existence of a link from another trustworthy site (see also Stewart 2003); and whether the site belongs to a well-known organization (brand name). Pamela Briggs and her colleagues suggested that heuristics about the interface dominate initial judgments about the reliability of advice in websites (2002).

Several institutional alternatives have emerged in response to the challenges posed by risky trade in informal markets.[9] As stated earlier, extending the horizons of relationships among agents by allowing repeated interactions,[10] or generating a dense normative context, as in some virtual communities, may generate the proper incentives to cooperate. But such structural modifications are often either unavailable or irrelevant. Other institutions capitalize on a few properties of Internet communication, such as low-cost emergent organization, large scale, and fast flow of information online. One possibility is simply posting information in sites dedicated to institutionalized gossip, such as blogs, discussion groups, and dedicated websites. The highly efficient flow of online information contributes to the fast circulation of such postings to relevant users.

Another alternative is to transform the problem of online trust into a problem of third-party competence using agencies that evaluate the trustworthiness of agents (Hardin 2002, 8). Information intermediaries, such as credit card companies and better business bureaus, and their online equivalents, are institutional solutions to the dilemmas involved in collecting and integrating large amounts of reputation information (Klein 1997). Such agencies can import their brand name and reputation from the offline world, but it is also inexpensive, compared to offline equivalents, to establish predominantly online services (such as TrustE and Verisign.) Such agencies provide information and even produce certificates about reliability and trustworthiness. Additional online mechanisms include professional reviews, ratings, and recommendation sites. At such sites, experts provide recommendations, favorites lists, and answers to questions from other users, who can sometimes rate the experts. Information is aggregated in databases, and sent to users in response to queries (Resnick and Varian 1997).

The most notable emergent solutions to the problem of risky trade are distributed reputation mechanisms, mostly referred to as reputation sites or reputation systems, to which I shortly turn. A reputation for trustworthiness (henceforth simply "reputation") substitutes for firsthand impressions, and is based on properties that others ascribe to agents. As an alternative to observations of future exchange partners, agents may need to rely on a reputation that is based on the experiences and impressions of (often unfamiliar) others who serve as proxies for judging trustworthiness.

A reputation provides valuable information required for trust judgments.[11] A good reputation of a second mover (the would-be trustee) should ideally enhance the trust level of the first mover (the would-be trustor) and increase the possibility of exchange, whereas a bad reputation can help prevent future losses for the first mover. At the same time, the ability of the first mover to trace the reputation of the second mover and possibly influence it in the future, provides additional incentives for the agent who moves second to honor the trust of the first mover. When an agent's trust has been compromised, the ability to damage the reputation of a shirker and thus potentially impair her future exchange functions as a sanctioning mechanism. Experimental work has demonstrated the importance of reputation for cooperation; most notably, work by Anatol Rapoport, Andreas Diekmann, and Axel Franzen demonstrates significantly higher levels of cooperation when reputations are accessible (1995; see also Bolton, Katok, and Ockenfels 2004; Keser 2002).

Reputation Systems

In recent years, we have witnessed the explosion of Web 2.0 collaborative endeavors for exchange and collective action, endeavors that rely heavily on endogenous input from peers. Examples range from collaborative encyclopedias and dictionaries to open source software, from Flash demonstrations and Internet-based social movement organizations to virtual communities and Internet-organized canvassing campaigns.

Many such projects rely for a variety of organizational functions on secondary collaborative institutions, that is, a family of institutions that aggregate large amounts of individual selections and generate social choices. Such systems allow agents to collaboratively and seamlessly perform tasks such as generating keywords to describe content (collaborative tagging), content management—that is, editing and rating content, moderating discussions and generating meta-moderation (moderating the moderators)[12]—producing reviews and recommendations of products and services, and even predictions of items that agents may appreciate, based on tastes of relevant others.[13] In the same vein, the Internet allows for the evolution of peer-based institutions for collecting and distributing reputation information on a massive scale.

Online reputation systems are instances of such secondary collaborative institutions and are arguably the most notable and promising emergent solutions to the problem of trust online (Dellarocas 2001; Resnick et al. 2000). Such systems enable exchange partners to rate and comment on the performance of one another and to aggregate a vast number of inputs from many exchange partners to generate reputations. Online reputation systems can be thought of as large-scale word-of-mouth networks (Dellarocas 2003), composed of large-scale databases that can accumulate massive amounts of information that is processed on request to generate responses to users' queries. Unlike websites dedicated to expert advice and unlike certifying agencies, reputation sites manifest a bottom-up approach where ratings and reviews can originate from all agents involved in exchange, not just experts.

The need for reputation intermediaries is acute for supporting trust in environments characterized by high risks and ineffective enforcement. The evolution of novel institutions for tracking, accumulating, and processing reputation information is not unique to the online realm (Dellarocas 2003; see also Greif 1989). But online, the large number of agents who converge into focal sites necessitates reputation systems in an unprecedented scale.

On the Internet, institutions can be ineffective in ensuring contract compliance and punishing shirkers. The often impersonal and singular nature of transactions disables the benefits of repeated exchange; embeddedness in a community that enables peer pressure and sanctions, and encourages norms of cooperativeness and trustworthiness, is by and large unavailable. When exchanging goods, the transacting parties are separated over time and space, no inspection of the traded item may be possible, its description may be inaccurate, and the seller may fail to provide proper packing and timely delivery (Keser 2002); hence the necessity and significance of reputation systems.

Reputation systems are established to enable users to benefit from the experience of other users who were involved in similar types of experiences. They enable agents to build reputations through a history of reviews, and consequently allow buyers to distinguish trustworthy from untrustworthy sellers (and vice versa). Once reputation systems have been established, they enable additional benefits for buyers: they encourage sellers to honor the trust of buyers, discourage untrustworthy sellers from participating in the market, and avoid crowding high-quality sellers out of the market in the absence of quality controls (Resnick et al. 2000; Resnick and Zeckhauser 2002). At their best, such systems would not only promote cooperative behavior, but would also enable agents to generalize their trust to other agents in such online environments.[14]

By its nature, a reputation management system is a public good, under which all would like to enjoy ratings and evaluations provided by others without contributing themselves. Market forces can lead to the emergence of mechanisms for collecting and disseminating reputation information, by entrepreneurs or clubs. But even as the provision problem of reputation systems is solved, the problem of motivating agents to provide feedback on the performance of their exchange partners remains.

Online environments have significant advantages over offline environments in terms of the transaction costs associated with obtaining reputation information. Acquiring relevant reputation information offline can be extremely costly. Reputation information is often private information possessed by particular individuals, and is spread through personal communication and rumors (Resnick et al. 2000). Gathering and verifying pieces of information about past transactions and synthesizing them into a coherent picture of the past performance of an agent are extremely costly. Compared to offline reputation intermediaries, online reputation systems enable easy collection, storage, retrieval, processing, and distribution of large amounts of reputation information, and thus dramatically reduce the costs of contributing and tracking reputations. Traditional obstacles to the collection of reputation information, such as geographical dispersion, distance, and national boundaries, are much more surpassable online. Online reputation systems also make use of graphical user interfaces and online forms, which enable clear structure and appealing visual presentation for capturing and distributing reputation information (Resnick et al. 2000).[15]

A notable advantage of the Internet for the development and success of reputation systems is the unprecedented large number of users that converge to focal exchange sites. Keep in mind that online reputation systems are a collaborative effort of a large number of agents. Large scale is necessary for the effectiveness of reputation systems. If a reputation management system is not based on many contributors, the resulting information can be anecdotal, fragmentary, and biased. Ideally, when individual feedbacks are honest and reliable, the observations and experiences of many users represent a vast collective experience.

For these reasons, using the Internet to locate reputation information can be much more efficient than offline alternatives; tracking reputations is much more immediate and less time consuming. Replicating such institutions offline is exponentially more expensive, and would most probably produce a more fragmentary outcome because of the dif-

ficulties of locating agents with particular kinds of information or expertise. The low costs of establishing and maintaining their infrastructure
are also good news for their sustainability.

Although primarily studied in economic exchange situations, such
systems are relevant in any context that involves many agents who can
rate and comment on the performance of many other agents. One possible application of such systems is for supporting the organization of dynamic ride sharing. Ride-sharing systems enable commuters to match
themselves to other commuters or drivers. Reputation systems relax
trust problems among commuters and drivers, for example, by authenti-
cating the identities of drivers and commuters, informing commuters
about the records of drivers and vice versa, and alerting them to possible hazards such as reckless driving, improper behaviors, and so on
(Resnick 2004). Howard Rheingold went even further and suggested
that decentralized reputation systems are key to creating smart mobs of
citizens that collaboratively generate reputations and capitalize on them
to engender collective action (2003). They provide a "flowing patchwork
of reputational nexuses," which is critical to supporting trust, especially
in large societies that lack the intimate and continuous dimension of interactions among agents (Shearmur and Klein 1997, 38).

The most popular, and studied, reputation management system is the
feedback forum created by eBay (see Resnick et al. 2006; see also Dellarocas 2003 and Kollock 1999). To produce feedback forum records,
every eBay trader is asked to rate her satisfaction from the performance
of her partner—that is, buyers can rate sellers and vice versa. The ratings can be positive, neutral, or negative, and can be supported by a
short textual comment. Ratings are aggregated in users' feedback profiles. Statistical data about a user's feedback profile is presented to potential traders on request. Similar reputation systems have been used
with some modifications in many other exchange sites.

An industry leader, eBay provides a marketplace for large scale peer-
to-peer exchange. Its website is consistently ranked among the most visited and stickiest websites. In 2003 its business cycle was $20 billion.
Given its huge scope, it is impossible for its staff to monitor every transaction. The feedback forum, as eBay's chief executive suggests, has allowed users to police themselves, and has been a necessary condition
for eBay's success ("Queen of the Online Flea Market," *Economist*, January 3, 2004, 48).[16]

Some evidence indeed demonstrates that feedback-forum-style reputation systems are instrumental for extracting gains from online exchange. For example, Paul Resnick and his colleagues conducted a natural experiment, where identical items (batches of vintage postcards)
were sold on eBay under newcomer identity and under a high reputation identity (2006). The price premium for the high reputation identity

(the return to reputation) was 8.1 percent. Additional support comes from laboratory investment games which made use of a reputation management system similar to the feedback forum. Agents were more willing to exchange with others who received positive feedbacks; the levels of investment by first movers and the amount reciprocated by second movers significantly increased (Bolton, Katok, and Ockenfels 2004; Keser 2002).

Yet certain potential problems can undermine the effectiveness of such institutions.[17] I touch on a few main problems, including the incentive incompatibility of providing feedback, bogus or dishonest feedback, and potential disappearance of agents. I also touch on certain proposed solutions to such problems.[18]

First, as observed earlier, reputation systems are public goods, and users may be motivated to free ride on evaluations provided by others, without contributing and providing evaluations themselves. Empirically, however, users seem to overcome this dilemma to a large degree, at least in the case of the feedback forum. An analysis of a large eBay dataset from 1999 shows that more than half of the transactions received feedback, even though providing feedback is voluntary (Resnick and Zeckhauser 2002).

Empirical research about the motivations to contribute to reputation systems is still lacking. One exception is a study by Dellarocas, Fan, and Wood that analyzed a large dataset from eBay's rare coin auctions (2004). The authors found a variety of motivations to contribute ratings. The majority of contributors, an estimated 50 percent to 70 percent, do so for strategic reasons (expectation of reciprocation by partner), but other motivations also come into play, like the warm glow of contribution, altruism, and reciprocity. The low cost of providing feedback (logging into one's account, checking a box and adding a textual comment) probably contributes to the high percentage of rated transactions, well above the zero-contribution free-rider hypothesis.[19] Studying the motivations to contribute to reputation systems is, however, still a work in progress.[20]

A second problem reputation systems face is to guarantee feedback honesty, overcoming incentives to strategically manipulate feedback. Reputation systems should be able to discriminate between honest ratings and ratings that are intentionally too hostile to competitors, or too rosy to friends (Resnick et al. 2000; Miller, Resnick, and Zeckhauser 2005). It should be noted that a small number of dishonest accusations can discourage agents from exchanging with the wrongfully accused person (Kollock 1999). On the other hand, a click circle—a clique of friends or colleagues recommending each other—can inflate the ratings of otherwise 'ordinary' sellers.

Chrysanthos Dellarocas proposed a controlled anonymity scheme to improve feedback honesty, according to which only the administrators of reputation systems would know the identity of sellers and buyers, and as a result buyers would decide to transact based on the terms of trade and seller reputation, reducing the effectiveness of unfair negative ratings (2001). Anonymity is recommended here as a path to minimize risks associated with unfair ratings while maintaining the ability to use the trader's reputation as a proxy for trustworthiness.[21] Other possibilities to minimize the perils of dishonest feedback involve software designed to detect click circles and screen out dishonest ratings, and possibly even monetary rewards for users whose ratings correlate with those of other users (for details, see Miller, Resnick, and Zeckhauser 2005).

Third, people can quite easily change their identity online. Consequently, agents who were pinned down as untrustworthy can resurface, assume new identities, and in a sense leave their negative trustworthiness ratings behind. To assist in avoiding disappearance of sellers, Eric Friedman and Paul Resnick suggested charging entry fees to reputation systems, and assigning users an average initial reputation to encourage them to build a reputation over time (2001). In exceptionally risky markets, authentication of identity by a trustworthy third party may still be required.

Reputation systems, like other secondary collaborative institutions, demonstrate the novel abilities to manipulate massive amounts of content efficiently and at low costs, using small contributions by many agents. Such systems are obviously not flawless, but at best, especially when used by many skilled and unbiased agents, they are promising tools for engendering cooperation in the absence of trust.

Conclusions

Generating trust online faces distinct challenges and unique opportunities. I concentrated on two features of the Internet that seem important for understanding the potentials of cooperation, with and without trust, online. On the one hand, the poverty of cues that conventionally support trust judgments makes it difficult to generate trust, and may prevent mutually beneficial exchange online, especially when exchange is singular and takes place among previously unacquainted partners with no shared time horizons. On the other hand, the Internet is a fertile ground for institutional innovation, and in our case conducive for collaborative institutions established to overcome the problem of trust by pooling together a large number of small reputational contributions (Lev-On and Hardin 2007).

I claimed that there are ways to compensate for the poverty of certain communication channels and to encourage cooperation, for instance, by enabling subjects to converse and make promises in conditions which come close to the speech-acts of promising familiar from daily life. The problem of assessing trustworthiness online and enabling the cognitive groundwork of trust can also be alleviated, among other ways, by the logic of repetition and time (when relevant), or by establishing institutions that change the incentive structure of the dilemma.

Herein lies the unique contribution of Internet communication for transforming the obstacles to cooperation. The Internet creates conditions that enable innovative large-scale institutions that capture and process massive amounts of reputation information. It does so by enabling entrepreneurs to generate the necessary conditions for many non-heroically motivated agents to (almost) costlessly rate others and benefit from rating by others. Such reputation systems allow agents to effectively police themselves by distinguishing among different types of agents, discouraging exchange with untrustworthy partners, and encouraging trustworthiness.

The design of functional and incentive-compatible reputation systems is an ongoing experiment. It takes a large dose of clever institutional engineering to minimize potential hazards and build enough trust to enable agents to benefit from the novel exchange opportunities online.

Notes

1. The view that trust and security are indistinguishable, and the suggestion that trust can best be generated through such means as cryptography and firewalls, are prevalent in the computer science literature (see Nissenbaum 2004, 156). Trust, however, should be distinguished from security. Even when sophisticated security mechanisms are present, additional difficulties can impede the formation of trust. Moreover, under some circumstances anonymity can facilitate exchange and trust (see later).

2. Two main concerns may reduce the attractiveness of the encapsulated account of trust in online settings. The first is the focus of the encapsulated account of trust on continuing relations as the main generators of trust. Russell Hardin grounded his conceptual account of trust on the existence of repeated interactions and ongoing relationship between trustor and trustee (2002). Such interactions commonly entail considerable knowledge of each other's incentives, commitments and character. But even if the frequency of such iterated interactions are "far and away the largest in ordinary interpersonal life" (25), their frequency online does not necessarily correspond to the ordinary interpersonal life equivalent. Online exchange can be infrequent and even singular, and thick relationships between users often fail to develop.

    The second concern involves the nature of rationality involved in trust judgments. Trust judgments can follow from a comprehensive comparison of the expected costs and benefits of potential courses of action (Gambetta 1988). But there is no prima facie reason to study only trust judgments that follow from such intentional and deliberative processes. A cognitive conception of trust can be fully consistent with the application of trust heuristics, which are in fact quite prevalent in sequential choice situations (Kramer 1999; Scholz 2000; Scholz and Lubell 1998). The application of heuristics may be necessary, even if at times they lead to flawed assessments of trustworthiness.

Therefore, while applying the encapsulated interest account of trust, some of the secondary assumptions about the nature of interactions between agents and the types of rationality applied are relaxed. This is done to enable conceptual validity and effectiveness when applied to online choice environments.

3. The definition is adapted from Roger Clarke (1999). Kathleen Wallace defined anonymity as "noncoordinatability of traits in a given respect" (1999, 23). Michael Froomkin defined it along two dimensions, traceability and source identification (1995).

4. In other contexts anonymity may have socially favorable consequence, for example when it is used to protect agents from others or to promote social customs largely seen as desirable. In such circumstances, anonymity can promote the expression and support of unpopular opinions, and can encourage information seeking, information exchange, and reaching out for help (Nissenbaum 1999; Wallace 1999). Online, Internet activists and libertarians celebrate the uses of anonymity for keeping personal data away from governments and corporations, and sometimes regard anonymity as the cornerstone of online trust. As Froomkin put it, "digital anonymity may be a rational response to a world in which the quantity of identifying data on each of us grows daily, and the data become ever easier for government and private parties to access" (1995). Clarke claimed that "the imposition of identification and authentication requirements, far from engendering trust, will undermine it" (1999).

5. Using an e-mail account from a respectable host (such as a well-known firm or university) provides an aura of respectability. This is in contrast to using a free e-mail address provided by an online services, where often the identities of users cannot be authenticated and users cannot be located if necessary (Kollock 1999).

6. The following few paragraphs are based on Bicchieri and Lev-On (2007).

7. In the lecture condition, subjects watched a videotape explaining the game, delivered by a lecturer who was not involved in the experiment. In the talk show condition subjects watched a videotaped discussion about the experiment, carried out by the videoconference group.

8. Unlike trust games, in social dilemma experiments there is only one decision period, and the assignment to one of two roles does not exist.

9. The discussion in the following paragraphs roughly follows Kollock (1999).

10. Experimental work shows that repetition may be more conductive to cooperation than reputation (see Bohnet and Huck 2004; Bolton, Katok, and Ockenfels 2004). See the discussion on reputation systems later in this chapter.

11. It should be noted, however, that basing trust judgments on reputation leaves the trustor vulnerable. A decision to trust another agent is oriented

to the future but based on past behavior, and so assumes consistency in human behavior (Sztompka 1999). The danger, of course, is a scenario in which an opportunistic agent invests in reputation and mimics trustworthy-making qualities, just to defect when the grand prize becomes available (Bacharach and Gambetta 2001).

12.   Let us look at the case of collaborative filtering of news stories. The ranking choices of agents have immediate design consequences, as the portal of the collaborative project is customized according to users' rankings, such that opinion pieces are presented according to their rating. The portal presents first those articles that members found especially interesting and relevant. In other words, the availability of content is determined by its popularity, and group members are first exposed to information that other group members think highly of. The portal is an immediate translation of readers' rankings, and hence reflects their tastes and serves as a sensitive barometer of public opinion.

13.   Probably the most famous collaborative system is Google, which has been revolutionary in using the linking decisions of large numbers of authors as a key to determine the relevance of possible answers to other users' queries.

14.   A survey of 274 Amazon auction marketplace buyers shows that the perceived effectiveness of reputation systems "engender[s] trust, not only in a few reputable sellers, but also in the entire community of sellers, which contributes to an effective online marketplace" (Pavlou and Gefen 2004, 37).

15.   Designers of reputation systems can manipulate the incentives of sellers to honor the trust of buyers by using different techniques of what is called information engineering. For example, by publishing the feedback from the most recent transactions, instead of or in addition to other forms of feedback, buyers are less able to capitalize on past positive ratings while providing low-quality goods or services at present (Dellarocas 2003). A further exploration of the consequences of different institutional designs of reputation systems is beyond the scope of this chapter.

16.   Six months after founding eBay.com, Pierre Omidyar published a letter announcing the establishment of the feedback forum: "Most people are honest. And they mean well. Some people go out of their way to make things right. I've heard great stories about the honesty of people here. But some people are dishonest. Or deceptive. This is true here, in the newsgroups, in the classifieds, and right next door. It's a fact of life. But here, those people can't hide. We'll drive them away. Protect others from them" (1995).

17.   The following few paragraphs are based on Resnick et al. (2000).

18.   This chapter does not aim at providing a thorough technical analysis or detailed design suggestions for future reputation systems. Instead, it points out general directions for advances in functional reputation systems.

19.   Providing feedback can be encouraged further merely by reminding users to rate their partners, or by introducing gains for providing ratings or losses for failing to do so. Feedback can be made mandatory, for example, by conditioning future exchange on providing feedback on past transactions.

20.   According to eBay's data, the overwhelming majority of feedback is posi-

tive. Sellers receive negative feedback only 1.2 percent of the time, and buyers 0.5 percent (Resnick and Zeckhauser 2002; see also Dellarocas, Fan, and Wood 2004). It is unclear, however, whether this inflation of positive ratings is an indicator of the success of the feedback forum in deterring moral hazard and encouraging successful transacting, or of its success in deterring negative ratings for fear of retaliation.

21. See the longer discussion of anonymity earlier in this chapter.

References

Bacharach, Michael, and Diego Gambetta. 2001. "Trust in Signs." In *Trust in Society*, edited by Karen S. Cook. New York: Russell Sage Foundation.

Ben-Ner, Avner, and Louis Putterman. 2003. "Trust in the New Economy." In *New Economy Handbook*, edited by Derek C. Jones. Amsterdam: Academic Press/Elsevier.

———. 2006. "Trust, Communication and Contracts: Experimental Evidence." Department of Economics working paper 2006–23. Providence, R.I.: Brown University.

Bicchieri, Cristina, and Azi Lev-On. 2007. "Computer-Mediated Communication and Cooperation in Social Dilemmas: An Experimental Analysis." *Politics, Philosophy and Economics* 6(2): 139–68.

Bicchieri, Cristina, Azi Lev-On, and Alex Chavez. 2009. "The Medium or the Message? Communication Richness and Relevance in Trust Games." *Synthese* (March 18, 2009).

Bohnet, Iris, and Yael Baytelman. 2007. "Institutions and Trust: Implications for Preferences, Beliefs and Behavior." *Rationality and Society* 19(1): 99–135.

Bohnet, Iris, and Steffen Huck. 2004. "Repetition and Reputation: Implications for Trust and Trustworthiness when Institutions Change." *American Economic Review* 94(2): 362–66.

Bolton, Gary E., Elena Katok, and Axel Ockenfels. 2004. "How Effective Are Electronic Reputation Mechanisms? An Experimental Investigation." *Management Science* 50(11): 1587–602.

Bos, Nathan, Darren Gergle, Judith S. Olson, and Gary M. Olson. 2001. "Being There Versus Seeing There: Trust via Video." In *CHI '01 Extended Abstracts on Human Factors in Computing Systems*, edited by Marilyn Mantei Tremaine. New York: ACM.

Briggs, Pamela, Bryan Burford, Antonella deAngeli, and Paula Lynch. 2002. "Trust in Online Advice." *Social Science Computer Review* 20(3): 321–32.

Brosig, Jeannette, Axel Ockenfels, and Joachim Weimann. 2003. "The Effect of Communication Media on Cooperation." *German Economic Review* 4(2): 217–41.

Charness, Gary, and Martin Dufwenberg. 2006. "Promises and Partnership." *Econometrica* 74(6): 1579–601.

Chidambaram, Laku. 1996. "Relational Development in Computer Supported Groups." *Management Information Systems Quarterly* 20(2): 142–65.

Clarke, Roger. 1999. "Identified, Anonymous and Pseudonymous Transactions:

The Spectrum of Choice." Presented at the User Identification & Privacy Protection Conference. Stockholm (June 14–15, 1999). Available at: http://www.anu.edu.au/people/Roger.Clarke/DV/UIPP99.html.

Cook, Karen S., and Robin M. Cooper. 2003. "Experimental Studies of Cooperation, Trust, and Social Exchange." In *Trust and Reciprocity: Interdisciplinary Lessons from Experimental Research*, edited by Elinor Ostrom and James Walker. New York: Russell Sage Foundation.

Cook, Karen S., and Russell Hardin. 2001. "Norms of Cooperativeness and Networks of Trust." In *Social Norms*, edited by Michael Hechter and Karl-Dieter Opp. New York: Russell Sage Foundation.

Dellarocas, Chrysanthos. 2001. "The Design of Reliable Trust Management Systems for Electronic Trading Communities." Sloan School of Management working paper 4180–01. Cambridge, Mass.: Massachusetts Institute of Technology.

———. 2003. "The Digitization of Word-of-Mouth: Promise and Challenges of Online Feedback Mechanisms." *Management Science* 49(10): 1407–424.

Dellarocas, Chrysanthos, Ming Fan, and Charles A. Wood. 2004. "Self-Interest, Reciprocity, and Participation in Online Reputation Systems." Sloan School of Management working paper 4500–04. Cambridge, Mass.: Massachusetts Institute of Technology.

DeSanctis, Gerardine, and Marshall S. Poole. 1994. "Capturing the Complexity in Advanced Technology Use: Adaptive Structuration Theory." *Organization Science* 5(2): 121–47.

Dutton, William H., and Adrian Shepherd. 2003. "Trust in the Internet: The Social Dynamics of an Experience Technology." Oil Research report no. 3. Oxford: Oxford Internet Institute. Available at: http://www.oii.ox.ac.uk/resources/publications/RR3.pdf.

Ellingsen, Tore, and Magnus Johannseeon. 2004. "Promises, Threats and Fairness." *Economic Journal* 114(3): 397–420.

Fogg, B. J., Tami Kameda, John Boyd, Jonathan Marshall, R. Sethi, M. Sockol, and T. Trowbridge. 2002. "Stanford-Makovsky Web Credibility Study 2002: Investigating What Makes Web Sites Credible Today." Technical report. Stanford, Calif.: Makovsky & Company and Stanford Persuasive Technology Lab.

Friedman, Eric, and Paul Resnick. 2001. "The Social Cost of Cheap Pseudonyms." *Journal of Economics and Management Strategy* 10(2): 173–99.

Frohlich, Norman, and Joe Oppenheimer. 1998. "Some Consequences of E-mail vs. Face-to-Face Communication in Experiment." *Journal of Economic Behavior and Organization* 35(3): 389–403.

Froomkin, A. Michael. 1995. "Anonymity and Its Enmities." *Journal of Online Law* Article 4. Available at: http://www.wm.edu/law/publications/jol/95_96/froomkin.html (accessed April 9, 2009).

Gambetta, Diego. 1988. "Can We Trust Trust?" In *Trust: Making and Breaking Cooperative Relations*. New York: Blackwell Publishing.

Greif, Avner. 1989. "Reputation and Coalitions in Medieval Trade: Evidence on the Maghribi Traders." *Journal of Economic History* 49(4): 857–82.

Hardin, Russell. 2002. *Trust and Trustworthiness*. New York: Russell Sage Foundation.

Iacono, C. Suzanne, and Suzanne Weisband. 1997. "Developing Trust in Virtual Teams." Paper presented at the Hawaii International Conference on System Sciences. Maui, Hawaii (January 3–6).

James, Harvey S. Jr. 2002. "The Trust Paradox: A Survey of Economic Inquiries into the Nature of Trust and Trustworthiness." *Journal of Economic Behavior and Organization* 47(3): 291–307.

Jarvenpaa, Sirkka L., and Dorothy E. Leidner. 1999. "Communication and Trust in Global Virtual Teams." *Organization Science* 10(6): 791–815.

Keser, Claudia. 2002. "Trust and Reputation Building in E-Commerce." *CIRANO* working paper 2002s-75. Montreal: Centre Interuniversitaire de Recherche en Analyse des Organisations. Available at: http://www.cirano.qc.ca/pdf/publication/2002s-75.pdf.

Kiesler, Sara, Jane Siegel, and Timothy W. McGuire. 1984. "Social Psychological Aspects of Computer-Mediated Communication." *American Psychologist* 39(10): 1123–134.

Kiesler, Sara, and Lee Sproull. 1992. "Group Decision Making and Communication Technology." *Organizational Behavior and Human Decision Processes* 52(1): 96–123.

Kirkman, Bradley L., Benson Rosen, Cristina B. Gibson, Paul E. Tesluk, and Simon O. McPherson. 2002. "Five Challenges to Virtual Team Success: Lessons from Sabre, Inc." *Academy of Management Executive* 16(1): 67–79.

Klein, Daniel B. 1997. "Trust for Hire: Voluntary Remedies for Quality and Safety." In *Reputation: Studies in the Voluntary Elicitation of Good Conduct*. Ann Arbor: University of Michigan Press.

Kollock, Peter. 1999. "The Production of Trust in Online Markets." In *Advances in Group Processes*, vol. 16, edited by Edward J. Lawler, Michael W. Macy, Shane R. Thye, and Henry A. Walker. Greenwich, Conn.: JAI Press.

Kramer, Roderick K. 1999. "Trust and Distrust in Organizations: Emerging Perspectives, Enduring Questions." *Annual Review of Psychology* 50(1999): 569–98.

Ledyard, John O. 1995. "Public Goods: A Survey of Experimental Research." In *Handbook of Experimental Economics*, edited by John H. Kagel and Alvin E. Roth. Princeton, N.J.: Princeton University Press.

Levi, Margaret, and Laura Stoker. 2000. "Political Trust and Trustworthiness." *Annual Review of Political Science* 3(2000): 475–507.

Levine, Noah. 1996. "Establishing Legal Accountability for Anonymous Communication in Cyberspace." *Columbia Law Review* 96(6): 1526–572.

Lev-On, Azi, and Russell Hardin. 2007. "Internet-Based Collaborations and Their Political Significance." *Journal of Information Technology and Politics* 4(2): 5–27.

McCabe, Kevin A., Vernon L. Smith, and Michael LePore. 2000. "Intentionality Detection and 'Mindreading': Why Does Game Form Matter?" *Proceedings of the National Academy of Sciences* 97(8): 4404–409.

McKnight, D. Harrison, and Norman L. Chervany. 1996. "The Meanings of Trust." MISRC working paper series 96–04. Duluth: University of Minnesota, Management Information Systems Research Center.

Messick, David M., and Marilyn B. Brewer. 1983. "Solving Social Dilemmas." In *Review of Personality and Social Psychology*, vol. 4, edited by Ladd Wheeler and Phillip Shaver. Beverly Hills, Calif.: Sage Publications.

Miller, Nolan, Paul Resnick, and Richard J. Zeckhauser. 2005. "Eliciting Informative Feedback: The Peer-Prediction Method." *Management Science* 51(9): 1359–373.,

Nissenbaum, Helen. 1999. "The Meaning of Anonymity in an Information Age." *The Information Society* 15(2): 141–44.

———. 2004. "Will Security Enhance Trust Online, or Supplant It?" In *Trust and Distrust in Organizations: Dilemmas and Approaches*, edited by Roderick M. Kramer and Karen S. Cook. New York: Russell Sage Foundation.

Omidyar, Pierre. 1995. "Our History." eBay Media Center. Available at: http://news.ebay.com/history.cfm (accessed April 9, 2009).

Parks, Malcolm R., and Kory Floyd. 1996. "Making Friends in Cyberspace." *Journal of Communication* 46(1): 80–97.

Pavlou, Paul A., and David Gefen. 2004. "Building Effective Online Marketplaces with Institution-Based Trust." *Information Systems Research* 15(1): 37–59.

Postmes, Tom, Russell Spears, and Martin Lea. 1998. "Breaching or Building Social Boundaries? SIDE-Effects of Computer-Mediated Communication." *Communication Research* 25(6): 689–715.

Postmes, Tom, Russell Spears, Khaled Sakhel, and Daphne De Groot. 2001. "Social Influence in Computer-Mediated Communication: The Effects of Anonymity on Group Behavior." *Personality and Social Psychology Bulletin* 27(10): 1243–254.

Rapoport, Anatol, Andreas Diekmann, and Axel Franzen. 1995. "Experiments with Social Traps IV: Reputations Effects in the Evolution of Cooperation." *Rationality and Society* 7(4): 431–41.

Resnick, Paul. 2004. "Impersonal Sociotechnical Capital, ICTs, and Collective Action among Strangers." In *Transforming Enterprise*, edited by William Dutton, Brian Kahin, Ramon O'Callaghan, and Andrew Wyckoff. Cambridge, Mass.: MIT Press.

Resnick, Paul, and Hal R. Varian. 1997. "Recommender Systems." *Communications of the ACM* 40(1): 56–58.

Resnick, Paul, and Richard Zeckhauser. 2002. "Trust among Strangers in Internet Transactions: Empirical Analysis of eBay's Reputation System." In *Advances in Applied Microeconomics*, vol. 11, *The Economics of the Internet and E-Commerce*, edited by Michael R. Baye. Amsterdam: Elsevier Science.

Resnick, Paul, Richard Zeckhauser, Eric Friedman, and Ko Kuwabara. 2000. "Reputation Systems." *Communications of the ACM* 43(1): 45–48.

Resnick, Paul, Richard Zeckhauser, John Swanson, and Kate Lockwood. 2006. "The Value of Reputation on eBay: A Controlled Experiment." *Experimental Economics* 9(2): 79–101.

Rheingold, Howard. 2003. *Smart Mobs: The Next Social Revolution*. Cambridge, Mass.: Perseus.

Rice, Ronald E., and Gail Love. 1987. "Electronic Emotion: Socioemotional Content in a Computer-Mediated Communication Network." *Communication Research* 14(1): 85–108.

Rocco, Elena. 1998. "Trust Breaks Down in Electronic Contexts but Can Be Repaired by Some Initial Face-to-Face Contact." *In Proceedings of the SIGCHI Conference on Human Factors in Computing Systems 1998*, edited by Clare-Marie

Karat, Arnold Lund, Joëlle Coutaz, and John Karat. New York: ACM Press/Addison-Wesley.

Sally, David. 1995. "Conversation and Cooperation in Social Dilemmas." *Rationality and Society* 7(1): 58–92.

Scholz, John T. 2000. "Trust, Taxes, and Compliance." In *Trust and Governance*, edited by Valerie Braithwaite and Margaret Levi. New York: Russell Sage Foundation.

Scholz, John T., and Mark Lubell. 1998. "Trust and Taxpaying: Testing the Heuristic Approach to Collective Action." *American Journal of Political Science* 42(2): 398–417.

Shearmur, Jeremy, and Daniel B. Klein. 1997. "Good Conduct in the Great Society: Adam Smith and the Role of Reputation." In *Reputation: Studies in the Voluntary Elicitation of Good Conduct*, edited by Daniel B. Klein. Ann Arbor: University of Michigan Press.

Shneiderman, Ben. 2000. "Designing Trust into Online Experiences." *Communications of the ACM* 43(1): 57–59.

Soukup, Charles. 2000. "Building a Theory of Multimedia CMC." *New Media and Society* 2(4): 407–25.

Spears, Russell, and Martin Lea. 1994. "Panacea or Panopticon? The Hidden Power in Computer-Mediated Communication." *Communication Research* 21(4): 427–59.

Sproull, Lee, and Sara Kiesler. 1986. "Reducing Social Context Cues: Electronic Mail in Organizational Communication." *Management Science* 32(11): 1492–512.

Stewart, Katherine J. 2003. "Trust Transfer on the World Wide Web." *Organization Science* 14(1): 5–17.

Sztompka, Piotr. 1999. *Trust: A Sociological Theory*. New York: Cambridge University Press.

Wallace, Kathleen A. 1999. "Anonymity." *Ethics and Information Society* 1(1): 23–35.

Walther, Joseph B. 1996. "Computer-Mediated Communication: Impersonal, Interpersonal, and Hyperpersonal Interaction." *Communication Research* 23(1): 3–43.

———. 1997. "Group and Interpersonal Effects in International Computer-Mediated Collaboration." *Human Communication Research* 23(3): 342–60.

Walther, Joseph B., Jeffrey F. Anderson, and David W. Park. 1994. "Interpersonal Effects in Computer-Mediated Interaction: A Meta-Analysis of Social and Antisocial Communication." *Communication Research* 21(4): 460–87.

Watt, Susan E., Martin Lea, and Russell Spears. 2002. "How Social Is Internet Communication? A Reappraisal of Bandwidth and Anonymity Effects." In *Virtual Society?* edited by Steve Woolgar. New York: Oxford University Press.

Wilson, Jeanne M., Susan G. Straus, and Bill McEvily. 2006. "All in Due Time: The Development of Trust in Computer-Mediated and Face-to-Face Teams." *Organizational Behavior and Human Decision Processes* 99(1): 16–33.

Zheng, Jun, Nathan Bos, Judith S. Olson, and Gary M. Olson. 2001. "Trust without Touch: Jumpstart Trust with Social Chat." In *CHI '01 Extended Abstracts on Human Factors in Computing Systems*, edited by Marilyn Mantei Tremaine. New York: ACM.

Index

Boldface numbers refer to figures and tables

ability, 216
administration, of online communities. *See* social control
advertising, 277–87
Akerlof, G., 73, 78
Allexperts.com, 218
Alter, 38. *See also* investment games
altruism, 42, 45–46, 68n6
Amazon.com, 33n6, 221, 313n14
analysis of variance (ANOVA), 85–86, 90, 204–5, 222
ANCOVA (analysis of covariance), 281
anonymity: as barrier to online trust formation, 294–95; benefits of, 312n4; definition of, 294; and feedback honesty, 309–10; information pool contributions, 278; laboratory experiment creation, 18; lemons problem solution condition, 82–83, 85, 86, 87, 90–91, 93, 96, 97–99, 101; risk of, 139–40, 145–47
ANOVA (analysis of variance), 85–86, 90, 204–5, 222
apology, 226–27, 229, 230–34
assessment of trustworthiness: barriers to, 293–96; empirical study of, 201–8; of exchange partners in goods and services markets, 198–201; factors in, 191–93, 293; in interpersonal environments, 195–96; in online reputation systems, 196–98; and relational definition of trust, 190–91; research considerations, 189, 208–9; in website design and structure, 194–95
asymmetric information. *See* information asymmetry
attitudes, trusting, 56
auctions, Internet. *See* Internet auctions
audio communications, 195, 295–96, 299
authentication, 17, 310
Axelrod, R., 110, 157

Ba, S., 112
backward induction, 42
banner advertising, 277–87
Barbie sales, 168
Barr, A., 112
Barrera, D., 25–26, 43, 58
Baytelman, Y., 300–301
Bearden, W., 56
behavioral trust, 216, 220, 227
behavior limitations, in perfect reputation systems, 24–27, 31–32
belief learning, 41
believability, 234
benevolence, 216–17
Ben-Ner, A., 300
betrayal, 275–76
Bicchieri, C., 300, 312n6